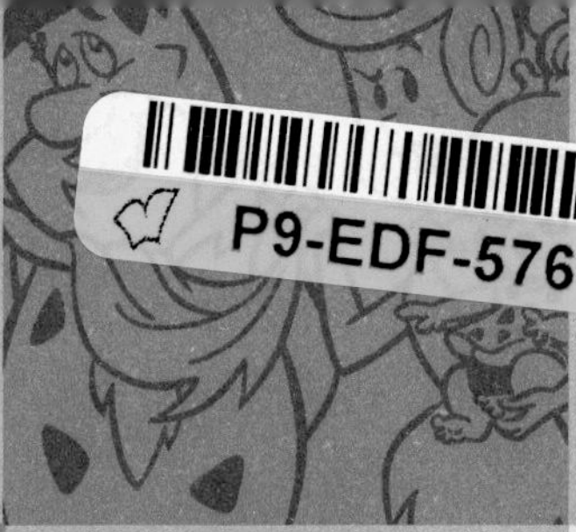

THE FLINTSTONES AND THE JETSONS

VOLUME 1

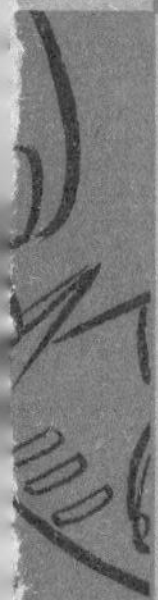

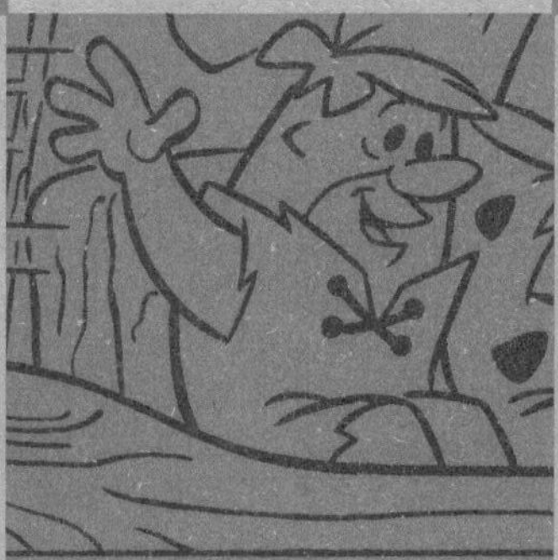

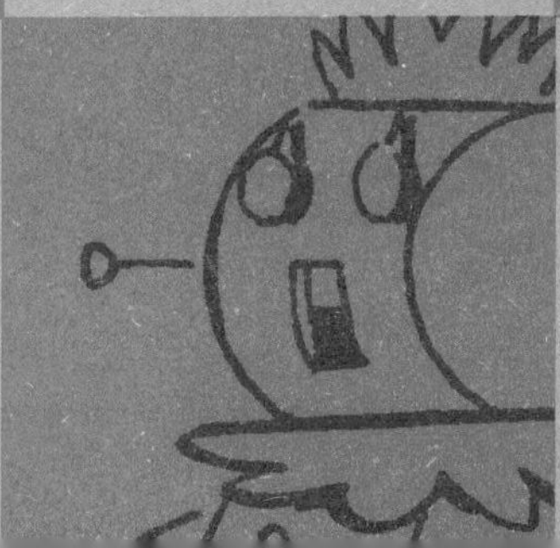

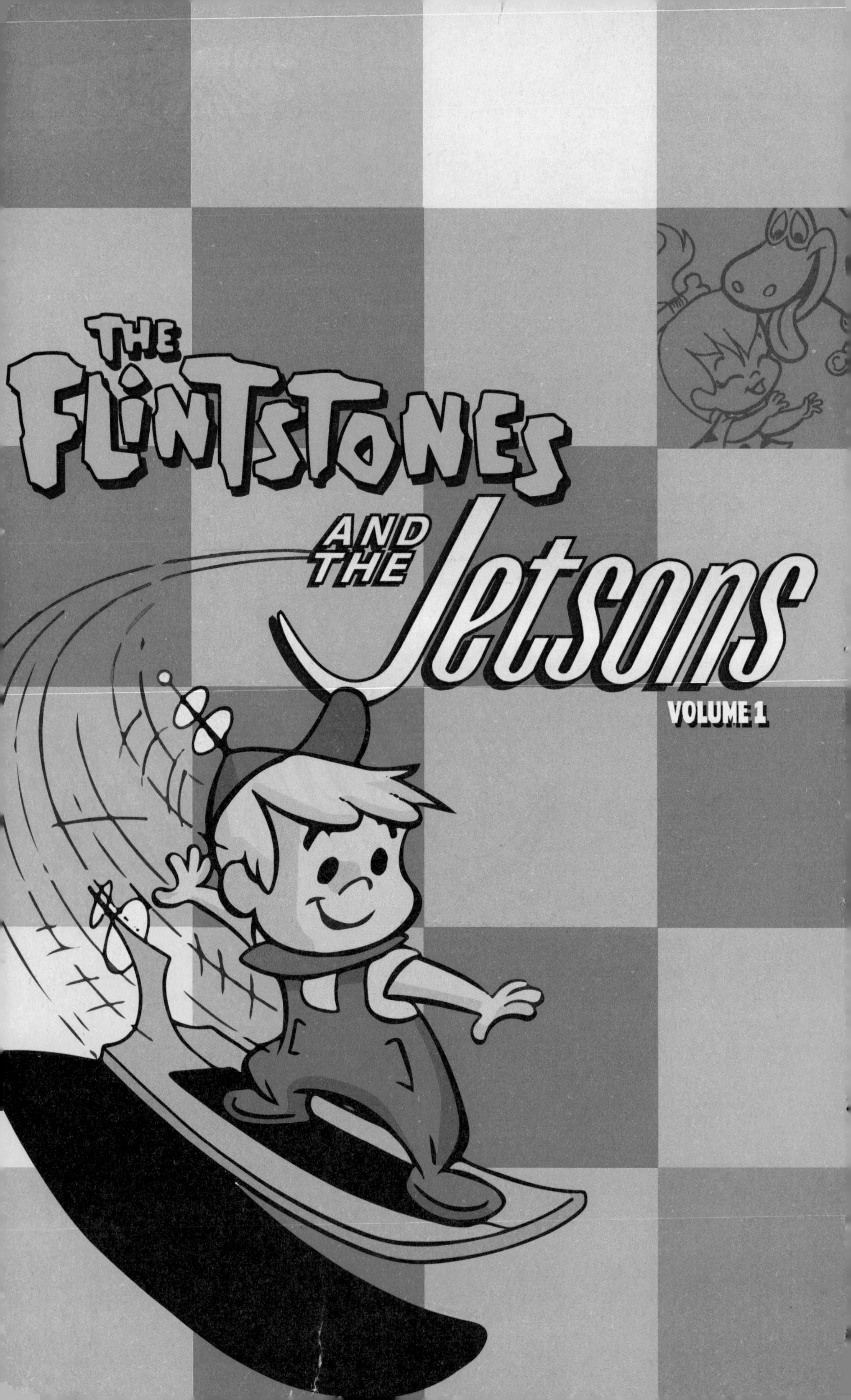
THE FLINTSTONES
AND THE Jetsons
VOLUME 1

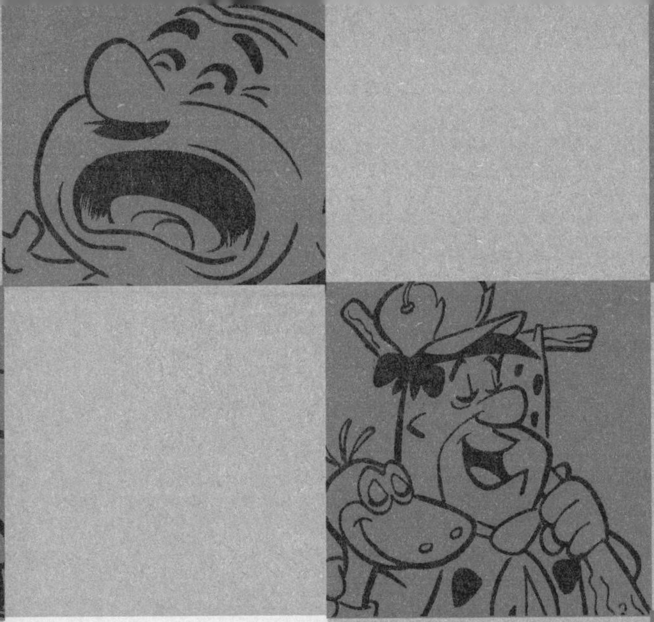

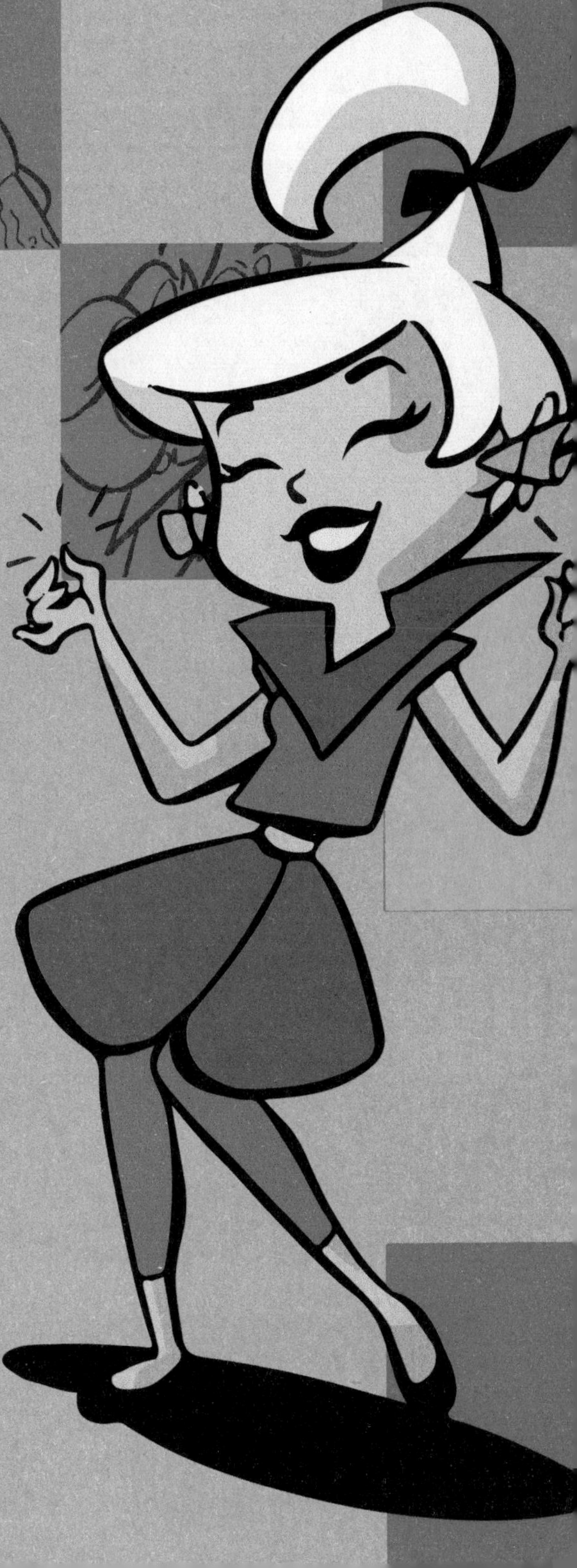

Writers
Robbie Busch • Mike Carlin • Sam Henderson
Michael Kupperman • Matt Wayne

Pencillers
Bill Alger • Ivan Brunetti • Thad Doria
Glen Hanson • Bill Wray

Inkers
Bill Alger • Ivan Brunetti • Mike DeCarlo
Stephen DeStefano • Tim Harkins • Bill Wray

Colorists
Bernie Mireault • Dave Tanguay • Rick Taylor

Letterers
John Costanza • Ken Lopez

Collection Cover Artist
Glen Hanson

BRONWYN TAGGART Editor - Original Series
JEB WOODARD Group Editor - Collected Editions • STEVE COOK Design Director - Books
MONIQUE GRUSPE Publication Design

BOB HARRAS Senior VP - Editor-in-Chief, DC Comics

DIANE NELSON President • DAN DiDIO Publisher • JIM LEE Publisher • GEOFF JOHNS President & Chief Creative Officer
AMIT DESAI Executive VP - Business & Marketing Strategy, Direct to Consumer & Global Franchise Management
SAM ADES Senior VP - Direct to Consumer • BOBBIE CHASE VP - Talent Development
MARK CHIARELLO Senior VP - Art, Design & Collected Editions • JOHN CUNNINGHAM Senior VP - Sales & Trade Marketing
ANNE DePIES Senior VP - Business Strategy, Finance & Administration • DON FALLETTI VP - Manufacturing Operations
LAWRENCE GANEM VP - Editorial Administration & Talent Relations • ALISON GILL Senior VP - Manufacturing & Operations
HANK KANALZ Senior VP - Editorial Strategy & Administration • JAY KOGAN VP - Legal Affairs
THOMAS LOFTUS VP - Business Affairs • JACK MAHAN VP - Business Affairs
NICK J. NAPOLITANO VP - Manufacturing Administration • EDDIE SCANNELL VP - Consumer Marketing
COURTNEY SIMMONS Senior VP - Publicity & Communications
JIM (SKI) SOKOLOWSKI VP - Comic Book Specialty Sales & Trade Marketing
NANCY SPEARS VP - Mass, Book, Digital Sales & Trade Marketing

THE FLINTSTONES AND THE JETSONS VOLUME 1

Published by DC Comics. Compilation and all new material Copyright © 2017 Hanna-Barbera. All Rights Reserved. Originally published
in single magazine form in THE FLINTSTONES AND THE JETSONS 1-6. Copyright © 1997, 1998 Hanna-Barbera. All Rights Reserved.
All characters, their distinctive likenesses and related elements featured in this publication are trademarks of Hanna-Barbera.
The stories, characters and incidents featured in this publication are entirely fictional. DC Comics does not read or accept unsolicited
submissions of ideas, stories or artwork.

DC Comics, 2900 West Alameda Ave., Burbank, CA 91505
Printed by LSC Communications, Owensville, MO, USA. 3/31/17. First Printing.
ISBN: 978-1-4012-7240-1

Library of Congress Cataloging-in-Publication Data is available.

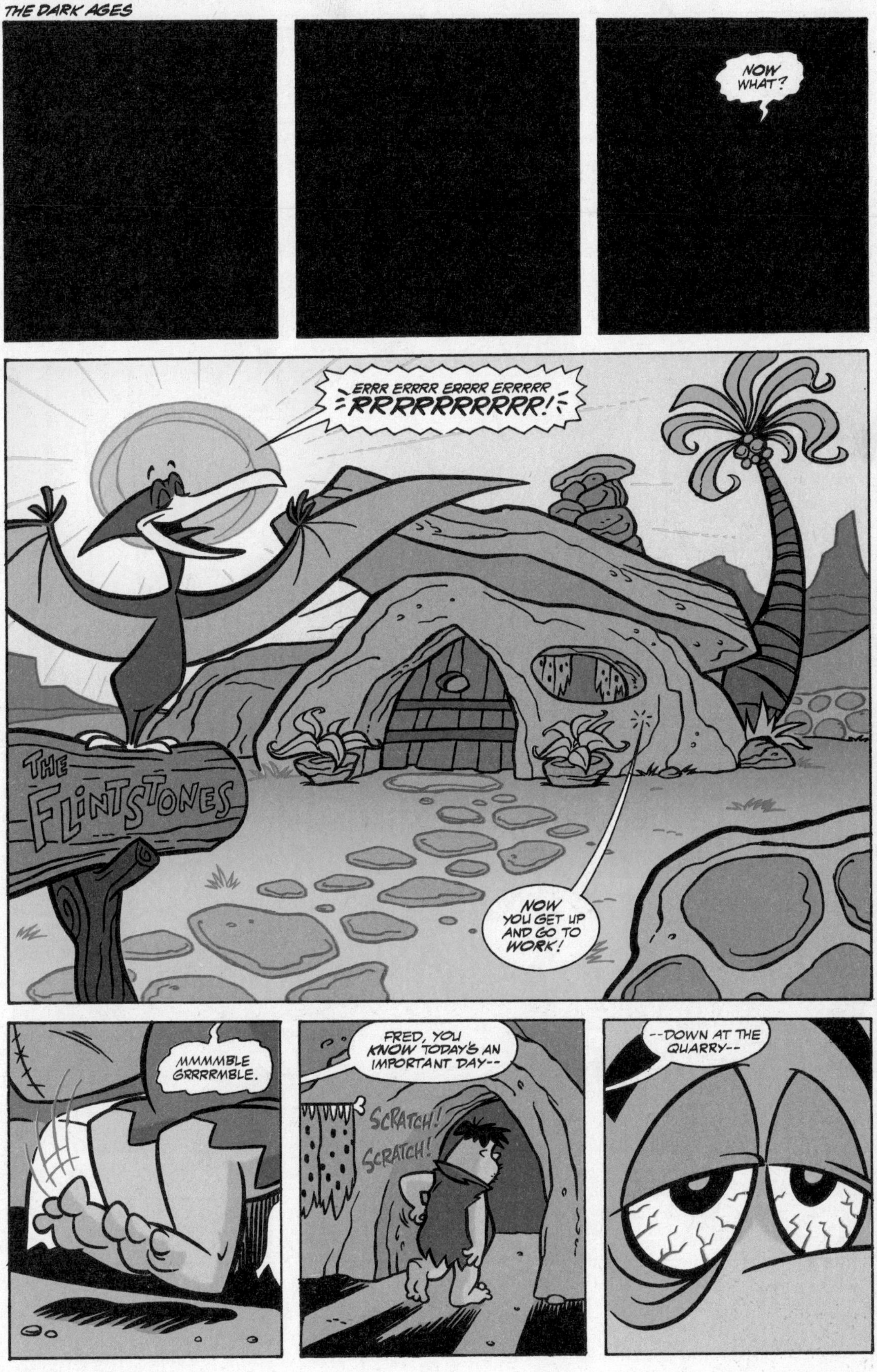
NOW WHAT?
ERRR ERRRR ERRRR ERRRRR RRRRRRRRRR!
THE FLINTSTONES
NOW YOU GET UP AND GO TO WORK!
MMMMBLE GRRRRMBLE.
FRED, YOU KNOW TODAY'S AN IMPORTANT DAY--
SCRATCH!
SCRATCH!
--DOWN AT THE QUARRY--

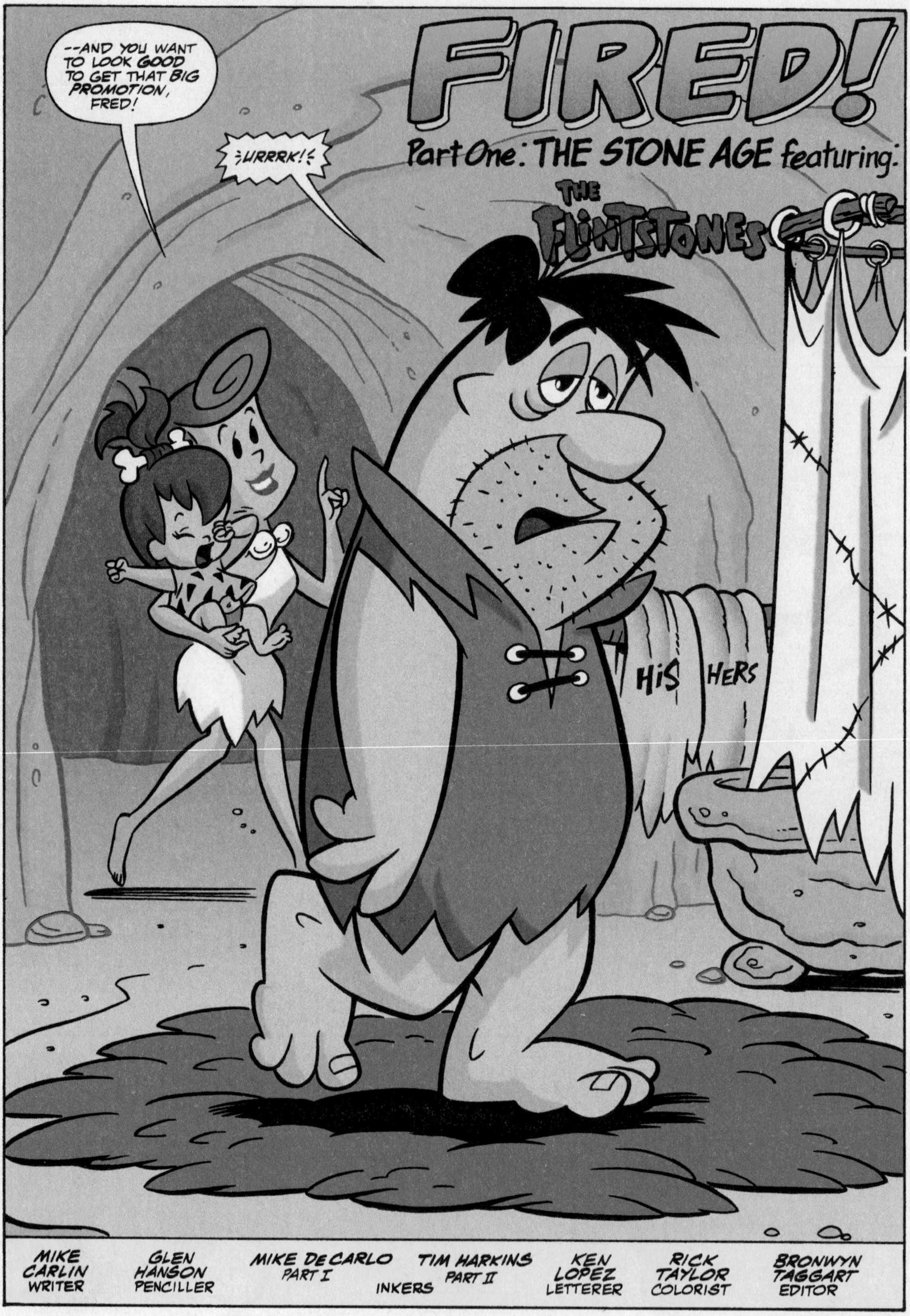
--AND YOU WANT TO LOOK GOOD TO GET THAT BIG PROMOTION, FRED!
URRRK!
FIRED!
Part One: THE STONE AGE featuring:
THE FLINTSTONES
HIS
HERS
MIKE CARLIN WRITER
GLEN HANSON PENCILLER
MIKE DECARLO PART I
TIM HARKINS PART II
INKERS
KEN LOPEZ LETTERER
RICK TAYLOR COLORIST
BRONWYN TAGGART EDITOR

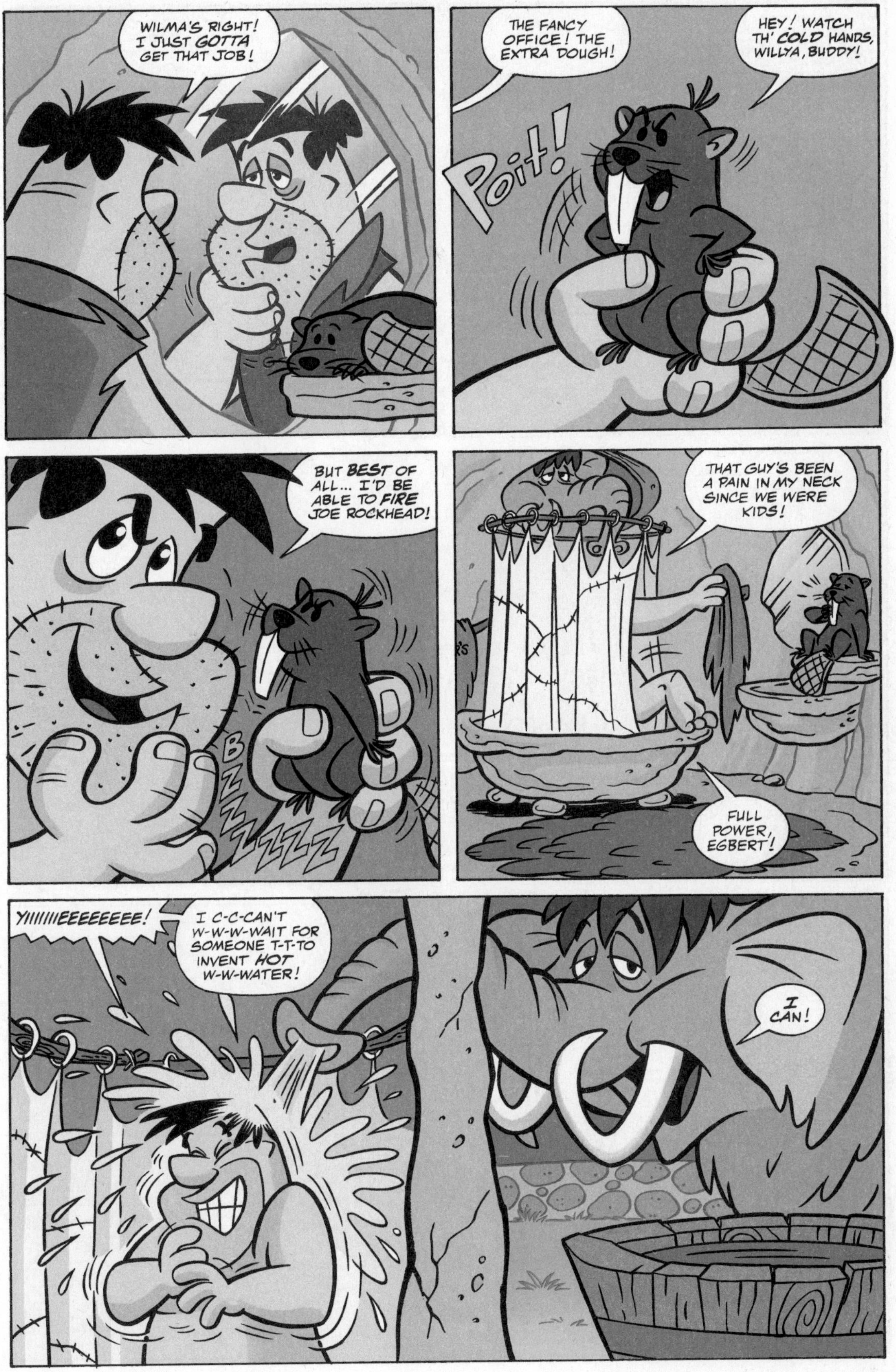
WILMA'S RIGHT! I JUST GOTTA GET THAT JOB!
THE FANCY OFFICE! THE EXTRA DOUGH!
HEY! WATCH TH' COLD HANDS, WILLYA, BUDDY!
Poit!
BUT BEST OF ALL... I'D BE ABLE TO FIRE JOE ROCKHEAD!
BZZZZZZZZ
THAT GUY'S BEEN A PAIN IN MY NECK SINCE WE WERE KIDS!
FULL POWER, EGBERT!
YIIIIIIIEEEEEEEE!
I C-C-CAN'T W-W-W-WAIT FOR SOMEONE T-T-TO INVENT HOT W-W-WATER!
I CAN!

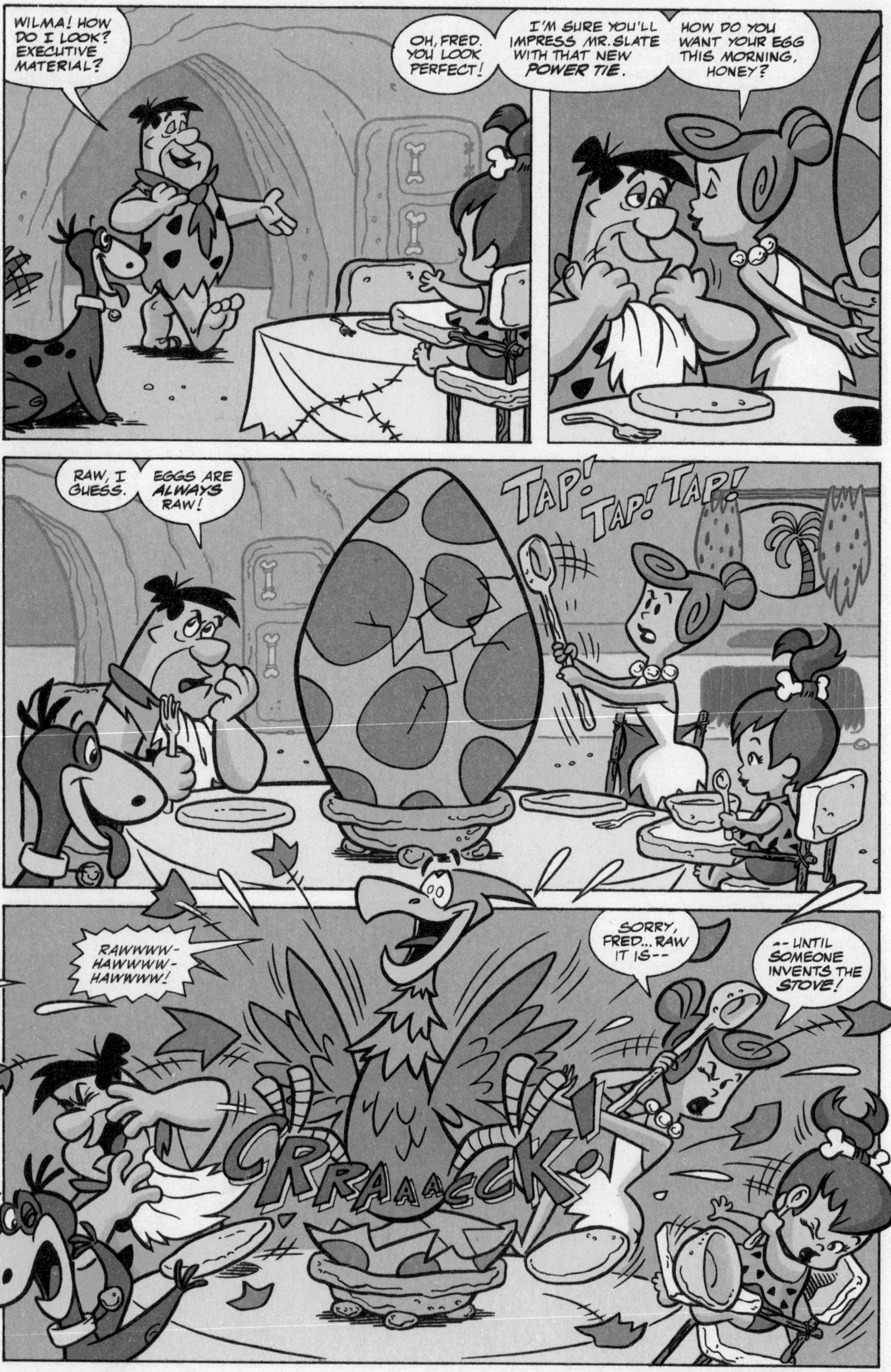

WILMA! HOW DO I LOOK? EXECUTIVE MATERIAL?
OH, FRED. YOU LOOK PERFECT!
I'M SURE YOU'LL IMPRESS MR. SLATE WITH THAT NEW POWER TIE.
HOW DO YOU WANT YOUR EGG THIS MORNING, HONEY?
RAW, I GUESS.
EGGS ARE ALWAYS RAW!
TAP! TAP! TAP!
RAWWWW-HAWWWW-HAWWWW!
SORRY, FRED... RAW IT IS--
--UNTIL SOMEONE INVENTS THE STOVE!
CRRAAACCK!

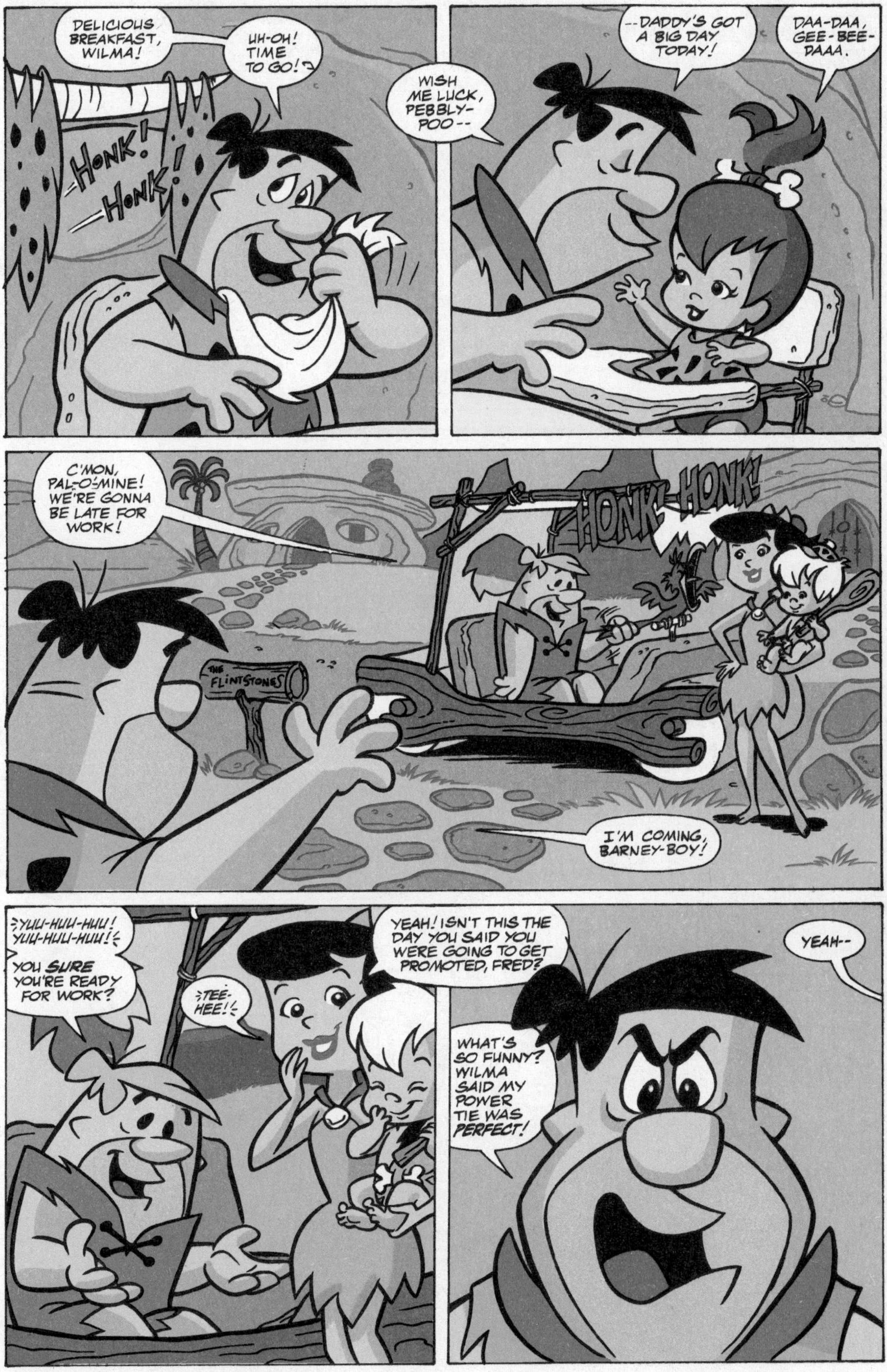
DELICIOUS BREAKFAST, WILMA!
UH-OH! TIME TO GO!
HONK! HONK!
WISH ME LUCK, PEBBLY-POO--
--DADDY'S GOT A BIG DAY TODAY!
DAA-DAA, GEE-BEE-DAAA.
C'MON, PAL-O-MINE! WE'RE GONNA BE LATE FOR WORK!
HONK! HONK!
THE FLINTSTONES
I'M COMING, BARNEY-BOY!
YUU-HUU-HUU! YUU-HUU-HUU!
YOU SURE YOU'RE READY FOR WORK?
TEE-HEE!
YEAH! ISN'T THIS THE DAY YOU SAID YOU WERE GOING TO GET PROMOTED, FRED?
YEAH--
WHAT'S SO FUNNY? WILMA SAID MY POWER TIE WAS PERFECT!

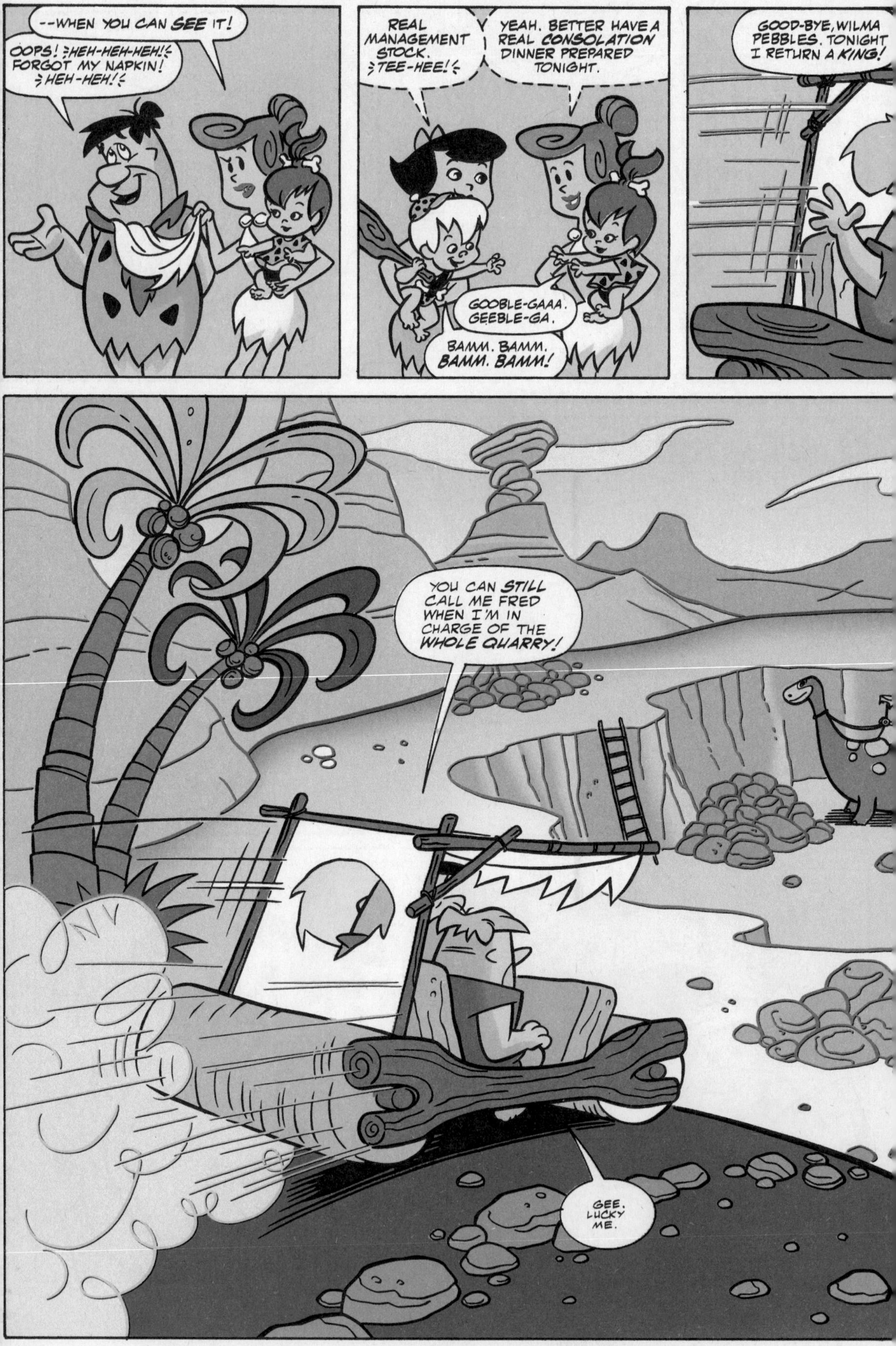
--WHEN YOU CAN SEE IT!
OOPS! HEH-HEH-HEH! FORGOT MY NAPKIN! HEH-HEH!
REAL MANAGEMENT STOCK. TEE-HEE!
YEAH. BETTER HAVE A REAL CONSOLATION DINNER PREPARED TONIGHT.
GOOBLE-GAAA. GEEBLE-GA.
BAMM. BAMM. BAMM. BAMM!
GOOD-BYE, WILMA PEBBLES. TONIGHT I RETURN A KING!
YOU CAN STILL CALL ME FRED WHEN I'M IN CHARGE OF THE WHOLE QUARRY!
GEE. LUCKY ME.

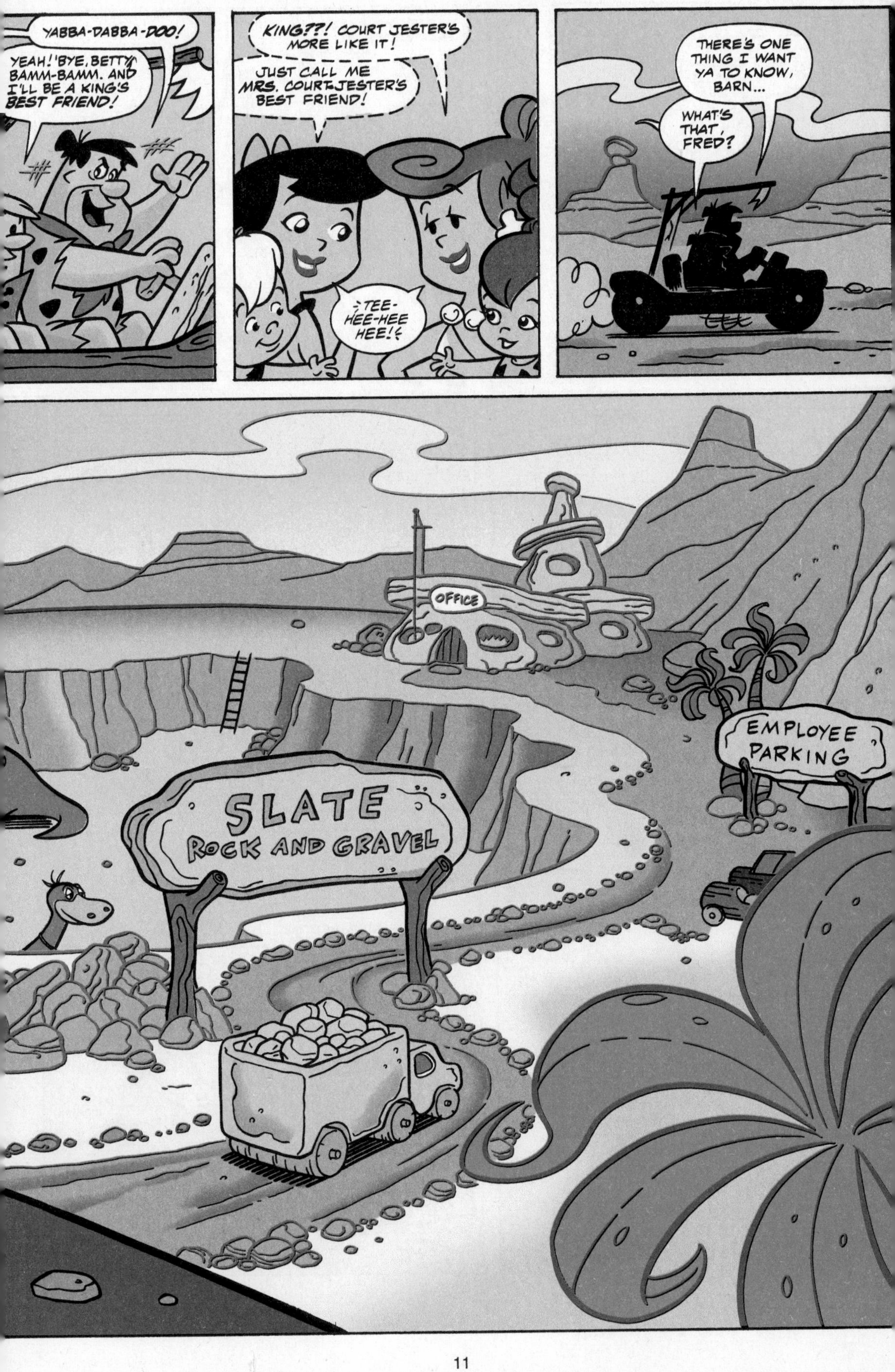
YABBA-DABBA-DOO!
YEAH! 'BYE, BETTY, BAMM-BAMM. AND I'LL BE A KING'S BEST FRIEND!
KING??! COURT JESTER'S MORE LIKE IT!
JUST CALL ME MRS. COURT-JESTER'S BEST FRIEND!
TEE-HEE-HEE HEE!
THERE'S ONE THING I WANT YA TO KNOW, BARN...
WHAT'S THAT, FRED?
OFFICE
SLATE ROCK AND GRAVEL
EMPLOYEE PARKING

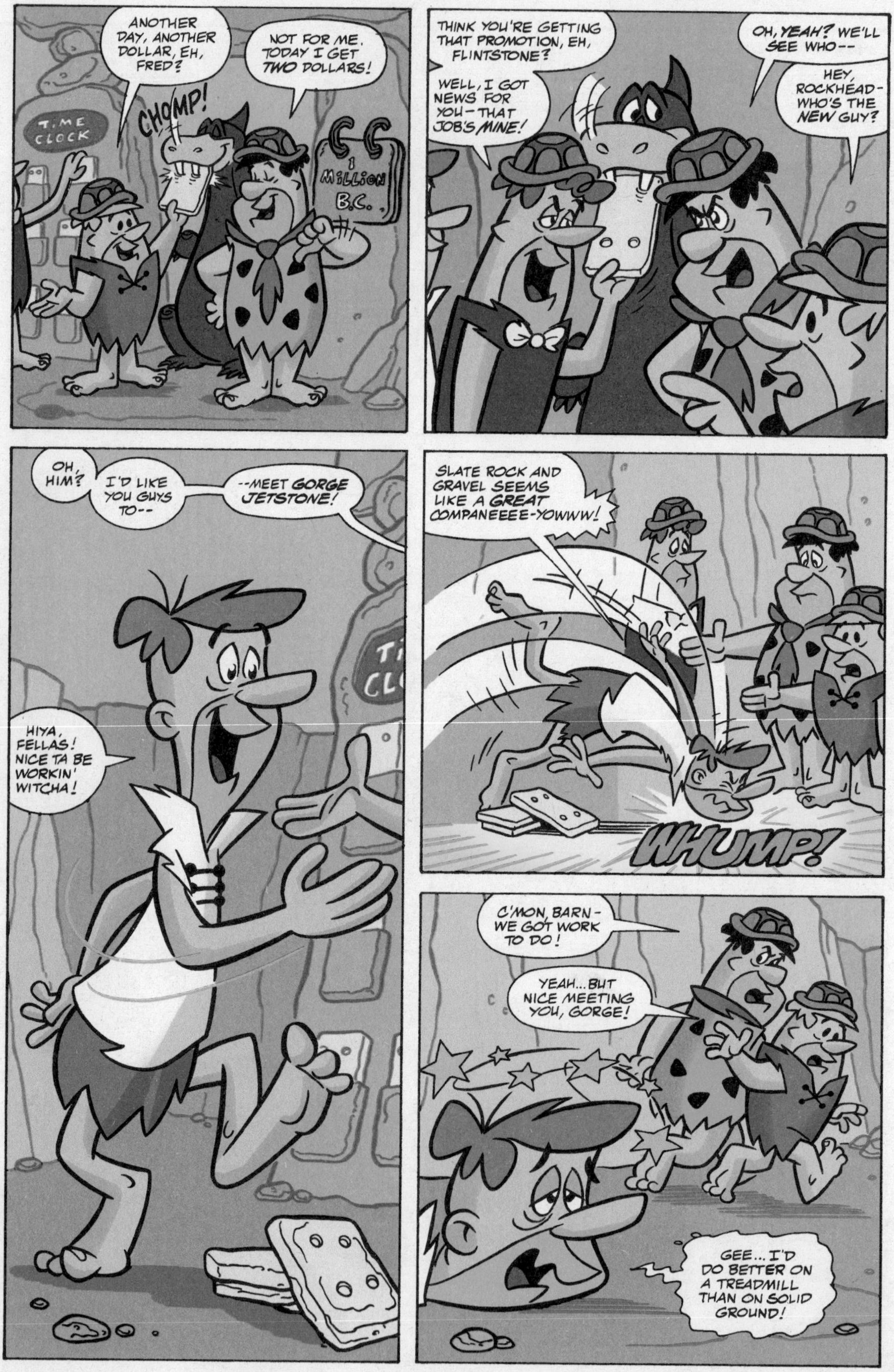
ANOTHER DAY, ANOTHER DOLLAR, EH, FRED?
NOT FOR ME. TODAY I GET TWO DOLLARS!
CHOMP!
TIME CLOCK
1 MILLION B.C.
THINK YOU'RE GETTING THAT PROMOTION, EH, FLINTSTONE?
WELL, I GOT NEWS FOR YOU-- THAT JOB'S MINE!
OH, YEAH? WE'LL SEE WHO--
HEY, ROCKHEAD-- WHO'S THE NEW GUY?
OH, HIM?
I'D LIKE YOU GUYS TO--
--MEET GORGE JETSTONE!
HIYA, FELLAS! NICE TA BE WORKIN' WITCHA!
SLATE ROCK AND GRAVEL SEEMS LIKE A GREAT COMPANEEEE-YOWWW!
WHUMP!
C'MON, BARN-- WE GOT WORK TO DO!
YEAH... BUT NICE MEETING YOU, GORGE!
GEE... I'D DO BETTER ON A TREADMILL THAN ON SOLID GROUND!

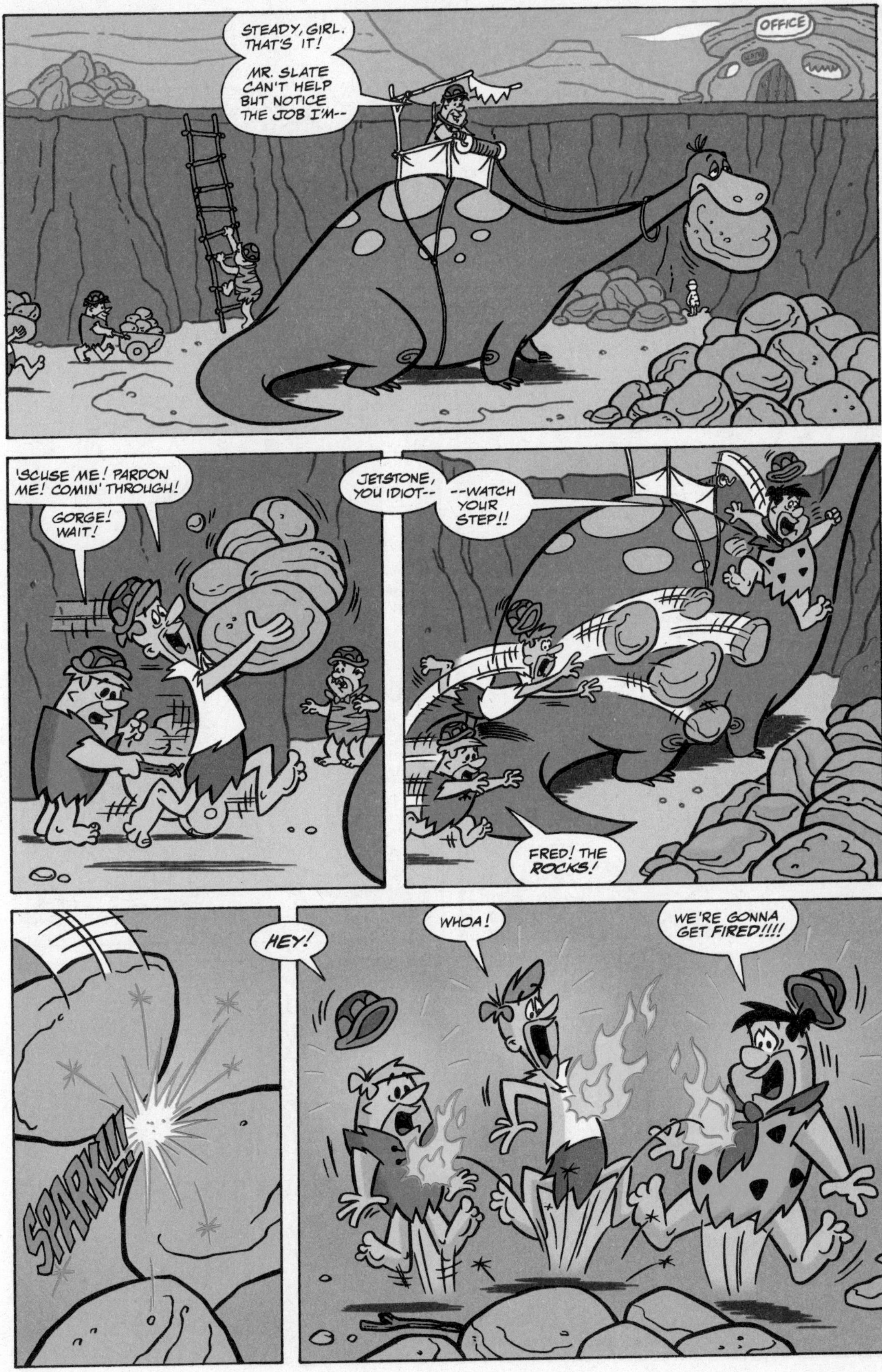
STEADY, GIRL. THAT'S IT!
MR. SLATE CAN'T HELP BUT NOTICE THE JOB I'M--
OFFICE
'SCUSE ME! PARDON ME! COMIN' THROUGH!
GORGE! WAIT!
JETSTONE, YOU IDIOT--
--WATCH YOUR STEP!!
FRED! THE ROCKS!
SPARK!!!
HEY!
WHOA!
WE'RE GONNA GET FIRED!!!!

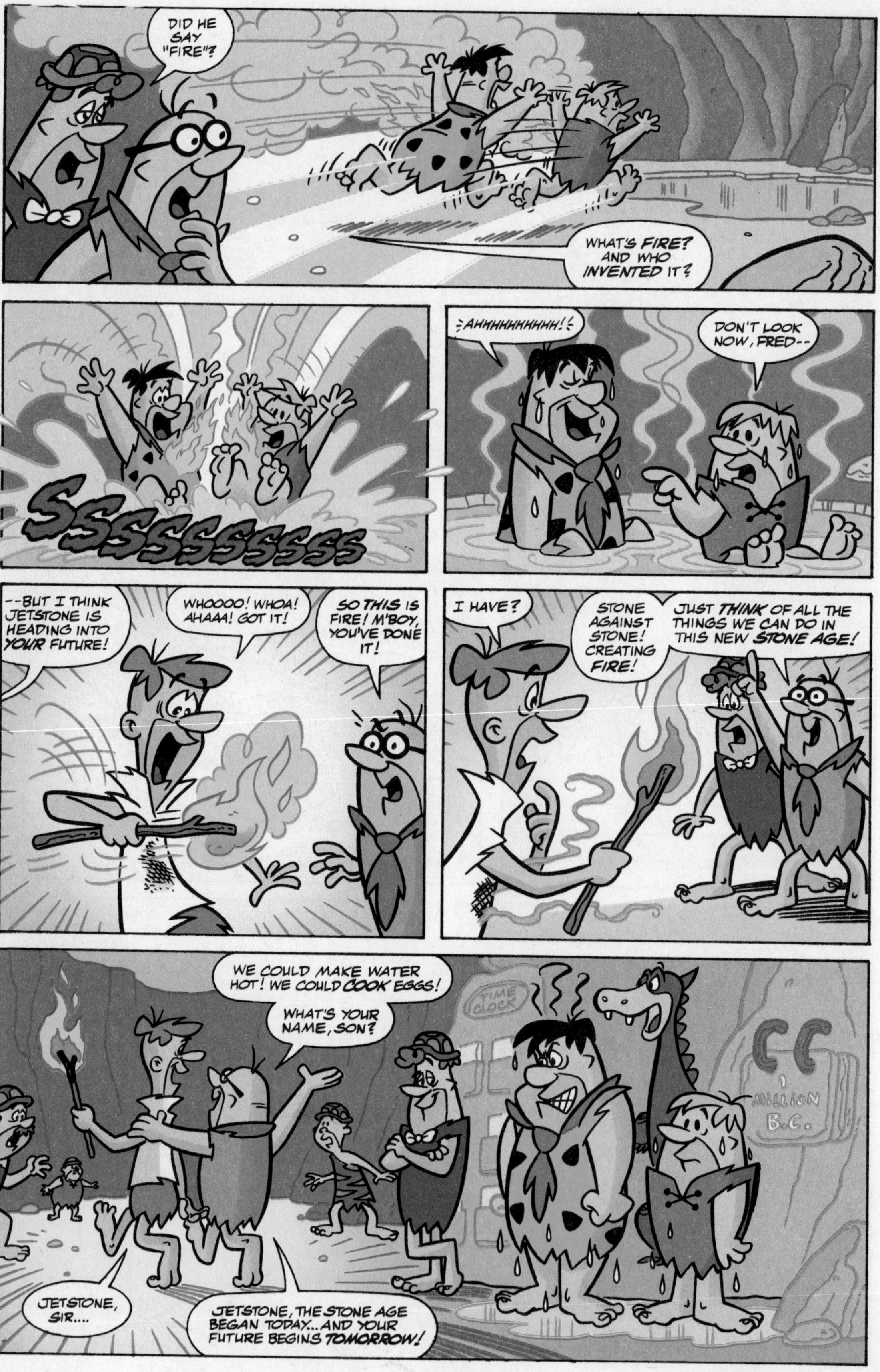
DID HE SAY "FIRE"?
WHAT'S FIRE? AND WHO INVENTED IT?
SSSSSSSSSS
AHHHHHHHHHH!
DON'T LOOK NOW, FRED--
--BUT I THINK JETSTONE IS HEADING INTO YOUR FUTURE!
WHOOOO! WHOA! AHAAA! GOT IT!
SO THIS IS FIRE! M'BOY, YOU'VE DONE IT!
I HAVE?
STONE AGAINST STONE! CREATING FIRE!
JUST THINK OF ALL THE THINGS WE CAN DO IN THIS NEW STONE AGE!
WE COULD MAKE WATER HOT! WE COULD COOK EGGS!
WHAT'S YOUR NAME, SON?
TIME CLOCK
1 MILLION B.C.
JETSTONE, SIR....
JETSTONE, THE STONE AGE BEGAN TODAY...AND YOUR FUTURE BEGINS TOMORROW!

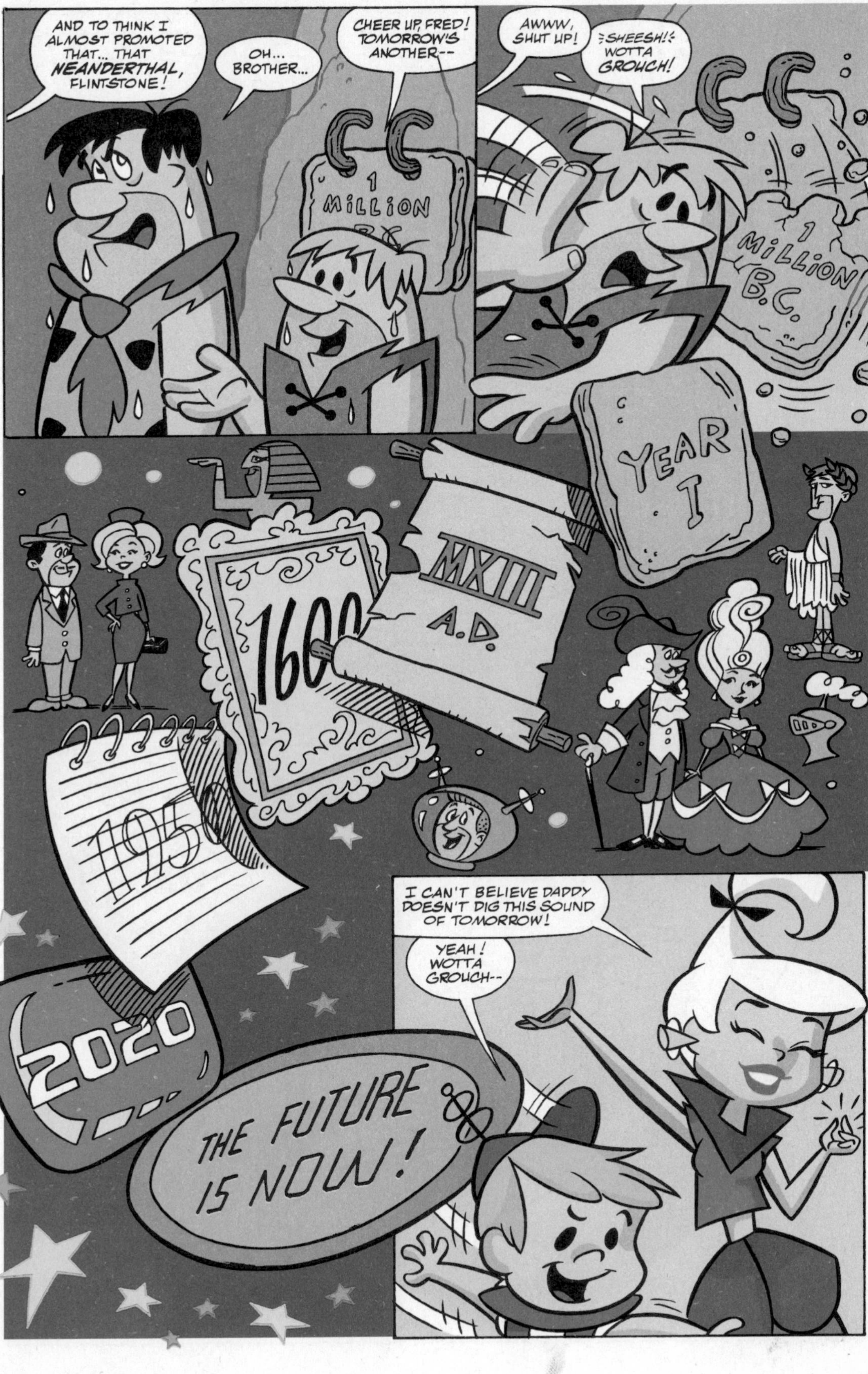
AND TO THINK I ALMOST PROMOTED THAT... THAT NEANDERTHAL, FLINTSTONE!
OH... BROTHER...
CHEER UP, FRED! TOMORROW'S ANOTHER--
1 MILLION B.C.
AWWW, SHUT UP!
SHEESH! WOTTA GROUCH!
1 MILLION B.C.
YEAR 1
MXIII A.D.
1600
1950
2020
THE FUTURE IS NOW!
I CAN'T BELIEVE DADDY DOESN'T DIG THIS SOUND OF TOMORROW!
YEAH! WOTTA GROUCH--

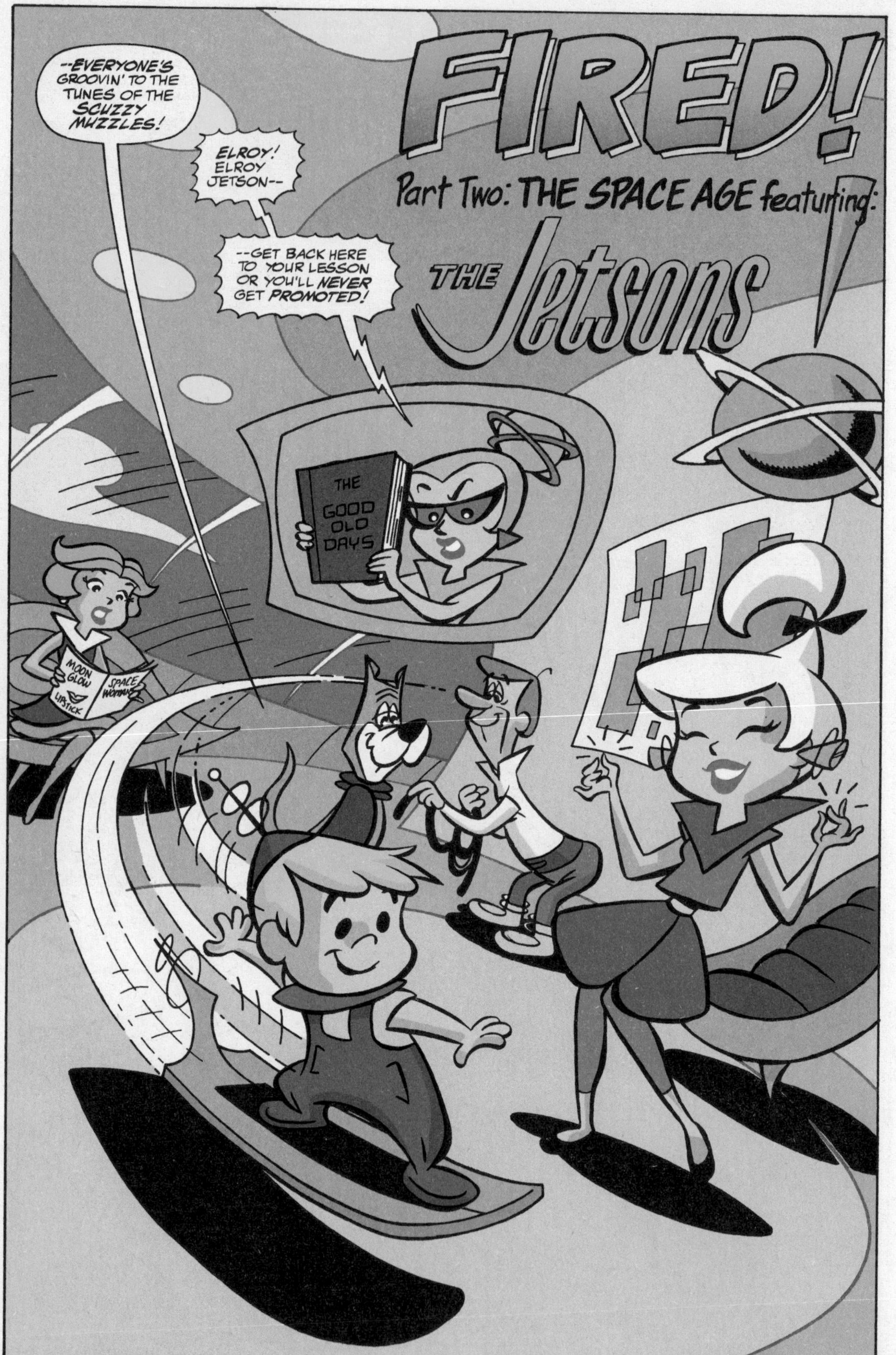
FIRED!
Part Two: THE SPACE AGE featuring:
THE Jetsons
--EVERYONE'S GROOVIN' TO THE TUNES OF THE SCUZZY MUZZLES!
ELROY! ELROY JETSON--
--GET BACK HERE TO YOUR LESSON OR YOU'LL NEVER GET PROMOTED!
THE GOOD OLD DAYS
MOON GLOW LIPSTICK
SPACE WOMAN

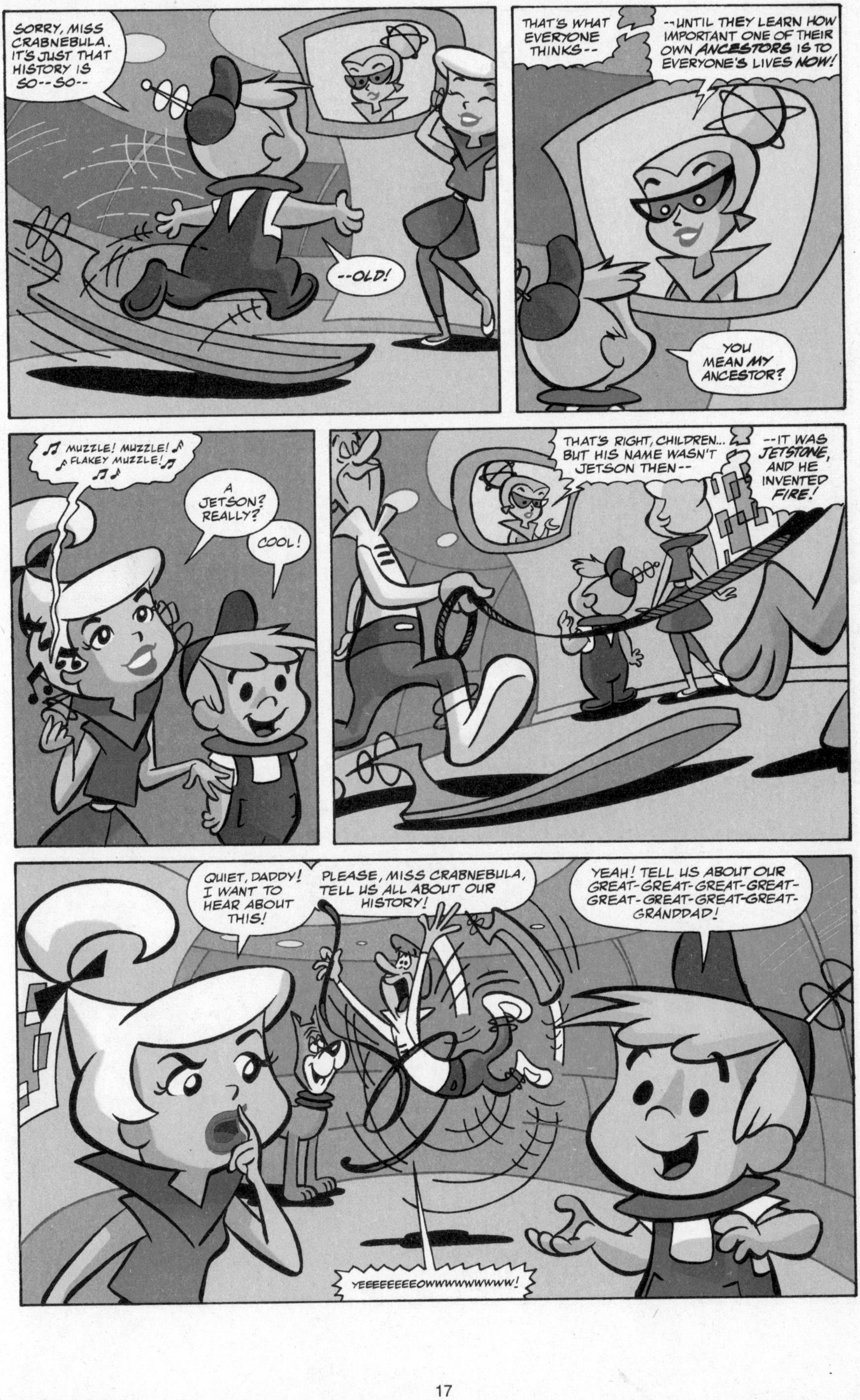

SORRY, MISS CRABNEBULA. IT'S JUST THAT HISTORY IS SO--SO--
--OLD!
THAT'S WHAT EVERYONE THINKS--
--UNTIL THEY LEARN HOW IMPORTANT ONE OF THEIR OWN ANCESTORS IS TO EVERYONE'S LIVES NOW!
YOU MEAN MY ANCESTOR?
♫ MUZZLE! MUZZLE! ♪ FLAKEY MUZZLE! ♫ ♫ ♪
A JETSON? REALLY?
COOL!
THAT'S RIGHT, CHILDREN... BUT HIS NAME WASN'T JETSON THEN--
--IT WAS JETSTONE, AND HE INVENTED FIRE!
QUIET, DADDY! I WANT TO HEAR ABOUT THIS!
PLEASE, MISS CRABNEBULA, TELL US ALL ABOUT OUR HISTORY!
YEAH! TELL US ABOUT OUR GREAT-GREAT-GREAT-GREAT-GREAT-GREAT-GREAT-GREAT-GRANDDAD!
YEEEEEEEEOWWWWWWWWW!

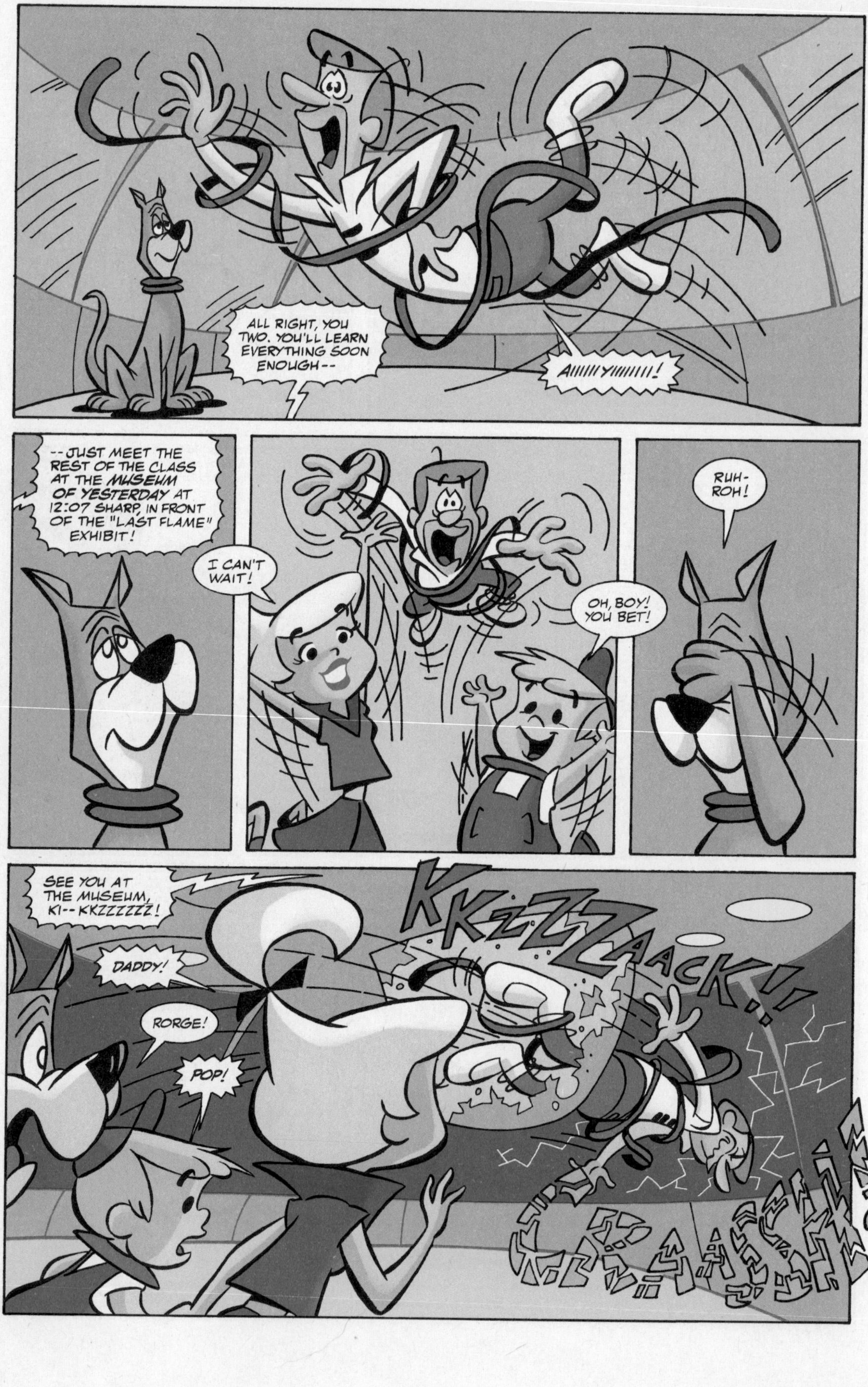
ALL RIGHT, YOU TWO. YOU'LL LEARN EVERYTHING SOON ENOUGH--
AIIIIIYIIIIIII!
--JUST MEET THE REST OF THE CLASS AT THE MUSEUM OF YESTERDAY AT 12:07 SHARP, IN FRONT OF THE "LAST FLAME" EXHIBIT!
I CAN'T WAIT!
OH, BOY! YOU BET!
RUH-ROH!
SEE YOU AT THE MUSEUM, KI--KKZZZZZZ!
KKZZZZAACK!!
DADDY!
RORGE!
POP!
CRAASSH!

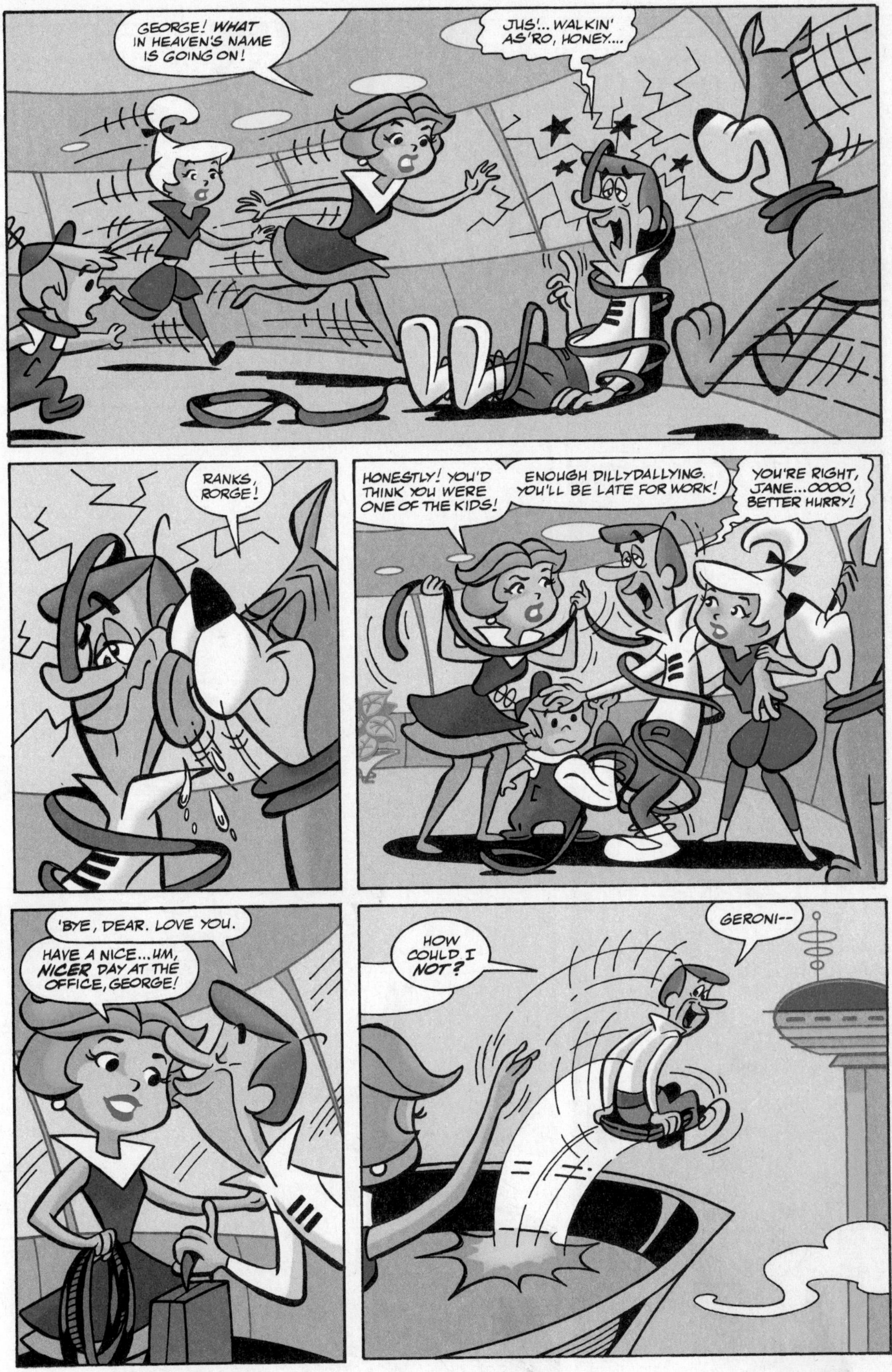
GEORGE! **WHAT** IN HEAVEN'S NAME IS GOING ON!
JUS'... WALKIN' AS'RO, HONEY....
RANKS, RORGE!
HONESTLY! YOU'D THINK YOU WERE ONE OF THE KIDS!
ENOUGH DILLYDALLYING. YOU'LL BE LATE FOR WORK!
YOU'RE RIGHT, JANE...OOOO, BETTER HURRY!
'BYE, DEAR. LOVE YOU.
HAVE A NICE...UM, **NICER** DAY AT THE OFFICE, GEORGE!
HOW COULD I **NOT?**
GERONI--

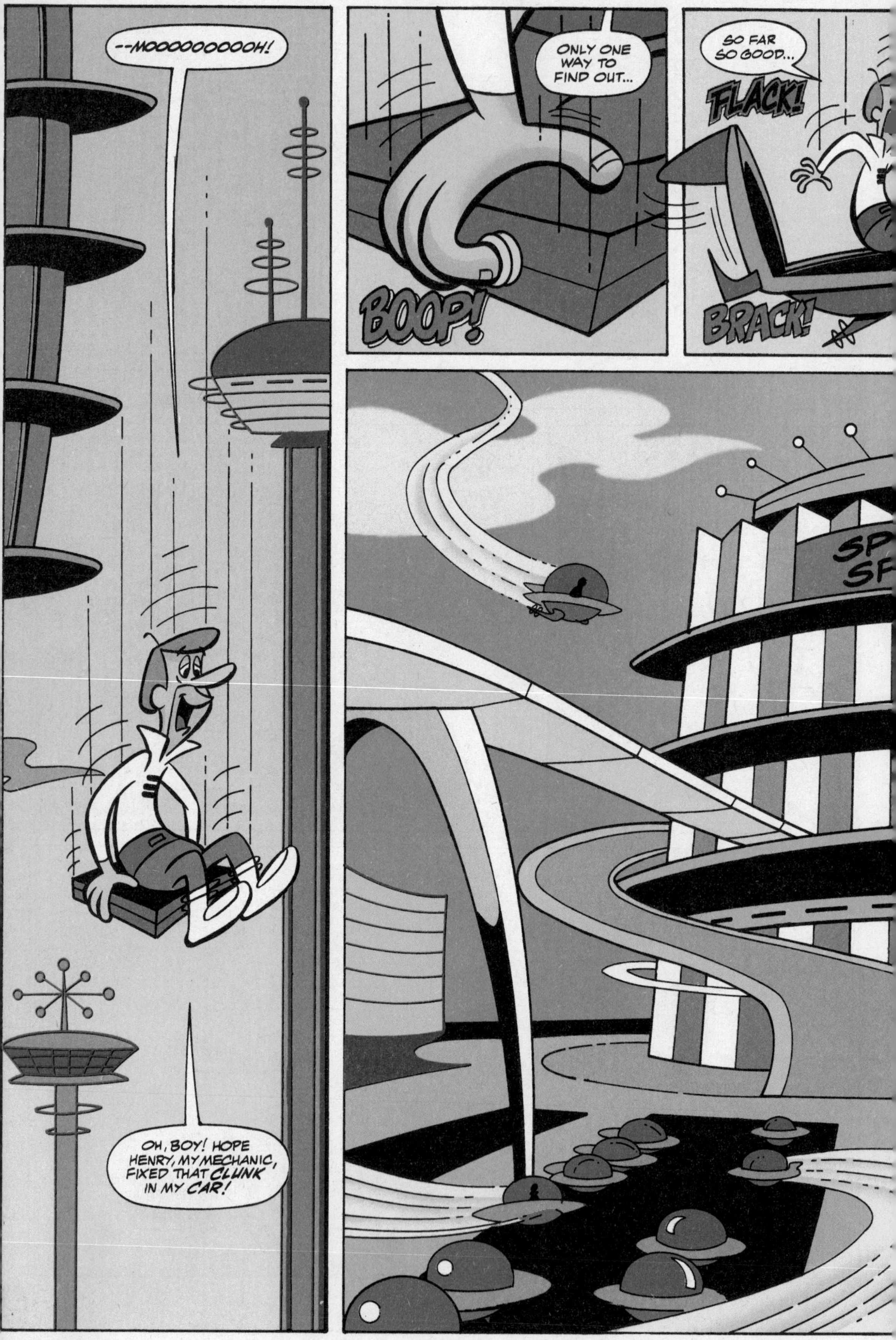
--MOOOOOOOOOOH!
OH, BOY! HOPE HENRY, MY MECHANIC, FIXED THAT CLUNK IN MY CAR!
ONLY ONE WAY TO FIND OUT...
BOOP!
SO FAR SO GOOD...
FLACK!
BRACK!

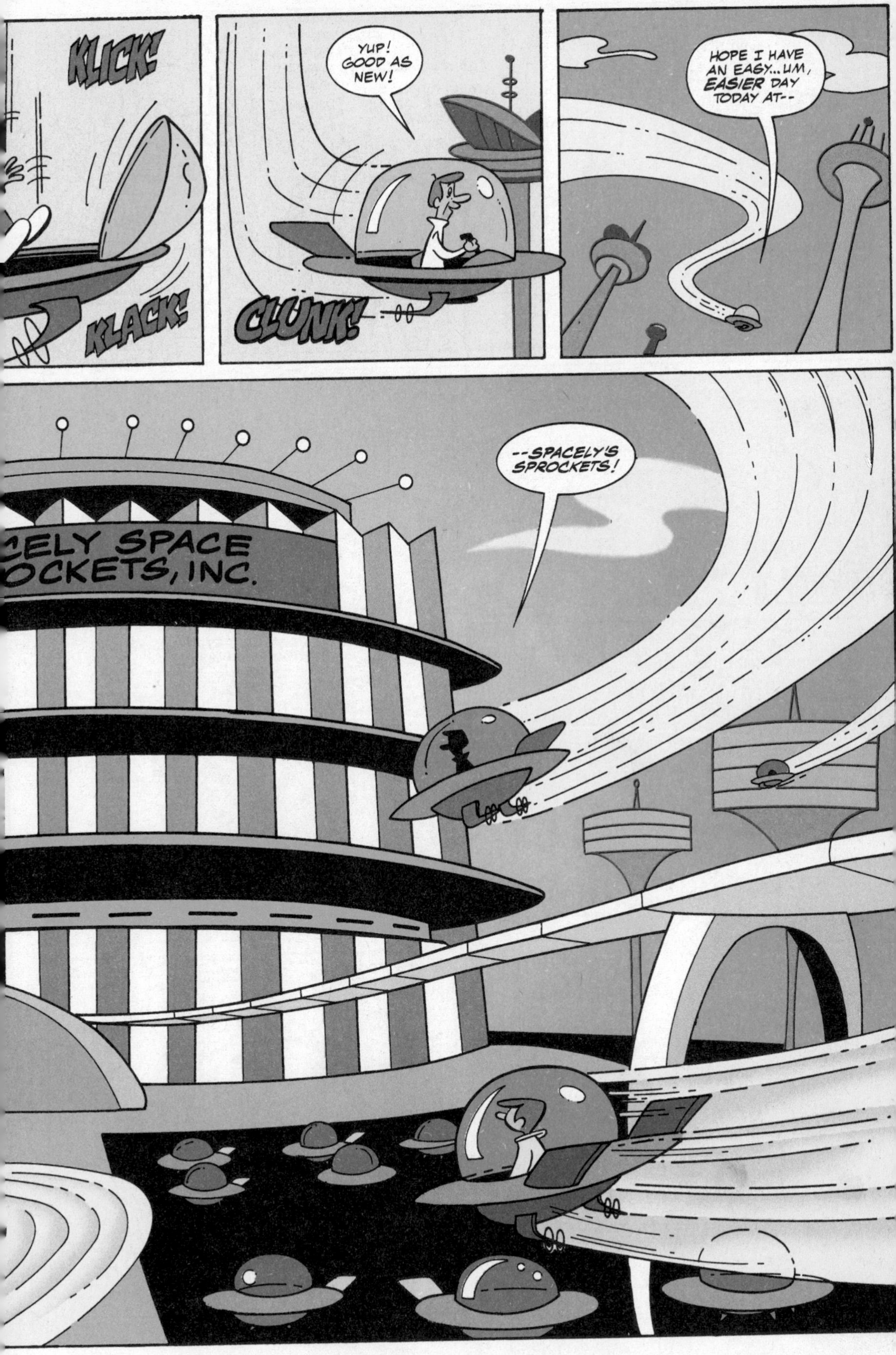
KLICK!
KLACK!
YUP! GOOD AS NEW!
CLUNK!
HOPE I HAVE AN EASY...UM, **EASIER** DAY TODAY AT--
CELY SPACE
OCKETS, INC.
--SPACELY'S SPROCKETS!

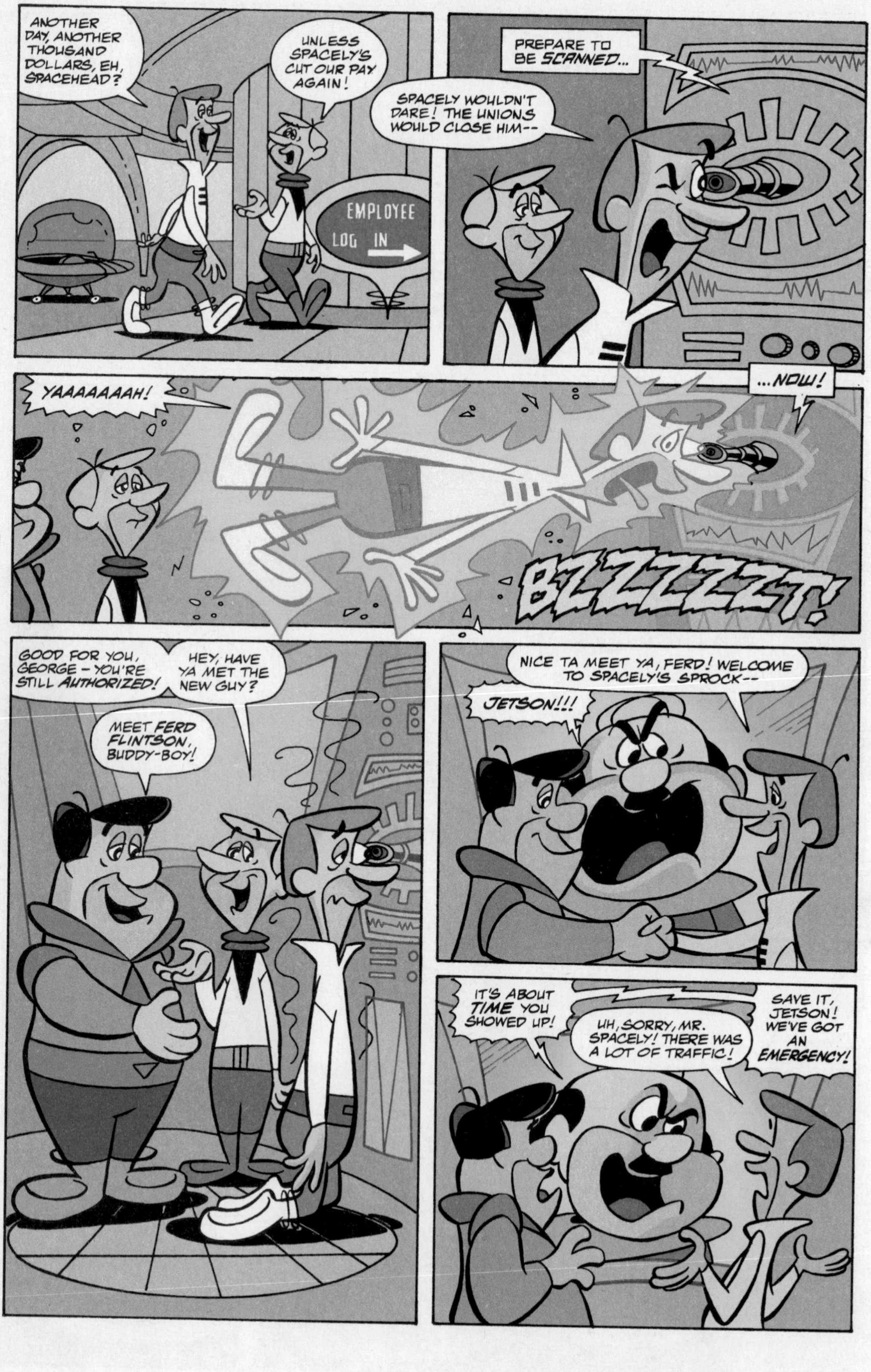
ANOTHER DAY, ANOTHER THOUSAND DOLLARS, EH, SPACEHEAD?
UNLESS SPACELY'S CUT OUR PAY AGAIN!
EMPLOYEE LOG IN
PREPARE TO BE *SCANNED*...
SPACELY WOULDN'T DARE! THE UNIONS WOULD CLOSE HIM--
YAAAAAAAH!
...NOW!
BZZZZZT!
GOOD FOR YOU, GEORGE – YOU'RE STILL *AUTHORIZED!*
HEY, HAVE YA MET THE NEW GUY?
MEET *FERD FLINTSON*, BUDDY-BOY!
NICE TA MEET YA, FERD! WELCOME TO SPACELY'S SPROCK--
JETSON!!!
IT'S ABOUT *TIME* YOU SHOWED UP!
UH, SORRY, MR. SPACELY! THERE WAS A LOT OF TRAFFIC!
SAVE IT, JETSON! WE'VE GOT AN *EMERGENCY!*

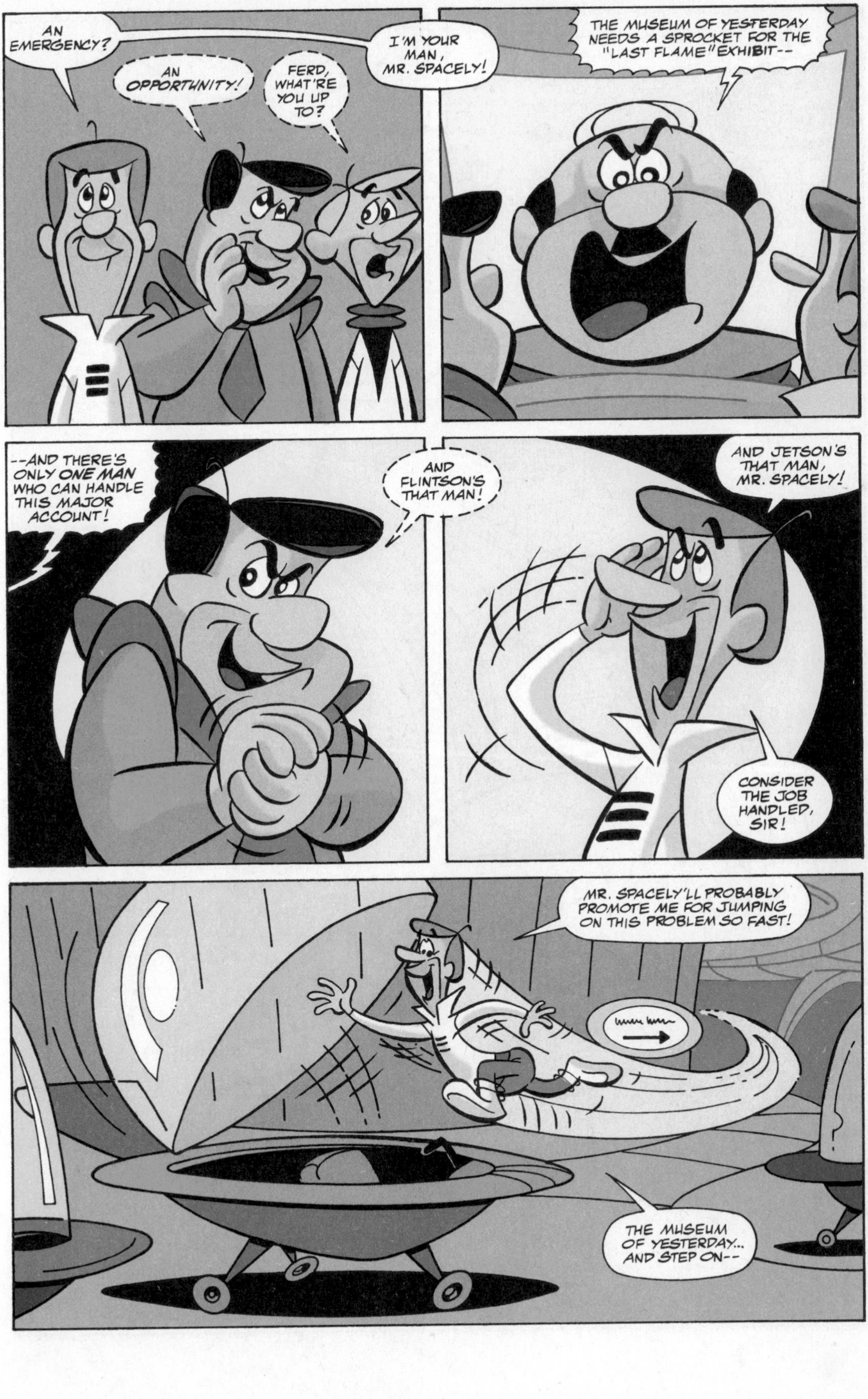
AN EMERGENCY?
AN OPPORTUNITY!
FERD, WHAT'RE YOU UP TO?
I'M YOUR MAN, MR. SPACELY!
THE MUSEUM OF YESTERDAY NEEDS A SPROCKET FOR THE "LAST FLAME" EXHIBIT--
--AND THERE'S ONLY ONE MAN WHO CAN HANDLE THIS MAJOR ACCOUNT!
AND FLINTSON'S THAT MAN!
AND JETSON'S THAT MAN, MR. SPACELY!
CONSIDER THE JOB HANDLED, SIR!
MR. SPACELY'LL PROBABLY PROMOTE ME FOR JUMPING ON THIS PROBLEM SO FAST!
THE MUSEUM OF YESTERDAY... AND STEP ON--

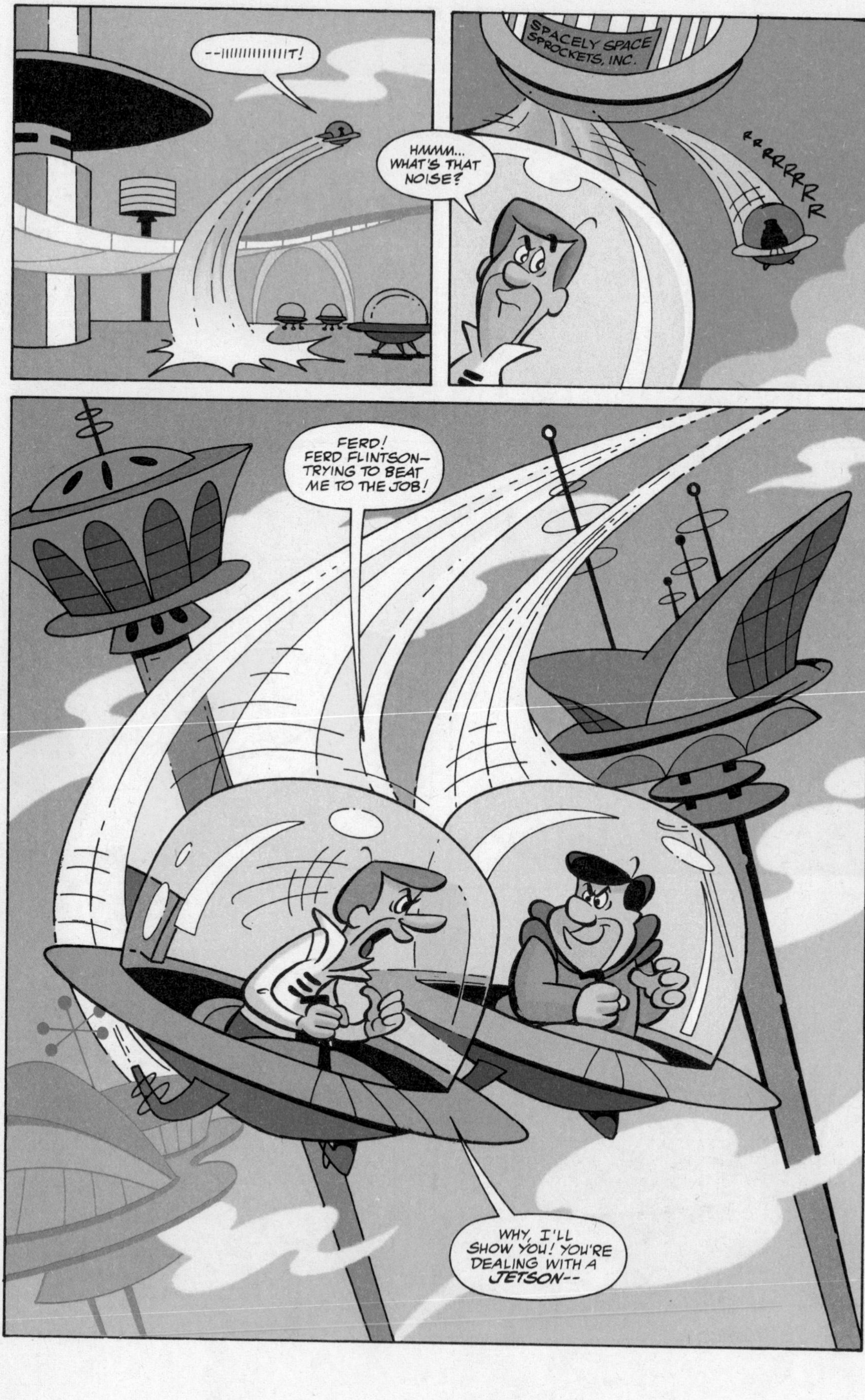
--IIIIIIIIIIIIT!
SPACELY SPACE SPROCKETS, INC.
HMMM... WHAT'S THAT NOISE?
RRRRRRRRR
FERD! FERD FLINTSON-- TRYING TO BEAT ME TO THE JOB!
WHY, I'LL SHOW YOU! YOU'RE DEALING WITH A JETSON--

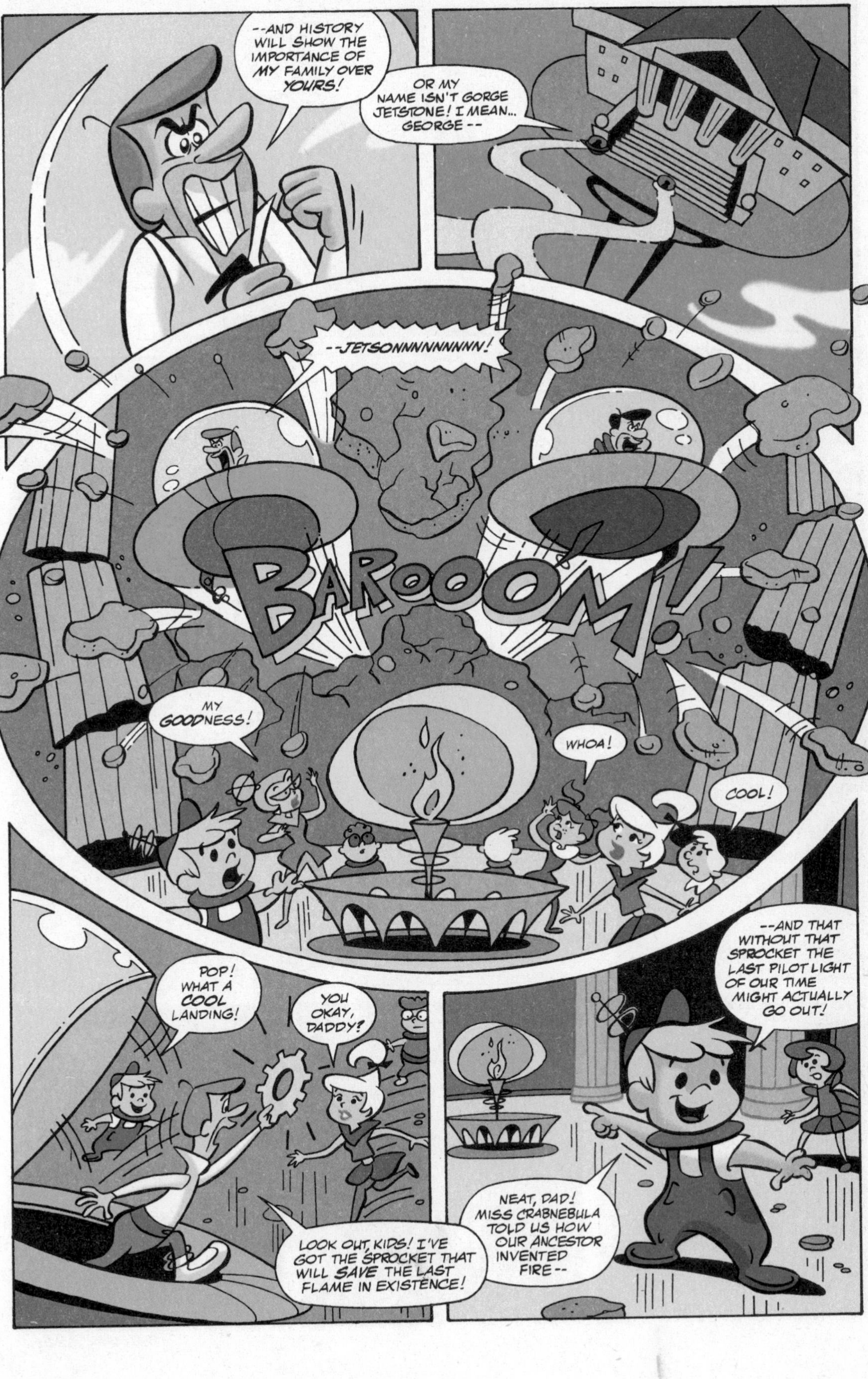
--AND HISTORY WILL SHOW THE IMPORTANCE OF MY FAMILY OVER YOURS!
OR MY NAME ISN'T GORGE JETSTONE! I MEAN... GEORGE--
--JETSONNNNNNNNN!
BAROOOOM!
MY GOODNESS!
WHOA!
COOL!
POP! WHAT A COOL LANDING!
YOU OKAY, DADDY?
LOOK OUT, KIDS! I'VE GOT THE SPROCKET THAT WILL SAVE THE LAST FLAME IN EXISTENCE!
NEAT, DAD! MISS CRABNEBULA TOLD US HOW OUR ANCESTOR INVENTED FIRE--
--AND THAT WITHOUT THAT SPROCKET THE LAST PILOT LIGHT OF OUR TIME MIGHT ACTUALLY GO OUT!

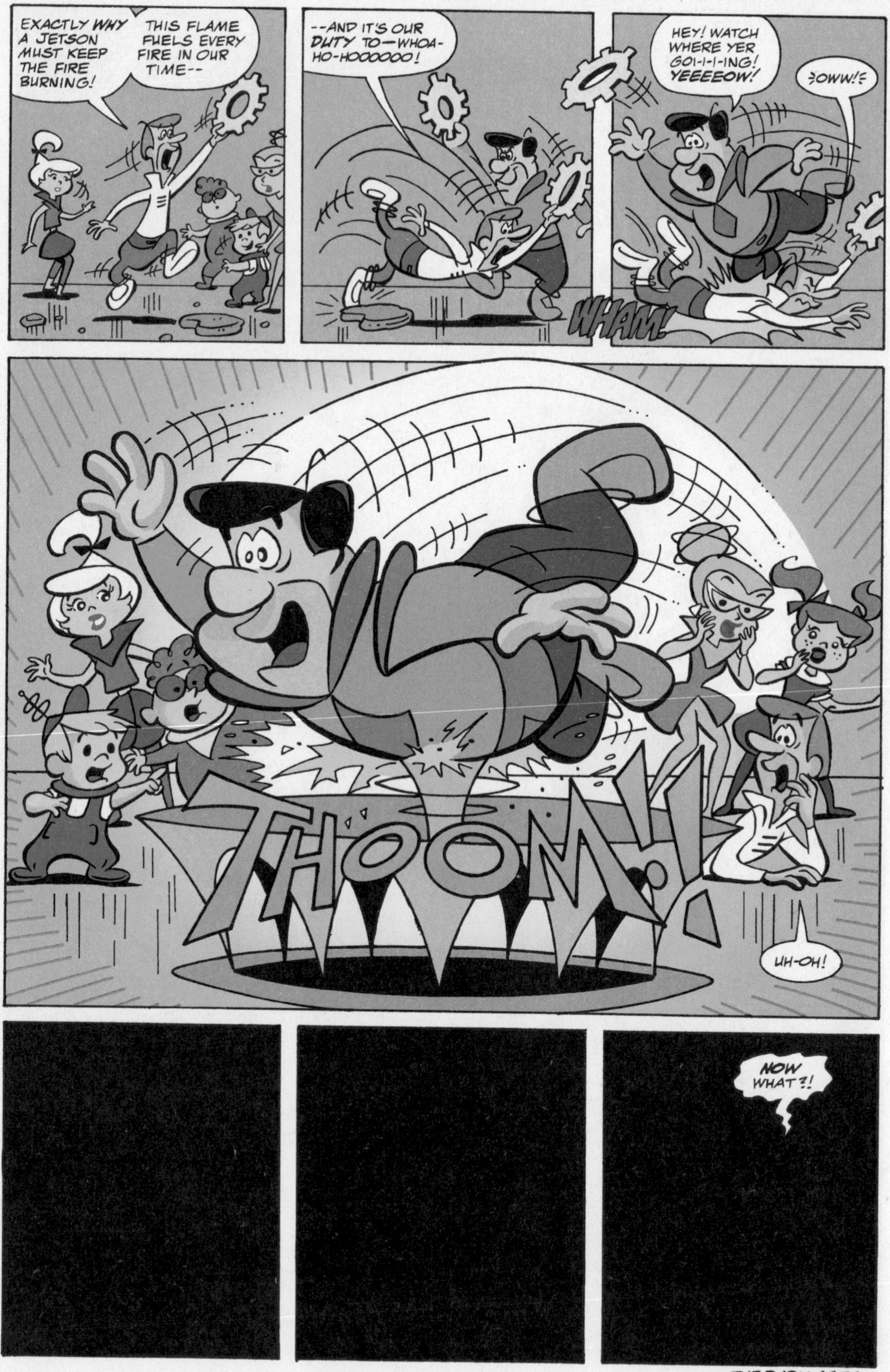
EXACTLY WHY A JETSON MUST KEEP THE FIRE BURNING!
THIS FLAME FUELS EVERY FIRE IN OUR TIME--
--AND IT'S OUR DUTY TO—WHOA-HO-HOOOOOO!
HEY! WATCH WHERE YER GOI-I-I-ING! YEEEEOW!
OWW!
WHAM!
THOOM!!
UH-OH!
NOW WHAT?!
THE DARK AGES...

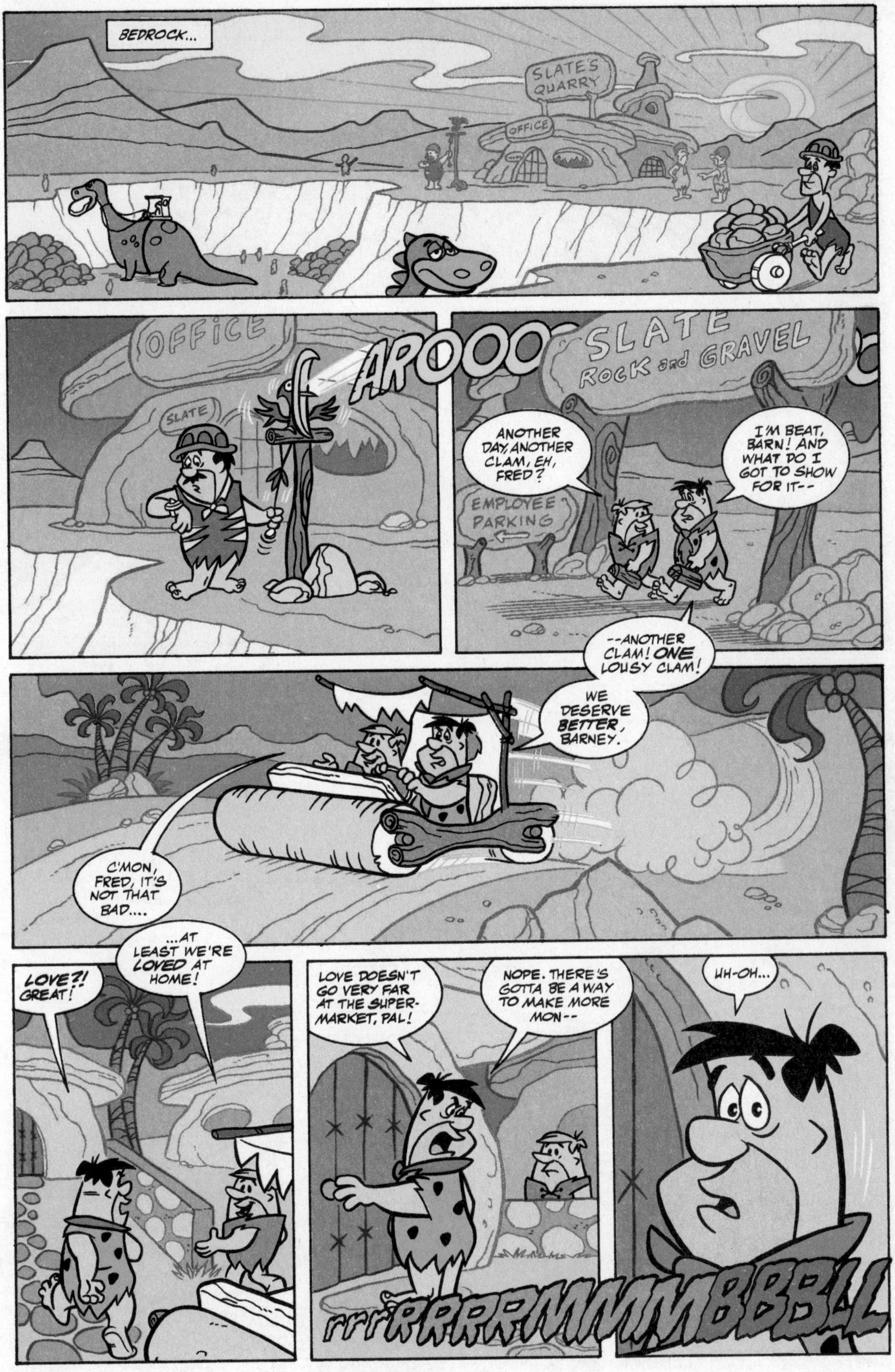
BEDROCK...
SLATE'S QUARRY
OFFICE
OFFICE
SLATE
AROOOO
SLATE Rock and GRAVEL
ANOTHER DAY, ANOTHER CLAM, EH, FRED?
I'M BEAT, BARN! AND WHAT DO I GOT TO SHOW FOR IT--
EMPLOYEE PARKING
--ANOTHER CLAM! ONE LOUSY CLAM!
WE DESERVE BETTER, BARNEY.
C'MON, FRED, IT'S NOT THAT BAD....
...AT LEAST WE'RE LOVED AT HOME!
LOVE?! GREAT!
LOVE DOESN'T GO VERY FAR AT THE SUPER-MARKET, PAL!
NOPE. THERE'S GOTTA BE A WAY TO MAKE MORE MON--
UH-OH...
rrrRRRRMMMMBBBLL

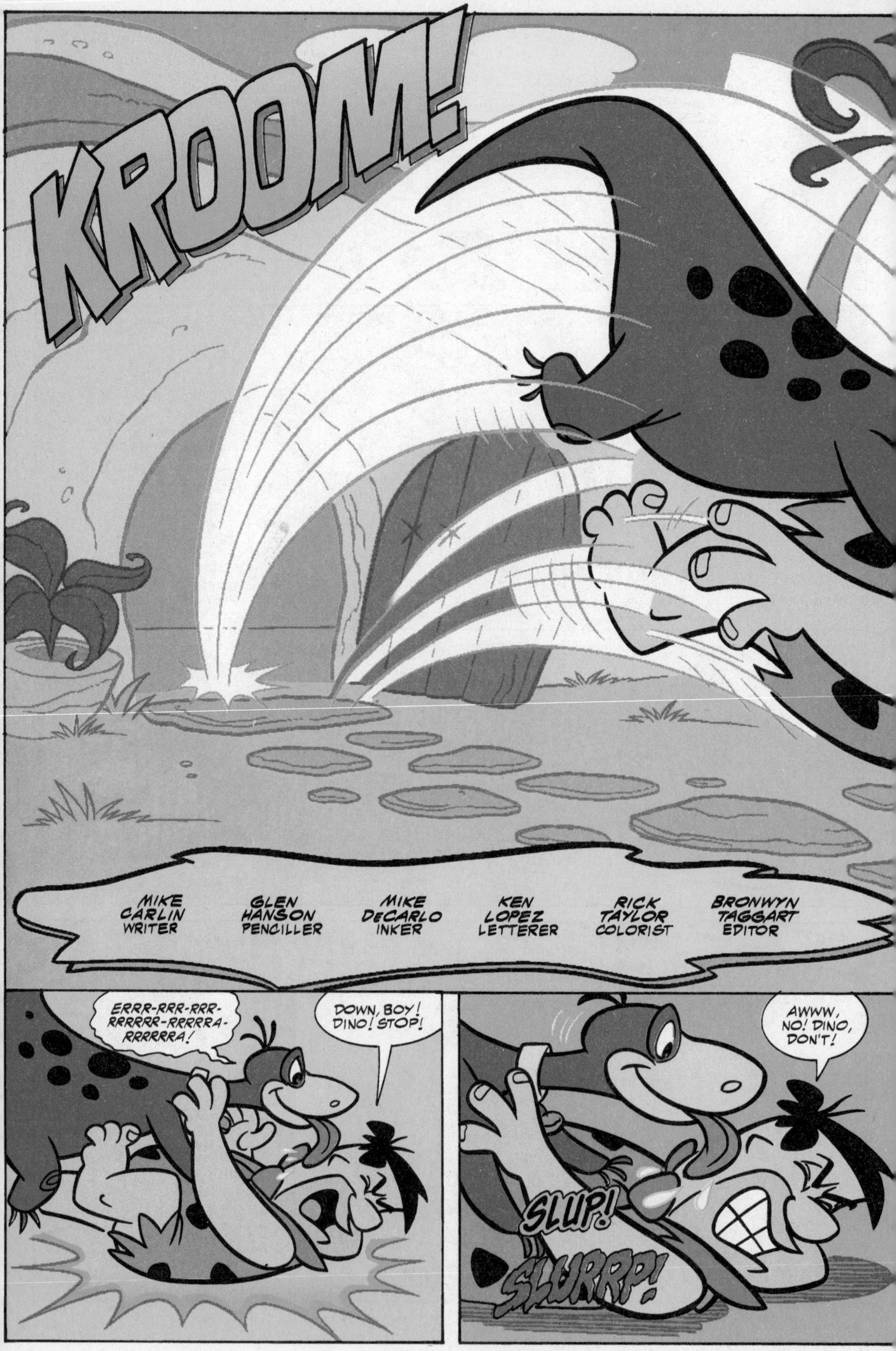
KROOM!
MIKE CARLIN WRITER
GLEN HANSON PENCILLER
MIKE DeCARLO INKER
KEN LOPEZ LETTERER
RICK TAYLOR COLORIST
BRONWYN TAGGART EDITOR
ERRR-RRR-RRR-RRRRRR-RRRRRA-RRRRRRA!
DOWN, BOY! DINO! STOP!
AWWW, NO! DINO, DON'T!
SLUP!
SLURRP!

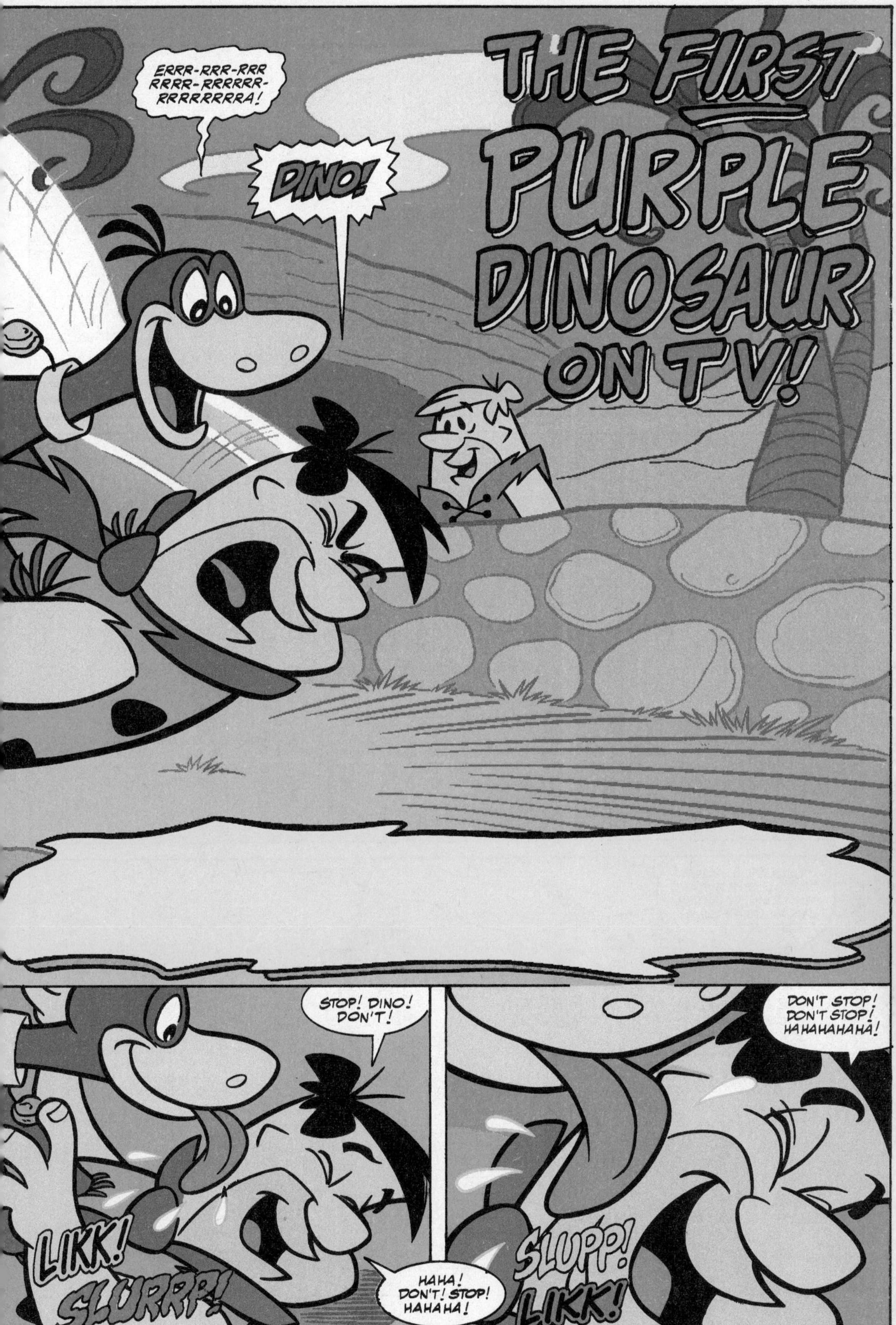
THE FIRST PURPLE DINOSAUR ON TV!
ERRR-RRR-RRR RRRR-RRRRRR-RRRRRRRRA!
DINO!
STOP! DINO! DON'T!
LIKK! SLURRP!
HAHA! DON'T! STOP! HAHAHA!
DON'T STOP! DON'T STOP! HAHAHAHAHA!
SLUPP! LIKK!

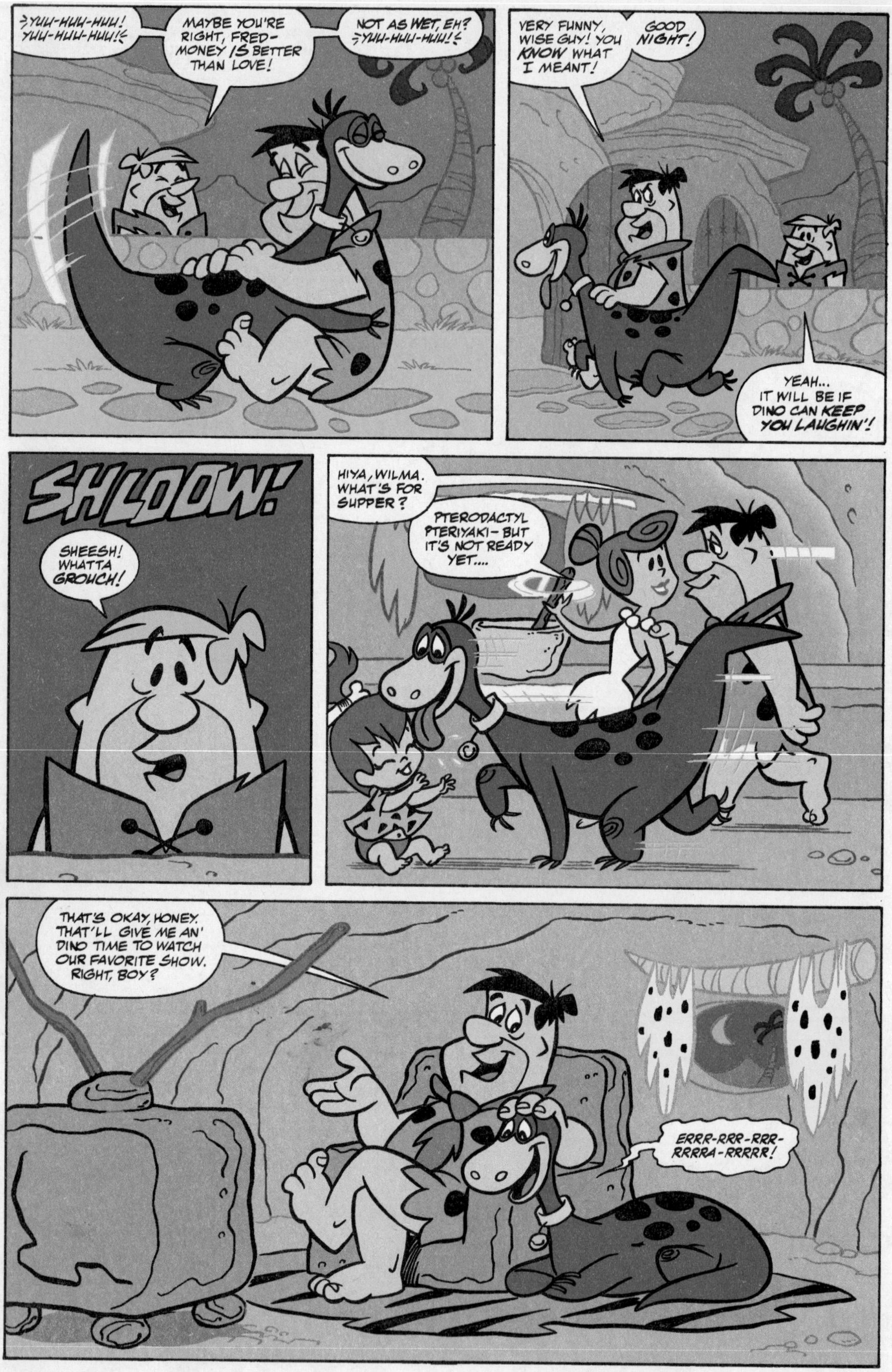

≈YUU-HUU-HUU! YUU-HUU-HUU!≈
MAYBE YOU'RE RIGHT, FRED-- MONEY IS BETTER THAN LOVE!
NOT AS WET, EH? ≈YUU-HUU-HUU!≈
VERY FUNNY, WISE GUY! YOU KNOW WHAT I MEANT!
GOOD NIGHT!
YEAH... IT WILL BE IF DINO CAN KEEP YOU LAUGHIN'!
SHLOOW!
SHEESH! WHATTA GROUCH!
HIYA, WILMA. WHAT'S FOR SUPPER?
PTERODACTYL PTERIYAKI-- BUT IT'S NOT READY YET....
THAT'S OKAY, HONEY. THAT'LL GIVE ME AN' DINO TIME TO WATCH OUR FAVORITE SHOW. RIGHT, BOY?
ERRR-RRR-RRR-RRRRA-RRRRR!

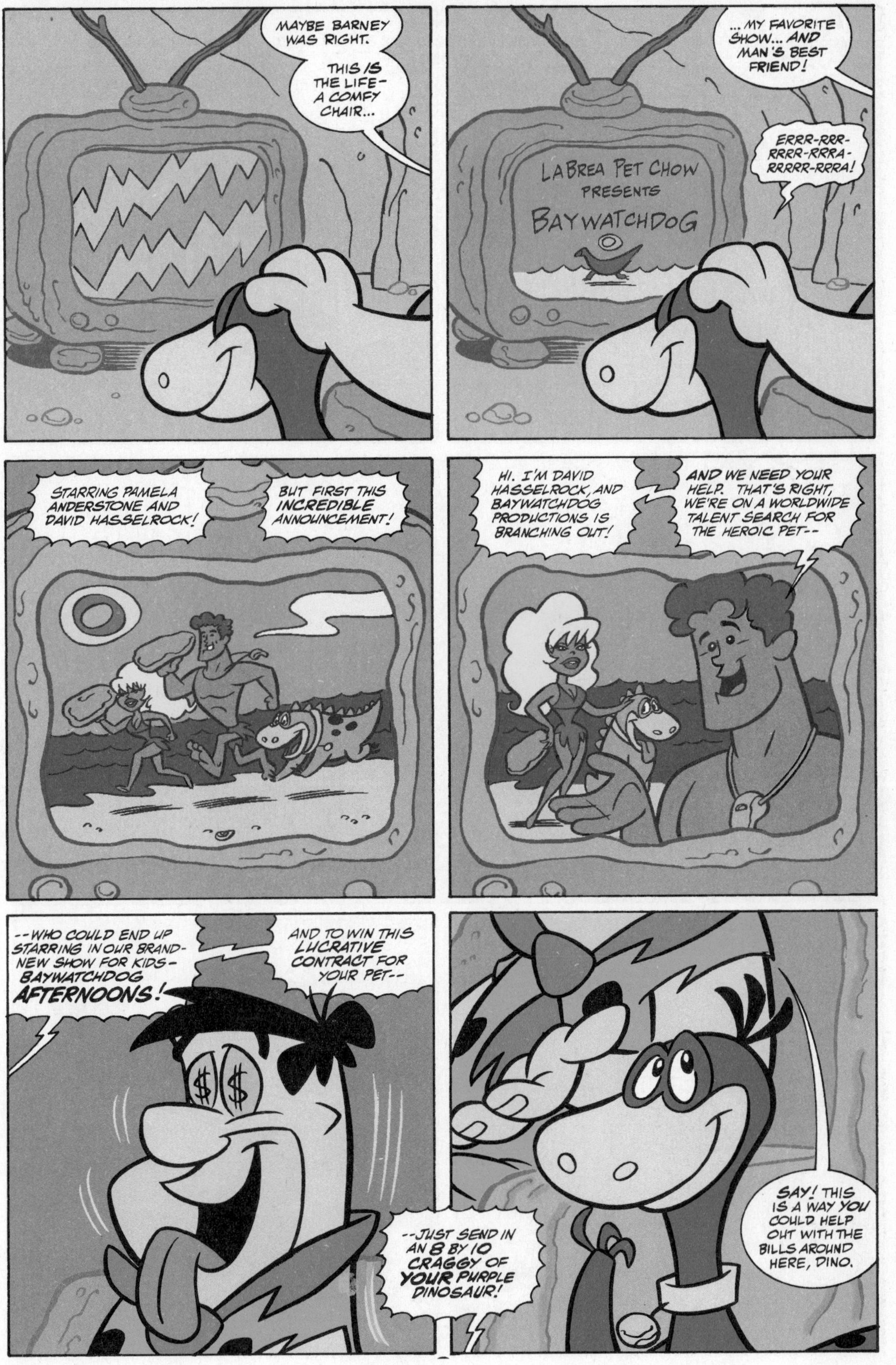
MAYBE BARNEY WAS RIGHT.
THIS IS THE LIFE-- A COMFY CHAIR...
...MY FAVORITE SHOW... AND MAN'S BEST FRIEND!
LA BREA PET CHOW PRESENTS BAYWATCHDOG
ERRR-RRR-RRRR-RRRA-RRRRR-RRRA!
STARRING PAMELA ANDERSTONE AND DAVID HASSELROCK!
BUT FIRST THIS INCREDIBLE ANNOUNCEMENT!
HI. I'M DAVID HASSELROCK, AND BAYWATCHDOG PRODUCTIONS IS BRANCHING OUT!
AND WE NEED YOUR HELP. THAT'S RIGHT, WE'RE ON A WORLDWIDE TALENT SEARCH FOR THE HEROIC PET--
--WHO COULD END UP STARRING IN OUR BRAND-NEW SHOW FOR KIDS-- BAYWATCHDOG AFTERNOONS!
AND TO WIN THIS LUCRATIVE CONTRACT FOR YOUR PET--
--JUST SEND IN AN 8 BY 10 CRAGGY OF YOUR PURPLE DINOSAUR!
SAY! THIS IS A WAY YOU COULD HELP OUT WITH THE BILLS AROUND HERE, DINO.

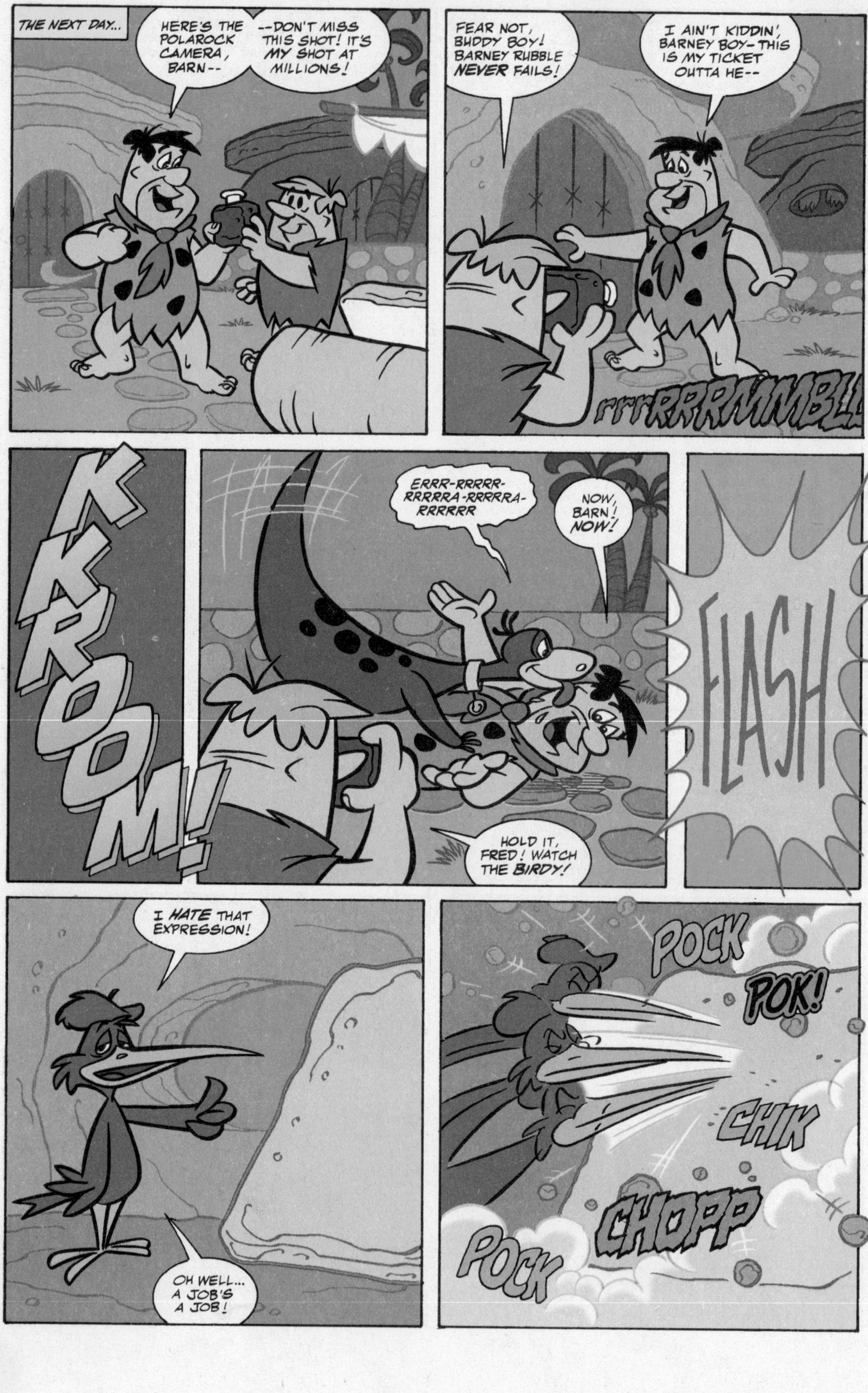
THE NEXT DAY...
HERE'S THE POLAROCK CAMERA, BARN--
--DON'T MISS THIS SHOT! IT'S MY SHOT AT MILLIONS!
FEAR NOT, BUDDY BOY! BARNEY RUBBLE NEVER FAILS!
I AIN'T KIDDIN', BARNEY BOY-- THIS IS MY TICKET OUTTA HE--
rrrRRRMMBLL
KKROOM!
ERRR-RRRRR-RRRRRA-RRRRRA-RRRRRR
NOW, BARN! NOW!
HOLD IT, FRED! WATCH THE BIRDY!
FLASH
I HATE THAT EXPRESSION!
OH WELL... A JOB'S A JOB!
POCK
POK!
CHIK
CHOPP
POCK

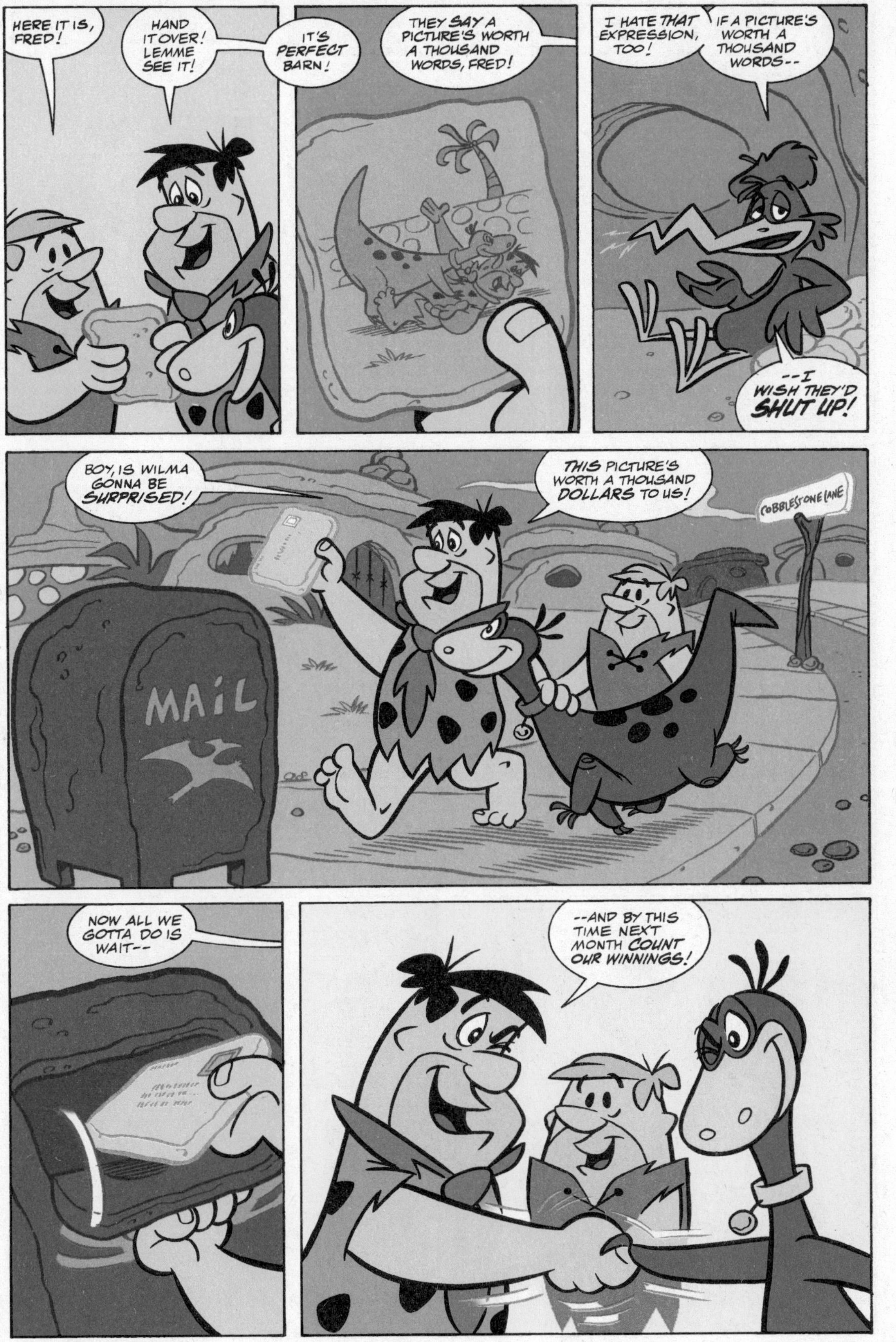
HERE IT IS, FRED!
HAND IT OVER! LEMME SEE IT!
IT'S PERFECT BARN!
THEY SAY A PICTURE'S WORTH A THOUSAND WORDS, FRED!
I HATE THAT EXPRESSION, TOO!
IF A PICTURE'S WORTH A THOUSAND WORDS--
--I WISH THEY'D SHUT UP!
BOY, IS WILMA GONNA BE SURPRISED!
THIS PICTURE'S WORTH A THOUSAND DOLLARS TO US!
COBBLESTONE LANE
MAIL
NOW ALL WE GOTTA DO IS WAIT--
--AND BY THIS TIME NEXT MONTH COUNT OUR WINNINGS!

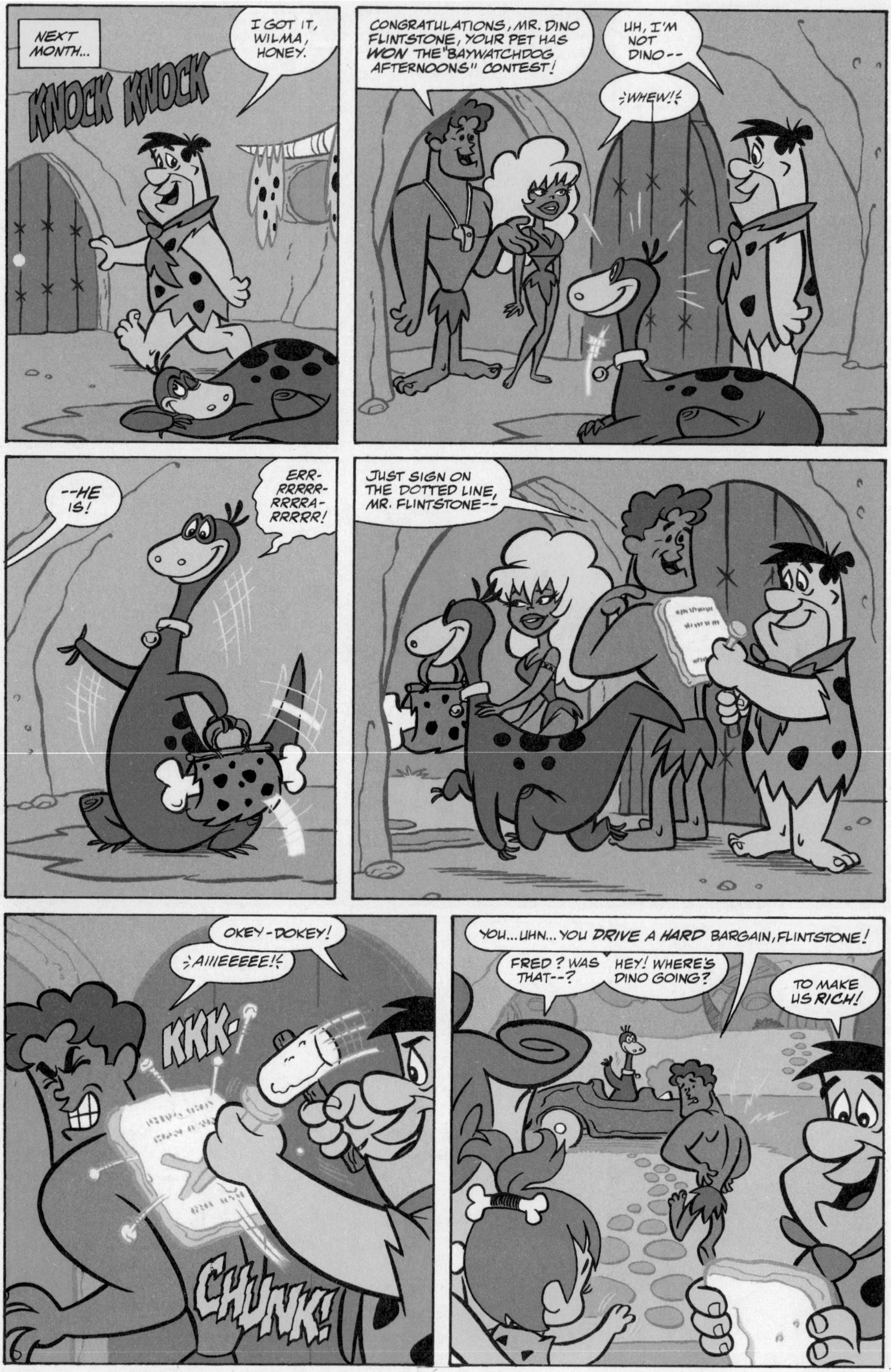
NEXT MONTH...
I GOT IT, WILMA, HONEY.
KNOCK KNOCK
CONGRATULATIONS, MR. DINO FLINTSTONE, YOUR PET HAS WON THE "BAYWATCHDOG AFTERNOONS" CONTEST!
UH, I'M NOT DINO--
WHEW!
--HE IS!
ERR-RRRRR-RRRRA-RRRRR!
JUST SIGN ON THE DOTTED LINE, MR. FLINTSTONE--
OKEY-DOKEY!
AIIIEEEEE!
KKK-
CHUNK!
YOU...UHN... YOU DRIVE A HARD BARGAIN, FLINTSTONE!
FRED? WAS THAT--?
HEY! WHERE'S DINO GOING?
TO MAKE US RICH!

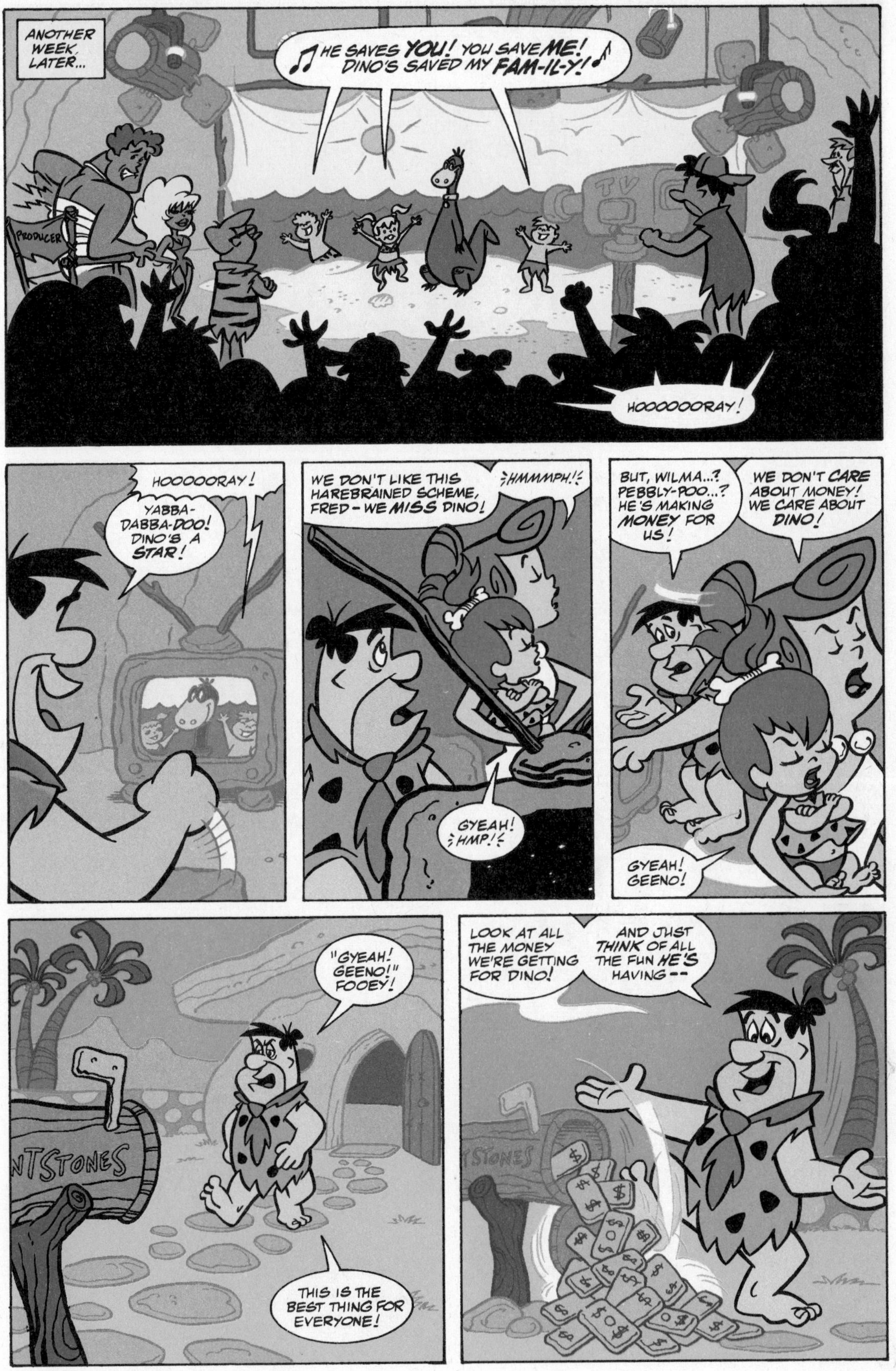
ANOTHER WEEK, LATER...
♫ HE SAVES YOU! YOU SAVE ME! DINO'S SAVED MY FAM-IL-Y! ♪
PRODUCER
TV
HOOOOOORAY!
HOOOOORAY!
YABBA-DABBA-DOO! DINO'S A STAR!
WE DON'T LIKE THIS HAREBRAINED SCHEME, FRED -- WE MISS DINO!
HMMMPH!
GYEAH! HMP!
BUT, WILMA...? PEBBLY-POO...? HE'S MAKING MONEY FOR US!
WE DON'T CARE ABOUT MONEY! WE CARE ABOUT DINO!
GYEAH! GEENO!
"GYEAH! GEENO!" FOOEY!
NTSTONES
THIS IS THE BEST THING FOR EVERYONE!
LOOK AT ALL THE MONEY WE'RE GETTING FOR DINO!
AND JUST THINK OF ALL THE FUN HE'S HAVING --
NTSTONES

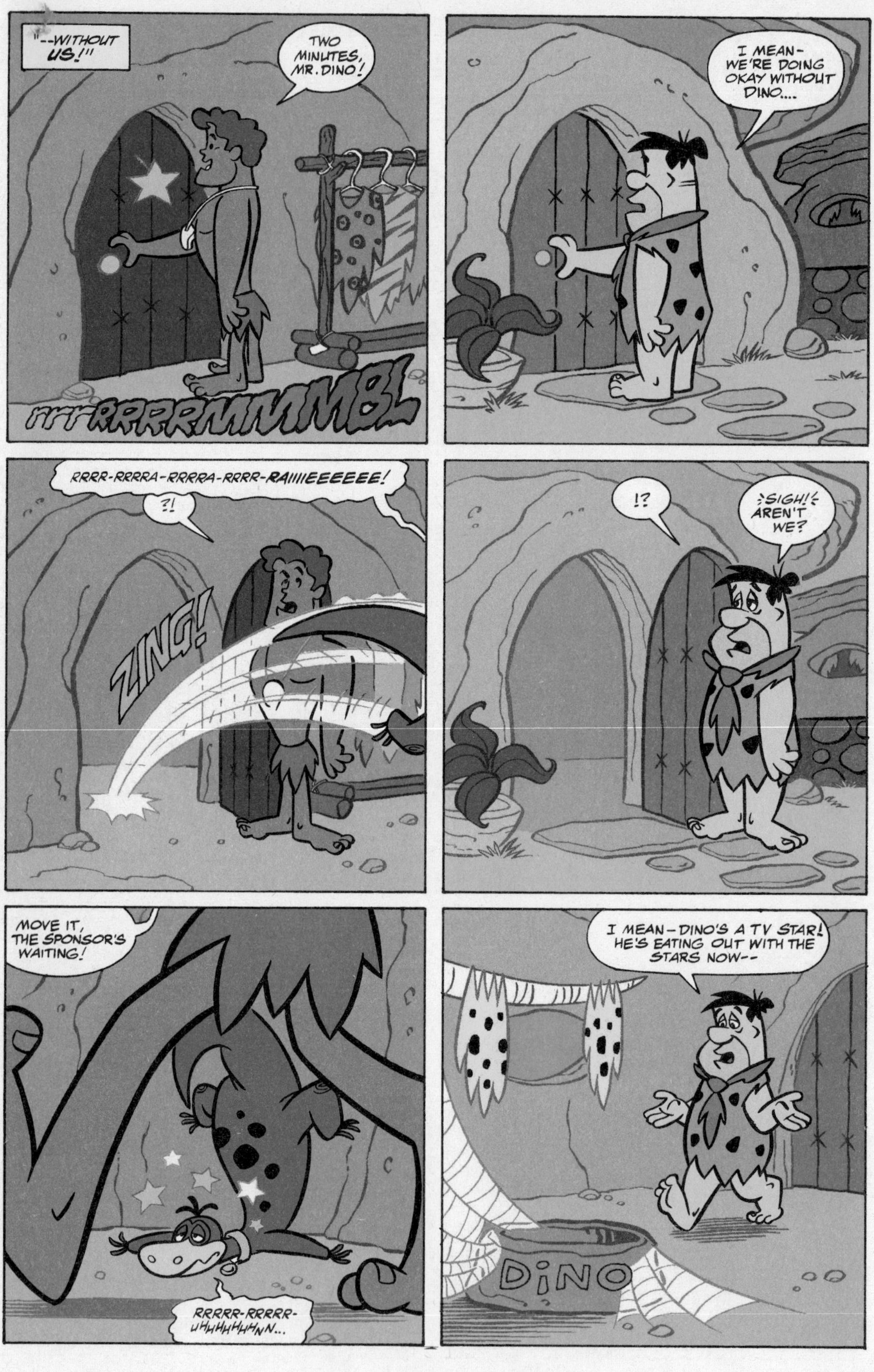
"--WITHOUT US!"
TWO MINUTES, MR. DINO!
rrrRRRRMMMBL
I MEAN- WE'RE DOING OKAY WITHOUT DINO....
RRRR-RRRRA-RRRRA-RRRR-RAIIIIEEEEEE!
?!
ZING!
!?
:SIGH!: AREN'T WE?
MOVE IT, THE SPONSOR'S WAITING!
RRRRR-RRRRR-UHHHHHHHNN...
I MEAN-DINO'S A TV STAR! HE'S EATING OUT WITH THE STARS NOW--
DINO

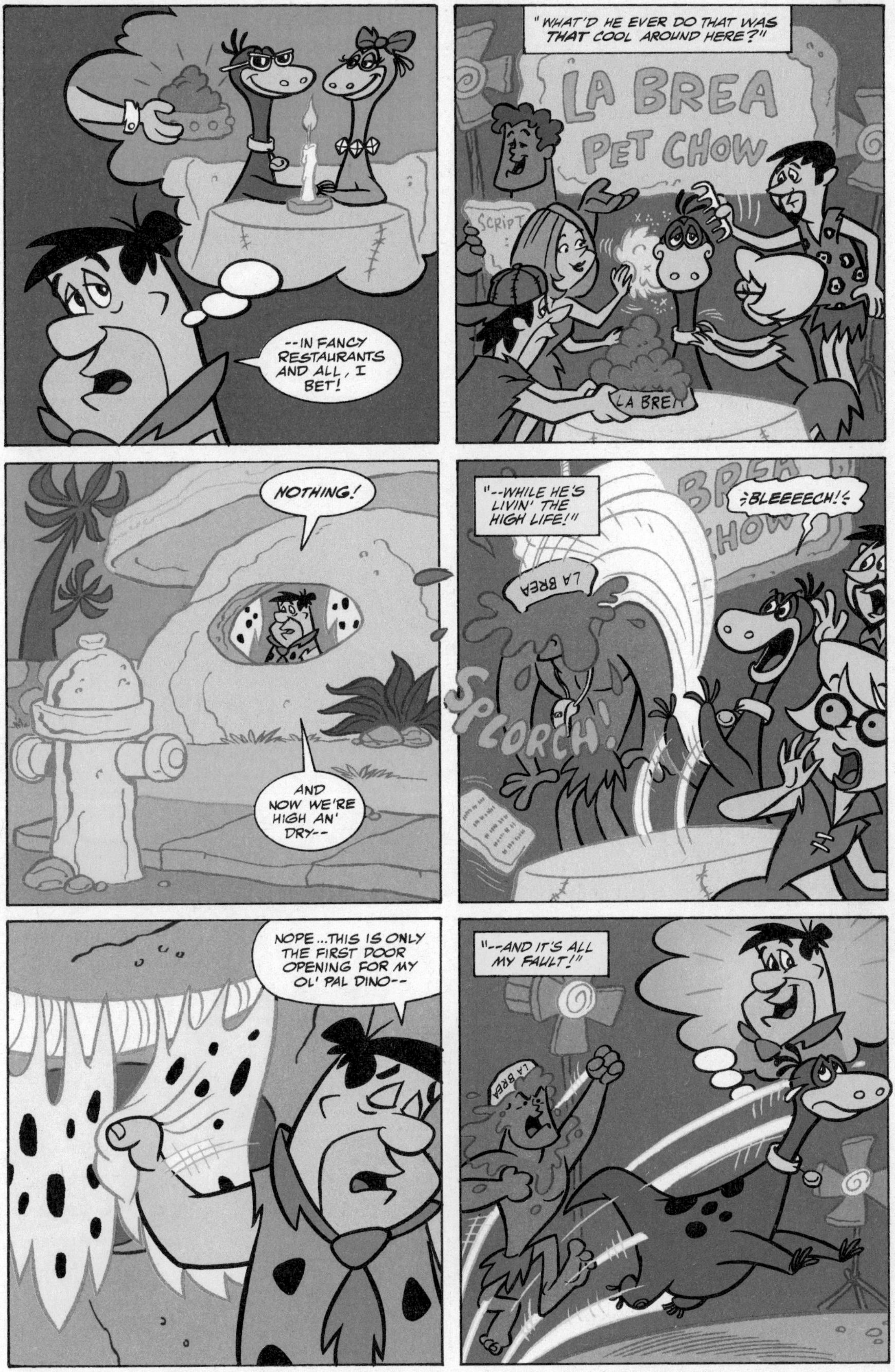
--IN FANCY RESTAURANTS AND ALL, I BET!
"WHAT'D HE EVER DO THAT WAS THAT COOL AROUND HERE?"
LA BREA PET CHOW
SCRIPT
LA BREA
NOTHING!
AND NOW WE'RE HIGH AN' DRY--
"--WHILE HE'S LIVIN' THE HIGH LIFE!"
BLEEEECH!
LA BREA
SPLORCH!
NOPE...THIS IS ONLY THE FIRST DOOR OPENING FOR MY OL' PAL DINO--
"--AND IT'S ALL MY FAULT!"
LA BREA

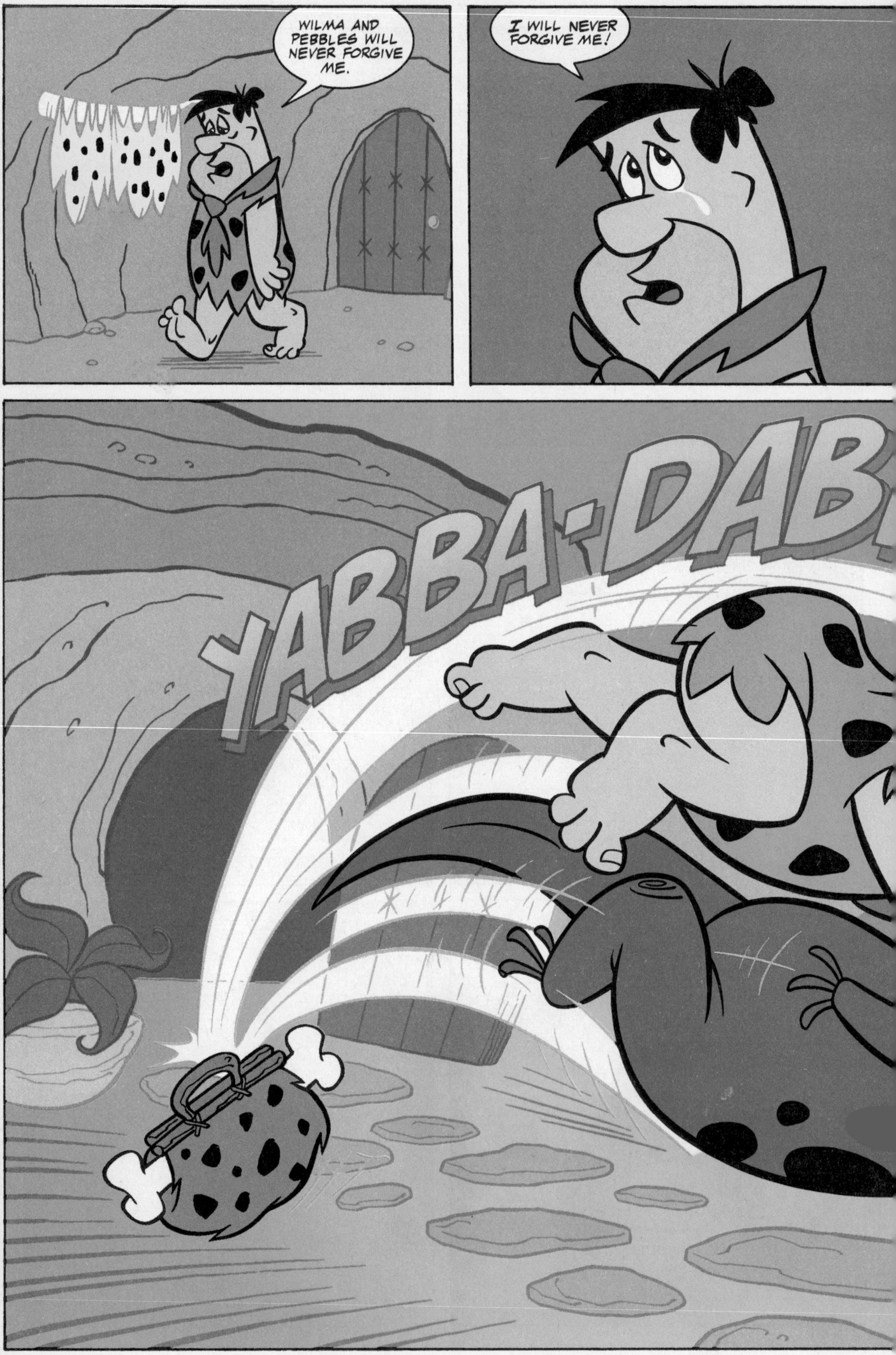
WILMA AND PEBBLES WILL NEVER FORGIVE ME.
I WILL NEVER FORGIVE ME!
YABBA-DAB

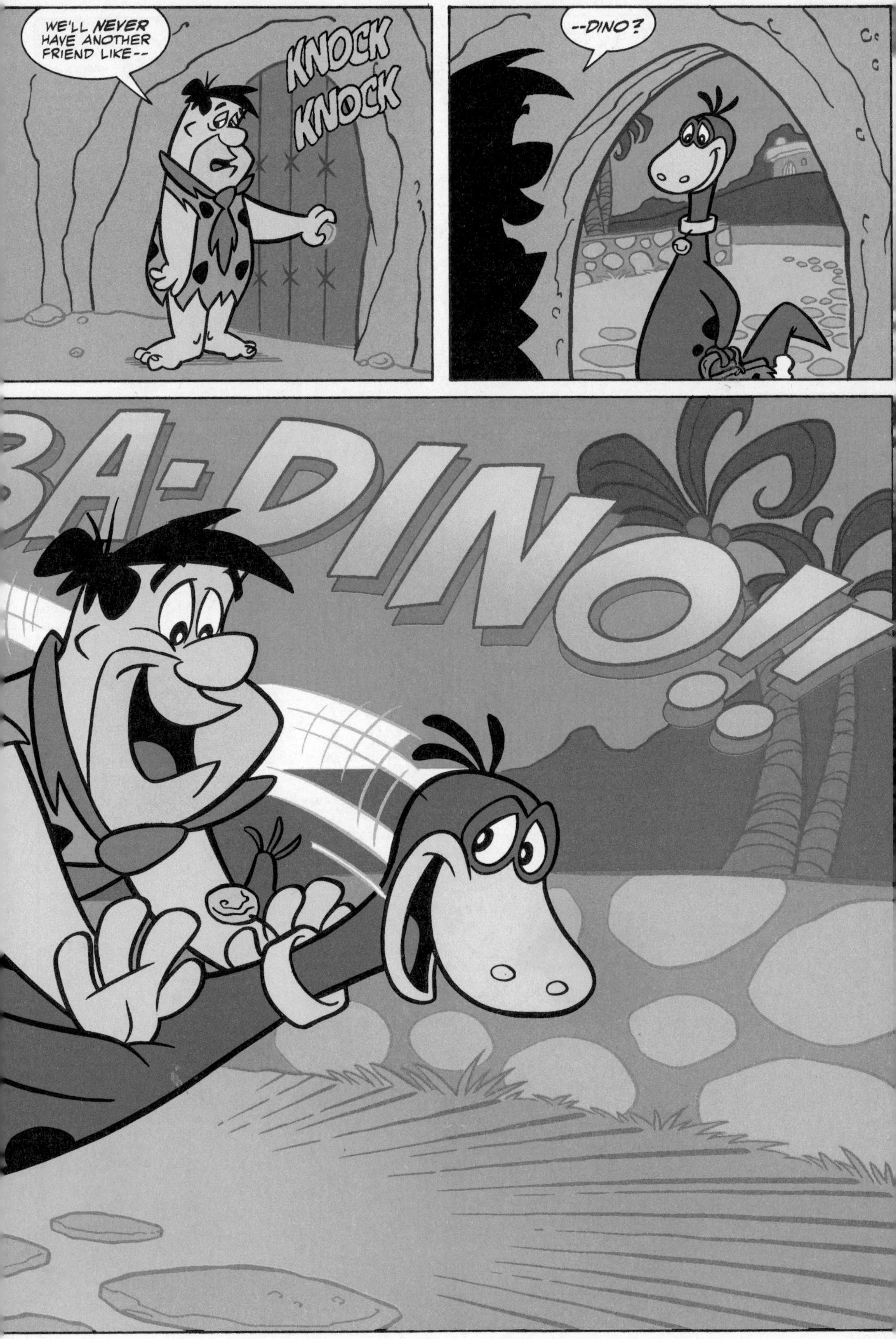

WE'LL NEVER HAVE ANOTHER FRIEND LIKE--
KNOCK KNOCK
--DINO?
BA-DINO!!

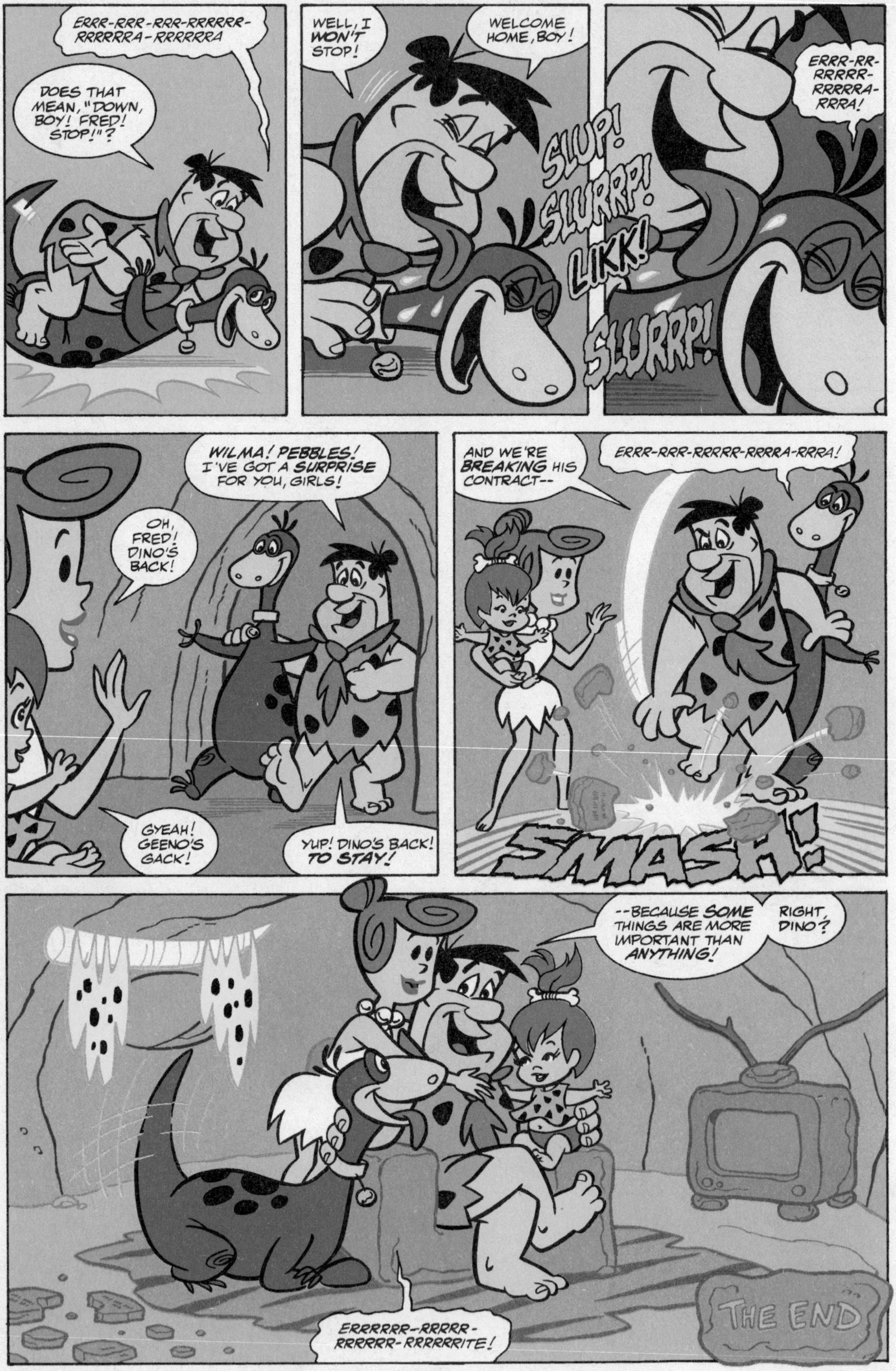

ERRR-RRR-RRR-RRRRRR-RRRRRRA-RRRRRRA
DOES THAT MEAN, "DOWN, BOY! FRED! STOP!"?
WELL, I WON'T STOP!
WELCOME HOME, BOY!
SLUP! SLURRP! LIKK! SLURRP!
ERRR-RR-RRRRR-RRRRRA-RRRA!
WILMA! PEBBLES! I'VE GOT A SURPRISE FOR YOU, GIRLS!
OH, FRED! DINO'S BACK!
GYEAH! GEENO'S GACK!
YUP! DINO'S BACK! TO STAY!
AND WE'RE BREAKING HIS CONTRACT--
ERRR-RRR-RRRRR-RRRRA-RRRA!
SMASH!
--BECAUSE SOME THINGS ARE MORE IMPORTANT THAN ANYTHING!
RIGHT, DINO?
ERRRRRR-RRRRR-RRRRRR-RRRRRRITE!
THE END

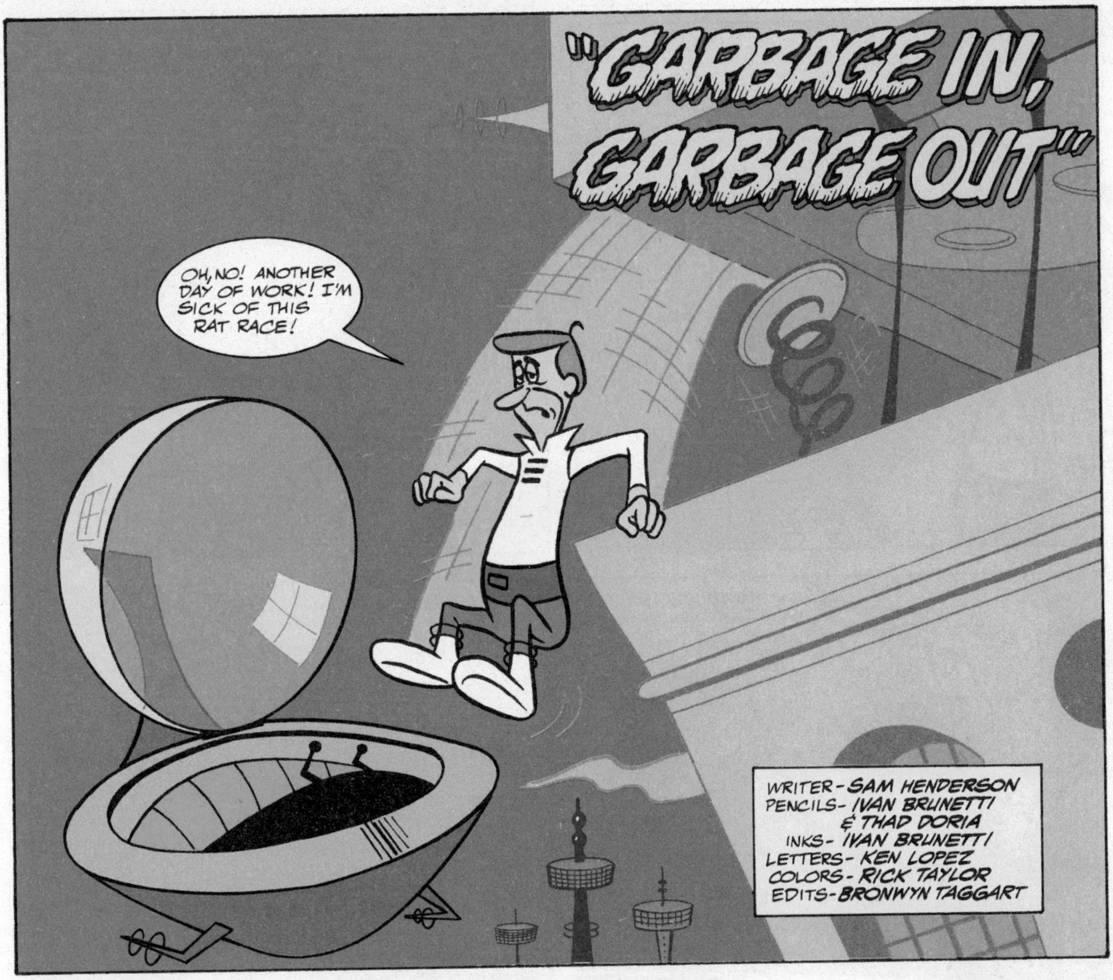
"GARBAGE IN, GARBAGE OUT"
OH, NO! ANOTHER DAY OF WORK! I'M SICK OF THIS RAT RACE!
WRITER- SAM HENDERSON
PENCILS- IVAN BRUNETTI & THAD DORIA
INKS- IVAN BRUNETTI
LETTERS- KEN LOPEZ
COLORS- RICK TAYLOR
EDITS- BRONWYN TAGGART

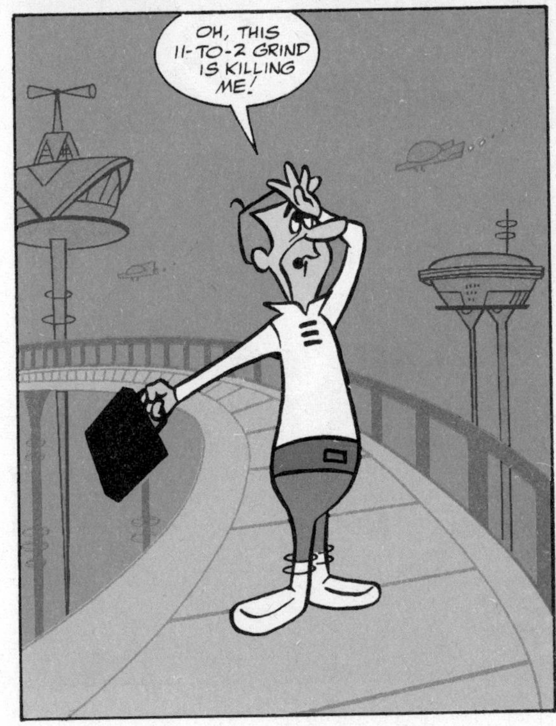
OH, THIS 11-TO-2 GRIND IS KILLING ME!

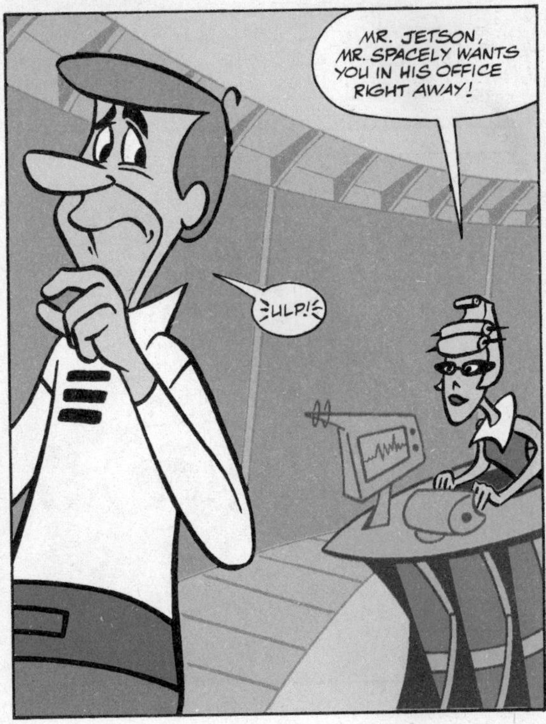
MR. JETSON, MR. SPACELY WANTS YOU IN HIS OFFICE RIGHT AWAY!
ULP!

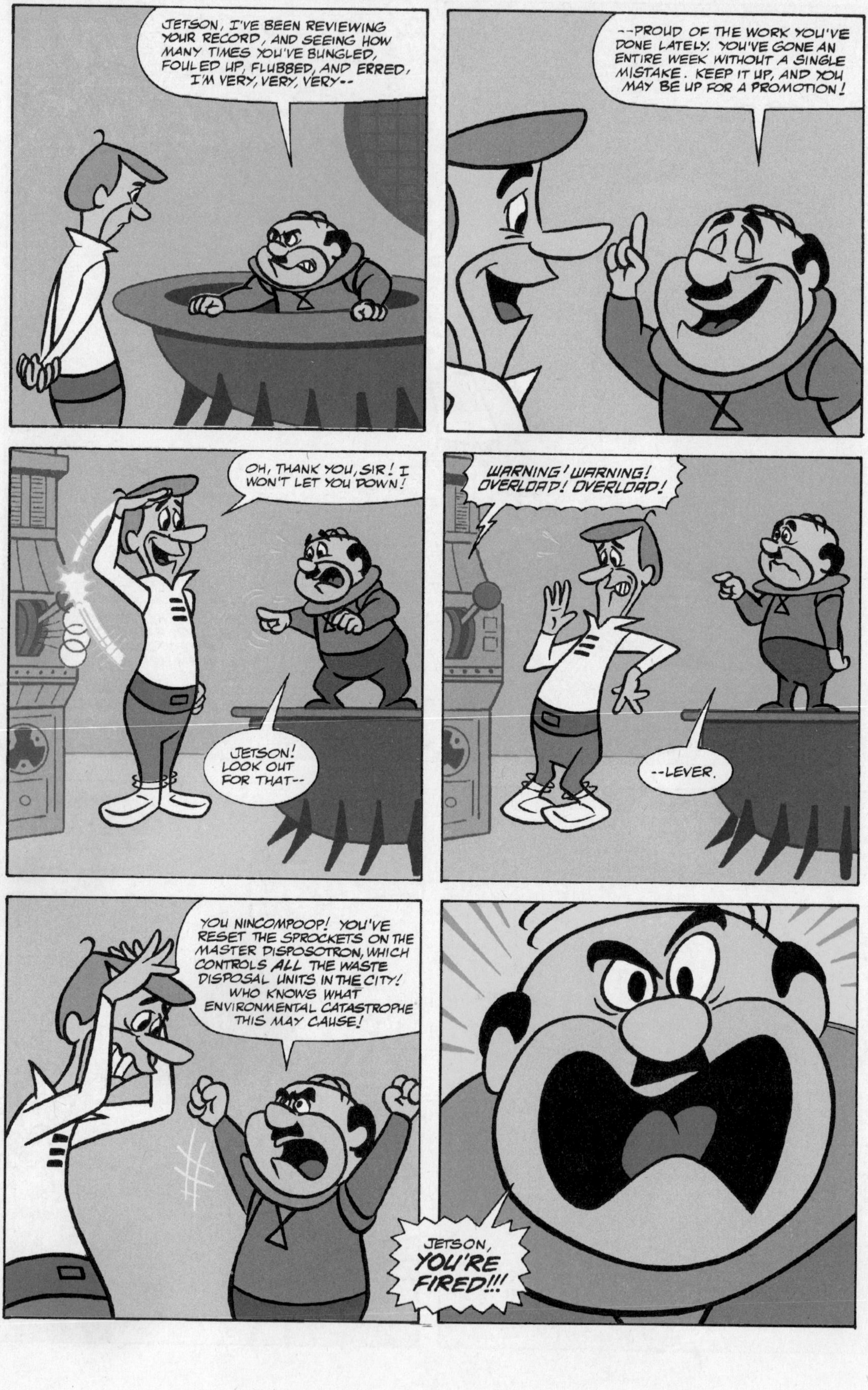
JETSON, I'VE BEEN REVIEWING YOUR RECORD, AND SEEING HOW MANY TIMES YOU'VE BUNGLED, FOULED UP, FLUBBED, AND ERRED, I'M VERY, VERY, VERY--
--PROUD OF THE WORK YOU'VE DONE LATELY. YOU'VE GONE AN ENTIRE WEEK WITHOUT A SINGLE MISTAKE. KEEP IT UP, AND YOU MAY BE UP FOR A PROMOTION!
OH, THANK YOU, SIR! I WON'T LET YOU DOWN!
JETSON! LOOK OUT FOR THAT--
WARNING! WARNING! OVERLOAD! OVERLOAD!
--LEVER.
YOU NINCOMPOOP! YOU'VE RESET THE SPROCKETS ON THE MASTER DISPOSOTRON, WHICH CONTROLS ALL THE WASTE DISPOSAL UNITS IN THE CITY! WHO KNOWS WHAT ENVIRONMENTAL CATASTROPHE THIS MAY CAUSE!
JETSON, YOU'RE FIRED!!!

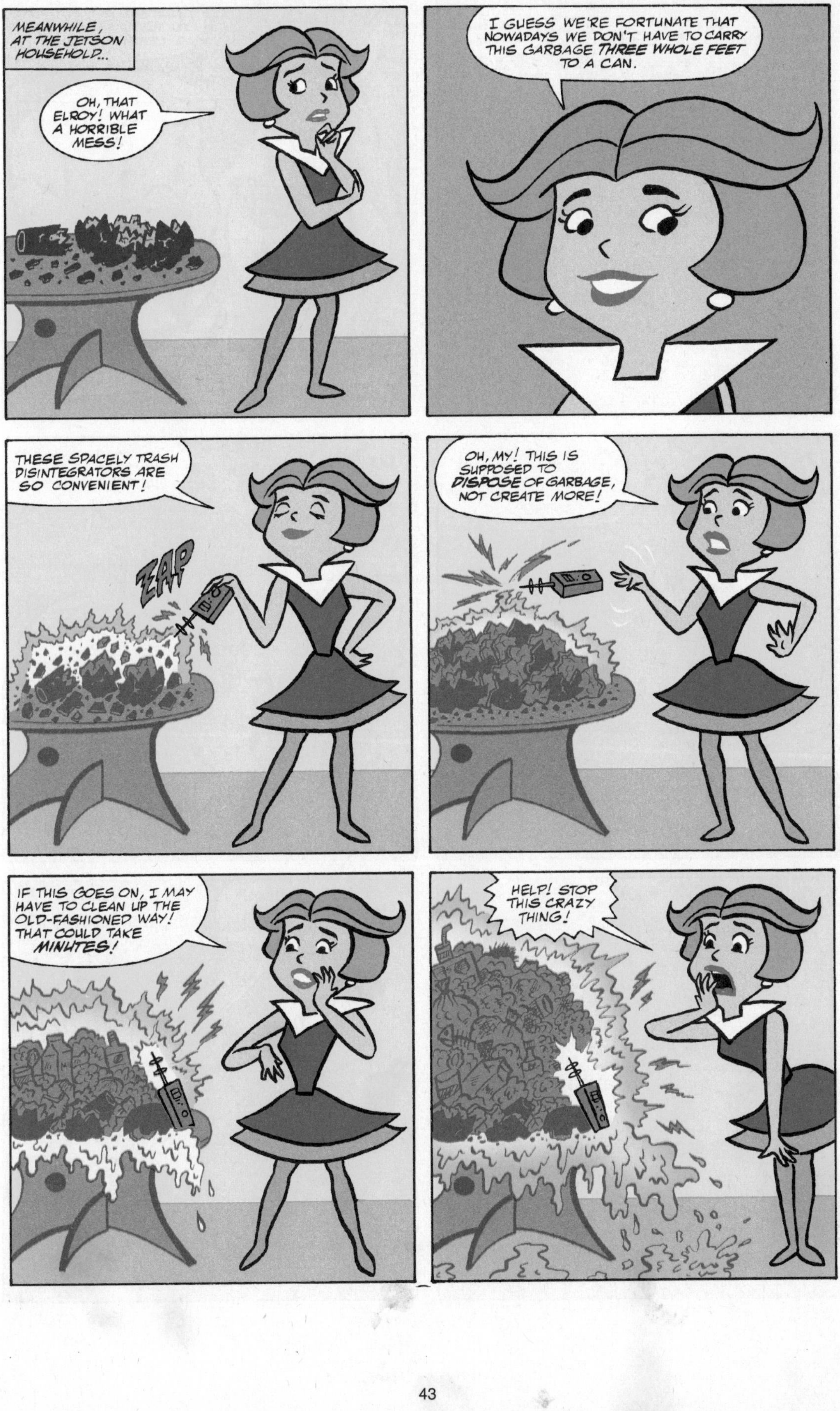
MEANWHILE, AT THE JETSON HOUSEHOLD...
OH, THAT ELROY! WHAT A HORRIBLE MESS!
I GUESS WE'RE FORTUNATE THAT NOWADAYS WE DON'T HAVE TO CARRY THIS GARBAGE THREE WHOLE FEET TO A CAN.
THESE SPACELY TRASH DISINTEGRATORS ARE SO CONVENIENT!
ZAP
OH, MY! THIS IS SUPPOSED TO DISPOSE OF GARBAGE, NOT CREATE MORE!
IF THIS GOES ON, I MAY HAVE TO CLEAN UP THE OLD-FASHIONED WAY! THAT COULD TAKE MINUTES!
HELP! STOP THIS CRAZY THING!

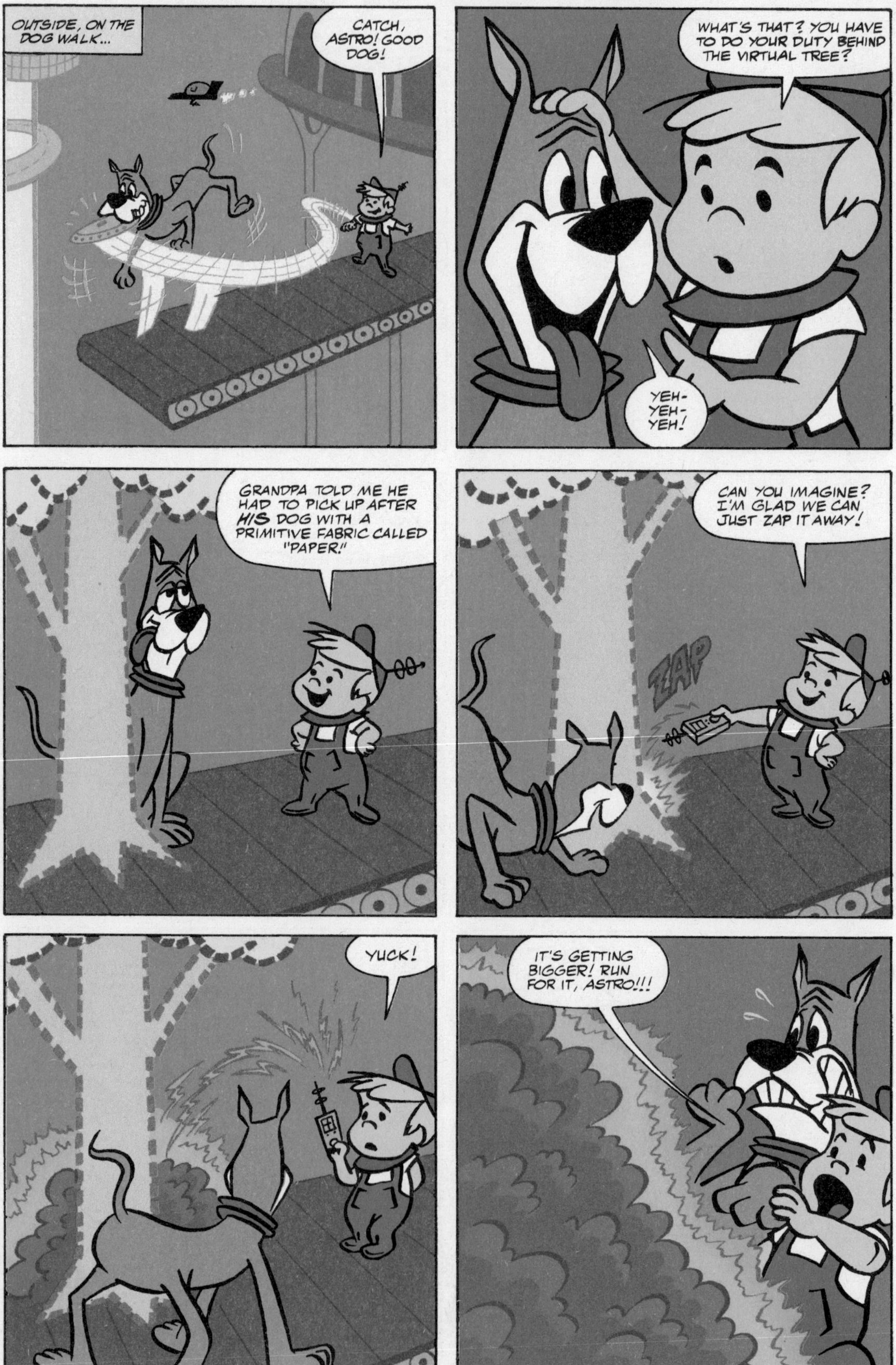
OUTSIDE, ON THE DOG WALK...
CATCH, ASTRO! GOOD DOG!
WHAT'S THAT? YOU HAVE TO DO YOUR DUTY BEHIND THE VIRTUAL TREE?
YEH-YEH-YEH!
GRANDPA TOLD ME HE HAD TO PICK UP AFTER HIS DOG WITH A PRIMITIVE FABRIC CALLED "PAPER."
CAN YOU IMAGINE? I'M GLAD WE CAN JUST ZAP IT AWAY!
ZAP
YUCK!
IT'S GETTING BIGGER! RUN FOR IT, ASTRO!!!

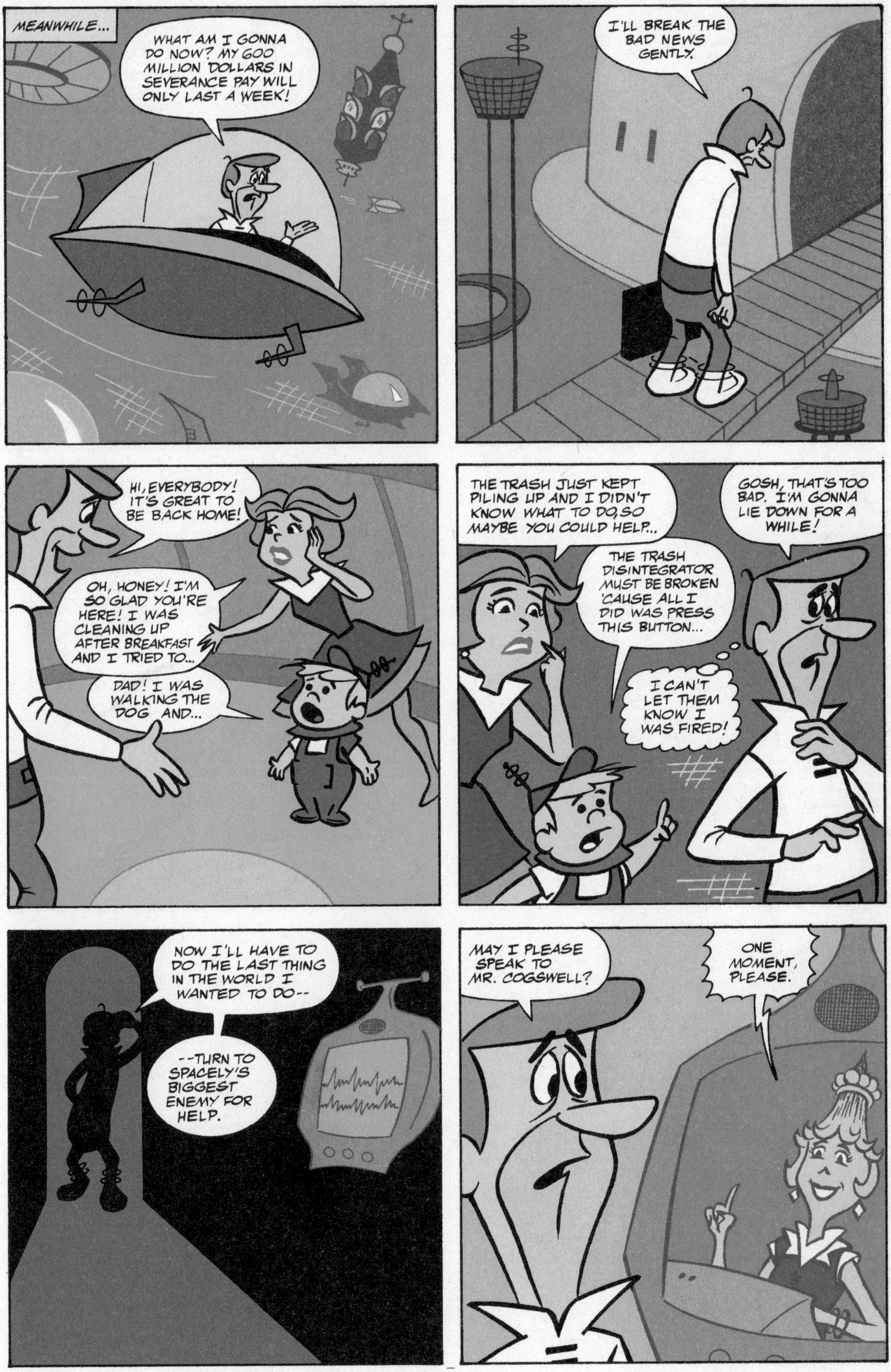
MEANWHILE...
WHAT AM I GONNA DO NOW? MY 600 MILLION DOLLARS IN SEVERANCE PAY WILL ONLY LAST A WEEK!
I'LL BREAK THE BAD NEWS GENTLY.
HI, EVERYBODY! IT'S GREAT TO BE BACK HOME!
OH, HONEY! I'M SO GLAD YOU'RE HERE! I WAS CLEANING UP AFTER BREAKFAST AND I TRIED TO...
DAD! I WAS WALKING THE DOG AND...
THE TRASH JUST KEPT PILING UP AND I DIDN'T KNOW WHAT TO DO, SO MAYBE YOU COULD HELP...
THE TRASH DISINTEGRATOR MUST BE BROKEN 'CAUSE ALL I DID WAS PRESS THIS BUTTON...
GOSH, THAT'S TOO BAD. I'M GONNA LIE DOWN FOR A WHILE!
I CAN'T LET THEM KNOW I WAS FIRED!
NOW I'LL HAVE TO DO THE LAST THING IN THE WORLD I WANTED TO DO--
--TURN TO SPACELY'S BIGGEST ENEMY FOR HELP.
MAY I PLEASE SPEAK TO MR. COGSWELL?
ONE MOMENT, PLEASE.

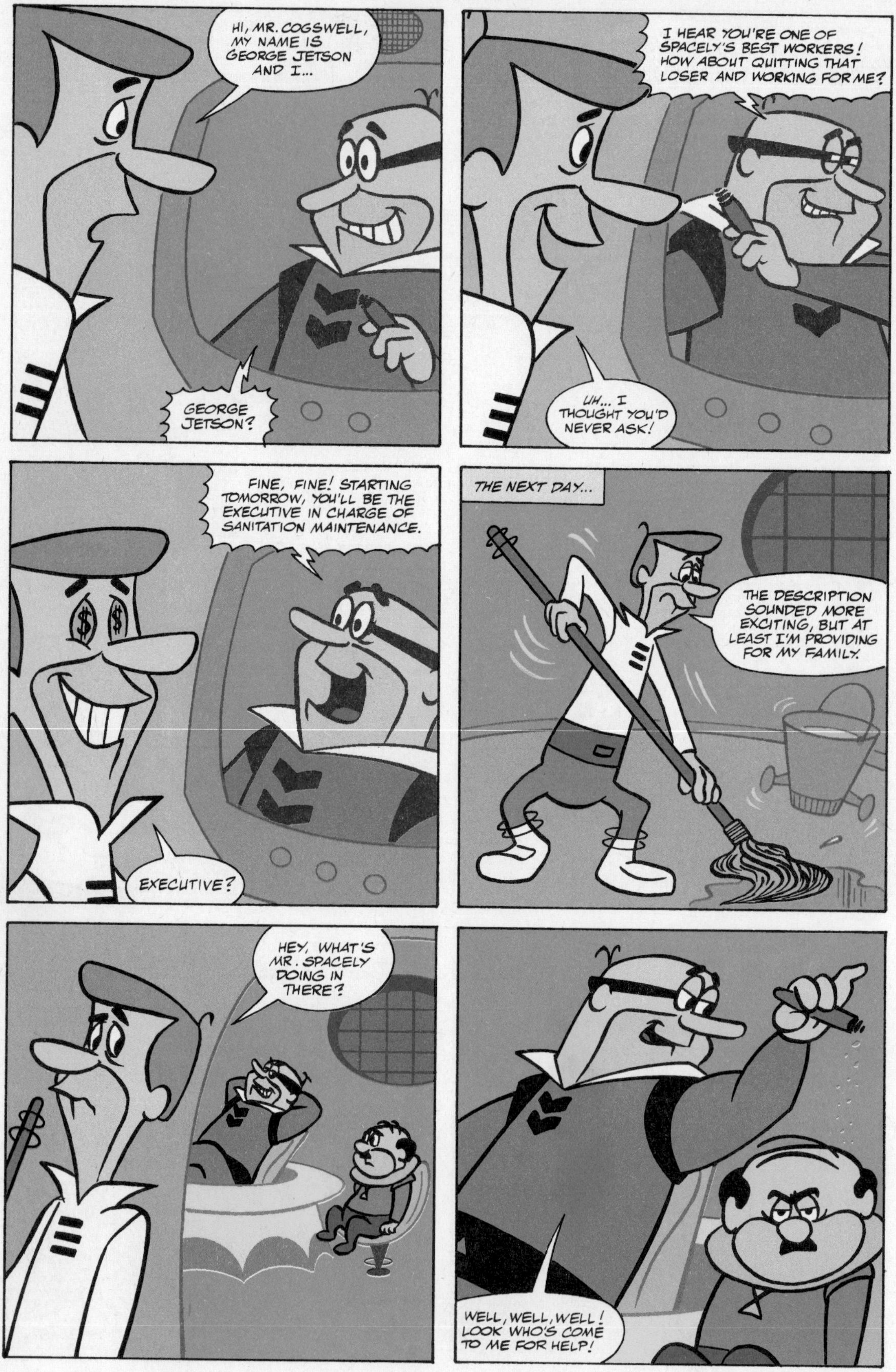
HI, MR. COGSWELL, MY NAME IS GEORGE JETSON AND I...
GEORGE JETSON?
I HEAR YOU'RE ONE OF SPACELY'S BEST WORKERS! HOW ABOUT QUITTING THAT LOSER AND WORKING FOR ME?
UH... I THOUGHT YOU'D NEVER ASK!
FINE, FINE! STARTING TOMORROW, YOU'LL BE THE EXECUTIVE IN CHARGE OF SANITATION MAINTENANCE.
EXECUTIVE?
THE NEXT DAY...
THE DESCRIPTION SOUNDED MORE EXCITING, BUT AT LEAST I'M PROVIDING FOR MY FAMILY.
HEY, WHAT'S MR. SPACELY DOING IN THERE?
WELL, WELL, WELL! LOOK WHO'S COME TO ME FOR HELP!

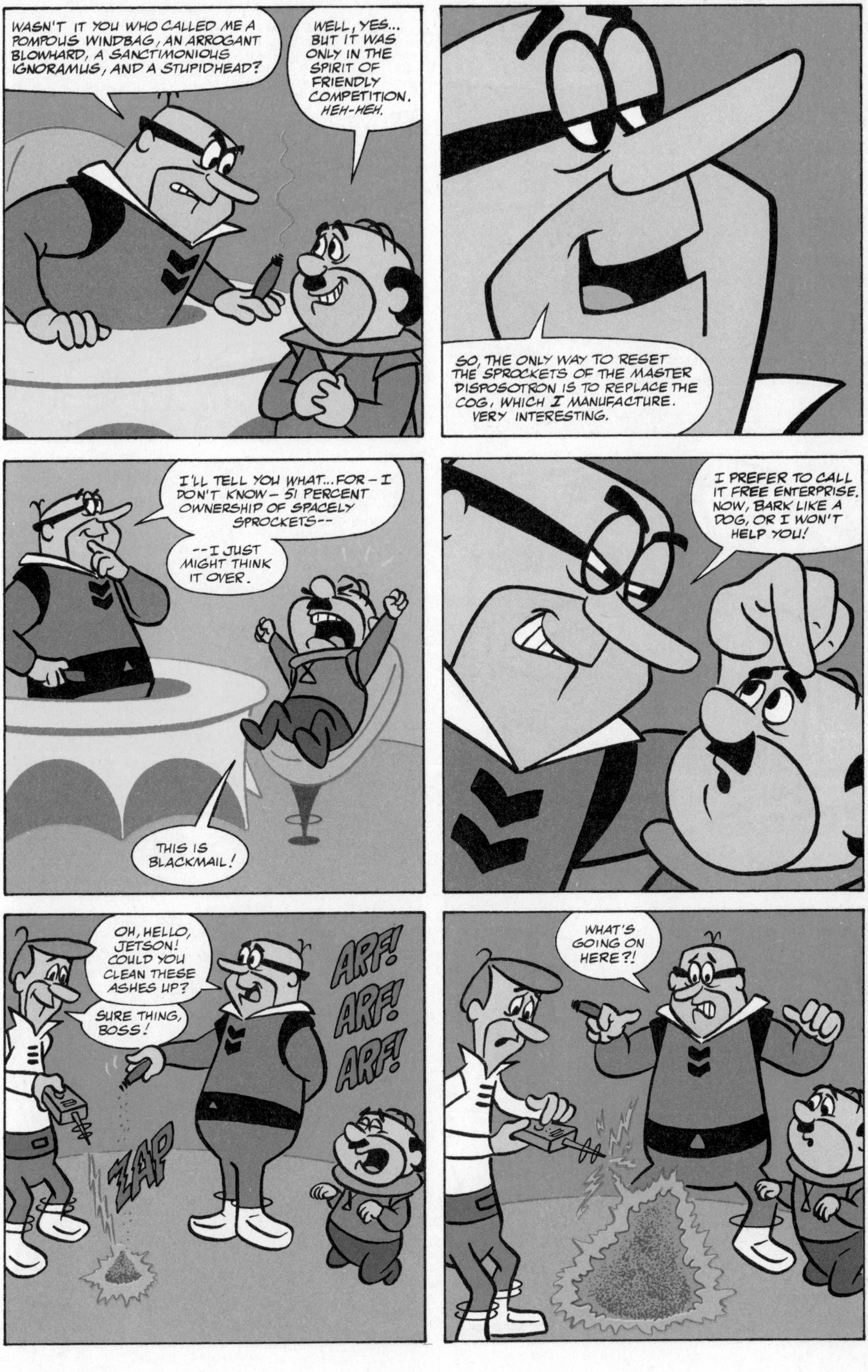
WASN'T IT YOU WHO CALLED ME A POMPOUS WINDBAG, AN ARROGANT BLOWHARD, A SANCTIMONIOUS IGNORAMUS, AND A STUPIDHEAD?
WELL, YES... BUT IT WAS ONLY IN THE SPIRIT OF FRIENDLY COMPETITION. HEH-HEH.
SO, THE ONLY WAY TO RESET THE SPROCKETS OF THE MASTER DISPOSOTRON IS TO REPLACE THE COG, WHICH I MANUFACTURE. VERY INTERESTING.
I'LL TELL YOU WHAT...FOR – I DON'T KNOW – 51 PERCENT OWNERSHIP OF SPACELY SPROCKETS--
--I JUST MIGHT THINK IT OVER.
THIS IS BLACKMAIL!
I PREFER TO CALL IT FREE ENTERPRISE. NOW, BARK LIKE A DOG, OR I WON'T HELP YOU!
OH, HELLO, JETSON! COULD YOU CLEAN THESE ASHES UP?
SURE THING, BOSS!
ARF! ARF! ARF!
ZAP
WHAT'S GOING ON HERE?!

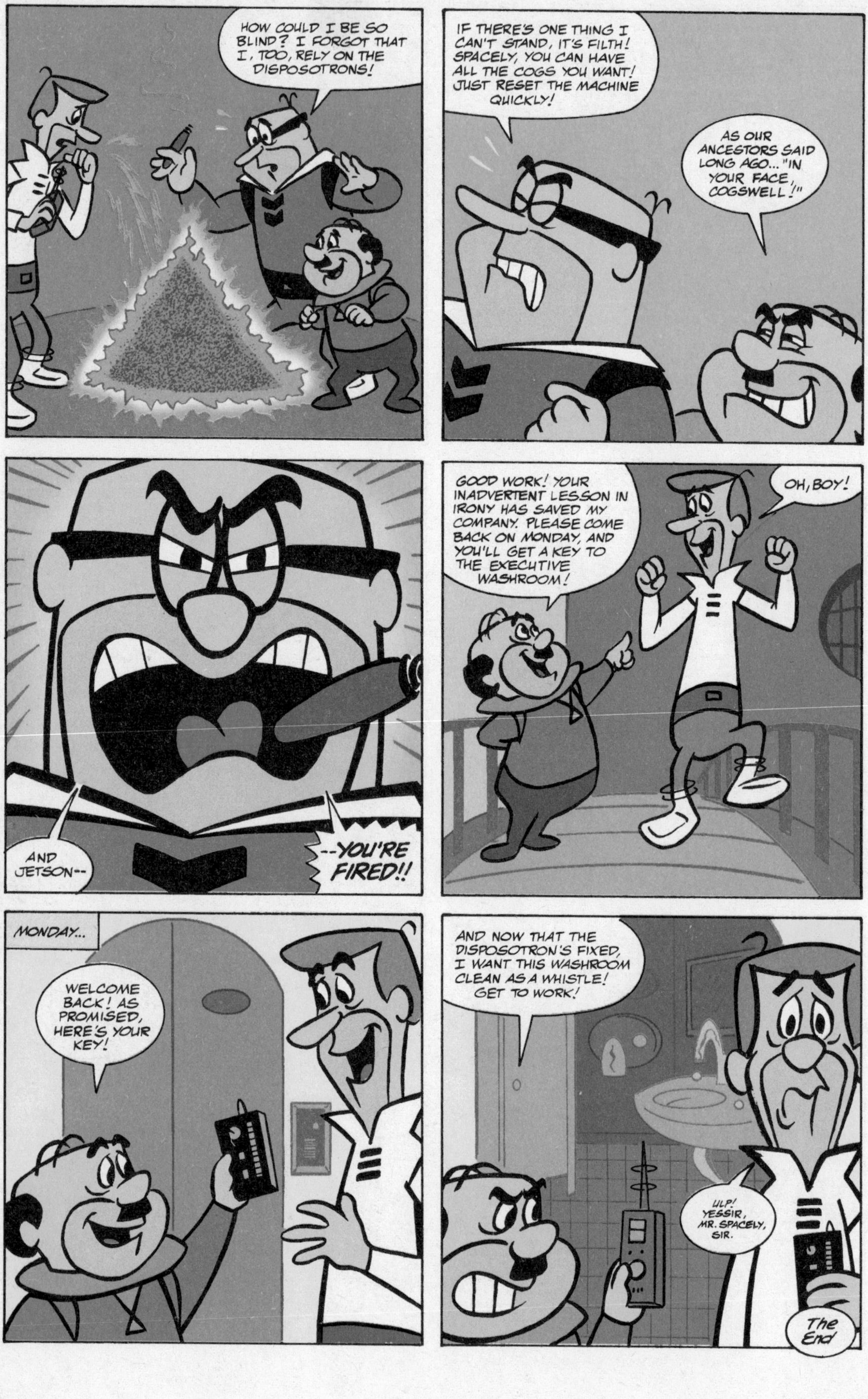

HOW COULD I BE SO BLIND? I FORGOT THAT I, TOO, RELY ON THE DISPOSOTRONS!
IF THERE'S ONE THING I CAN'T STAND, IT'S FILTH! SPACELY, YOU CAN HAVE ALL THE COGS YOU WANT! JUST RESET THE MACHINE QUICKLY!
AS OUR ANCESTORS SAID LONG AGO... "IN YOUR FACE, COGSWELL!"
AND JETSON--
--YOU'RE FIRED!!
GOOD WORK! YOUR INADVERTENT LESSON IN IRONY HAS SAVED MY COMPANY. PLEASE COME BACK ON MONDAY, AND YOU'LL GET A KEY TO THE EXECUTIVE WASHROOM!
OH, BOY!
MONDAY...
WELCOME BACK! AS PROMISED, HERE'S YOUR KEY!
AND NOW THAT THE DISPOSOTRON'S FIXED, I WANT THIS WASHROOM CLEAN AS A WHISTLE! GET TO WORK!
ULP! YESSIR, MR. SPACELY, SIR.
The End

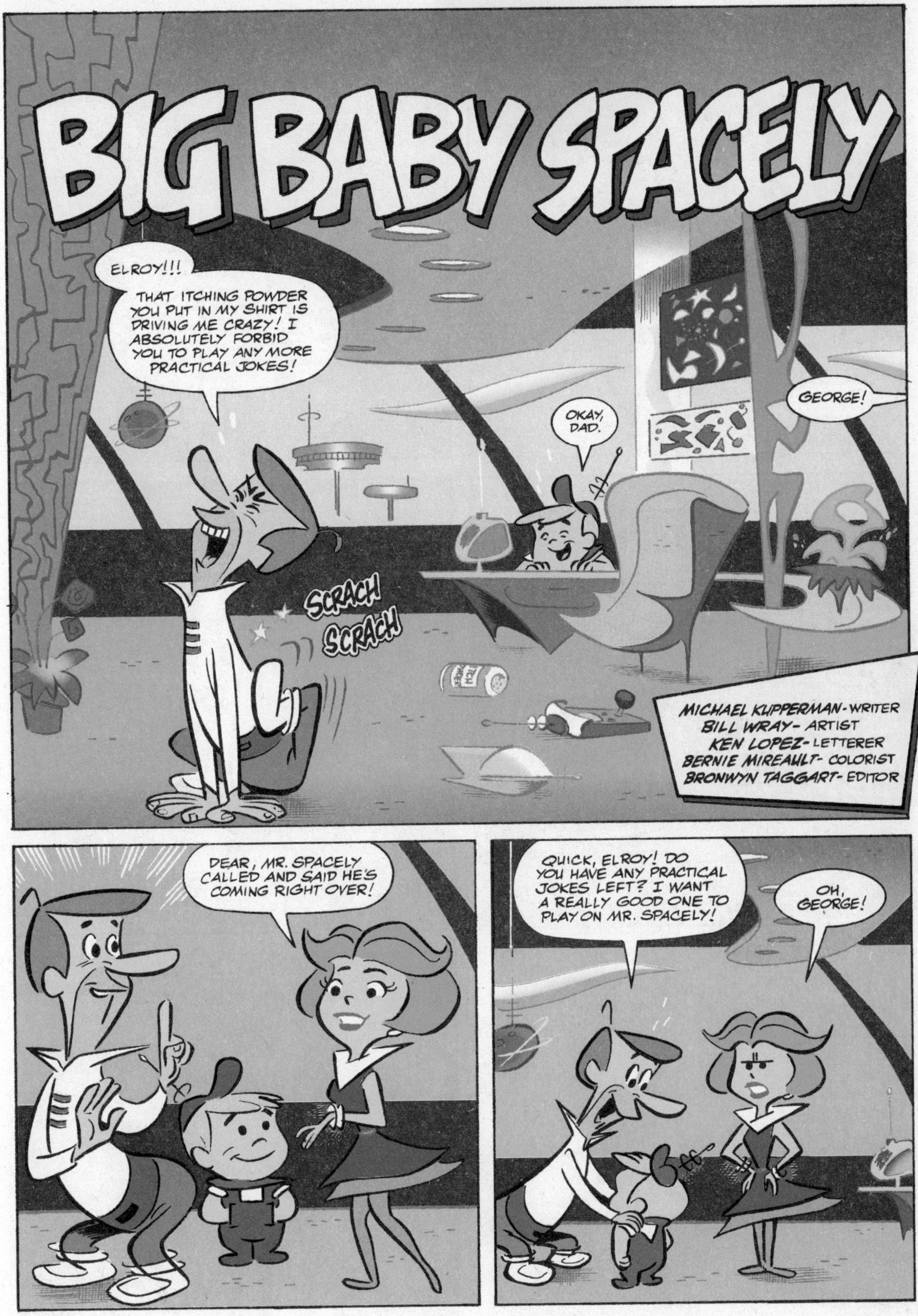
BIG BABY SPACELY
ELROY!!!
THAT ITCHING POWDER YOU PUT IN MY SHIRT IS DRIVING ME CRAZY! I ABSOLUTELY FORBID YOU TO PLAY ANY MORE PRACTICAL JOKES!
OKAY, DAD.
GEORGE!
SCRACH SCRACH
MICHAEL KUPPERMAN-WRITER
BILL WRAY- ARTIST
KEN LOPEZ- LETTERER
BERNIE MIREAULT- COLORIST
BRONWYN TAGGART- EDITOR
DEAR, MR. SPACELY CALLED AND SAID HE'S COMING RIGHT OVER!
QUICK, ELROY! DO YOU HAVE ANY PRACTICAL JOKES LEFT? I WANT A REALLY GOOD ONE TO PLAY ON MR. SPACELY!
OH, GEORGE!

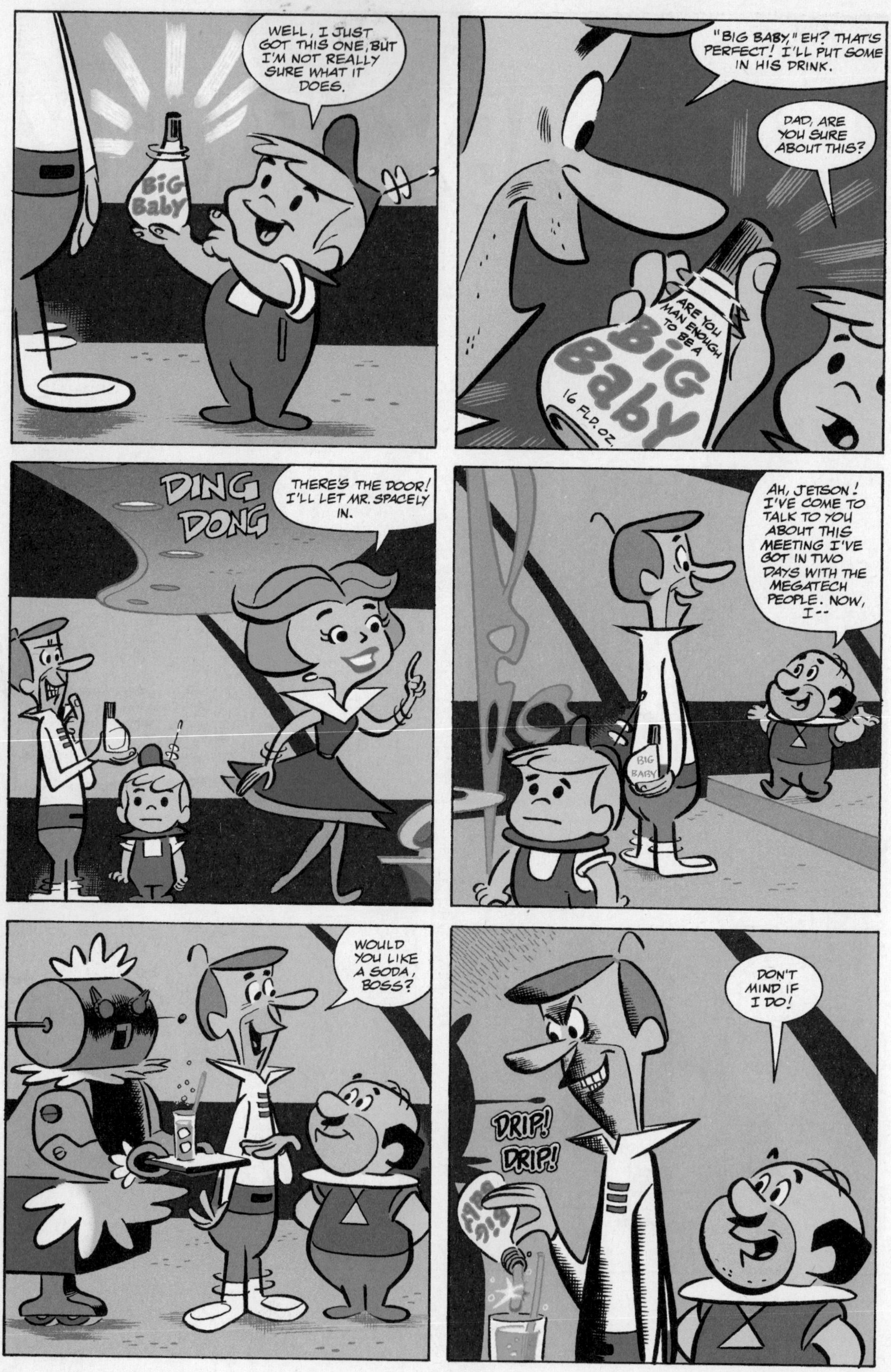
WELL, I JUST GOT THIS ONE, BUT I'M NOT REALLY SURE WHAT IT DOES.
BIG Baby
"BIG BABY," EH? THAT'S PERFECT! I'LL PUT SOME IN HIS DRINK.
DAD, ARE YOU SURE ABOUT THIS?
ARE YOU MAN ENOUGH TO BE A BIG Baby 16 FLD. OZ.
DING DONG
THERE'S THE DOOR! I'LL LET MR. SPACELY IN.
AH, JETSON! I'VE COME TO TALK TO YOU ABOUT THIS MEETING I'VE GOT IN TWO DAYS WITH THE MEGATECH PEOPLE. NOW, I--
BIG BABY
WOULD YOU LIKE A SODA, BOSS?
DON'T MIND IF I DO!
DRIP! DRIP!

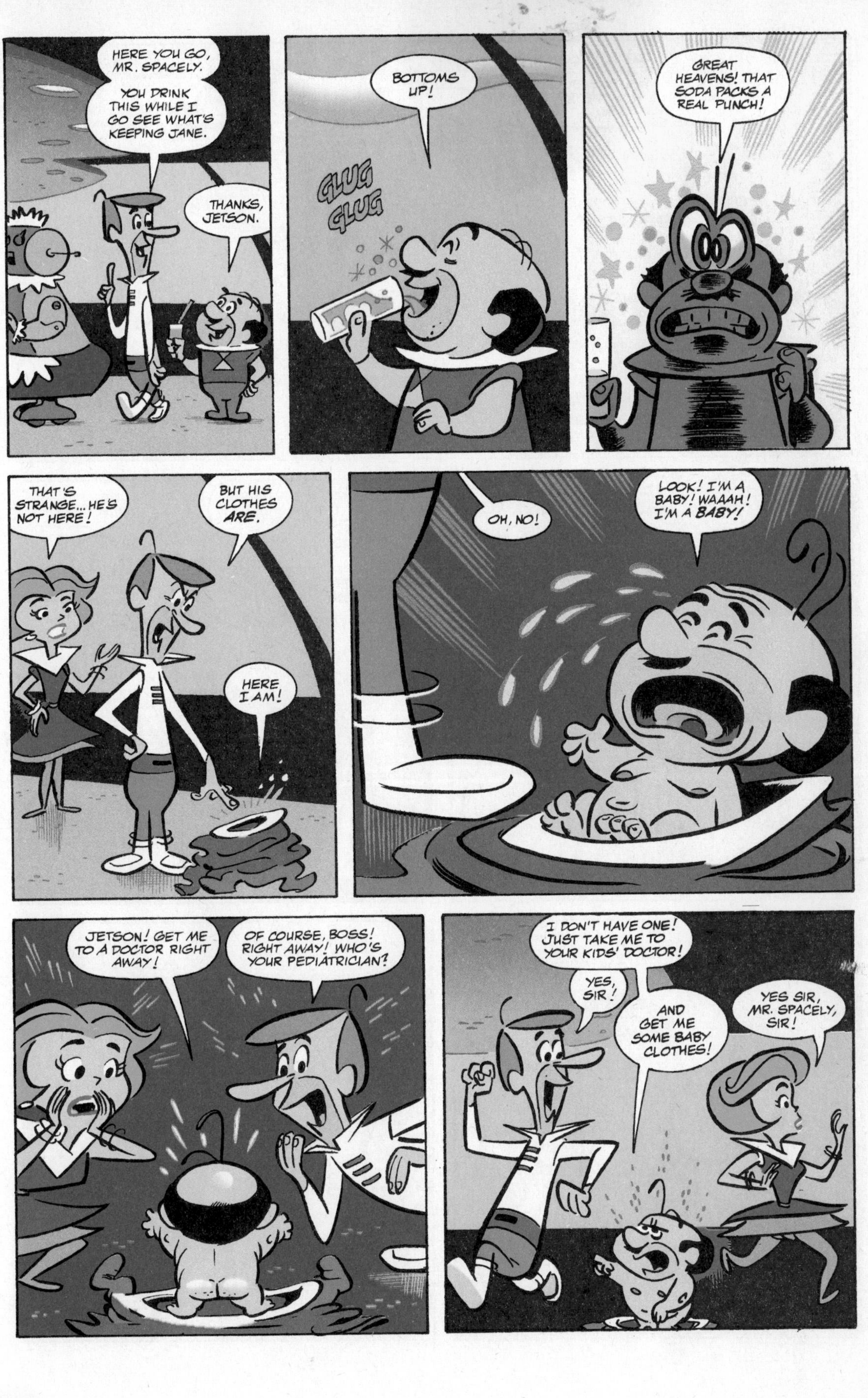
HERE YOU GO, MR. SPACELY.
YOU DRINK THIS WHILE I GO SEE WHAT'S KEEPING JANE.
THANKS, JETSON.
BOTTOMS UP!
GLUG GLUG
GREAT HEAVENS! THAT SODA PACKS A REAL PUNCH!
THAT'S STRANGE... HE'S NOT HERE!
BUT HIS CLOTHES ARE.
HERE I AM!
OH, NO!
LOOK! I'M A BABY! WAAAH! I'M A BABY!
JETSON! GET ME TO A DOCTOR RIGHT AWAY!
OF COURSE, BOSS! RIGHT AWAY! WHO'S YOUR PEDIATRICIAN?
I DON'T HAVE ONE! JUST TAKE ME TO YOUR KIDS' DOCTOR!
YES, SIR!
AND GET ME SOME BABY CLOTHES!
YES SIR, MR. SPACELY, SIR!

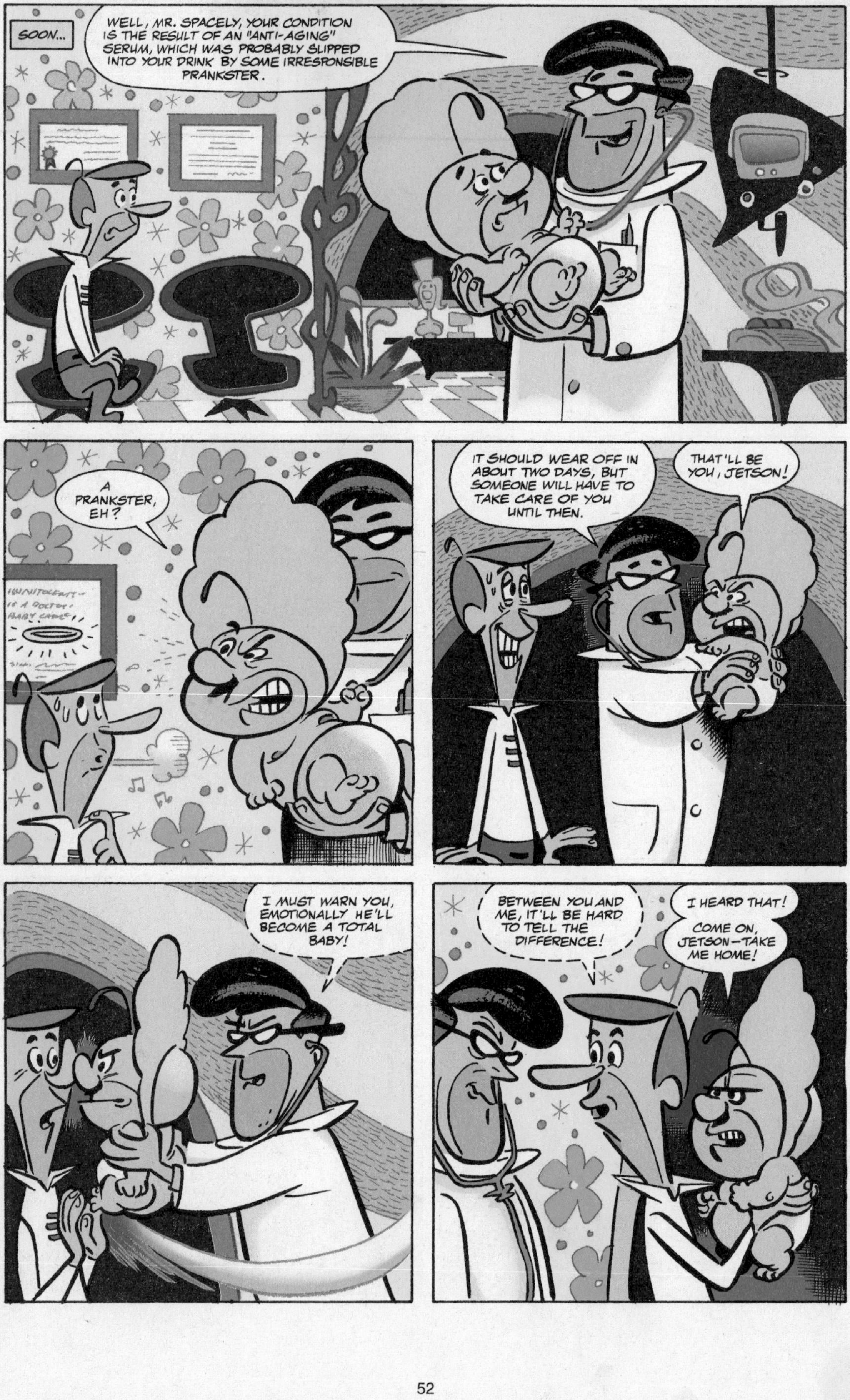
SOON...
WELL, MR. SPACELY, YOUR CONDITION IS THE RESULT OF AN "ANTI-AGING" SERUM, WHICH WAS PROBABLY SLIPPED INTO YOUR DRINK BY SOME IRRESPONSIBLE PRANKSTER.
A PRANKSTER, EH?
IT SHOULD WEAR OFF IN ABOUT TWO DAYS, BUT SOMEONE WILL HAVE TO TAKE CARE OF YOU UNTIL THEN.
THAT'LL BE YOU, JETSON!
I MUST WARN YOU, EMOTIONALLY HE'LL BECOME A TOTAL BABY!
BETWEEN YOU AND ME, IT'LL BE HARD TO TELL THE DIFFERENCE!
I HEARD THAT!
COME ON, JETSON—TAKE ME HOME!

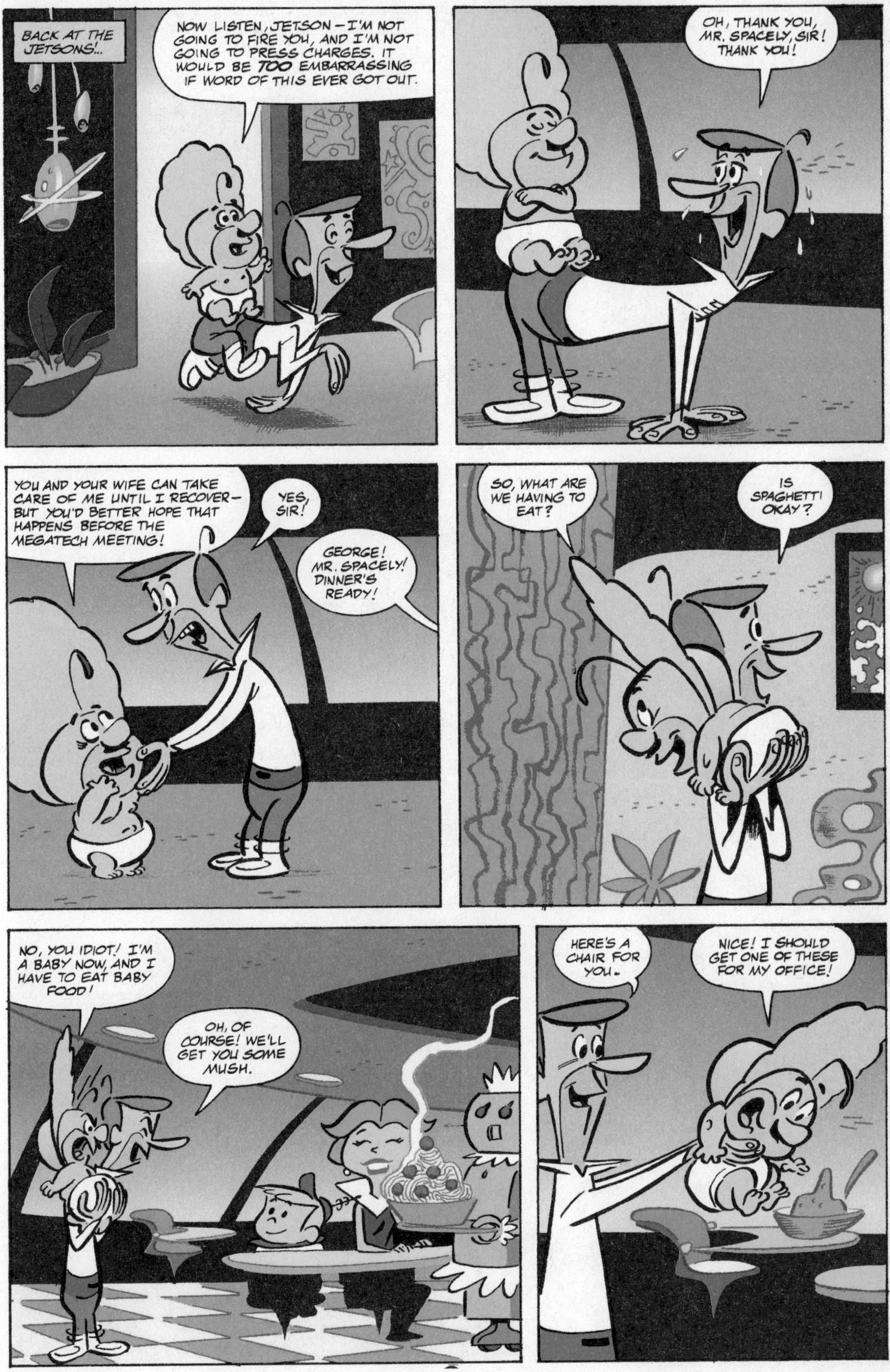
BACK AT THE JETSONS!..
NOW LISTEN, JETSON — I'M NOT GOING TO FIRE YOU, AND I'M NOT GOING TO PRESS CHARGES. IT WOULD BE TOO EMBARRASSING IF WORD OF THIS EVER GOT OUT.
OH, THANK YOU, MR. SPACELY, SIR! THANK YOU!
YOU AND YOUR WIFE CAN TAKE CARE OF ME UNTIL I RECOVER— BUT YOU'D BETTER HOPE THAT HAPPENS BEFORE THE MEGATECH MEETING!
YES, SIR!
GEORGE! MR. SPACELY! DINNER'S READY!
SO, WHAT ARE WE HAVING TO EAT?
IS SPAGHETTI OKAY?
NO, YOU IDIOT! I'M A BABY NOW, AND I HAVE TO EAT BABY FOOD!
OH, OF COURSE! WE'LL GET YOU SOME MUSH.
HERE'S A CHAIR FOR YOU.
NICE! I SHOULD GET ONE OF THESE FOR MY OFFICE!

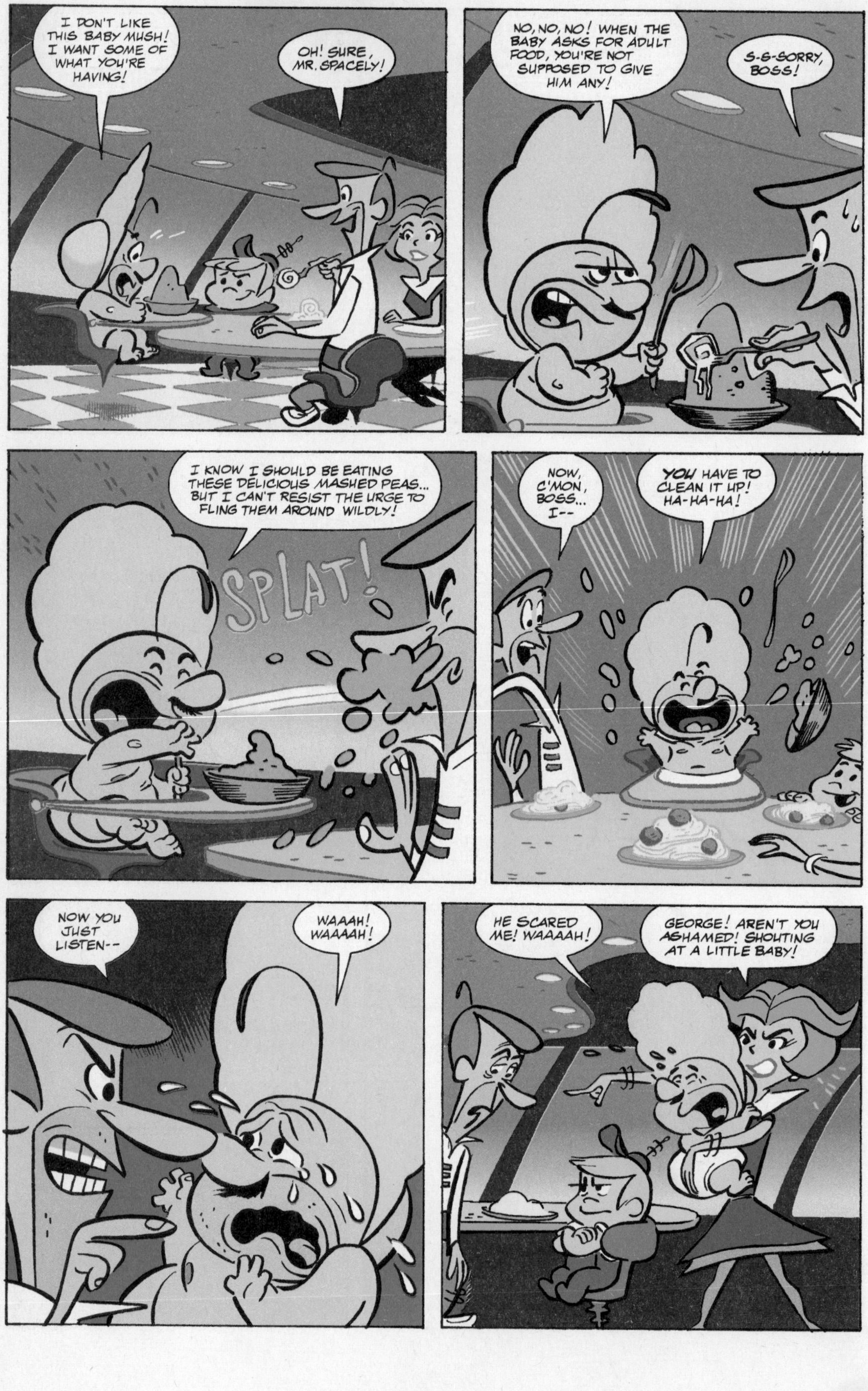
I DON'T LIKE THIS BABY MUSH! I WANT SOME OF WHAT YOU'RE HAVING!
OH! SURE, MR. SPACELY!
NO, NO, NO! WHEN THE BABY ASKS FOR ADULT FOOD, YOU'RE NOT SUPPOSED TO GIVE HIM ANY!
S-S-SORRY, BOSS!
I KNOW I SHOULD BE EATING THESE DELICIOUS MASHED PEAS... BUT I CAN'T RESIST THE URGE TO FLING THEM AROUND WILDLY!
SPLAT!
NOW, C'MON, BOSS... I--
YOU HAVE TO CLEAN IT UP! HA-HA-HA!
NOW YOU JUST LISTEN--
WAAAH! WAAAAH!
HE SCARED ME! WAAAAH!
GEORGE! AREN'T YOU ASHAMED! SHOUTING AT A LITTLE BABY!

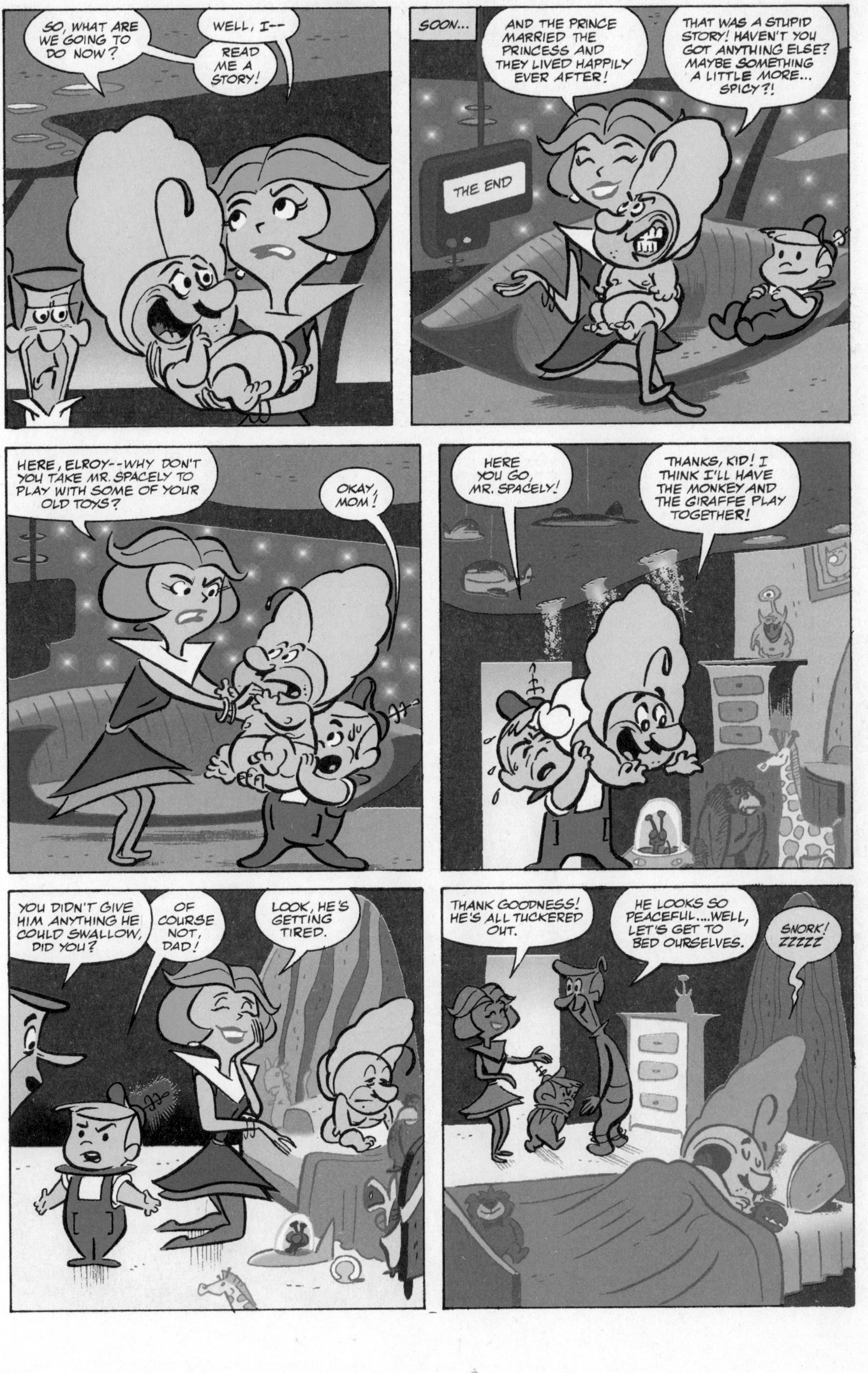

SO, WHAT ARE WE GOING TO DO NOW?
WELL, I--
READ ME A STORY!
SOON...
AND THE PRINCE MARRIED THE PRINCESS AND THEY LIVED HAPPILY EVER AFTER!
THAT WAS A STUPID STORY! HAVEN'T YOU GOT ANYTHING ELSE? MAYBE SOMETHING A LITTLE MORE... SPICY?!
THE END
HERE, ELROY--WHY DON'T YOU TAKE MR. SPACELY TO PLAY WITH SOME OF YOUR OLD TOYS?
OKAY, MOM!
HERE YOU GO, MR. SPACELY!
THANKS, KID! I THINK I'LL HAVE THE MONKEY AND THE GIRAFFE PLAY TOGETHER!
YOU DIDN'T GIVE HIM ANYTHING HE COULD SWALLOW, DID YOU?
OF COURSE NOT, DAD!
LOOK, HE'S GETTING TIRED.
THANK GOODNESS! HE'S ALL TUCKERED OUT.
HE LOOKS SO PEACEFUL....WELL, LET'S GET TO BED OURSELVES.
SNORK! ZZZZZ

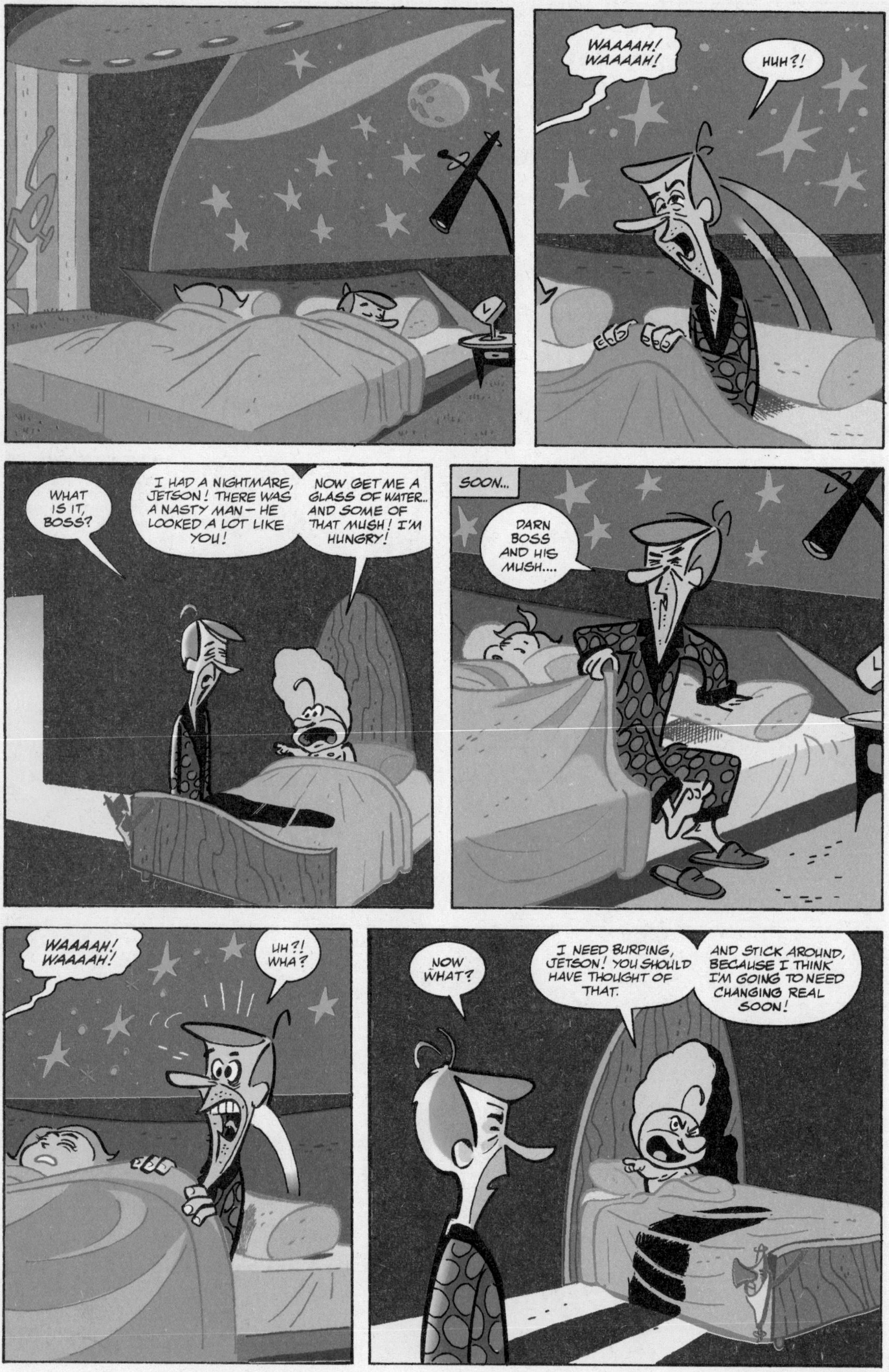
WAAAAH! WAAAAH!
HUH?!
WHAT IS IT, BOSS?
I HAD A NIGHTMARE, JETSON! THERE WAS A NASTY MAN — HE LOOKED A LOT LIKE YOU!
NOW GET ME A GLASS OF WATER... AND SOME OF THAT MUSH! I'M HUNGRY!
SOON...
DARN BOSS AND HIS MUSH....
WAAAAH! WAAAAH!
UH?! WHA?
NOW WHAT?
I NEED BURPING, JETSON! YOU SHOULD HAVE THOUGHT OF THAT.
AND STICK AROUND, BECAUSE I THINK I'M GOING TO NEED CHANGING REAL SOON!

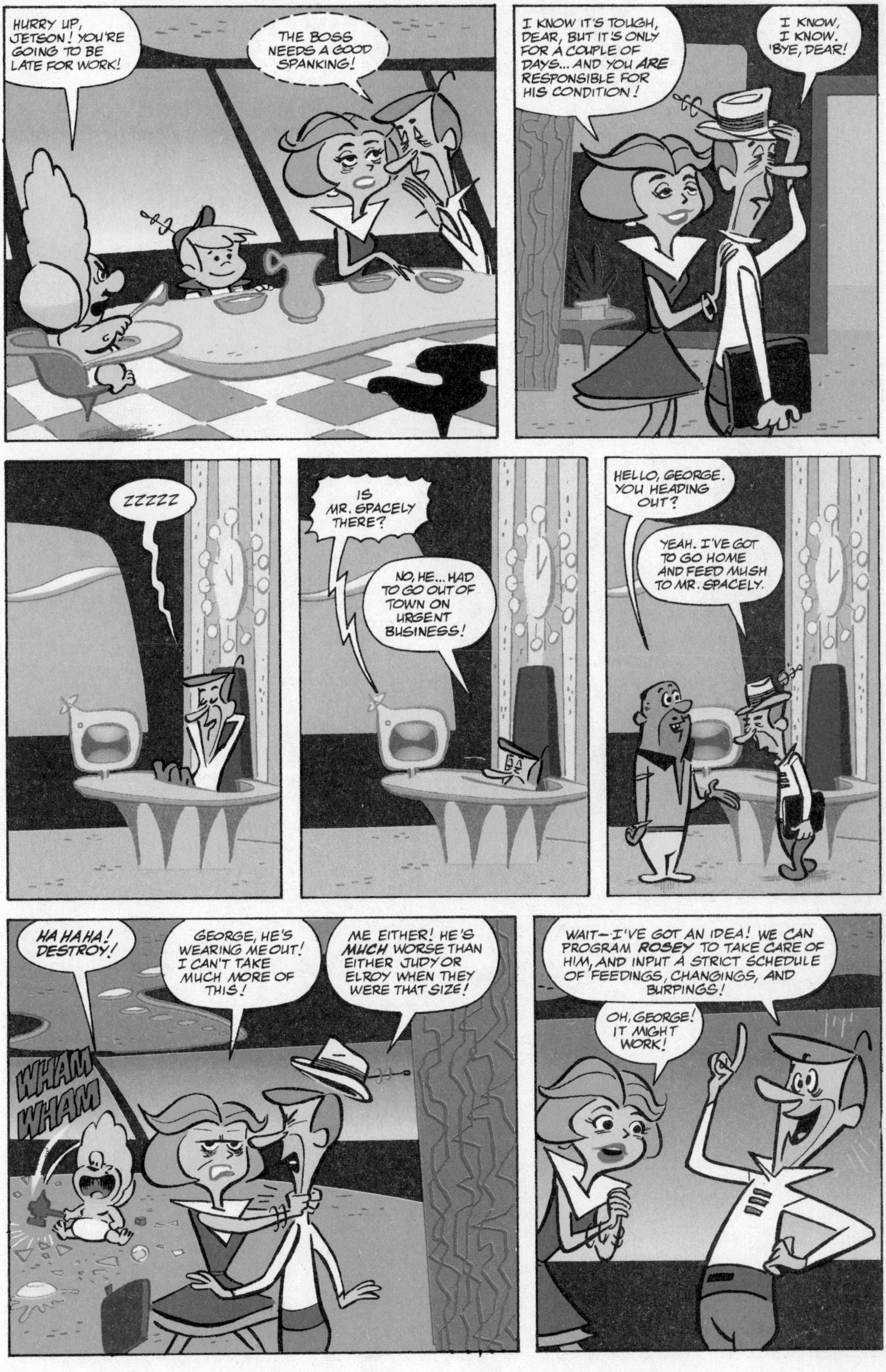

HURRY UP, JETSON! YOU'RE GOING TO BE LATE FOR WORK!
THE BOSS NEEDS A GOOD SPANKING!
I KNOW IT'S TOUGH, DEAR, BUT IT'S ONLY FOR A COUPLE OF DAYS... AND YOU ARE RESPONSIBLE FOR HIS CONDITION!
I KNOW, I KNOW. 'BYE, DEAR!
ZZZZZ
IS MR. SPACELY THERE?
NO, HE... HAD TO GO OUT OF TOWN ON URGENT BUSINESS!
HELLO, GEORGE. YOU HEADING OUT?
YEAH. I'VE GOT TO GO HOME AND FEED MUSH TO MR. SPACELY.
HA HA HA! DESTROY!
GEORGE, HE'S WEARING ME OUT! I CAN'T TAKE MUCH MORE OF THIS!
ME EITHER! HE'S MUCH WORSE THAN EITHER JUDY OR ELROY WHEN THEY WERE THAT SIZE!
WHAM WHAM
WAIT—I'VE GOT AN IDEA! WE CAN PROGRAM ROSEY TO TAKE CARE OF HIM, AND INPUT A STRICT SCHEDULE OF FEEDINGS, CHANGINGS, AND BURPINGS!
OH, GEORGE! IT MIGHT WORK!

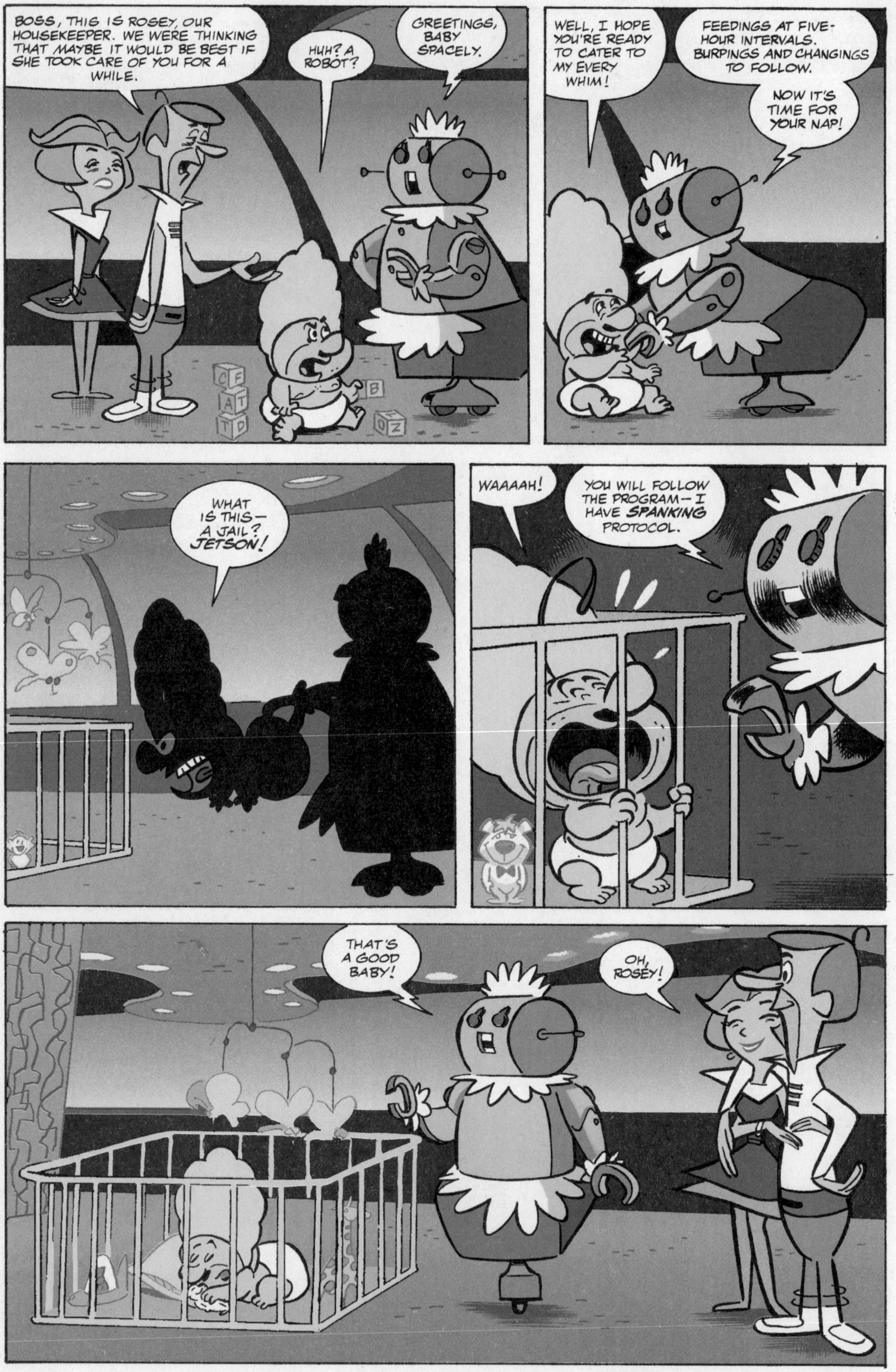
BOSS, THIS IS ROSEY, OUR HOUSEKEEPER. WE WERE THINKING THAT MAYBE IT WOULD BE BEST IF SHE TOOK CARE OF YOU FOR A WHILE.
HUH? A ROBOT?
GREETINGS, BABY SPACELY.
WELL, I HOPE YOU'RE READY TO CATER TO MY EVERY WHIM!
FEEDINGS AT FIVE-HOUR INTERVALS. BURPINGS AND CHANGINGS TO FOLLOW.
NOW IT'S TIME FOR YOUR NAP!
WHAT IS THIS— A JAIL? JETSON!
WAAAAH!
YOU WILL FOLLOW THE PROGRAM— I HAVE SPANKING PROTOCOL.
THAT'S A GOOD BABY!
OH, ROSEY!

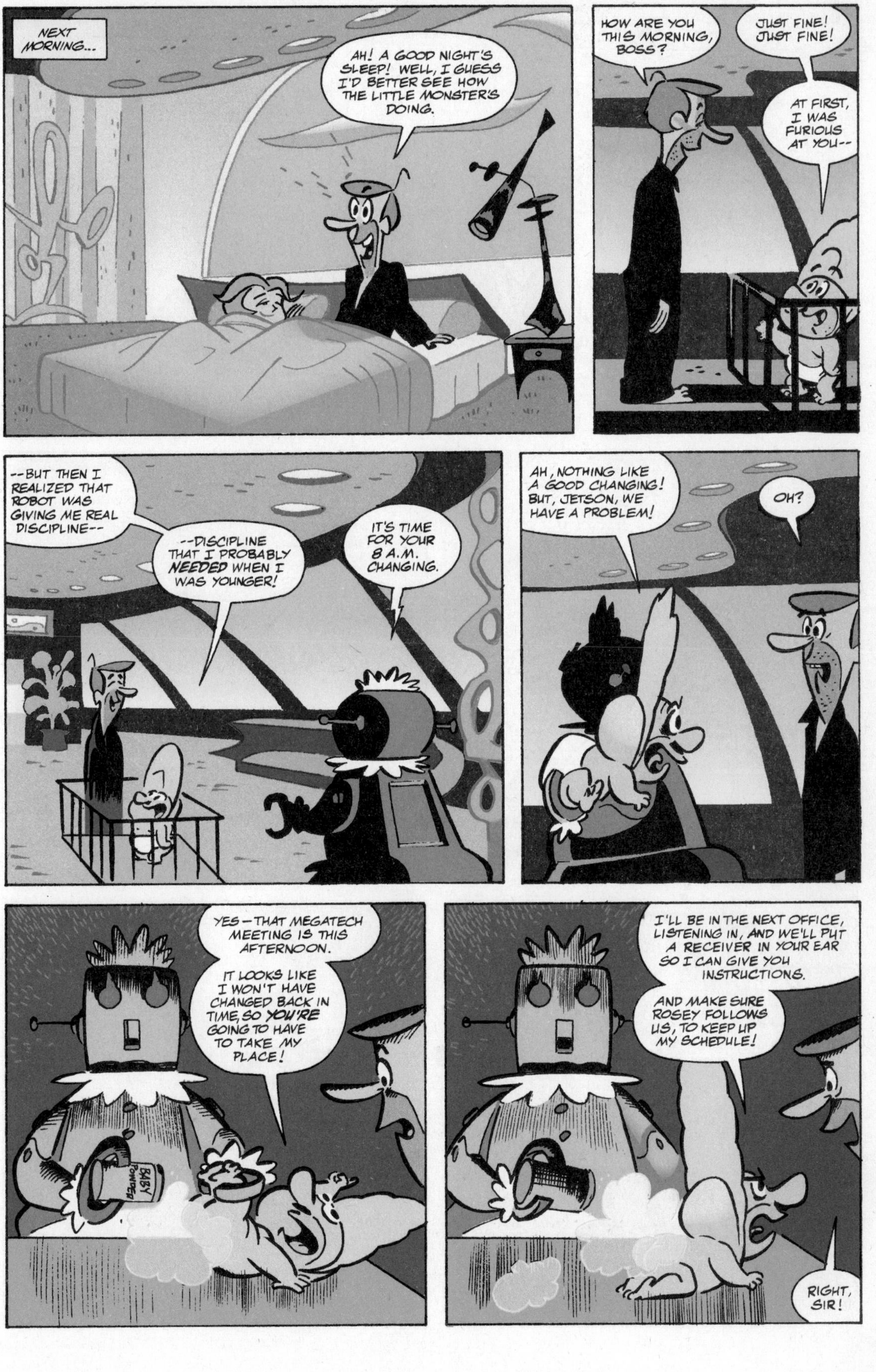
NEXT MORNING...
AH! A GOOD NIGHT'S SLEEP! WELL, I GUESS I'D BETTER SEE HOW THE LITTLE MONSTER'S DOING.
HOW ARE YOU THIS MORNING, BOSS?
JUST FINE! JUST FINE!
AT FIRST, I WAS FURIOUS AT YOU--
--BUT THEN I REALIZED THAT ROBOT WAS GIVING ME REAL DISCIPLINE--
--DISCIPLINE THAT I PROBABLY NEEDED WHEN I WAS YOUNGER!
IT'S TIME FOR YOUR 8 A.M. CHANGING.
AH, NOTHING LIKE A GOOD CHANGING! BUT, JETSON, WE HAVE A PROBLEM!
OH?
YES—THAT MEGATECH MEETING IS THIS AFTERNOON.
IT LOOKS LIKE I WON'T HAVE CHANGED BACK IN TIME, SO YOU'RE GOING TO HAVE TO TAKE MY PLACE!
BABY POWDER
I'LL BE IN THE NEXT OFFICE, LISTENING IN, AND WE'LL PUT A RECEIVER IN YOUR EAR SO I CAN GIVE YOU INSTRUCTIONS.
AND MAKE SURE ROSEY FOLLOWS US, TO KEEP UP MY SCHEDULE!
RIGHT, SIR!

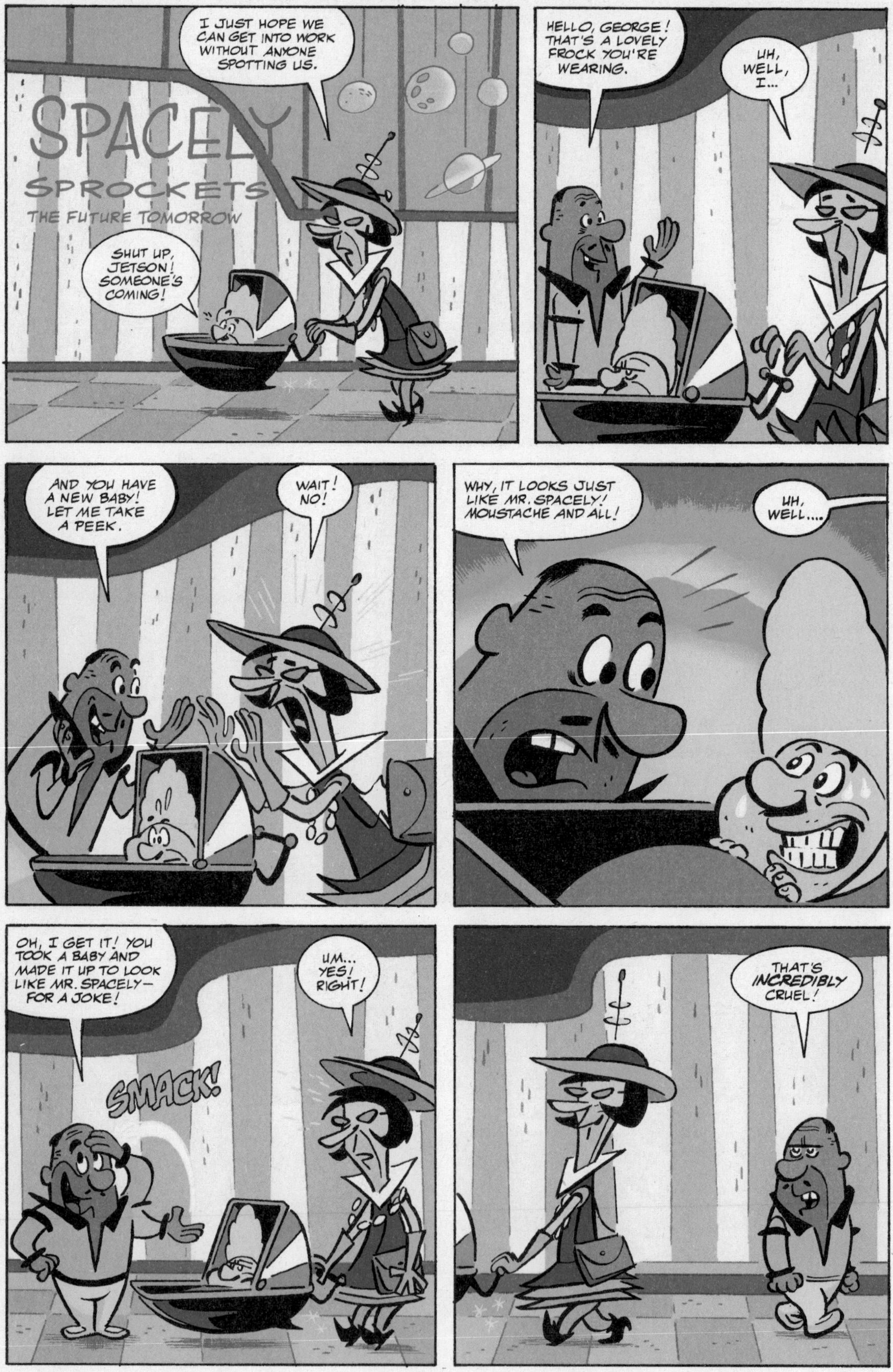
I JUST HOPE WE CAN GET INTO WORK WITHOUT ANYONE SPOTTING US.
SPACELY SPROCKETS
THE FUTURE TOMORROW
SHUT UP, JETSON! SOMEONE'S COMING!
HELLO, GEORGE! THAT'S A LOVELY FROCK YOU'RE WEARING.
UH, WELL, I...
AND YOU HAVE A NEW BABY! LET ME TAKE A PEEK.
WAIT! NO!
WHY, IT LOOKS JUST LIKE MR. SPACELY! MOUSTACHE AND ALL!
UH, WELL....
OH, I GET IT! YOU TOOK A BABY AND MADE IT UP TO LOOK LIKE MR. SPACELY— FOR A JOKE!
UM... YES! RIGHT!
SMACK!
THAT'S INCREDIBLY CRUEL!

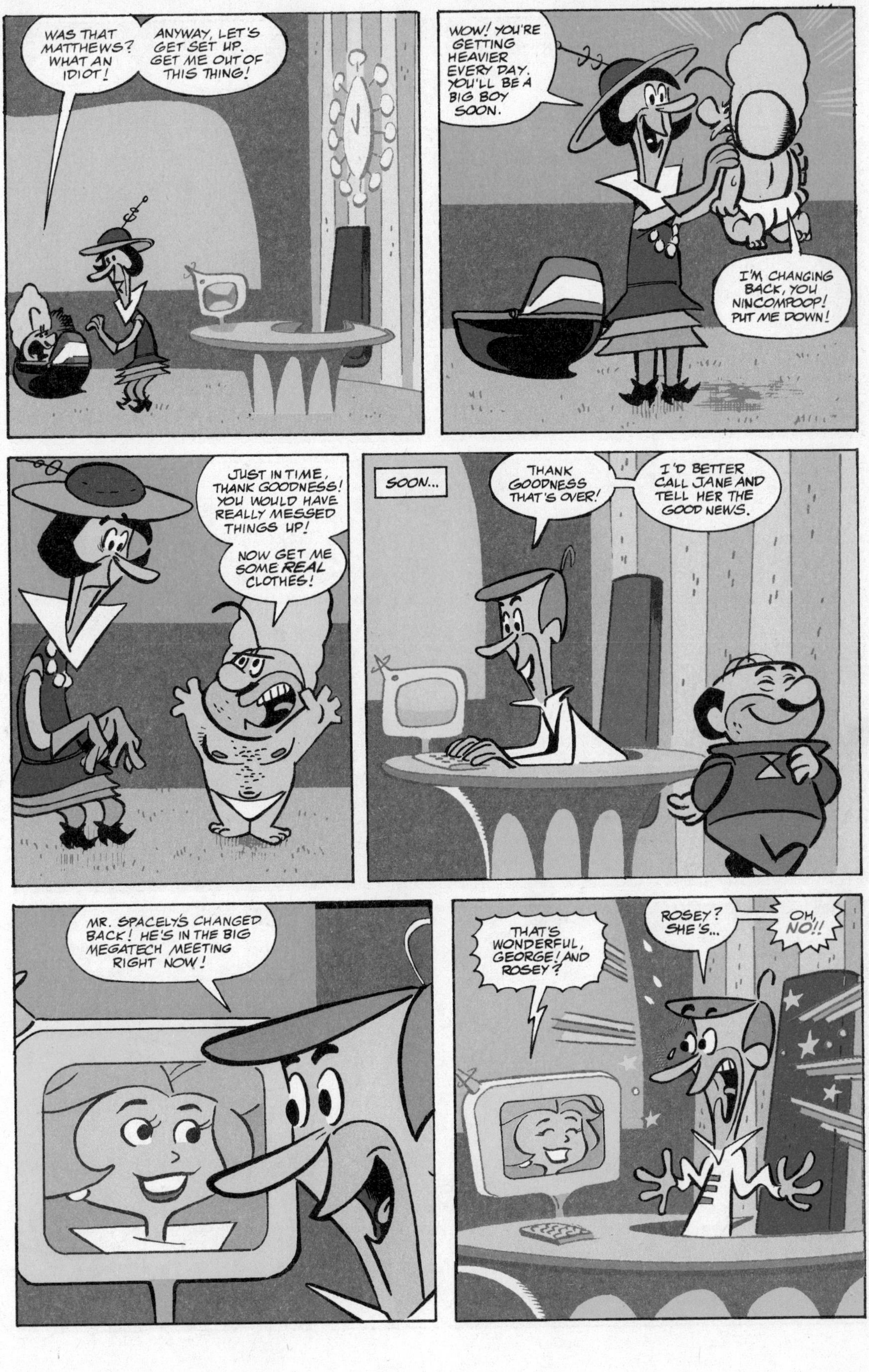
WAS THAT MATTHEWS? WHAT AN IDIOT!
ANYWAY, LET'S GET SET UP. GET ME OUT OF THIS THING!
WOW! YOU'RE GETTING HEAVIER EVERY DAY. YOU'LL BE A BIG BOY SOON.
I'M CHANGING BACK, YOU NINCOMPOOP! PUT ME DOWN!
JUST IN TIME, THANK GOODNESS! YOU WOULD HAVE REALLY MESSED THINGS UP!
NOW GET ME SOME REAL CLOTHES!
SOON...
THANK GOODNESS THAT'S OVER!
I'D BETTER CALL JANE AND TELL HER THE GOOD NEWS.
MR. SPACELY'S CHANGED BACK! HE'S IN THE BIG MEGATECH MEETING RIGHT NOW!
THAT'S WONDERFUL, GEORGE! AND ROSEY?
ROSEY? SHE'S...
OH, NO!!

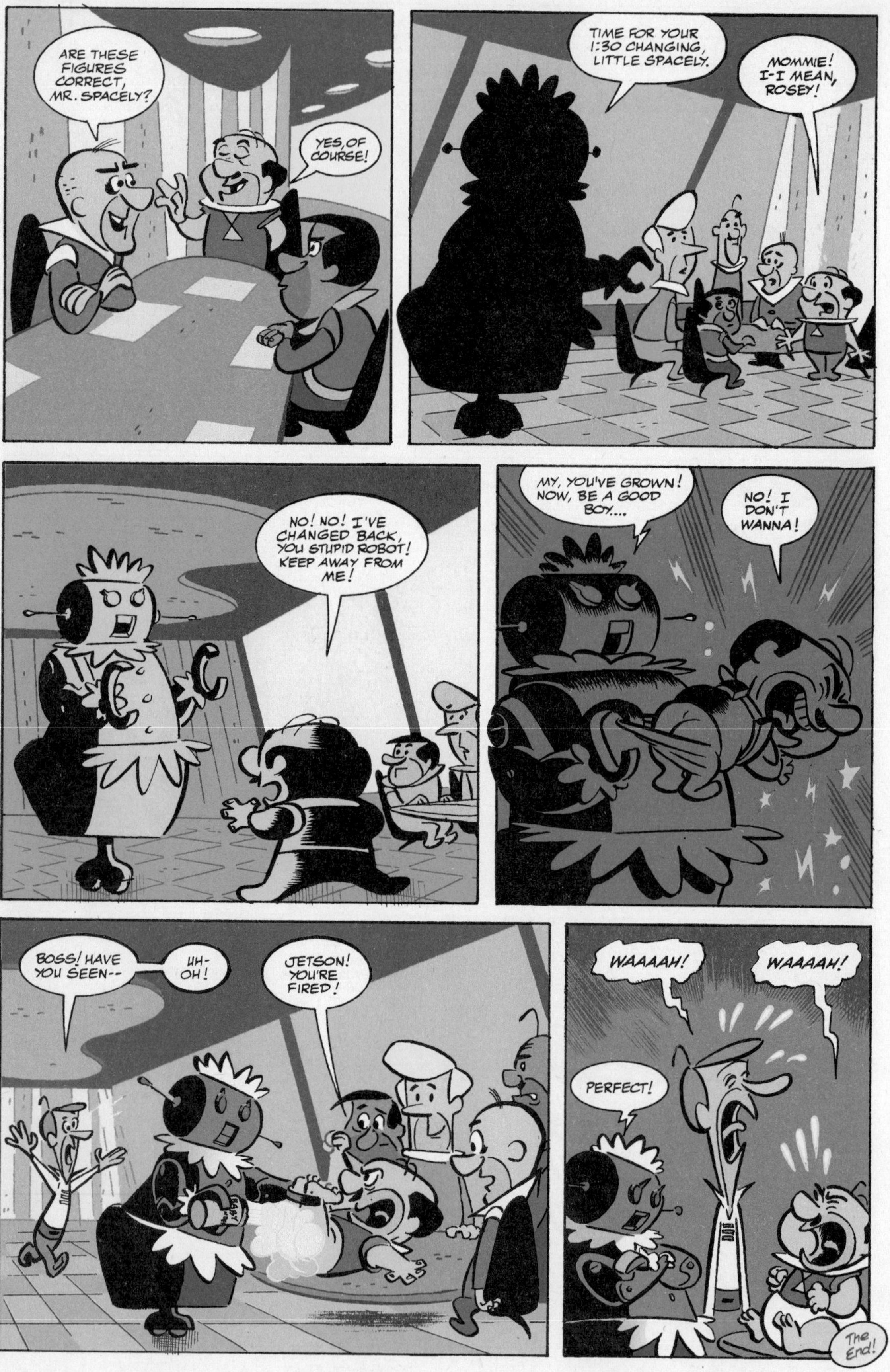
ARE THESE FIGURES CORRECT, MR. SPACELY?
YES, OF COURSE!
TIME FOR YOUR 1:30 CHANGING, LITTLE SPACELY.
MOMMIE! I-I MEAN, ROSEY!
NO! NO! I'VE CHANGED BACK, YOU STUPID ROBOT! KEEP AWAY FROM ME!
MY, YOU'VE GROWN! NOW, BE A GOOD BOY....
NO! I DON'T WANNA!
BOSS! HAVE YOU SEEN--
UH-OH!
JETSON! YOU'RE FIRED!
WAAAAH!
WAAAAH!
PERFECT!
The End!

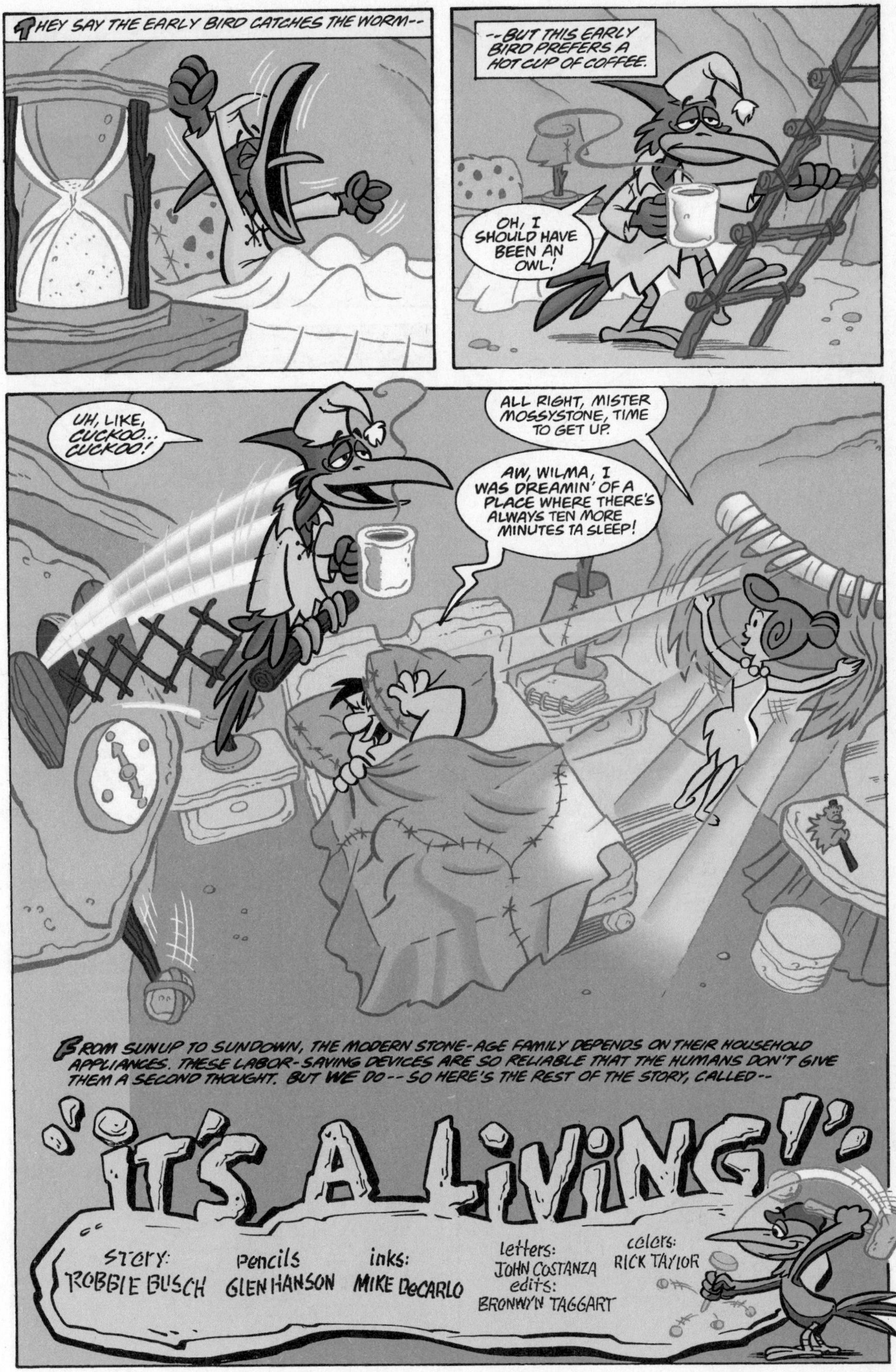
THEY SAY THE EARLY BIRD CATCHES THE WORM--
--BUT THIS EARLY BIRD PREFERS A HOT CUP OF COFFEE.
OH, I SHOULD HAVE BEEN AN OWL!
UH, LIKE, CUCKOO... CUCKOO!
ALL RIGHT, MISTER MOSSYSTONE, TIME TO GET UP.
AW, WILMA, I WAS DREAMIN' OF A PLACE WHERE THERE'S ALWAYS TEN MORE MINUTES TA SLEEP!
FROM SUNUP TO SUNDOWN, THE MODERN STONE-AGE FAMILY DEPENDS ON THEIR HOUSEHOLD APPLIANCES. THESE LABOR-SAVING DEVICES ARE SO RELIABLE THAT THE HUMANS DON'T GIVE THEM A SECOND THOUGHT. BUT WE DO-- SO HERE'S THE REST OF THE STORY, CALLED--
"IT'S A LIVING!"
story: ROBBIE BUSCH
pencils GLEN HANSON
inks: MIKE DeCARLO
letters: JOHN COSTANZA
edits: BRONWYN TAGGART
colors: RICK TAYLOR

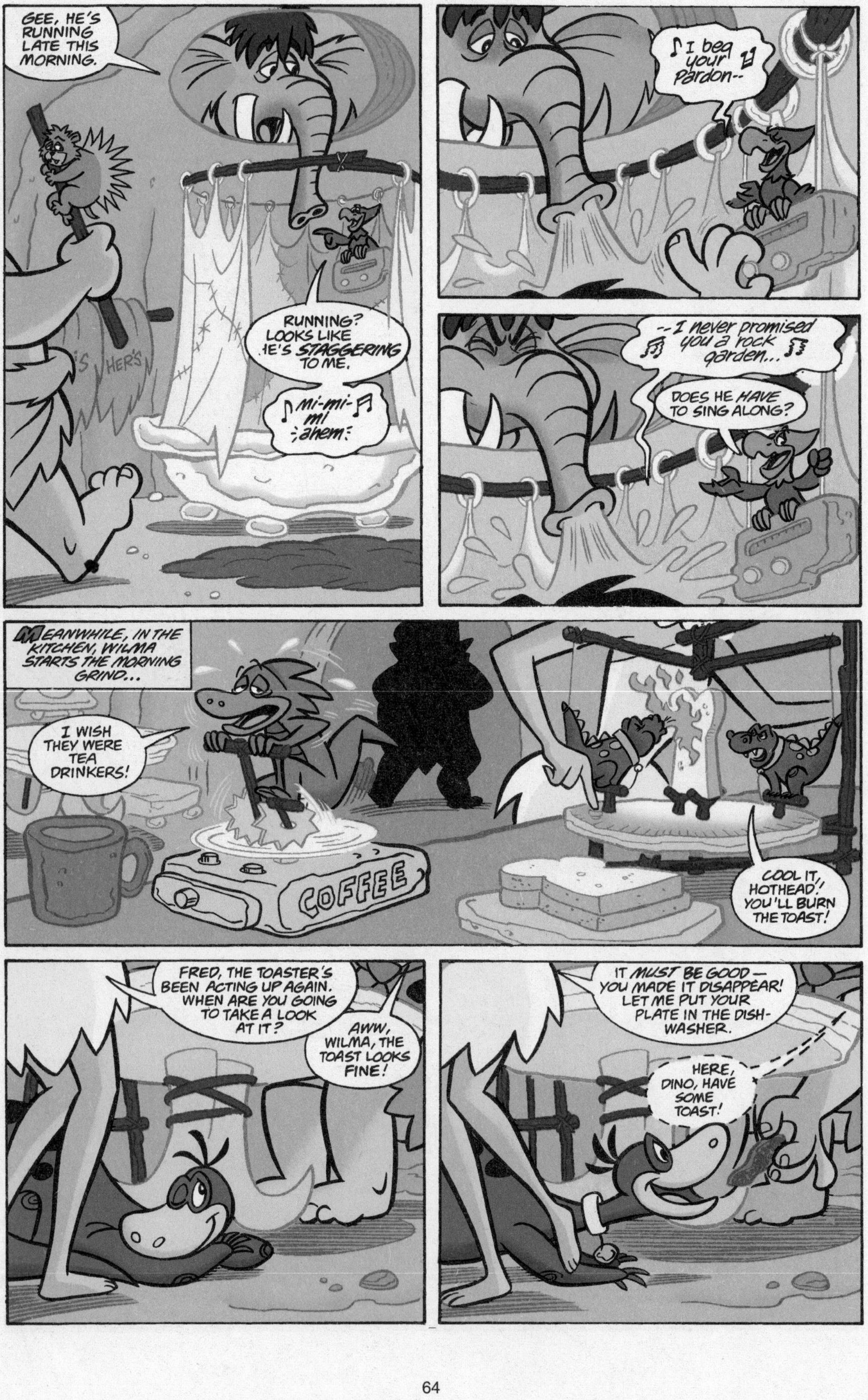

GEE, HE'S RUNNING LATE THIS MORNING.
RUNNING? LOOKS LIKE HE'S STAGGERING TO ME.
♪ MI-MI-MI ♫ AHEM
♪ I beg your pardon--
--I never promised you a rock garden... ♫
DOES HE HAVE TO SING ALONG?
MEANWHILE, IN THE KITCHEN, WILMA STARTS THE MORNING GRIND...
I WISH THEY WERE TEA DRINKERS!
COFFEE
COOL IT, HOTHEAD! YOU'LL BURN THE TOAST!
FRED, THE TOASTER'S BEEN ACTING UP AGAIN. WHEN ARE YOU GOING TO TAKE A LOOK AT IT?
AWW, WILMA, THE TOAST LOOKS FINE!
IT MUST BE GOOD — YOU MADE IT DISAPPEAR! LET ME PUT YOUR PLATE IN THE DISH-WASHER.
HERE, DINO, HAVE SOME TOAST!

I'VE ALWAYS LOVED THE WATER--

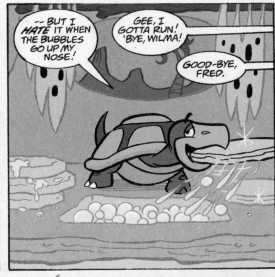

-- BUT I *HATE* IT WHEN THE BUBBLES GO UP MY NOSE!

GEE, I GOTTA RUN! 'BYE, WILMA!

GOOD-BYE, FRED.

HONK! HONK!

GET A MOVE ON, BARN'! I DON'T WANNA BE LATE FOR WORK!

I'M COMIN', FRED! I'M COMIN'!

STOP

I CAN'T WAIT 'TIL YOUR BARBECUE TONIGHT.

YEAH, THAT NEW GRILL OF OURS TURNS OUT A GREAT BRONTOSAURUS BURGER.

GO

I LIKE THE WOOD PANELING ON THOSE NEW MODEL CARS.

ME TOO, BUT I'M ON A DIET.

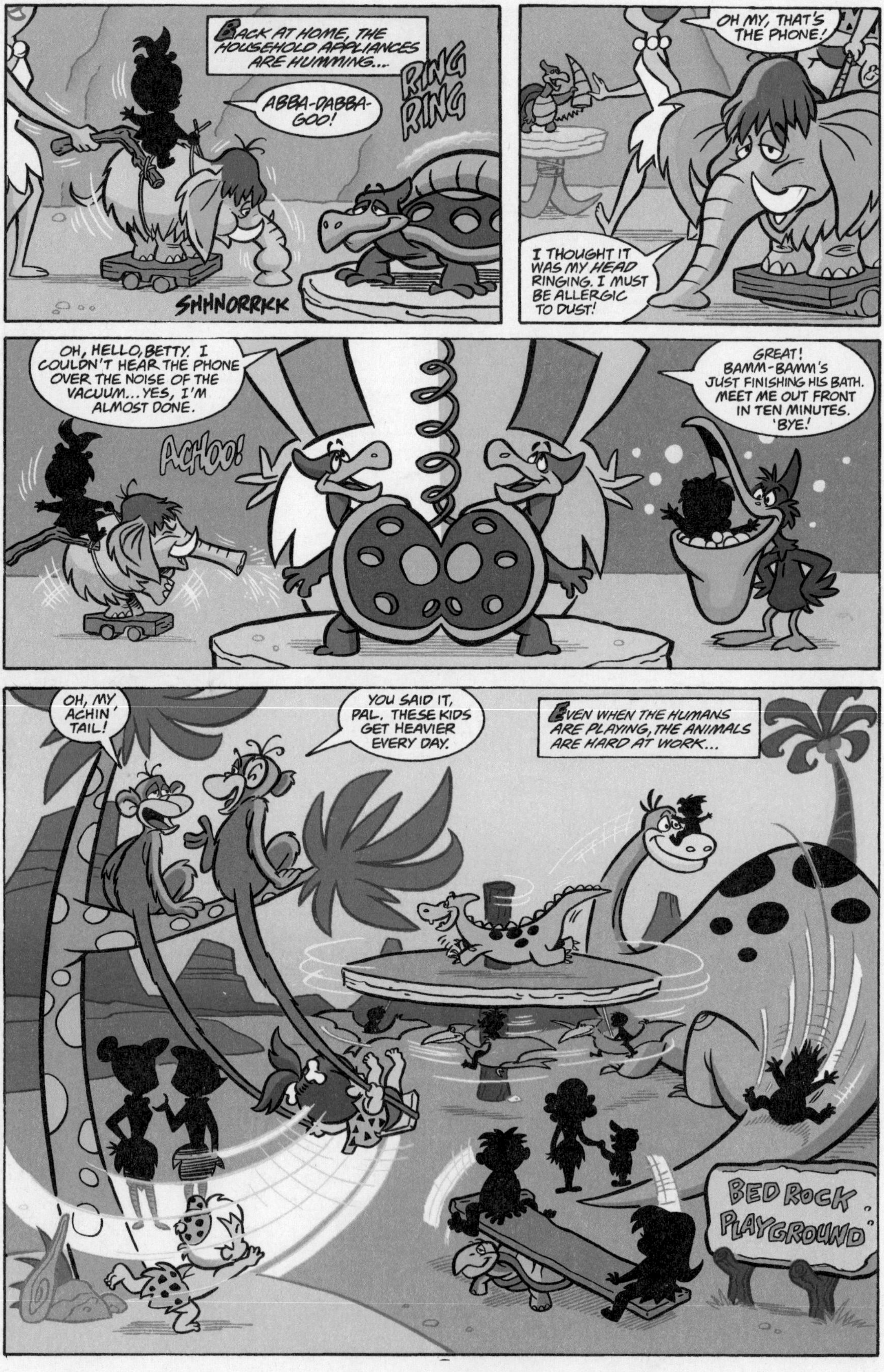
BACK AT HOME, THE HOUSEHOLD APPLIANCES ARE HUMMING...
ABBA-DABBA-GOO!
RING RING
SHHNORRKK
OH MY, THAT'S THE PHONE!
I THOUGHT IT WAS MY HEAD RINGING. I MUST BE ALLERGIC TO DUST!
OH, HELLO, BETTY. I COULDN'T HEAR THE PHONE OVER THE NOISE OF THE VACUUM... YES, I'M ALMOST DONE.
ACHOO!
GREAT! BAMM-BAMM'S JUST FINISHING HIS BATH. MEET ME OUT FRONT IN TEN MINUTES. 'BYE!
OH, MY ACHIN' TAIL!
YOU SAID IT, PAL. THESE KIDS GET HEAVIER EVERY DAY.
EVEN WHEN THE HUMANS ARE PLAYING, THE ANIMALS ARE HARD AT WORK...
BED ROCK PLAYGROUND

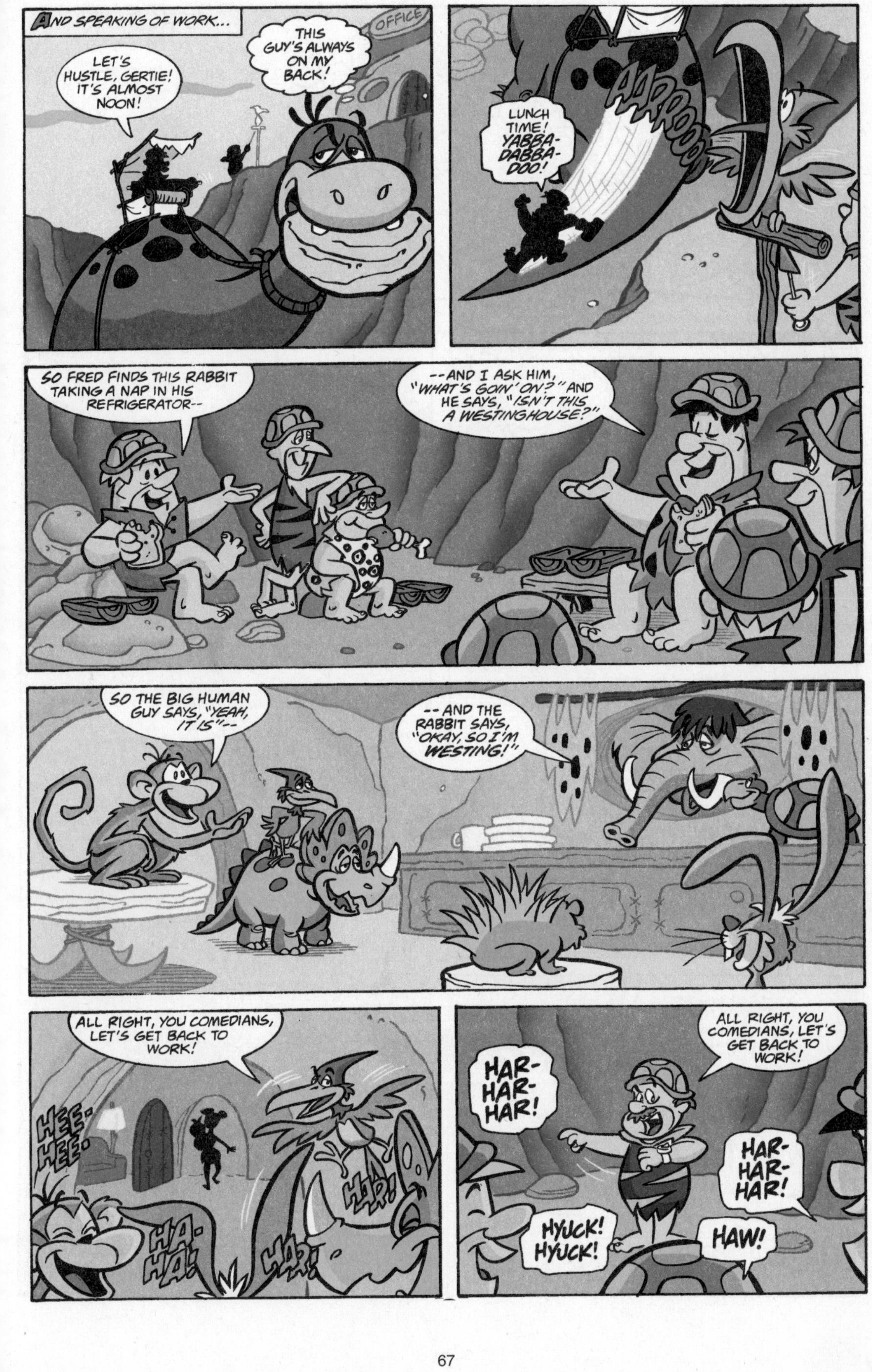
AND SPEAKING OF WORK...
LET'S HUSTLE, GERTIE! IT'S ALMOST NOON!
THIS GUY'S ALWAYS ON MY BACK!
OFFICE
LUNCH TIME! YABBA-DABBA-DOO!
AAROOO
SO FRED FINDS THIS RABBIT TAKING A NAP IN HIS REFRIGERATOR--
--AND I ASK HIM, "WHAT'S GOIN' ON?" AND HE SAYS, "ISN'T THIS A WESTINGHOUSE?"
SO THE BIG HUMAN GUY SAYS, "YEAH, IT IS"--
--AND THE RABBIT SAYS, "OKAY, SO I'M WESTING!"
ALL RIGHT, YOU COMEDIANS, LET'S GET BACK TO WORK!
HEE-HEE-HEE
HA-HA!
HAR!
HAR!
ALL RIGHT, YOU COMEDIANS, LET'S GET BACK TO WORK!
HAR-HAR-HAR!
HAR-HAR-HAR!
HYUCK! HYUCK!
HAW!

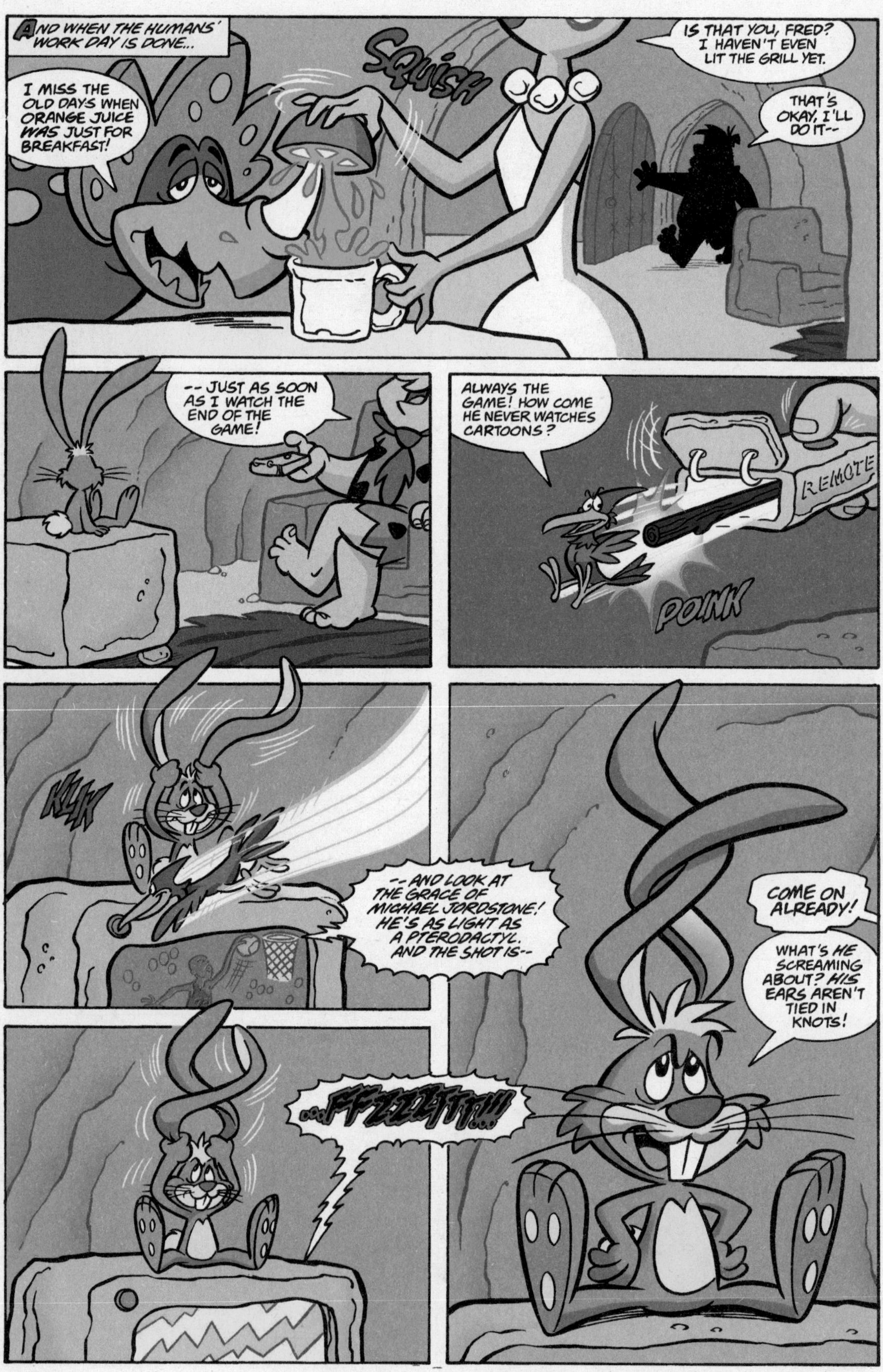
AND WHEN THE HUMANS' WORK DAY IS DONE...
I MISS THE OLD DAYS WHEN ORANGE JUICE WAS JUST FOR BREAKFAST!
SQUISH
IS THAT YOU, FRED? I HAVEN'T EVEN LIT THE GRILL YET.
THAT'S OKAY, I'LL DO IT--
--JUST AS SOON AS I WATCH THE END OF THE GAME!
ALWAYS THE GAME! HOW COME HE NEVER WATCHES CARTOONS?
REMOTE
POINK
KLIK
--AND LOOK AT THE GRACE OF MICHAEL JORDSTONE! HE'S AS LIGHT AS A PTERODACTYL. AND THE SHOT IS--
COME ON ALREADY!
WHAT'S HE SCREAMING ABOUT? HIS EARS AREN'T TIED IN KNOTS!
...FFZZZZTTT!!!...

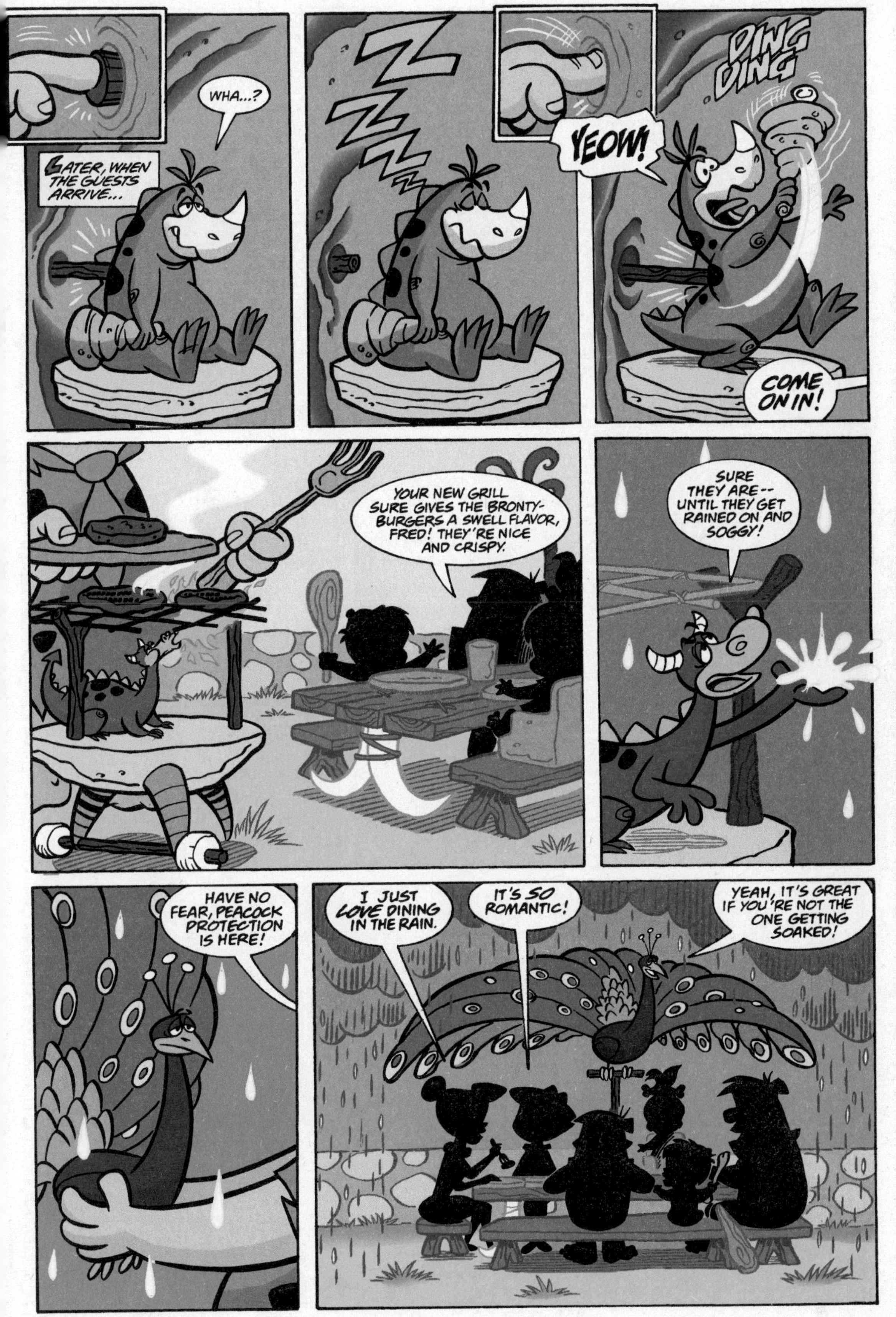

WHA...?
LATER, WHEN THE GUESTS ARRIVE...
DING DING
YEOW!
COME ON IN!
YOUR NEW GRILL SURE GIVES THE BRONTY-BURGERS A SWELL FLAVOR, FRED! THEY'RE NICE AND CRISPY.
SURE THEY ARE-- UNTIL THEY GET RAINED ON AND SOGGY!
HAVE NO FEAR, PEACOCK PROTECTION IS HERE!
I JUST LOVE DINING IN THE RAIN.
IT'S SO ROMANTIC!
YEAH, IT'S GREAT IF YOU'RE NOT THE ONE GETTING SOAKED!

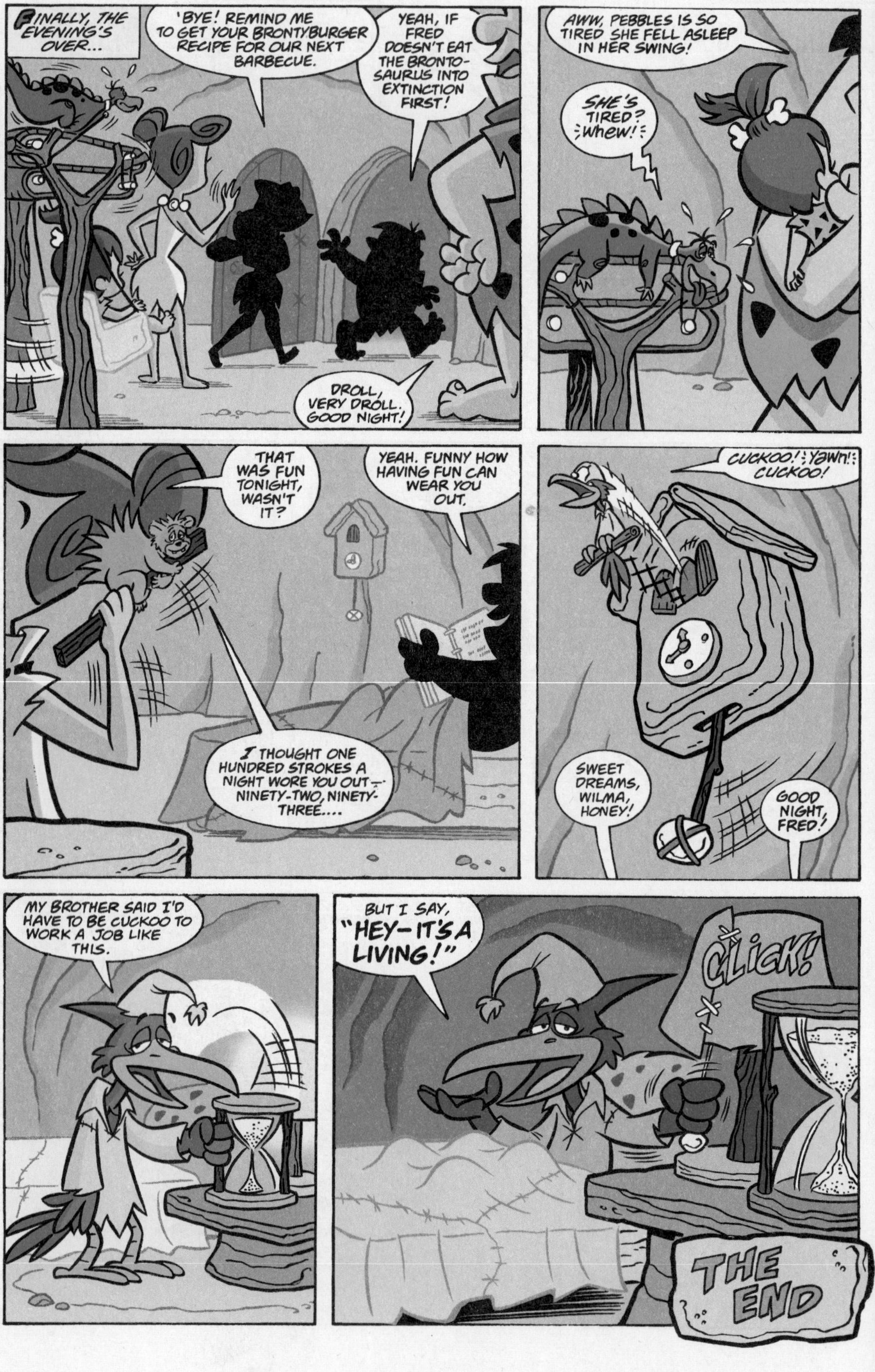
FINALLY, THE EVENING'S OVER...
'BYE! REMIND ME TO GET YOUR BRONTYBURGER RECIPE FOR OUR NEXT BARBECUE.
YEAH, IF FRED DOESN'T EAT THE BRONTOSAURUS INTO EXTINCTION FIRST!
DROLL, VERY DROLL. GOOD NIGHT!
AWW, PEBBLES IS SO TIRED SHE FELL ASLEEP IN HER SWING!
SHE'S TIRED? WHEW!
THAT WAS FUN TONIGHT, WASN'T IT?
YEAH. FUNNY HOW HAVING FUN CAN WEAR YOU OUT.
I THOUGHT ONE HUNDRED STROKES A NIGHT WORE YOU OUT— NINETY-TWO, NINETY-THREE....
CUCKOO! YAWN! CUCKOO!
SWEET DREAMS, WILMA, HONEY!
GOOD NIGHT, FRED!
MY BROTHER SAID I'D HAVE TO BE CUCKOO TO WORK A JOB LIKE THIS.
BUT I SAY, "HEY—IT'S A LIVING!"
CLICK!
THE END

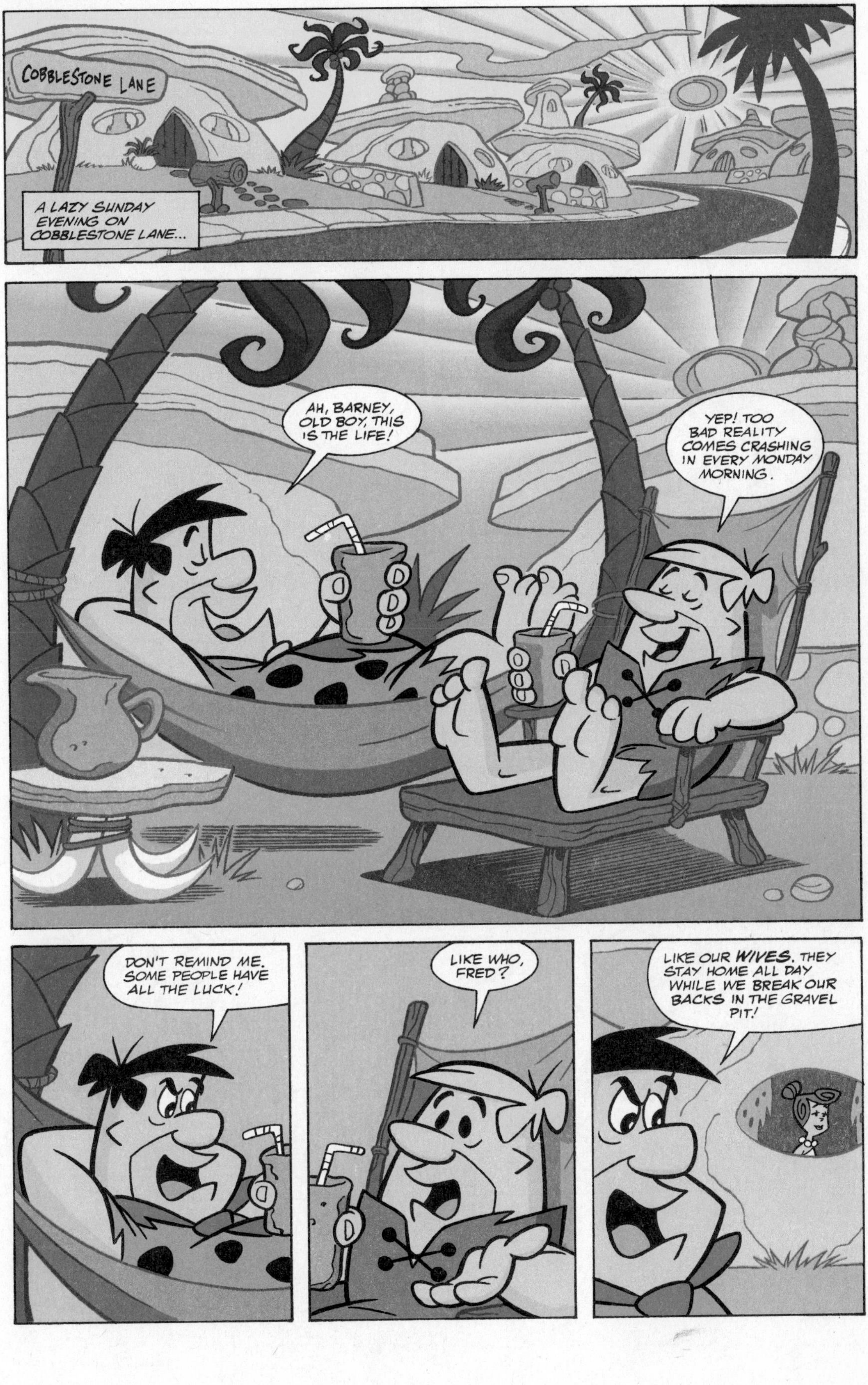
COBBLESTONE LANE
A LAZY SUNDAY EVENING ON COBBLESTONE LANE...
AH, BARNEY, OLD BOY, THIS IS THE LIFE!
YEP! TOO BAD REALITY COMES CRASHING IN EVERY MONDAY MORNING.
DON'T REMIND ME. SOME PEOPLE HAVE ALL THE LUCK!
LIKE WHO, FRED?
LIKE OUR WIVES. THEY STAY HOME ALL DAY WHILE WE BREAK OUR BACKS IN THE GRAVEL PIT!

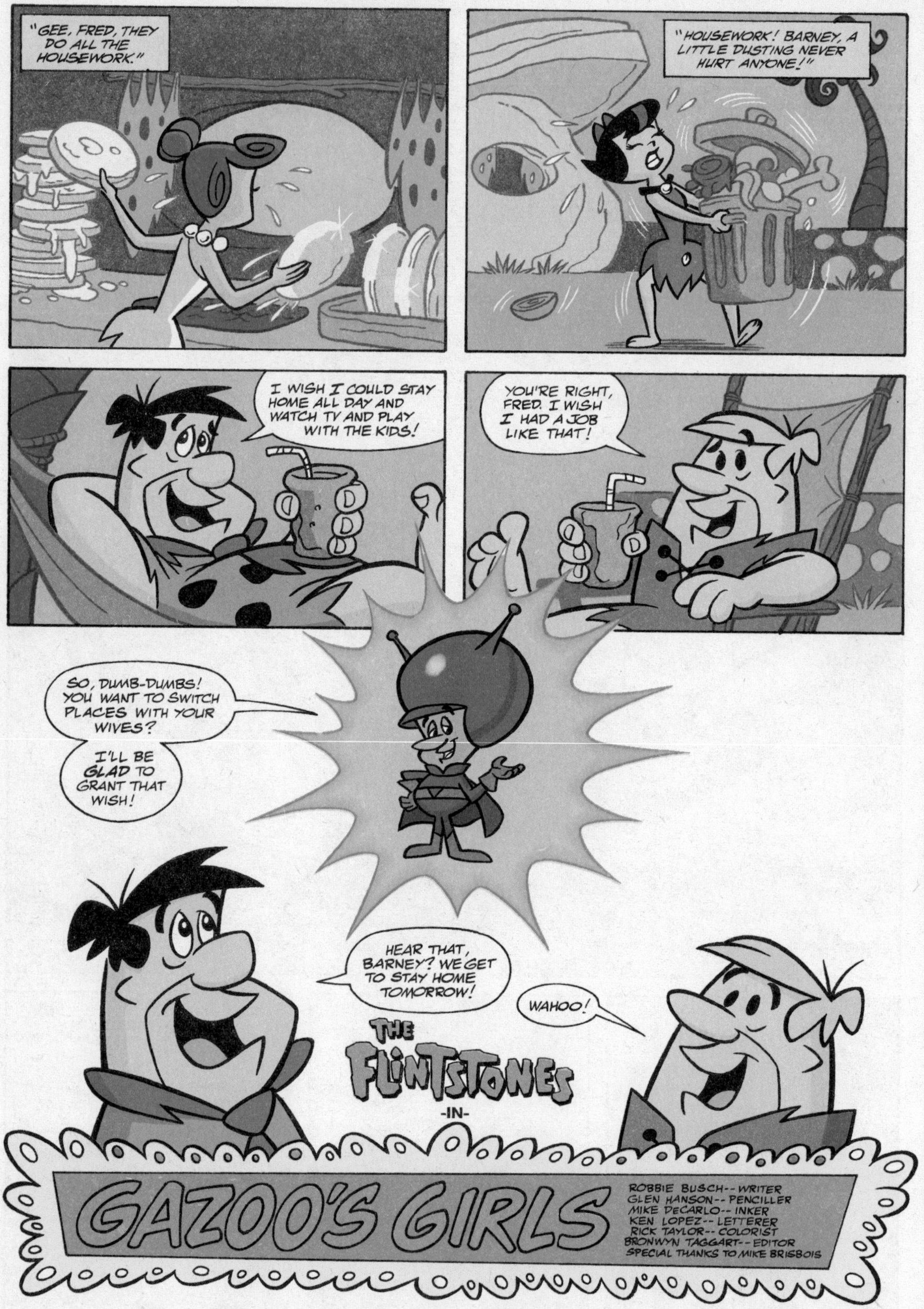
"GEE, FRED, THEY DO ALL THE HOUSEWORK."
"HOUSEWORK! BARNEY, A LITTLE DUSTING NEVER HURT ANYONE!"
I WISH I COULD STAY HOME ALL DAY AND WATCH TV AND PLAY WITH THE KIDS!
YOU'RE RIGHT, FRED. I WISH I HAD A JOB LIKE THAT!
SO, DUMB-DUMBS! YOU WANT TO SWITCH PLACES WITH YOUR WIVES?
I'LL BE GLAD TO GRANT THAT WISH!
HEAR THAT, BARNEY? WE GET TO STAY HOME TOMORROW!
WAHOO!
THE FLINTSTONES
-IN-
GAZOO'S GIRLS
ROBBIE BUSCH-- WRITER
GLEN HANSON-- PENCILLER
MIKE DECARLO-- INKER
KEN LOPEZ-- LETTERER
RICK TAYLOR-- COLORIST
BRONWYN TAGGART-- EDITOR
SPECIAL THANKS TO MIKE BRISBOIS

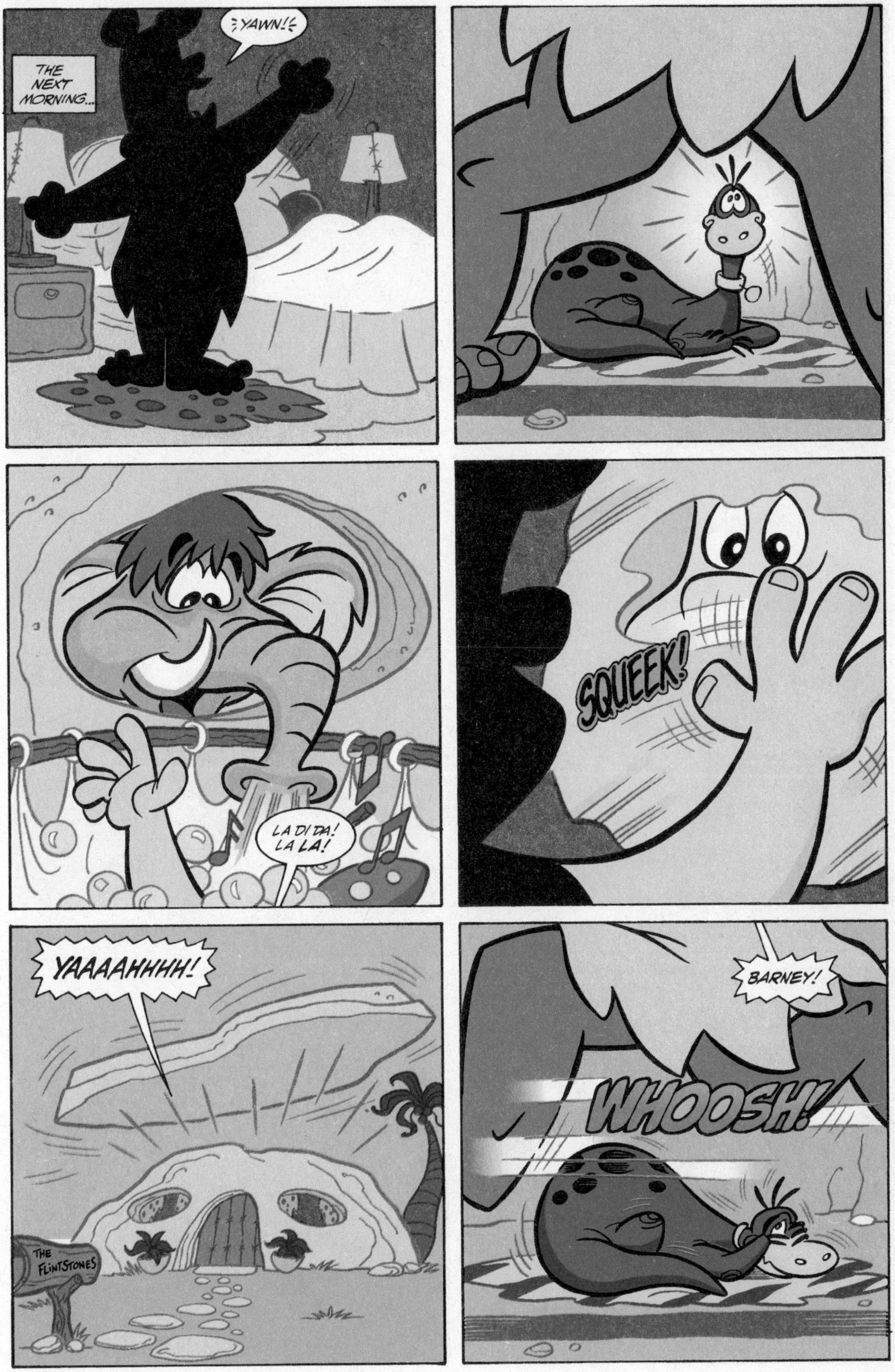
THE NEXT MORNING...
YAWN!
LA DI DA! LA LA!
SQUEEK!
YAAAAHHHH!
THE FLINTSTONES
BARNEY!
WHOOSH!

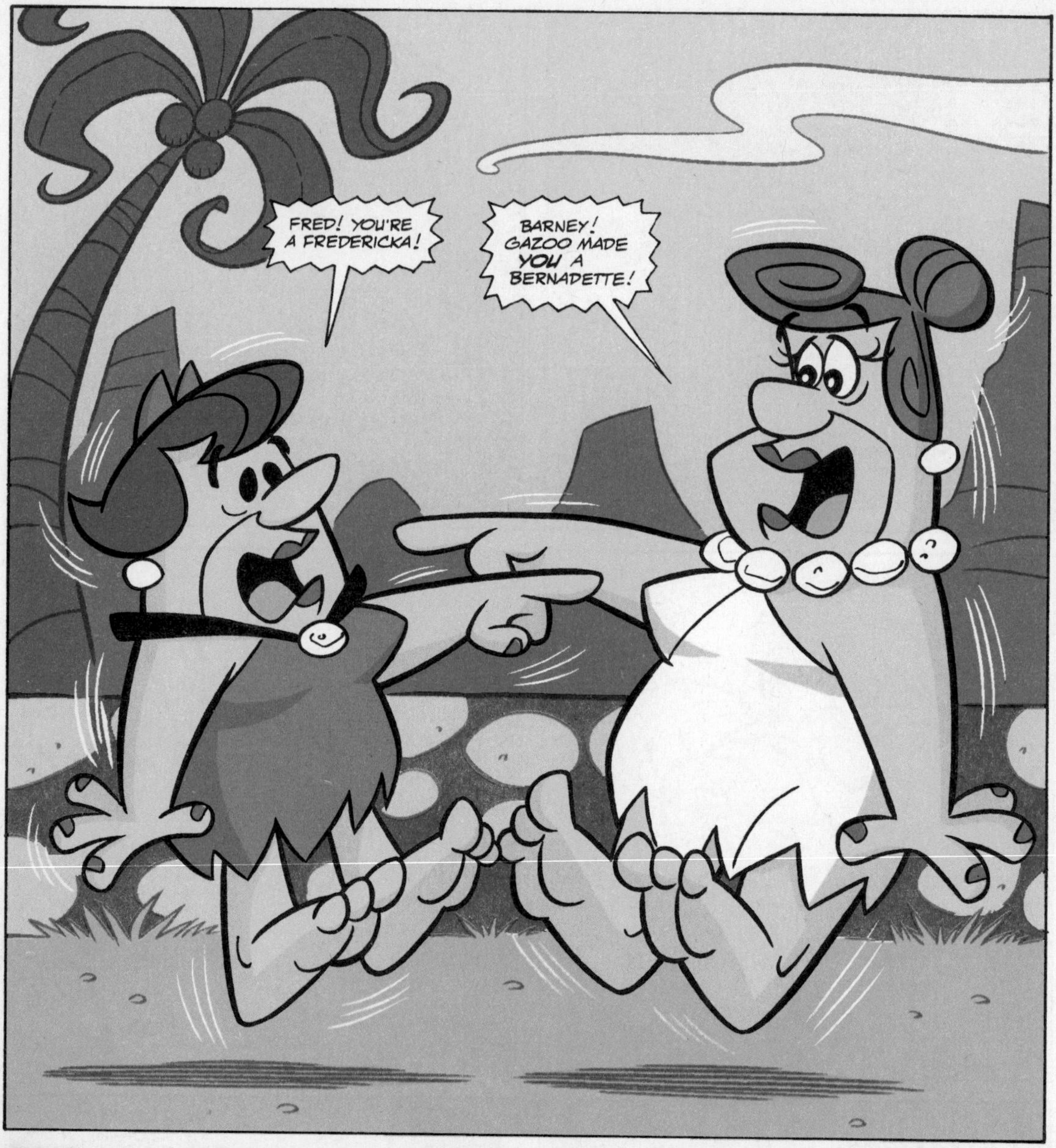
FRED! YOU'RE A FREDERICKA!
BARNEY! GAZOO MADE YOU A BERNADETTE!

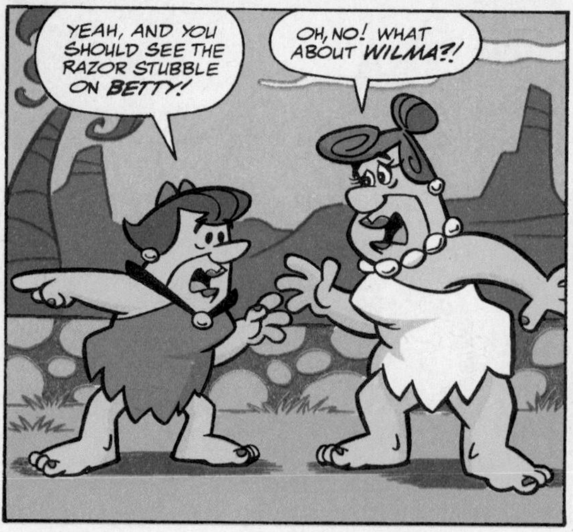
YEAH, AND YOU SHOULD SEE THE RAZOR STUBBLE ON BETTY!
OH, NO! WHAT ABOUT WILMA?!

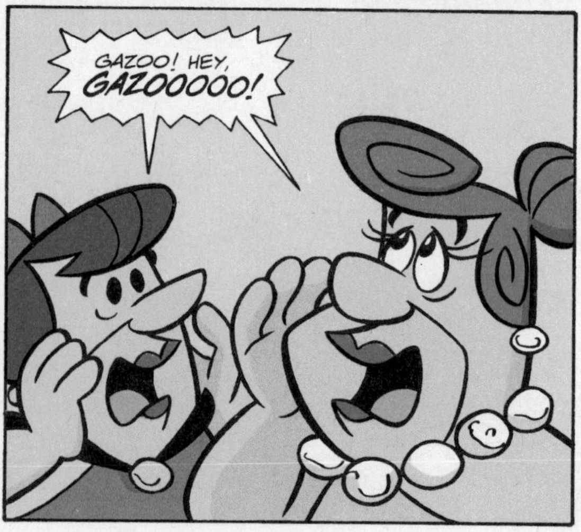
GAZOO! HEY, GAZOOOOO!

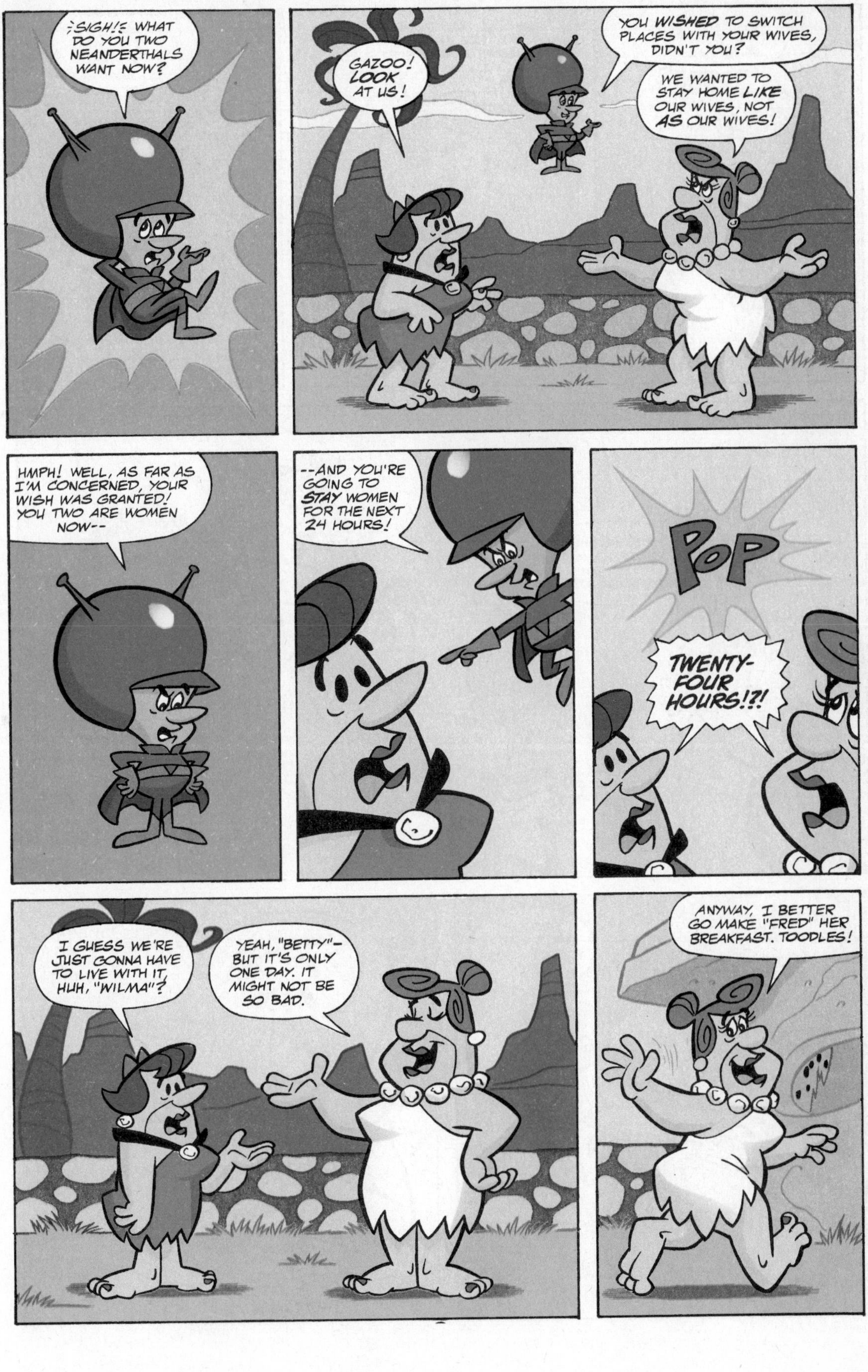

:SIGH!: WHAT DO YOU TWO NEANDERTHALS WANT NOW?
GAZOO! LOOK AT US!
YOU WISHED TO SWITCH PLACES WITH YOUR WIVES, DIDN'T YOU?
WE WANTED TO STAY HOME LIKE OUR WIVES, NOT AS OUR WIVES!
HMPH! WELL, AS FAR AS I'M CONCERNED, YOUR WISH WAS GRANTED! YOU TWO ARE WOMEN NOW--
--AND YOU'RE GOING TO STAY WOMEN FOR THE NEXT 24 HOURS!
POP
TWENTY-FOUR HOURS!?!
I GUESS WE'RE JUST GONNA HAVE TO LIVE WITH IT, HUH, "WILMA"?
YEAH, "BETTY"— BUT IT'S ONLY ONE DAY. IT MIGHT NOT BE SO BAD.
ANYWAY, I BETTER GO MAKE "FRED" HER BREAKFAST. TOODLES!

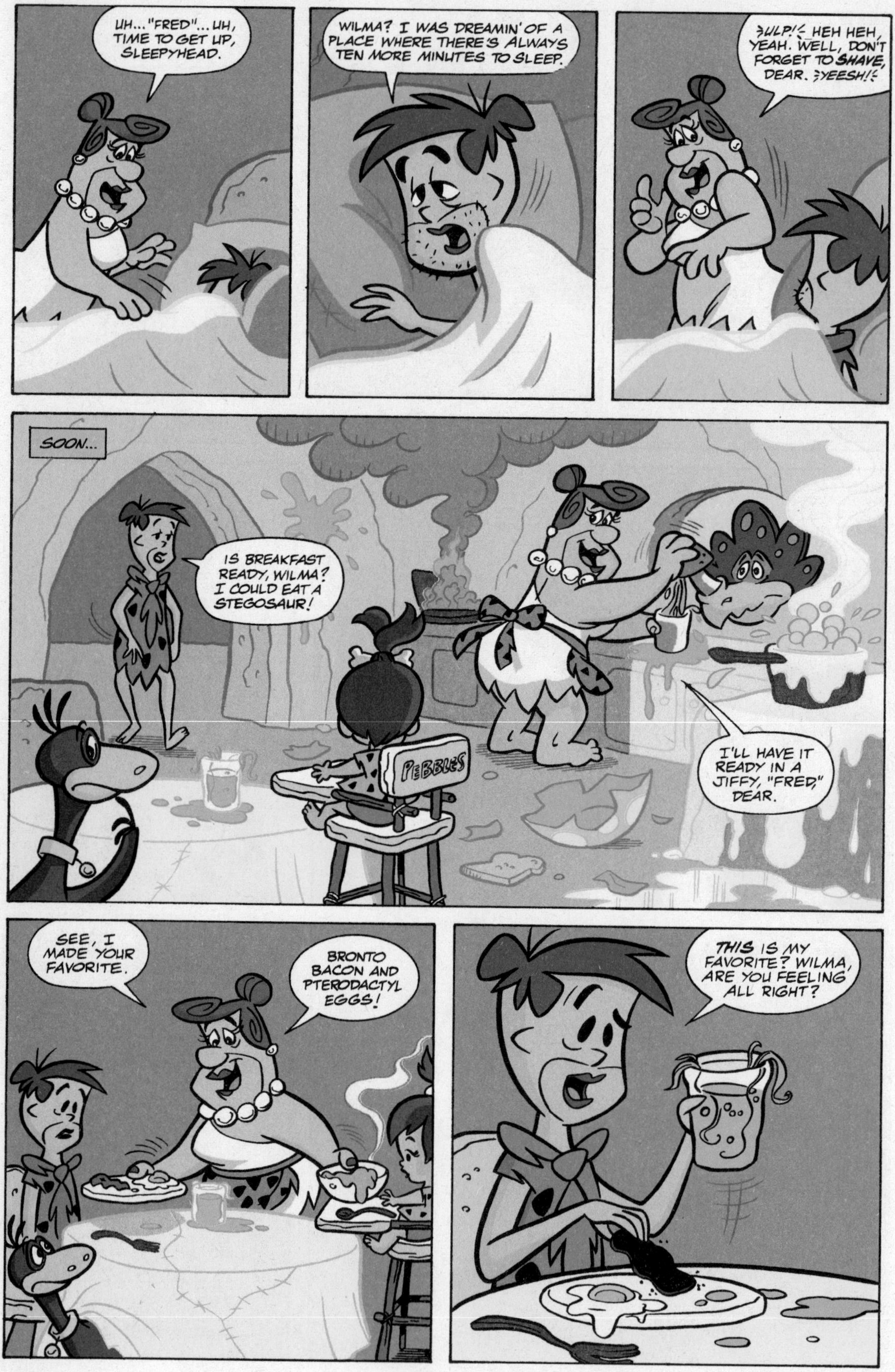
UH..."FRED"...UH, TIME TO GET UP, SLEEPYHEAD.
WILMA? I WAS DREAMIN' OF A PLACE WHERE THERE'S ALWAYS TEN MORE MINUTES TO SLEEP.
ULP! HEH HEH, YEAH. WELL, DON'T FORGET TO SHAVE, DEAR. *YEESH!*
SOON...
IS BREAKFAST READY, WILMA? I COULD EAT A STEGOSAUR!
PEBBLES
I'LL HAVE IT READY IN A JIFFY, "FRED," DEAR.
SEE, I MADE YOUR FAVORITE.
BRONTO BACON AND PTERODACTYL EGGS!
THIS IS MY FAVORITE? WILMA, ARE YOU FEELING ALL RIGHT?

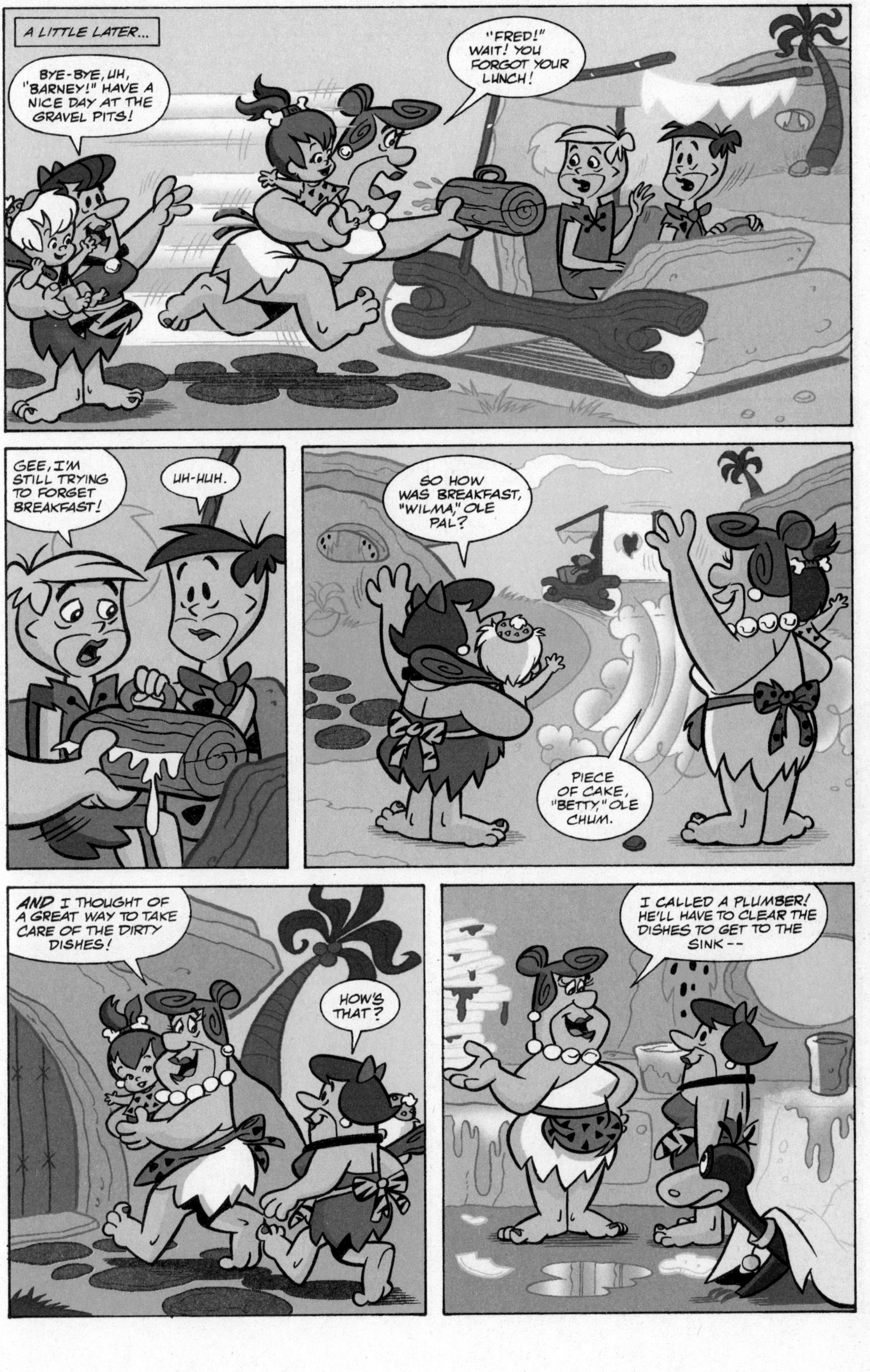

A LITTLE LATER...
BYE-BYE, UH, "BARNEY!" HAVE A NICE DAY AT THE GRAVEL PITS!
"FRED!" WAIT! YOU FORGOT YOUR LUNCH!
GEE, I'M STILL TRYING TO FORGET BREAKFAST!
UH-HUH.
SO HOW WAS BREAKFAST, "WILMA," OLE PAL?
PIECE OF CAKE, "BETTY," OLE CHUM.
AND I THOUGHT OF A GREAT WAY TO TAKE CARE OF THE DIRTY DISHES!
HOW'S THAT?
I CALLED A PLUMBER! HE'LL HAVE TO CLEAR THE DISHES TO GET TO THE SINK --

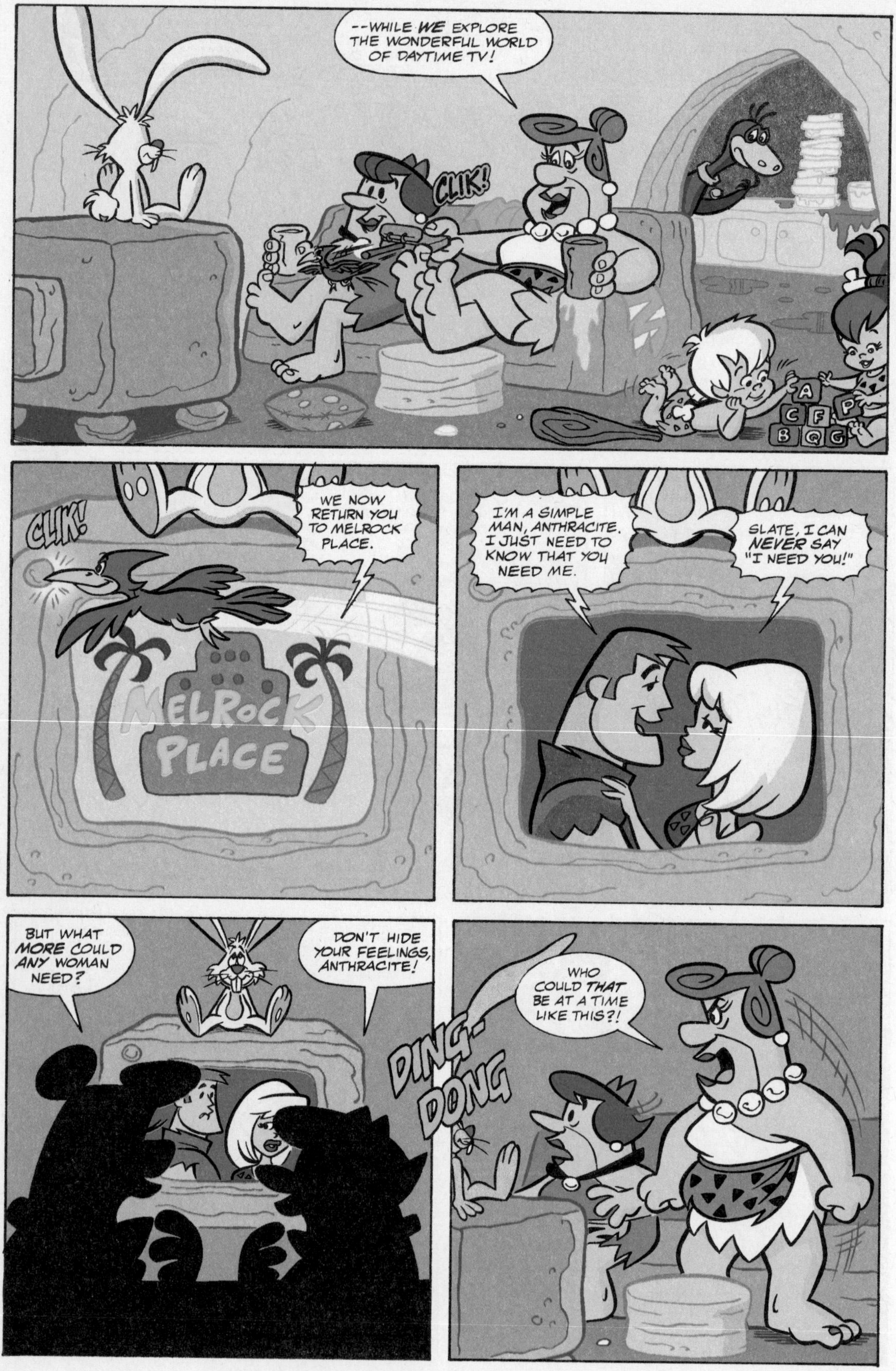
--WHILE WE EXPLORE THE WONDERFUL WORLD OF DAYTIME TV!
CLIK!
A
C F P
B Q G
CLIK!
WE NOW RETURN YOU TO MELROCK PLACE.
MELROCK PLACE
I'M A SIMPLE MAN, ANTHRACITE. I JUST NEED TO KNOW THAT YOU NEED ME.
SLATE, I CAN NEVER SAY "I NEED YOU!"
BUT WHAT MORE COULD ANY WOMAN NEED?
DON'T HIDE YOUR FEELINGS, ANTHRACITE!
DING-DONG
WHO COULD THAT BE AT A TIME LIKE THIS?!

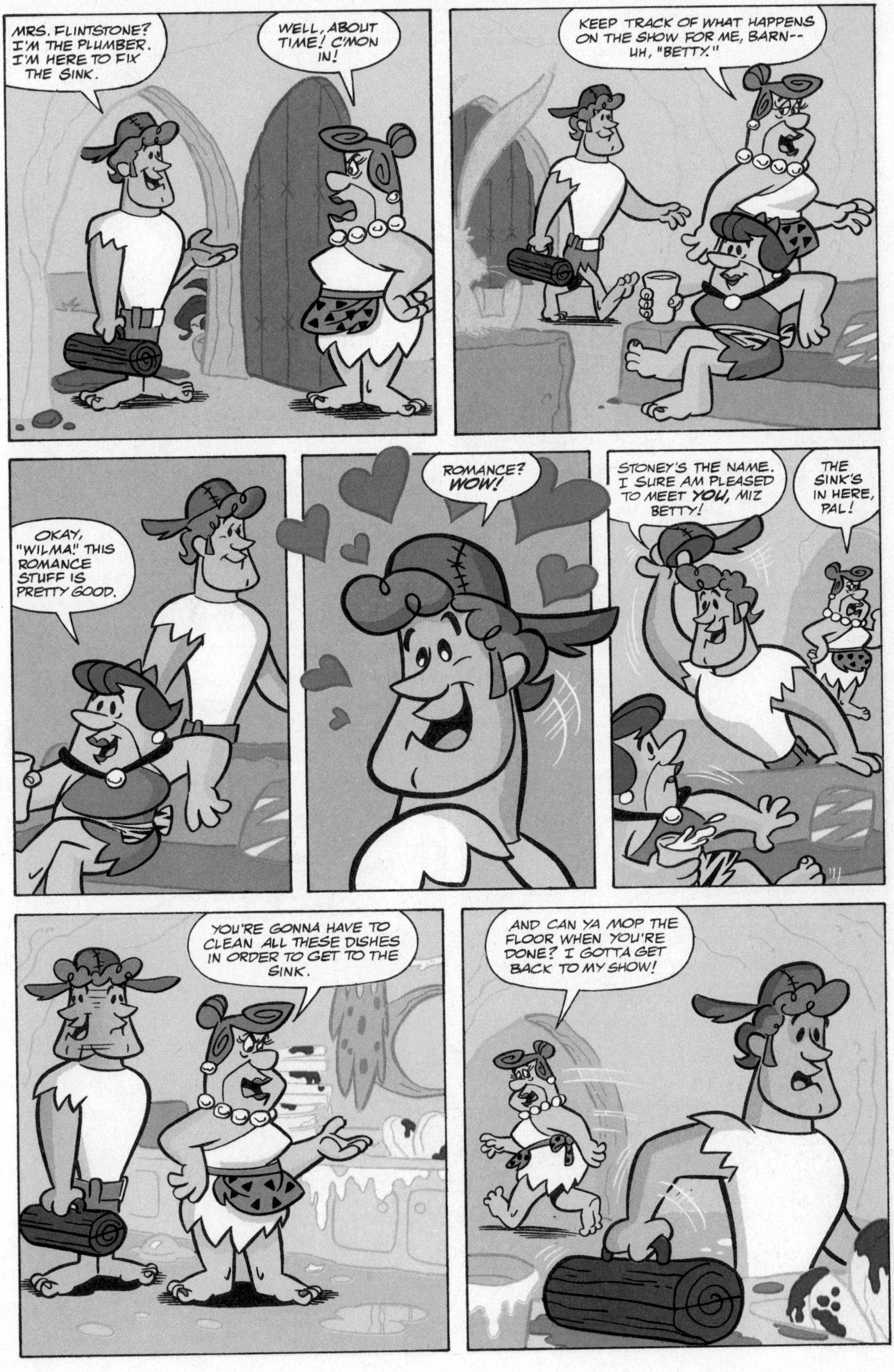
MRS. FLINTSTONE? I'M THE PLUMBER. I'M HERE TO FIX THE SINK.
WELL, ABOUT TIME! C'MON IN!
KEEP TRACK OF WHAT HAPPENS ON THE SHOW FOR ME, BARN-- UH, "BETTY."
OKAY, "WILMA." THIS ROMANCE STUFF IS PRETTY GOOD.
ROMANCE? WOW!
STONEY'S THE NAME. I SURE AM PLEASED TO MEET YOU, MIZ BETTY!
THE SINK'S IN HERE, PAL!
YOU'RE GONNA HAVE TO CLEAN ALL THESE DISHES IN ORDER TO GET TO THE SINK.
AND CAN YA MOP THE FLOOR WHEN YOU'RE DONE? I GOTTA GET BACK TO MY SHOW!

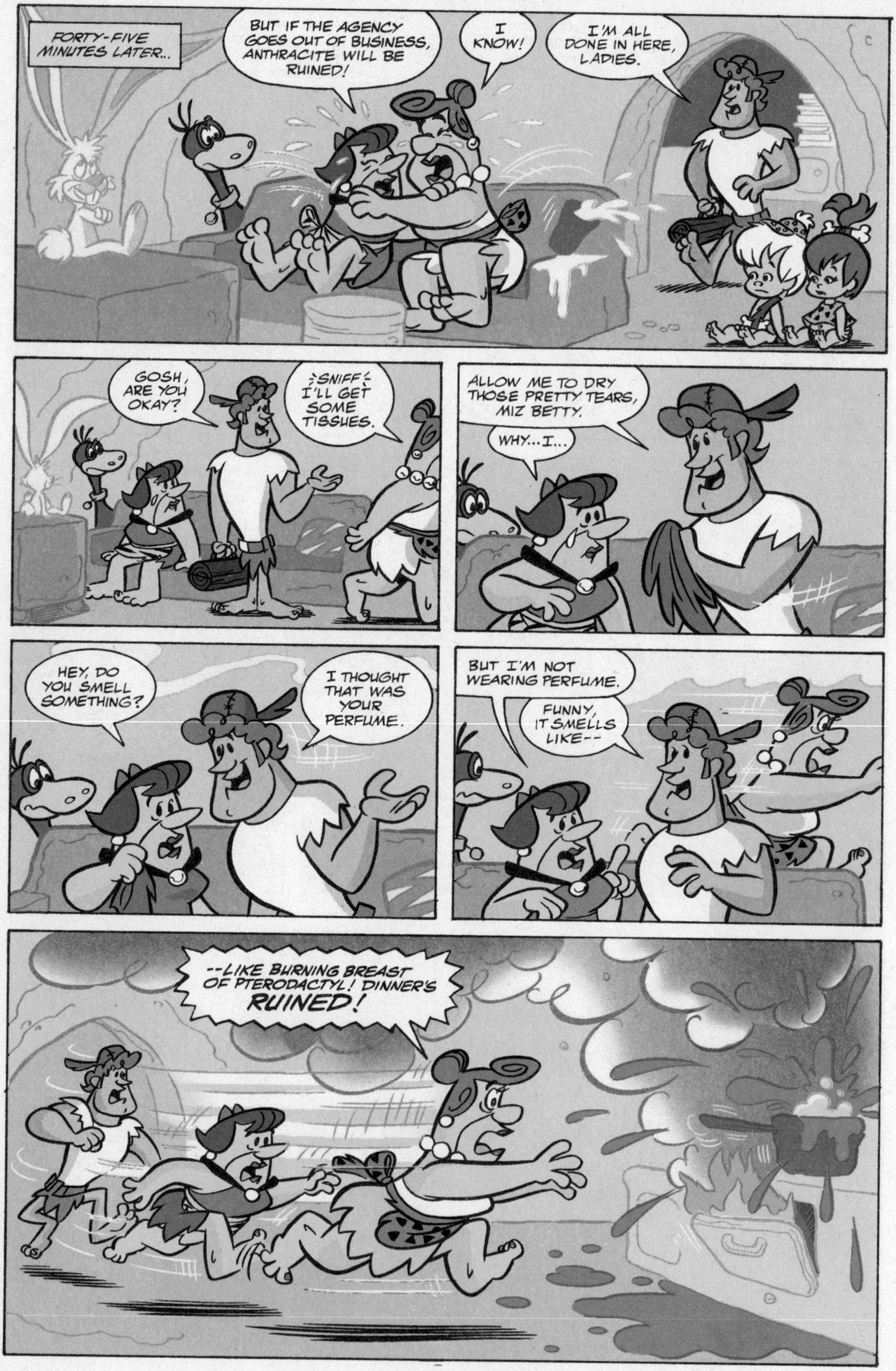
FORTY-FIVE MINUTES LATER...
BUT IF THE AGENCY GOES OUT OF BUSINESS, ANTHRACITE WILL BE RUINED!
I KNOW!
I'M ALL DONE IN HERE, LADIES.
GOSH, ARE YOU OKAY?
SNIFF I'LL GET SOME TISSUES.
ALLOW ME TO DRY THOSE PRETTY TEARS, MIZ BETTY.
WHY... I...
HEY, DO YOU SMELL SOMETHING?
I THOUGHT THAT WAS YOUR PERFUME.
BUT I'M NOT WEARING PERFUME.
FUNNY, IT SMELLS LIKE--
--LIKE BURNING BREAST OF PTERODACTYL! DINNER'S RUINED!

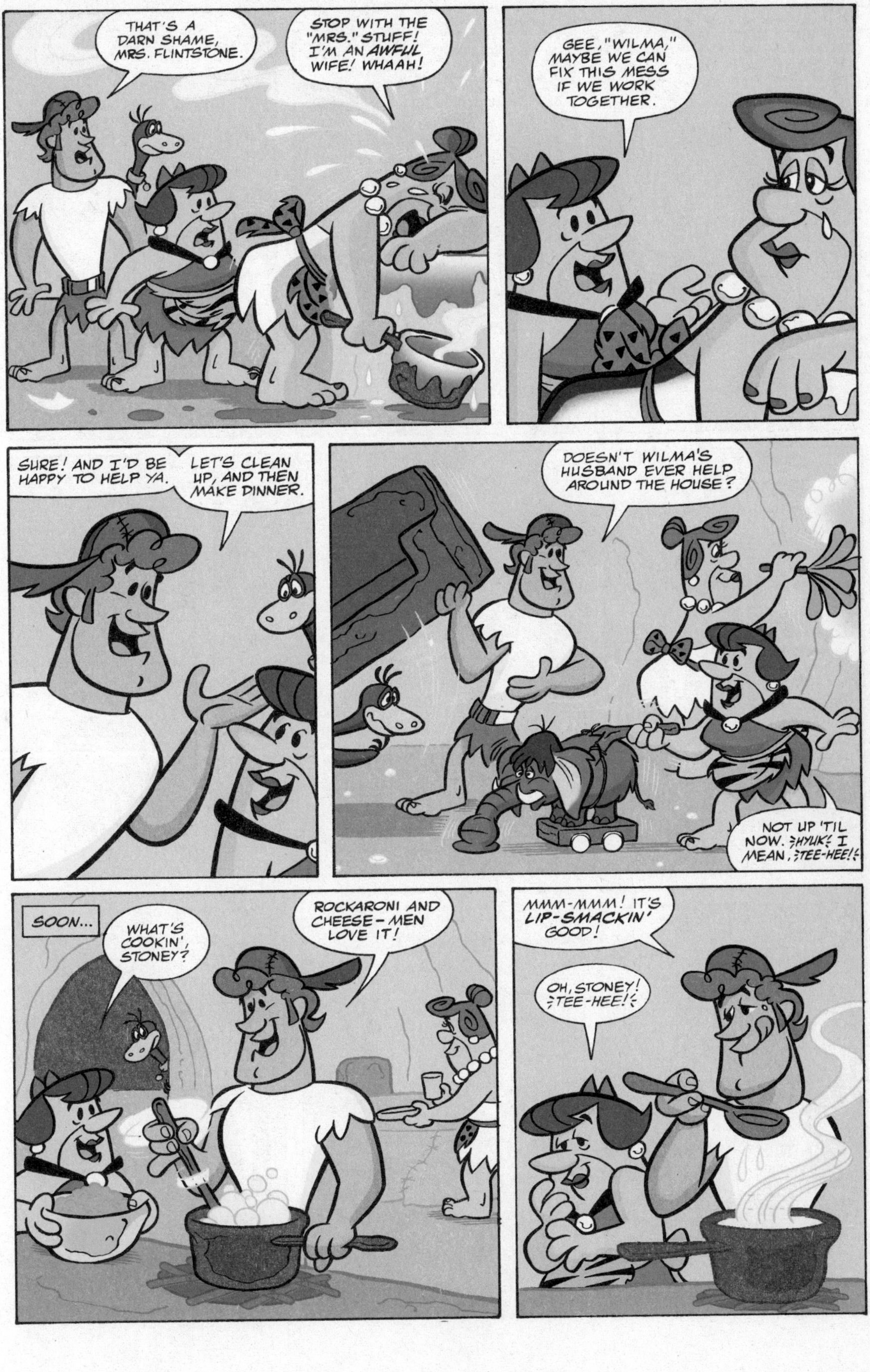
THAT'S A DARN SHAME, MRS. FLINTSTONE.
STOP WITH THE "MRS." STUFF! I'M AN AWFUL WIFE! WHAAH!
GEE, "WILMA," MAYBE WE CAN FIX THIS MESS IF WE WORK TOGETHER.
SURE! AND I'D BE HAPPY TO HELP YA.
LET'S CLEAN UP, AND THEN MAKE DINNER.
DOESN'T WILMA'S HUSBAND EVER HELP AROUND THE HOUSE?
NOT UP 'TIL NOW. HYUK! I MEAN, TEE-HEE!
SOON...
WHAT'S COOKIN', STONEY?
ROCKARONI AND CHEESE—MEN LOVE IT!
MMM-MMM! IT'S LIP-SMACKIN' GOOD!
OH, STONEY! TEE-HEE!

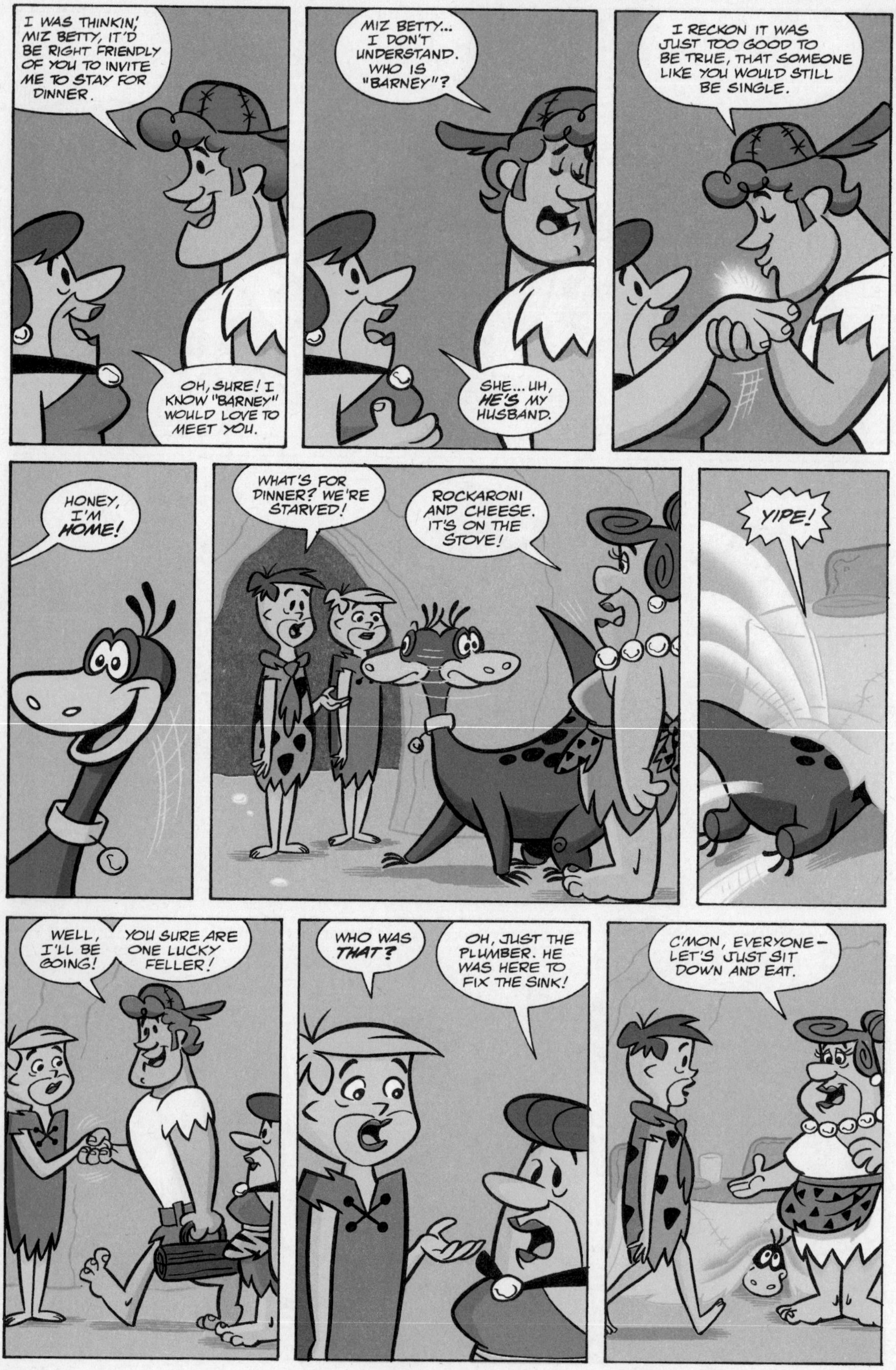
I WAS THINKIN', MIZ BETTY, IT'D BE RIGHT FRIENDLY OF YOU TO INVITE ME TO STAY FOR DINNER.
OH, SURE! I KNOW "BARNEY" WOULD LOVE TO MEET YOU.
MIZ BETTY... I DON'T UNDERSTAND. WHO IS "BARNEY"?
SHE... UH, HE'S MY HUSBAND.
I RECKON IT WAS JUST TOO GOOD TO BE TRUE, THAT SOMEONE LIKE YOU WOULD STILL BE SINGLE.
HONEY, I'M HOME!
WHAT'S FOR DINNER? WE'RE STARVED!
ROCKARONI AND CHEESE. IT'S ON THE STOVE!
YIPE!
WELL, I'LL BE GOING!
YOU SURE ARE ONE LUCKY FELLER!
WHO WAS THAT?
OH, JUST THE PLUMBER. HE WAS HERE TO FIX THE SINK!
C'MON, EVERYONE-LET'S JUST SIT DOWN AND EAT.

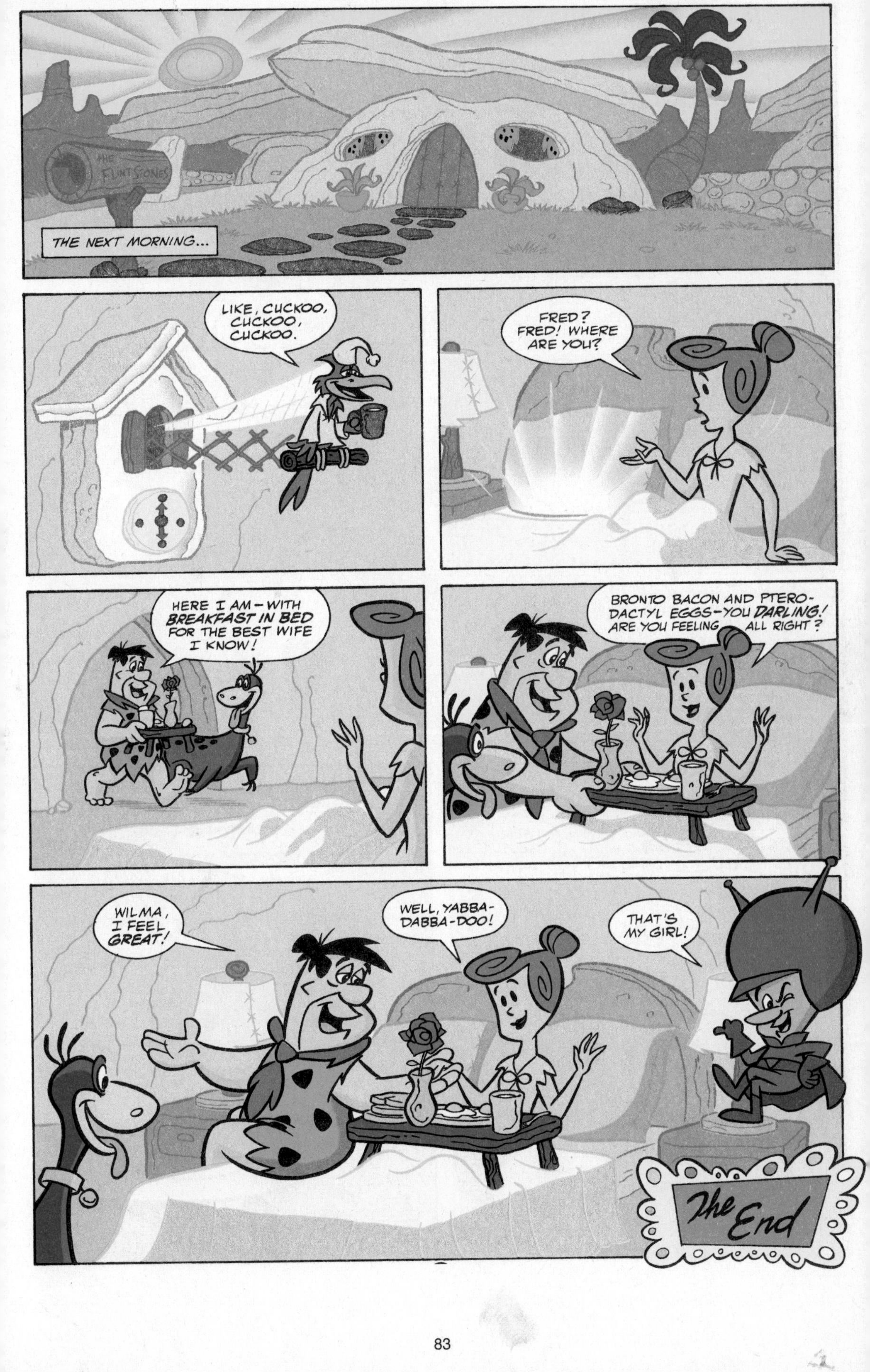

THE FLINTSTONES
THE NEXT MORNING...
LIKE, CUCKOO, CUCKOO, CUCKOO.
FRED? FRED! WHERE ARE YOU?
HERE I AM—WITH BREAKFAST IN BED FOR THE BEST WIFE I KNOW!
BRONTO BACON AND PTERO-DACTYL EGGS—YOU DARLING! ARE YOU FEELING ALL RIGHT?
WILMA, I FEEL GREAT!
WELL, YABBA-DABBA-DOO!
THAT'S MY GIRL!
The End

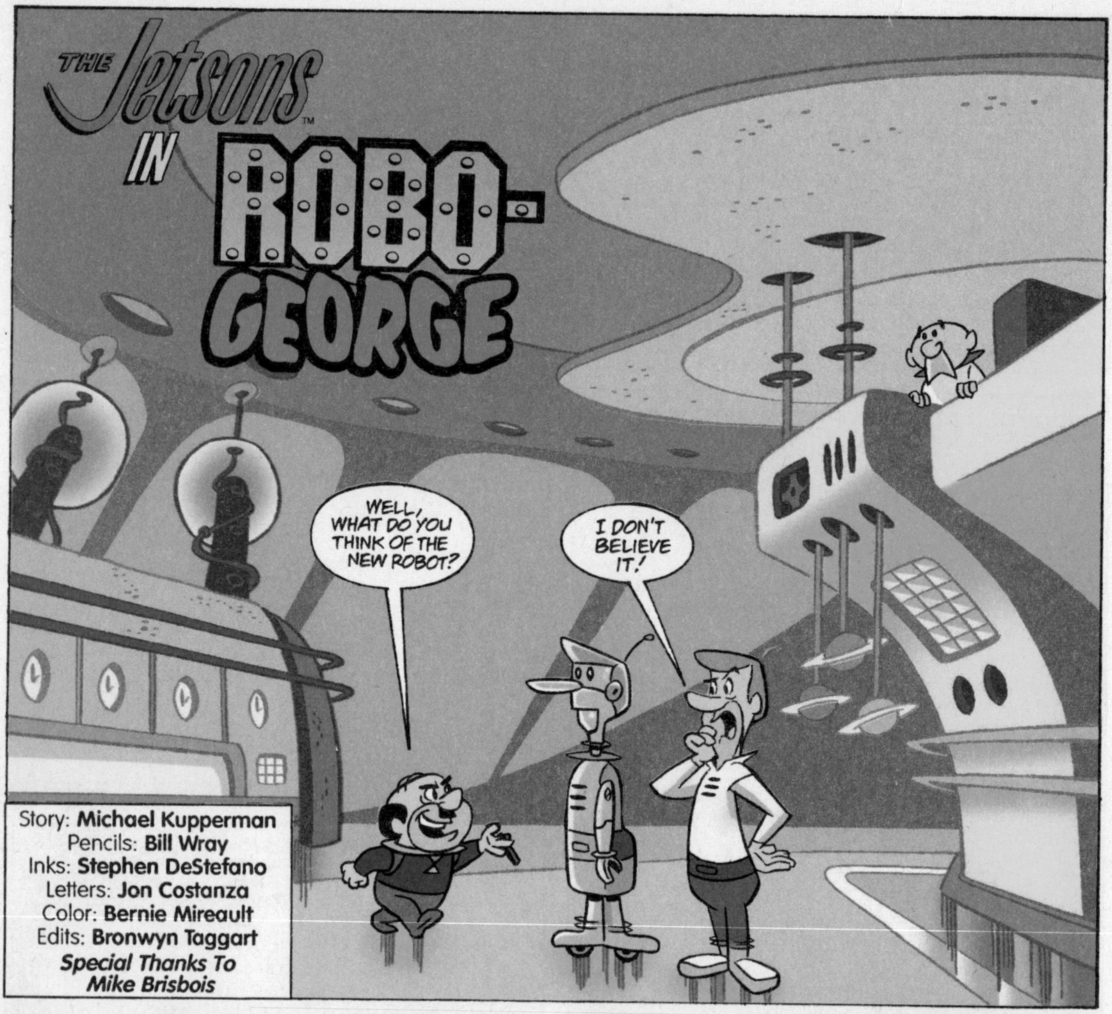
THE Jetsons™
IN ROBO-GEORGE
WELL, WHAT DO YOU THINK OF THE NEW ROBOT?
I DON'T BELIEVE IT!
Story: Michael Kupperman
Pencils: Bill Wray
Inks: Stephen DeStefano
Letters: Jon Costanza
Color: Bernie Mireault
Edits: Bronwyn Taggart
Special Thanks To Mike Brisbois

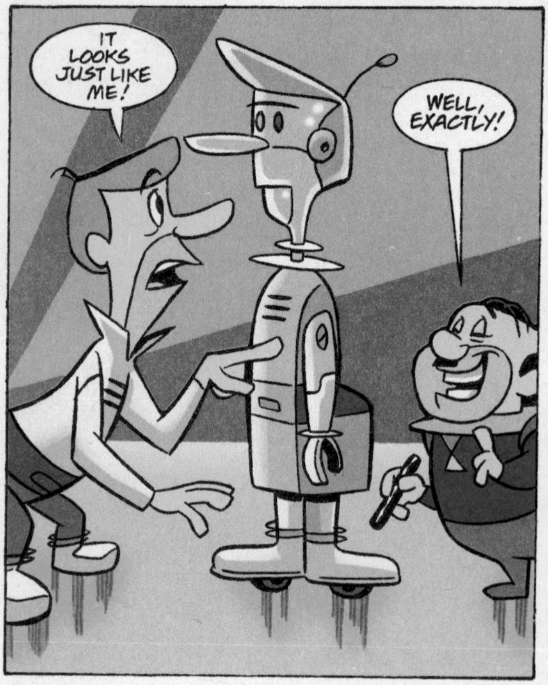
IT LOOKS JUST LIKE ME!
WELL, EXACTLY!

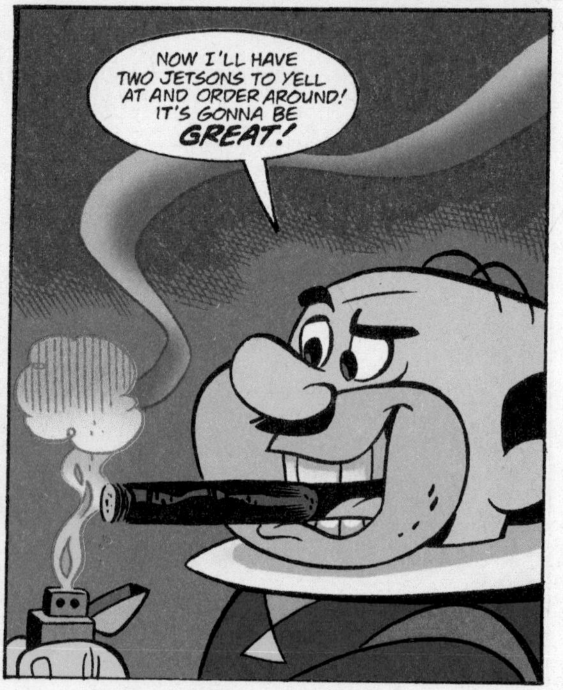
NOW I'LL HAVE TWO JETSONS TO YELL AT AND ORDER AROUND! IT'S GONNA BE GREAT!

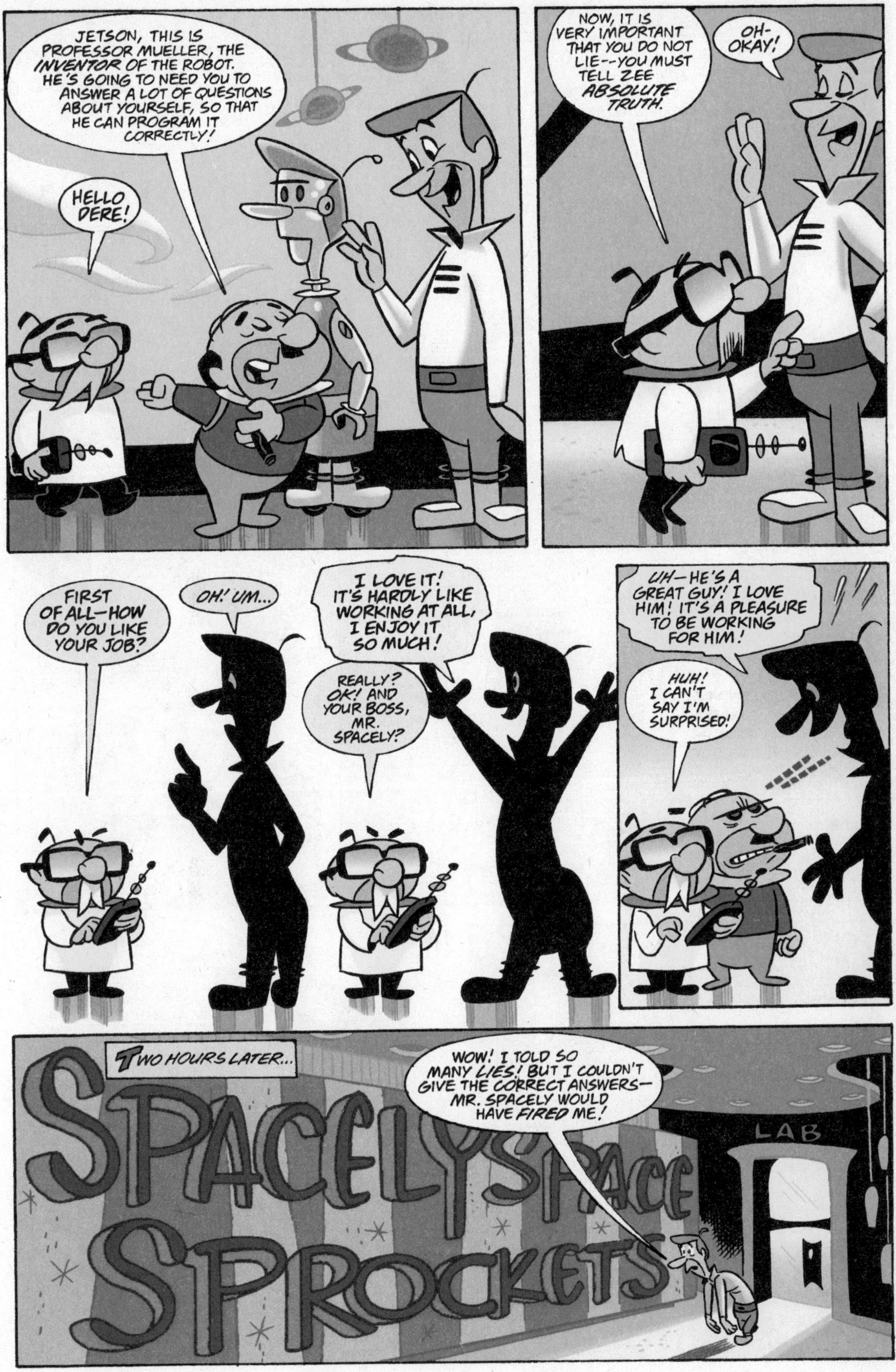

JETSON, THIS IS PROFESSOR MUELLER, THE INVENTOR OF THE ROBOT. HE'S GOING TO NEED YOU TO ANSWER A LOT OF QUESTIONS ABOUT YOURSELF, SO THAT HE CAN PROGRAM IT CORRECTLY!
HELLO DERE!
NOW, IT IS VERY IMPORTANT THAT YOU DO NOT LIE--YOU MUST TELL ZEE ABSOLUTE TRUTH.
OH-OKAY!
FIRST OF ALL—HOW DO YOU LIKE YOUR JOB?
OH! UM...
I LOVE IT! IT'S HARDLY LIKE WORKING AT ALL, I ENJOY IT SO MUCH!
REALLY? OK! AND YOUR BOSS, MR. SPACELY?
UH—HE'S A GREAT GUY! I LOVE HIM! IT'S A PLEASURE TO BE WORKING FOR HIM!
HUH! I CAN'T SAY I'M SURPRISED!
TWO HOURS LATER...
SPACELY SPACE SPROCKETS
WOW! I TOLD SO MANY LIES! BUT I COULDN'T GIVE THE CORRECT ANSWERS—MR. SPACELY WOULD HAVE FIRED ME!
LAB

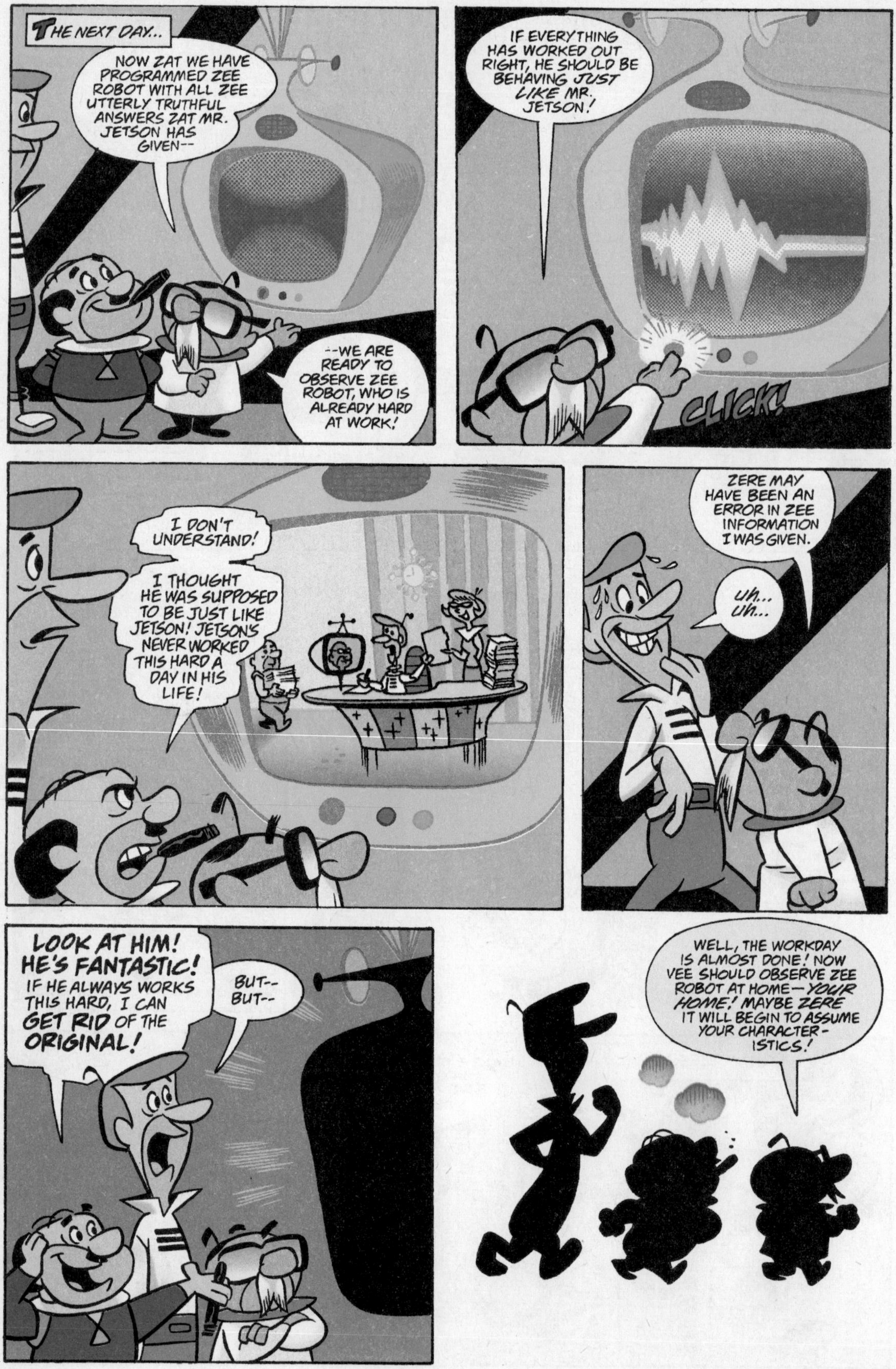
THE NEXT DAY...
NOW ZAT WE HAVE PROGRAMMED ZEE ROBOT WITH ALL ZEE UTTERLY TRUTHFUL ANSWERS ZAT MR. JETSON HAS GIVEN--
--WE ARE READY TO OBSERVE ZEE ROBOT, WHO IS ALREADY HARD AT WORK!
IF EVERYTHING HAS WORKED OUT RIGHT, HE SHOULD BE BEHAVING JUST LIKE MR. JETSON!
CLICK!
I DON'T UNDERSTAND!
I THOUGHT HE WAS SUPPOSED TO BE JUST LIKE JETSON! JETSON'S NEVER WORKED THIS HARD A DAY IN HIS LIFE!
ZERE MAY HAVE BEEN AN ERROR IN ZEE INFORMATION I WAS GIVEN.
uh... uh...
LOOK AT HIM! HE'S FANTASTIC! IF HE ALWAYS WORKS THIS HARD, I CAN GET RID OF THE ORIGINAL!
BUT-- BUT--
WELL, THE WORKDAY IS ALMOST DONE! NOW VEE SHOULD OBSERVE ZEE ROBOT AT HOME—YOUR HOME! MAYBE ZERE IT WILL BEGIN TO ASSUME YOUR CHARACTER-ISTICS!

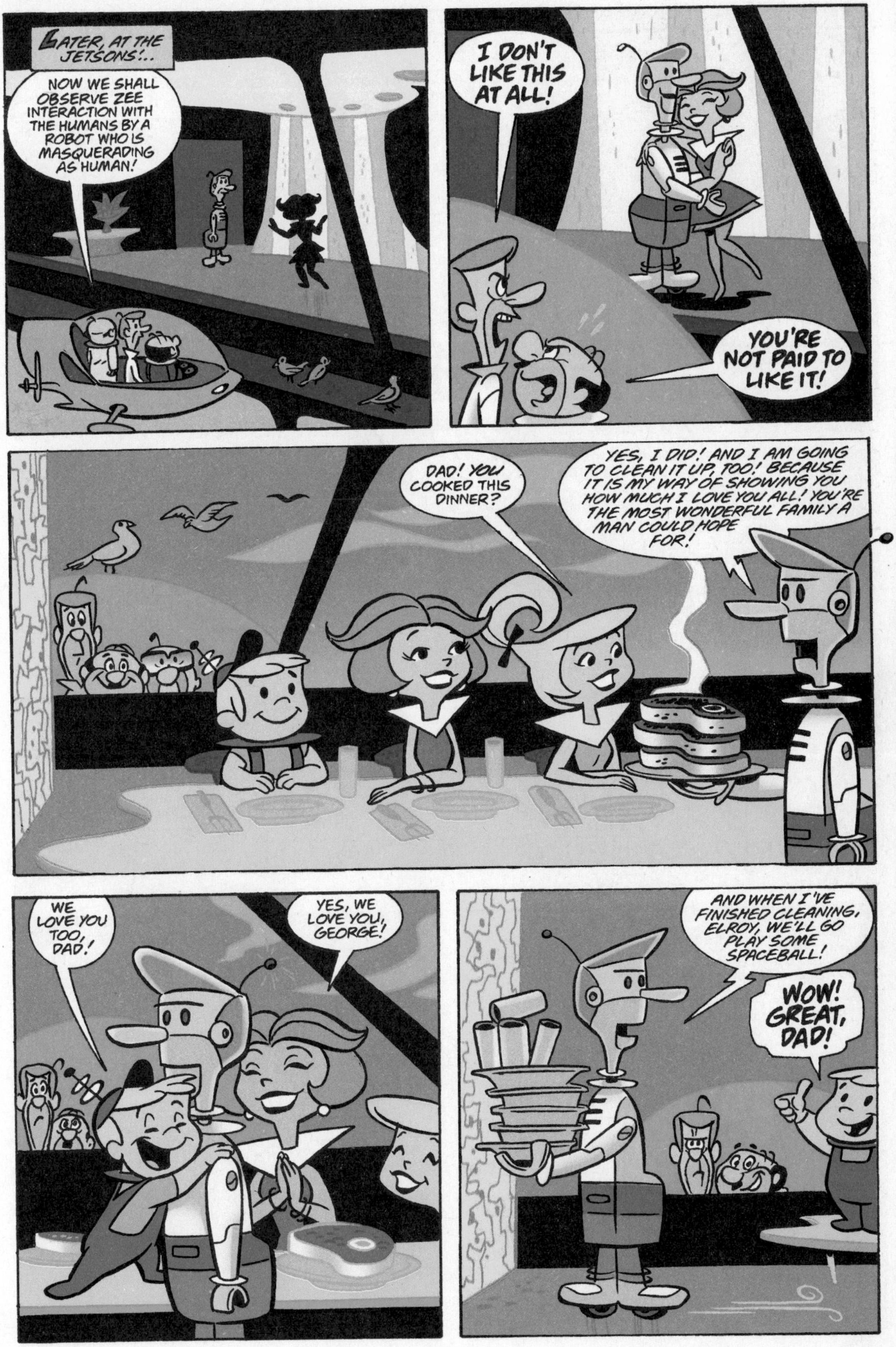
LATER, AT THE JETSONS'...
NOW WE SHALL OBSERVE ZEE INTERACTION WITH THE HUMANS BY A ROBOT WHO IS MASQUERADING AS HUMAN!
I DON'T LIKE THIS AT ALL!
YOU'RE NOT PAID TO LIKE IT!
DAD! YOU COOKED THIS DINNER?
YES, I DID! AND I AM GOING TO CLEAN IT UP, TOO! BECAUSE IT IS MY WAY OF SHOWING YOU HOW MUCH I LOVE YOU ALL! YOU'RE THE MOST WONDERFUL FAMILY A MAN COULD HOPE FOR!
WE LOVE YOU TOO, DAD!
YES, WE LOVE YOU, GEORGE!
AND WHEN I'VE FINISHED CLEANING, ELROY, WE'LL GO PLAY SOME SPACEBALL!
WOW! GREAT, DAD!

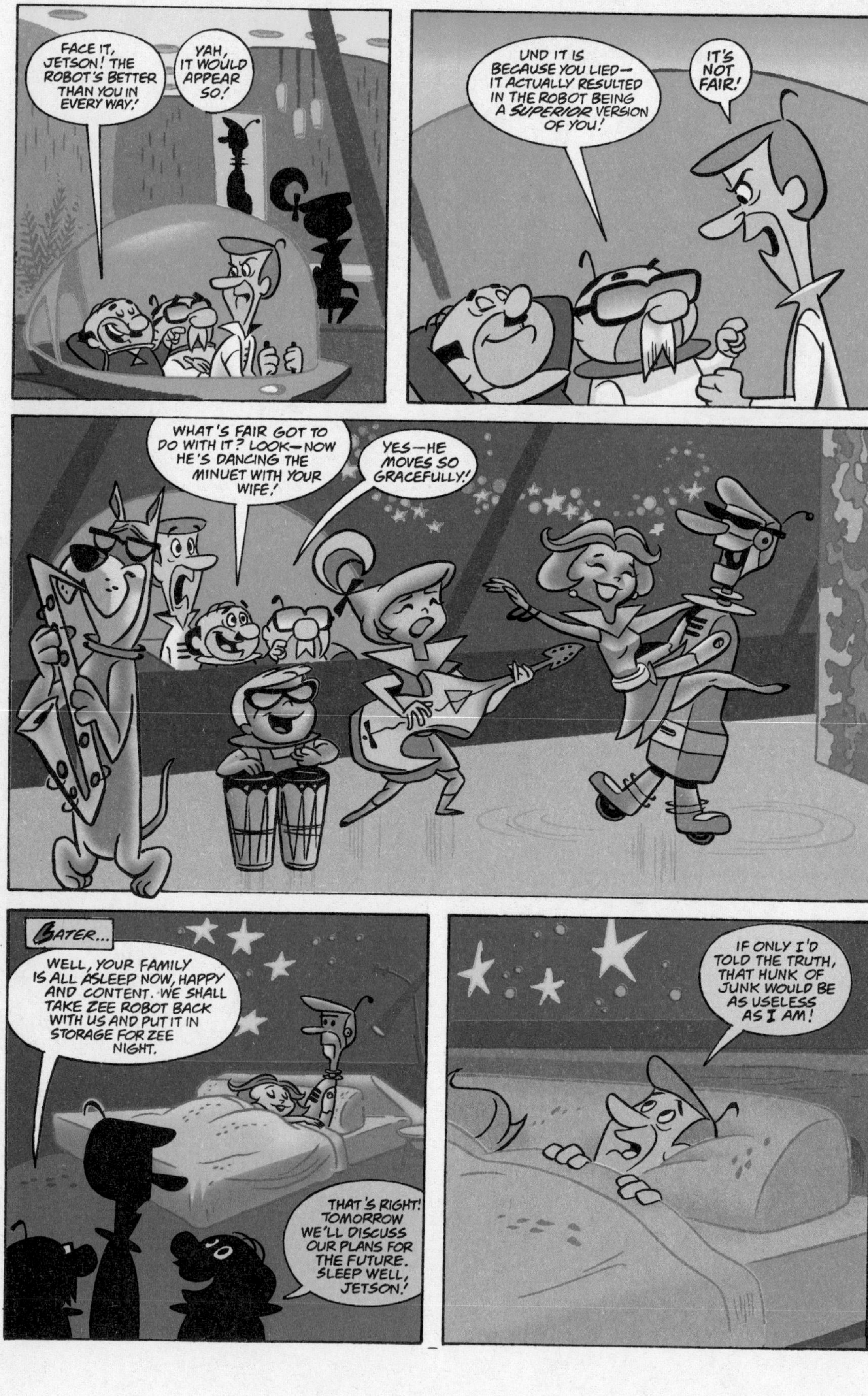
FACE IT, JETSON! THE ROBOT'S BETTER THAN YOU IN EVERY WAY!
YAH, IT WOULD APPEAR SO!
UND IT IS BECAUSE YOU LIED— IT ACTUALLY RESULTED IN THE ROBOT BEING A SUPERIOR VERSION OF YOU!
IT'S NOT FAIR!
WHAT'S FAIR GOT TO DO WITH IT? LOOK—NOW HE'S DANCING THE MINUET WITH YOUR WIFE!
YES—HE MOVES SO GRACEFULLY!
LATER...
WELL, YOUR FAMILY IS ALL ASLEEP NOW, HAPPY AND CONTENT. WE SHALL TAKE ZEE ROBOT BACK WITH US AND PUT IT IN STORAGE FOR ZEE NIGHT.
THAT'S RIGHT! TOMORROW WE'LL DISCUSS OUR PLANS FOR THE FUTURE. SLEEP WELL, JETSON!
IF ONLY I'D TOLD THE TRUTH, THAT HUNK OF JUNK WOULD BE AS USELESS AS I AM!

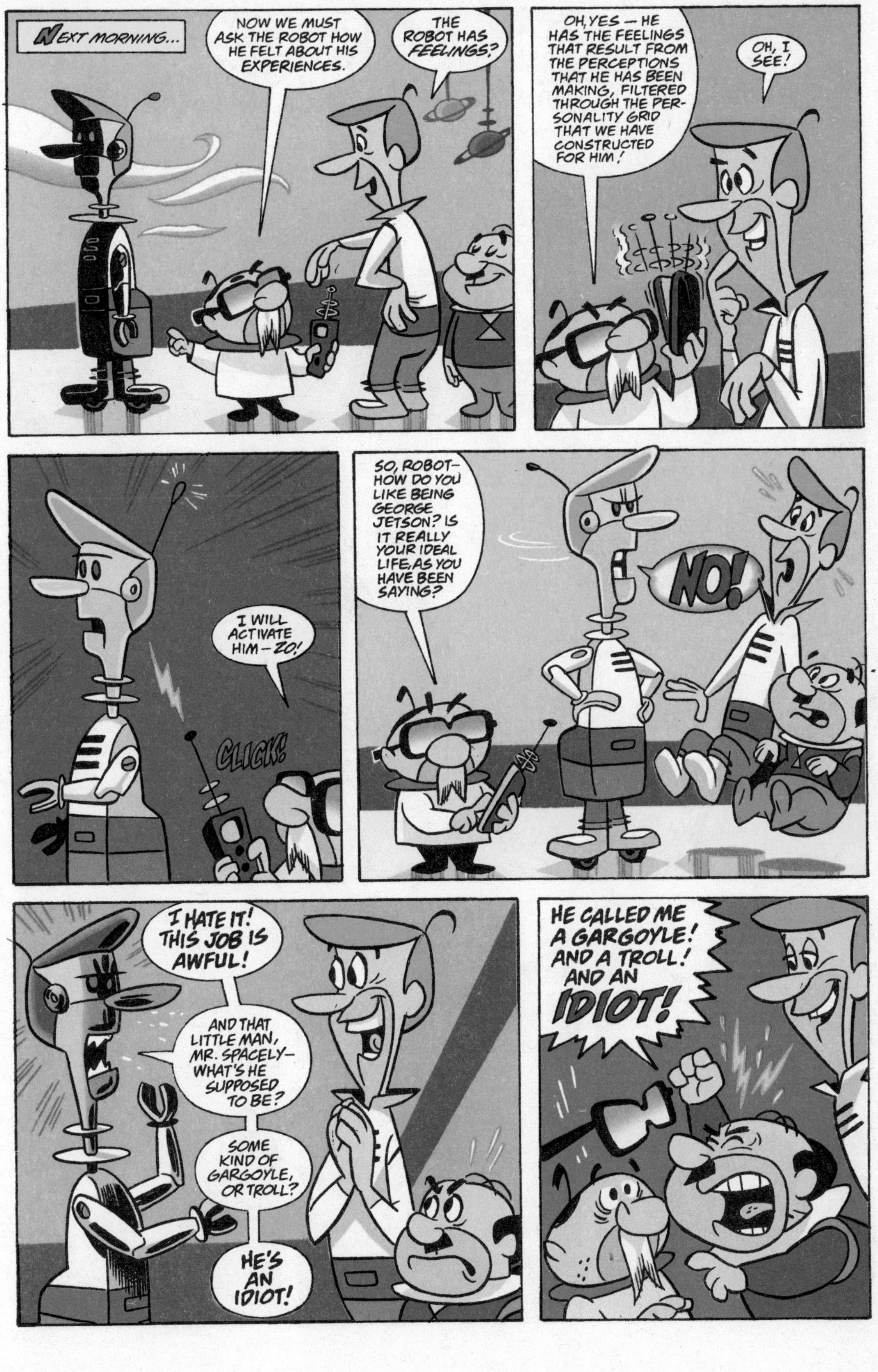
NEXT MORNING...
NOW WE MUST ASK THE ROBOT HOW HE FELT ABOUT HIS EXPERIENCES.
THE ROBOT HAS FEELINGS?
OH, YES — HE HAS THE FEELINGS THAT RESULT FROM THE PERCEPTIONS THAT HE HAS BEEN MAKING, FILTERED THROUGH THE PERSONALITY GRID THAT WE HAVE CONSTRUCTED FOR HIM!
OH, I SEE!
I WILL ACTIVATE HIM—ZO!
CLICK!
SO, ROBOT—HOW DO YOU LIKE BEING GEORGE JETSON? IS IT REALLY YOUR IDEAL LIFE, AS YOU HAVE BEEN SAYING?
NO!
I HATE IT! THIS JOB IS AWFUL!
AND THAT LITTLE MAN, MR. SPACELY—WHAT'S HE SUPPOSED TO BE?
SOME KIND OF GARGOYLE, OR TROLL?
HE'S AN IDIOT!
HE CALLED ME A GARGOYLE! AND A TROLL! AND AN IDIOT!

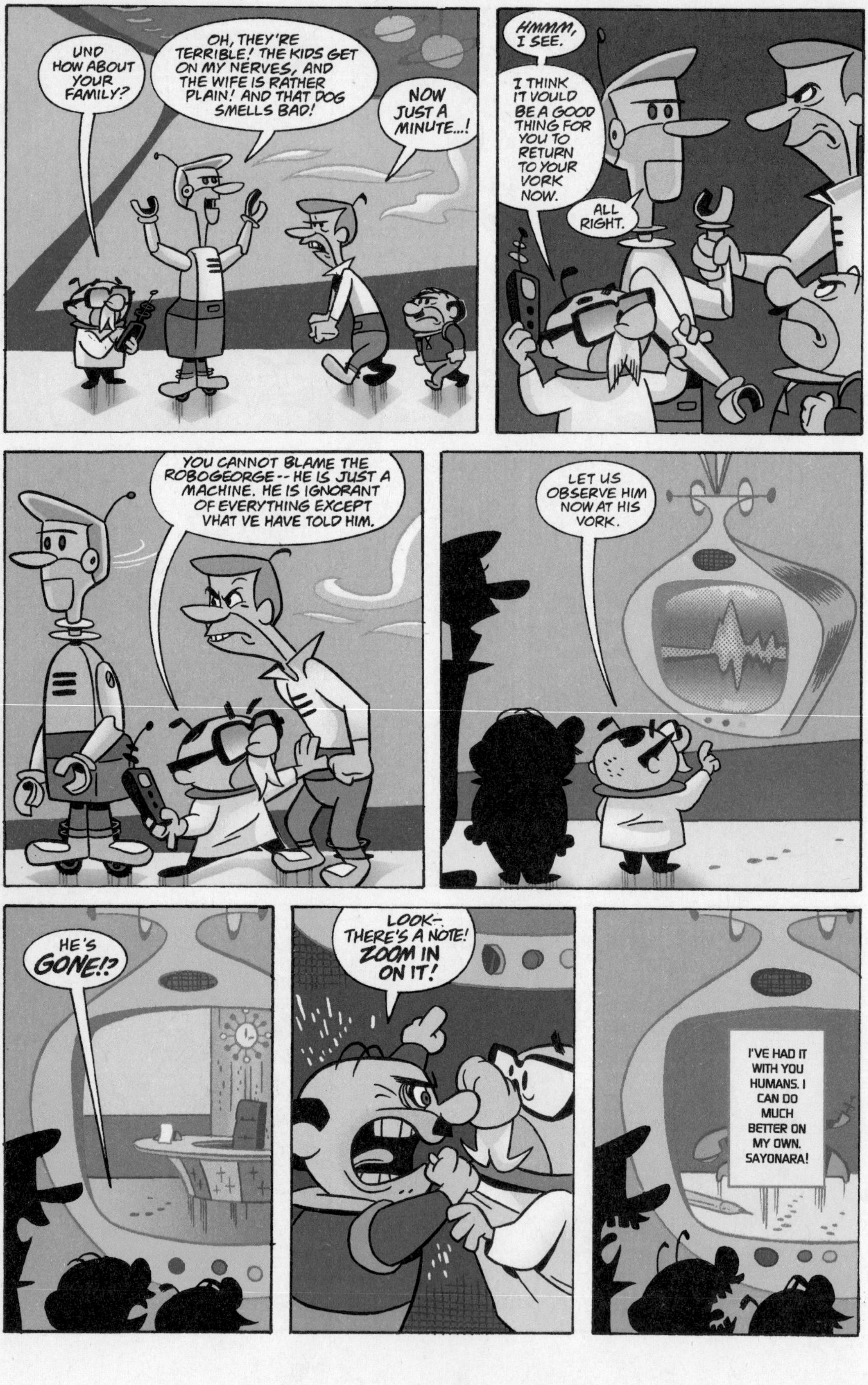
UND HOW ABOUT YOUR FAMILY?
OH, THEY'RE TERRIBLE! THE KIDS GET ON MY NERVES, AND THE WIFE IS RATHER PLAIN! AND THAT DOG SMELLS BAD!
NOW JUST A MINUTE...!
HMMM, I SEE.
I THINK IT VOULD BE A GOOD THING FOR YOU TO RETURN TO YOUR VORK NOW.
ALL RIGHT.
YOU CANNOT BLAME THE ROBOGEORGE-- HE IS JUST A MACHINE. HE IS IGNORANT OF EVERYTHING EXCEPT VHAT VE HAVE TOLD HIM.
LET US OBSERVE HIM NOW AT HIS VORK.
HE'S GONE!?
LOOK-- THERE'S A NOTE! ZOOM IN ON IT!
I'VE HAD IT WITH YOU HUMANS. I CAN DO MUCH BETTER ON MY OWN. SAYONARA!

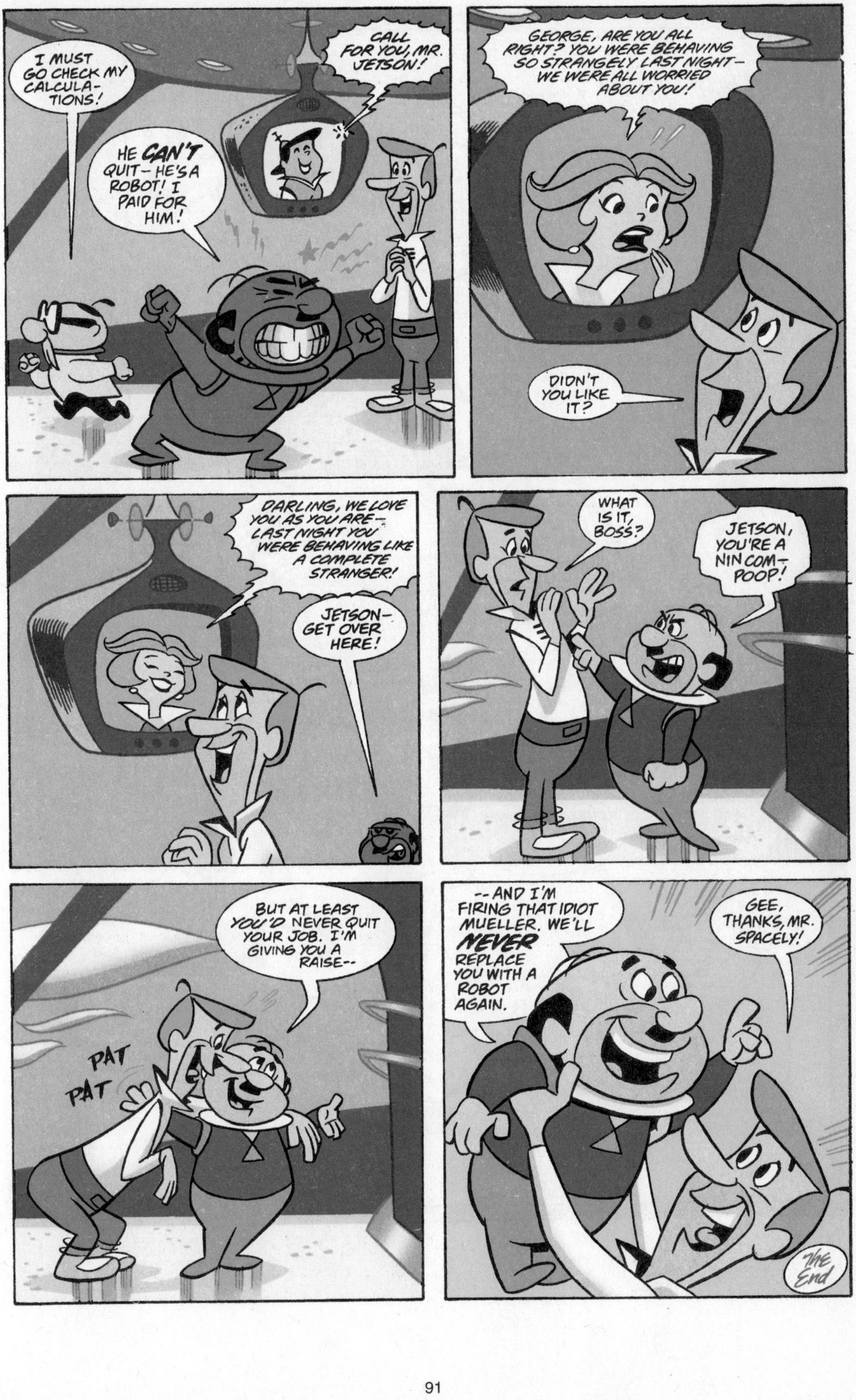
I MUST GO CHECK MY CALCULATIONS!
CALL FOR YOU, MR. JETSON!
HE CAN'T QUIT— HE'S A ROBOT! I PAID FOR HIM!
GEORGE, ARE YOU ALL RIGHT? YOU WERE BEHAVING SO STRANGELY LAST NIGHT— WE WERE ALL WORRIED ABOUT YOU!
DIDN'T YOU LIKE IT?
DARLING, WE LOVE YOU AS YOU ARE— LAST NIGHT YOU WERE BEHAVING LIKE A COMPLETE STRANGER!
JETSON— GET OVER HERE!
WHAT IS IT, BOSS?
JETSON, YOU'RE A NINCOMPOOP!
BUT AT LEAST YOU'D NEVER QUIT YOUR JOB. I'M GIVING YOU A RAISE--
PAT PAT
--AND I'M FIRING THAT IDIOT MUELLER. WE'LL NEVER REPLACE YOU WITH A ROBOT AGAIN.
GEE, THANKS, MR. SPACELY!
The End

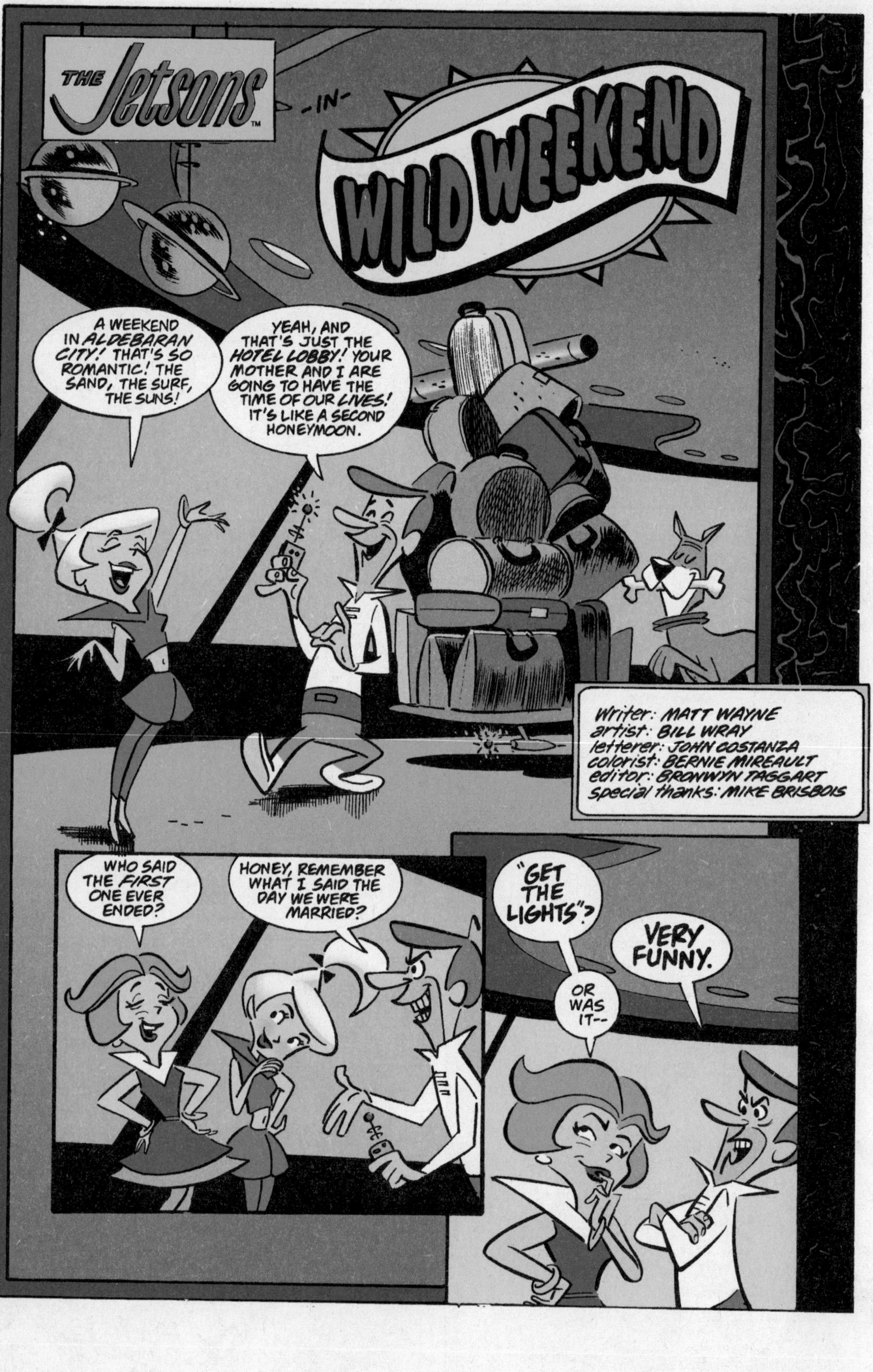
THE Jetsons™
-IN-
WILD WEEKEND
A WEEKEND IN ALDEBARAN CITY! THAT'S SO ROMANTIC! THE SAND, THE SURF, THE SUNS!
YEAH, AND THAT'S JUST THE HOTEL LOBBY! YOUR MOTHER AND I ARE GOING TO HAVE THE TIME OF OUR LIVES! IT'S LIKE A SECOND HONEYMOON.
Writer: MATT WAYNE
artist: BILL WRAY
letterer: JOHN COSTANZA
colorist: BERNIE MIREAULT
editor: BRONWYN TAGGART
special thanks: MIKE BRISBOIS
WHO SAID THE FIRST ONE EVER ENDED?
HONEY, REMEMBER WHAT I SAID THE DAY WE WERE MARRIED?
"GET THE LIGHTS"?
OR WAS IT--
VERY FUNNY.

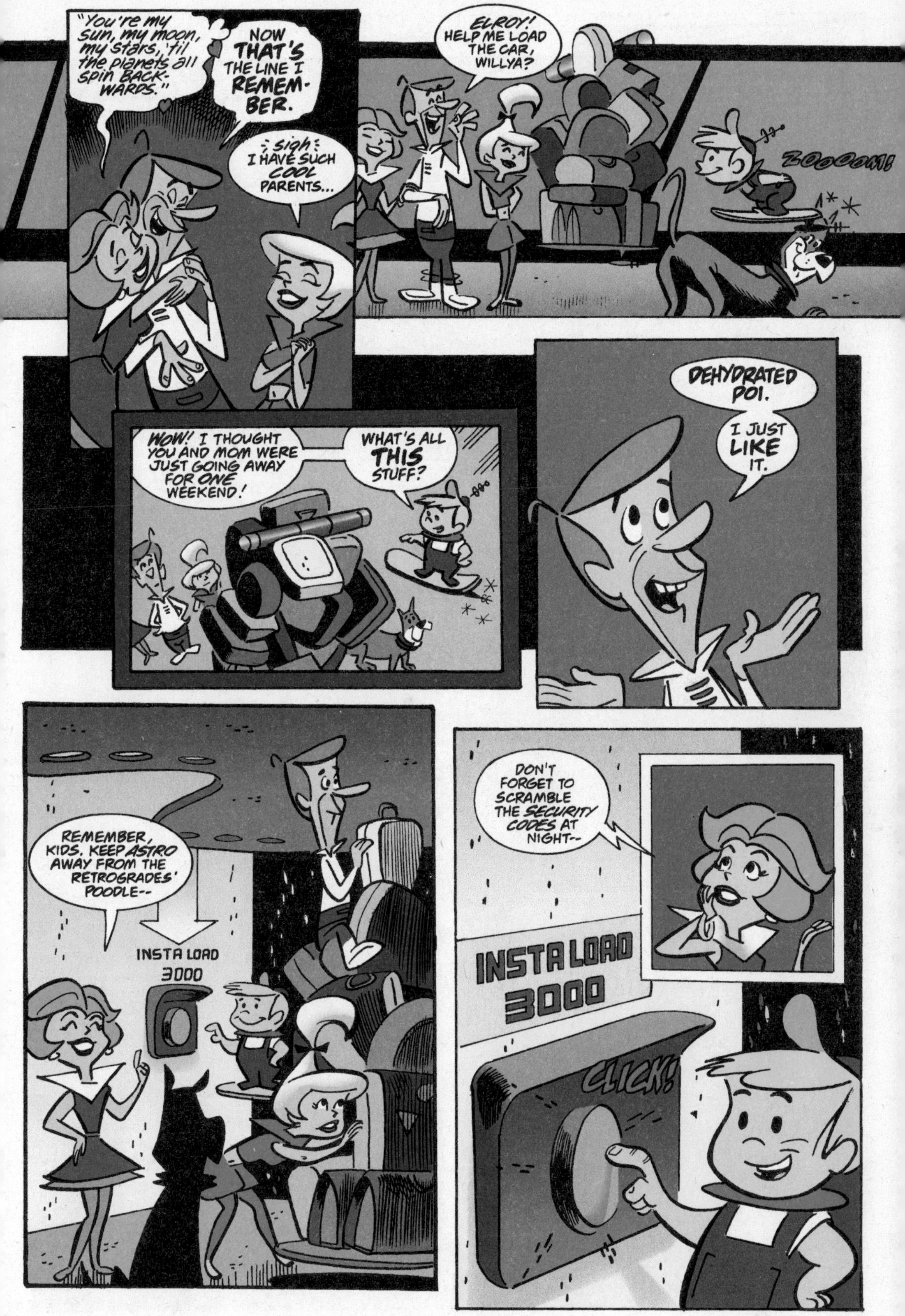
"You're my sun, my moon, my stars, 'til the planets all spin BACKWARDS."
NOW THAT'S THE LINE I REMEMBER.
:sigh: I HAVE SUCH COOL PARENTS...
ELROY! HELP ME LOAD THE CAR, WILLYA?
ZOOOOOM!
WOW! I THOUGHT YOU AND MOM WERE JUST GOING AWAY FOR ONE WEEKEND!
WHAT'S ALL THIS STUFF?
DEHYDRATED POI.
I JUST LIKE IT.
REMEMBER, KIDS. KEEP ASTRO AWAY FROM THE RETROGRADES' POODLE--
INSTA LOAD 3000
DON'T FORGET TO SCRAMBLE THE SECURITY CODES AT NIGHT--
INSTA LOAD 3000
CLICK!

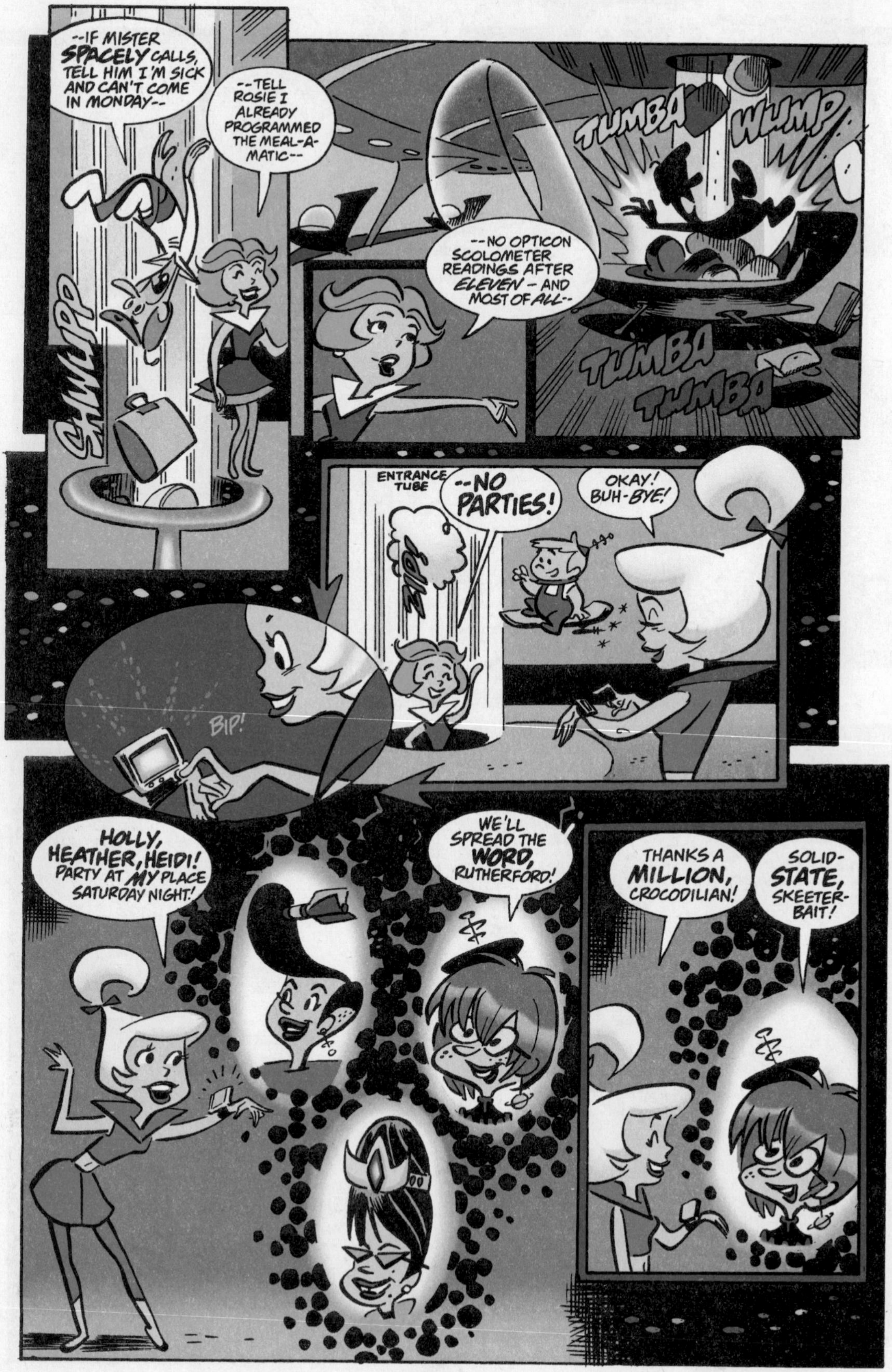
--IF MISTER SPACELY CALLS, TELL HIM I'M SICK AND CAN'T COME IN MONDAY--
--TELL ROSIE I ALREADY PROGRAMMED THE MEAL-A-MATIC--
SHWUPP
--NO OPTICON SCOLOMETER READINGS AFTER ELEVEN -- AND MOST OF ALL--
TUMBA WUMP
TUMBA TUMBA
ENTRANCE TUBE
--NO PARTIES!
OKAY! BUH-BYE!
ZIP!
BIP!
HOLLY, HEATHER, HEIDI! PARTY AT MY PLACE SATURDAY NIGHT!
WE'LL SPREAD THE WORD, RUTHERFORD!
THANKS A MILLION, CROCODILIAN!
SOLID-STATE, SKEETER-BAIT!

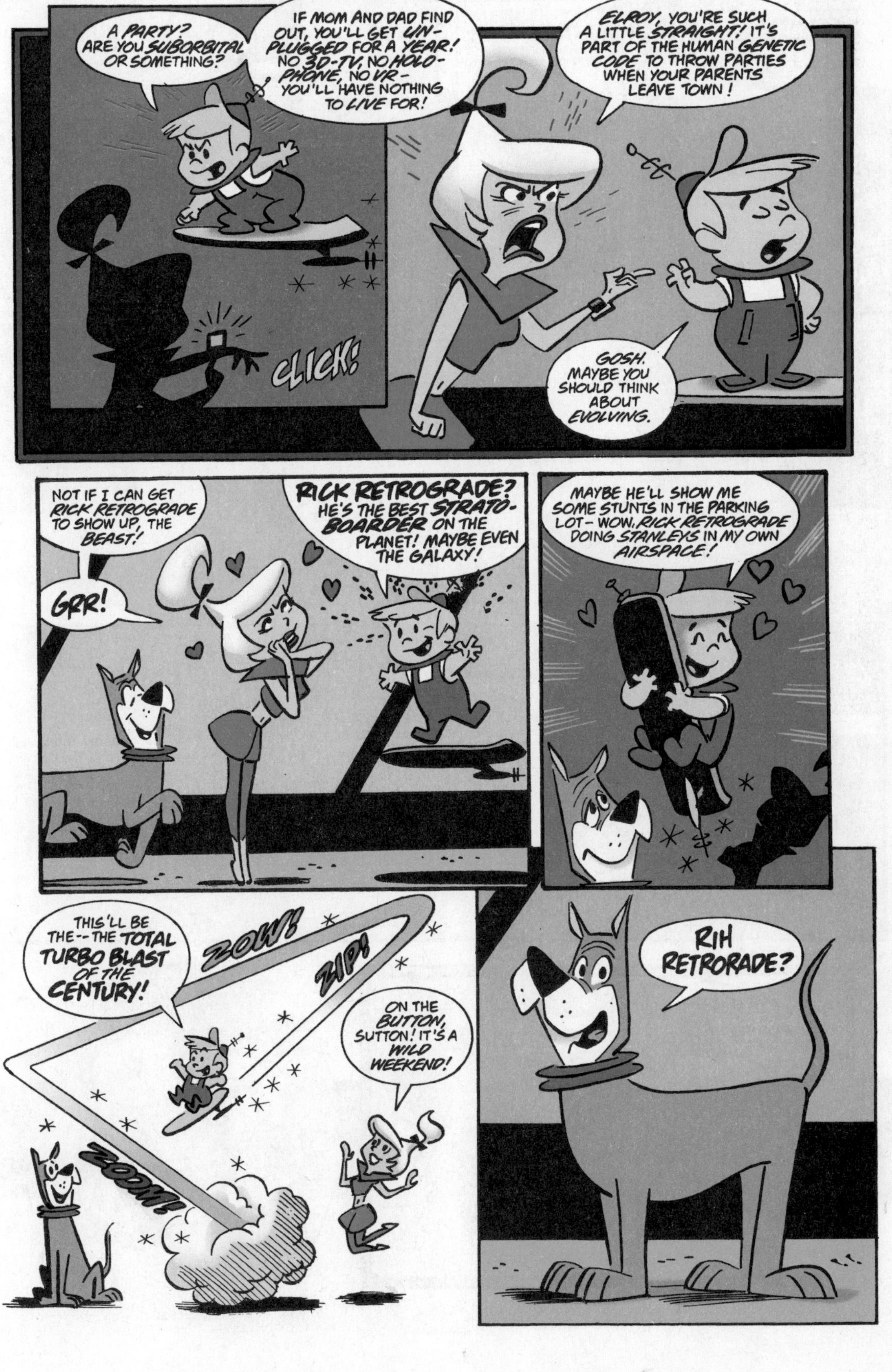
A PARTY? ARE YOU SUBORBITAL OR SOMETHING?
IF MOM AND DAD FIND OUT, YOU'LL GET UN-PLUGGED FOR A YEAR! NO 3D-TV, NO HOLO-PHONE, NO VR- YOU'LL HAVE NOTHING TO LIVE FOR!
CLICK!
ELROY, YOU'RE SUCH A LITTLE STRAIGHT! IT'S PART OF THE HUMAN GENETIC CODE TO THROW PARTIES WHEN YOUR PARENTS LEAVE TOWN!
GOSH. MAYBE YOU SHOULD THINK ABOUT EVOLVING.
NOT IF I CAN GET RICK RETROGRADE TO SHOW UP, THE BEAST!
GRR!
RICK RETROGRADE? HE'S THE BEST STRATO-BOARDER ON THE PLANET! MAYBE EVEN THE GALAXY!
MAYBE HE'LL SHOW ME SOME STUNTS IN THE PARKING LOT- WOW, RICK RETROGRADE DOING STANLEYS IN MY OWN AIRSPACE!
THIS'LL BE THE--THE TOTAL TURBO BLAST OF THE CENTURY!
ZOW!
ZIP!
ON THE BUTTON, SUTTON! IT'S A WILD WEEKEND!
ZOOM!
RIH RETRORADE?

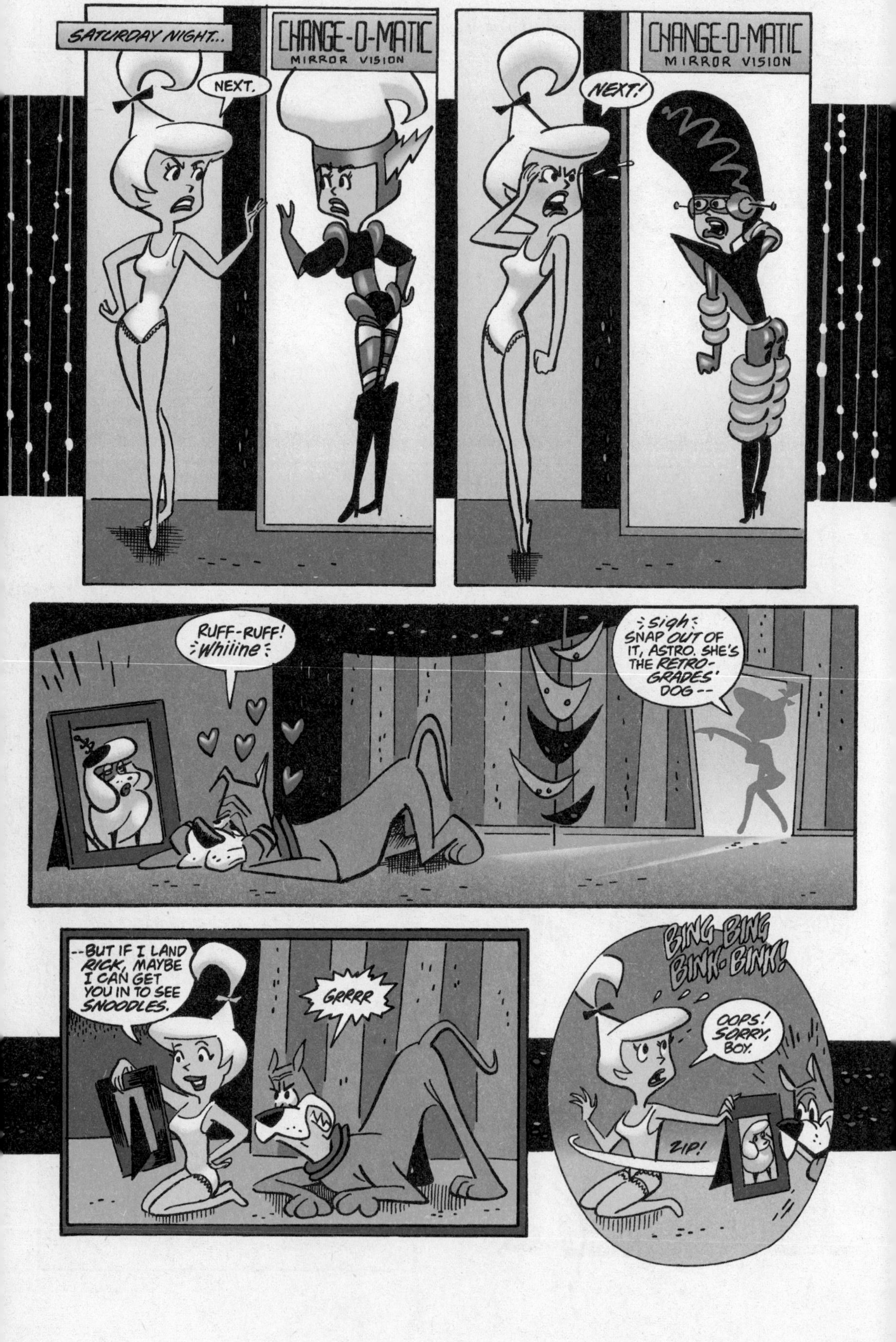
SATURDAY NIGHT...
CHANGE-O-MATIC
MIRROR VISION
NEXT.
CHANGE-O-MATIC
MIRROR VISION
NEXT!
RUFF-RUFF! Whiiine
Sigh SNAP OUT OF IT, ASTRO. SHE'S THE RETRO-GRADES' DOG--
--BUT IF I LAND RICK, MAYBE I CAN GET YOU IN TO SEE SNOODLES.
GRRRR
BING BING BINK-BINK!
OOPS! SORRY, BOY.
ZIP!

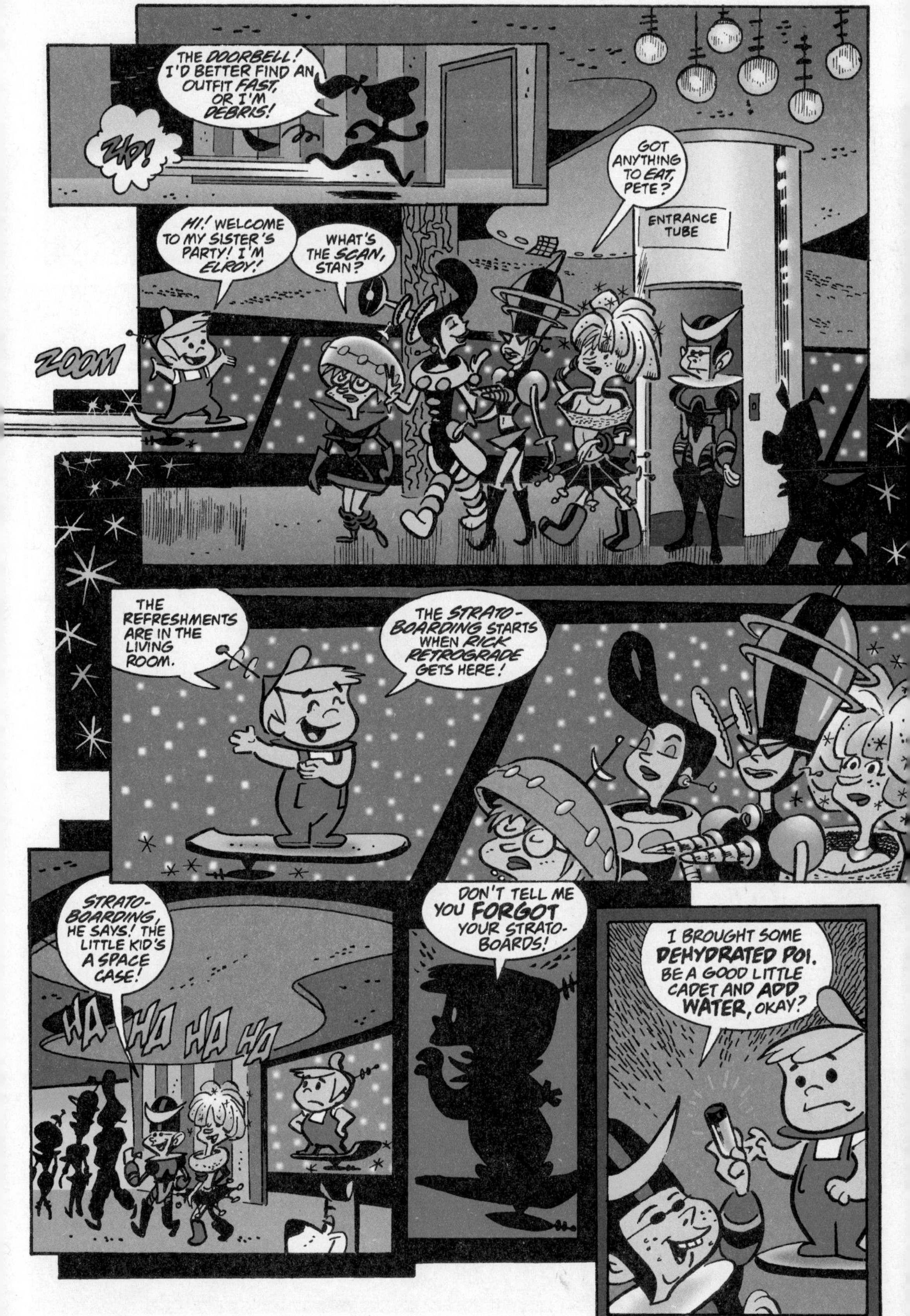
THE DOORBELL! I'D BETTER FIND AN OUTFIT FAST, OR I'M DEBRIS!
ZIP!
GOT ANYTHING TO EAT, PETE?
ENTRANCE TUBE
HI! WELCOME TO MY SISTER'S PARTY! I'M ELROY!
WHAT'S THE SCAN, STAN?
ZOOM
THE REFRESHMENTS ARE IN THE LIVING ROOM.
THE STRATO-BOARDING STARTS WHEN RICK RETROGRADE GETS HERE!
STRATO-BOARDING, HE SAYS! THE LITTLE KID'S A SPACE CASE!
HA HA HA HA
DON'T TELL ME YOU FORGOT YOUR STRATO-BOARDS!
I BROUGHT SOME DEHYDRATED POI. BE A GOOD LITTLE CADET AND ADD WATER, OKAY?

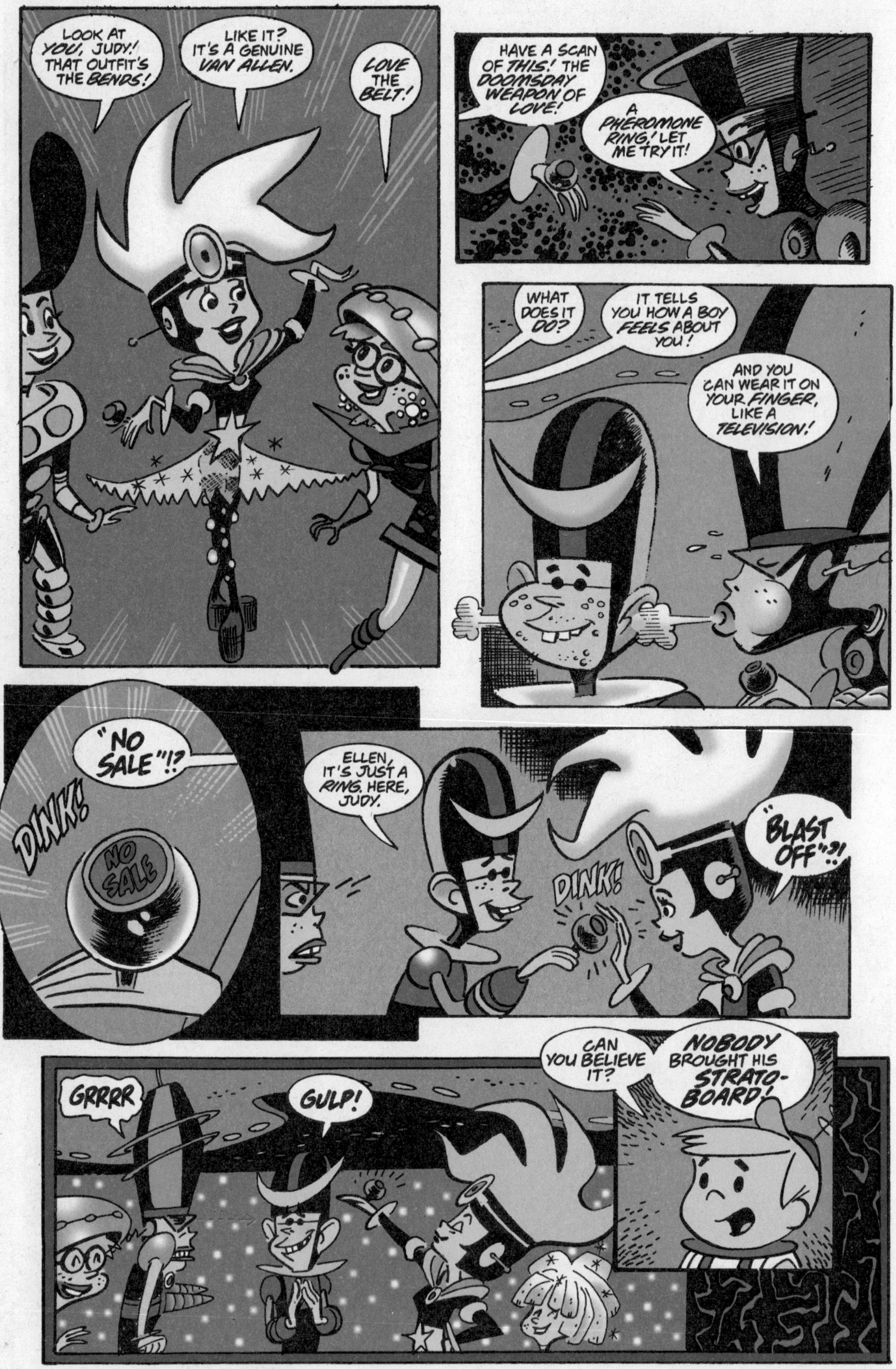
LOOK AT YOU, JUDY! THAT OUTFIT'S THE BENDS!
LIKE IT? IT'S A GENUINE VAN ALLEN.
LOVE THE BELT!
HAVE A SCAN OF THIS! THE DOOMSDAY WEAPON OF LOVE!
A PHEROMONE RING! LET ME TRY IT!
WHAT DOES IT DO?
IT TELLS YOU HOW A BOY FEELS ABOUT YOU!
AND YOU CAN WEAR IT ON YOUR FINGER, LIKE A TELEVISION!
"NO SALE"!?
DINK!
NO SALE
ELLEN, IT'S JUST A RING. HERE, JUDY.
DINK!
"BLAST OFF"?!
GRRRR
GULP!
CAN YOU BELIEVE IT?
NOBODY BROUGHT HIS STRATO-BOARD!

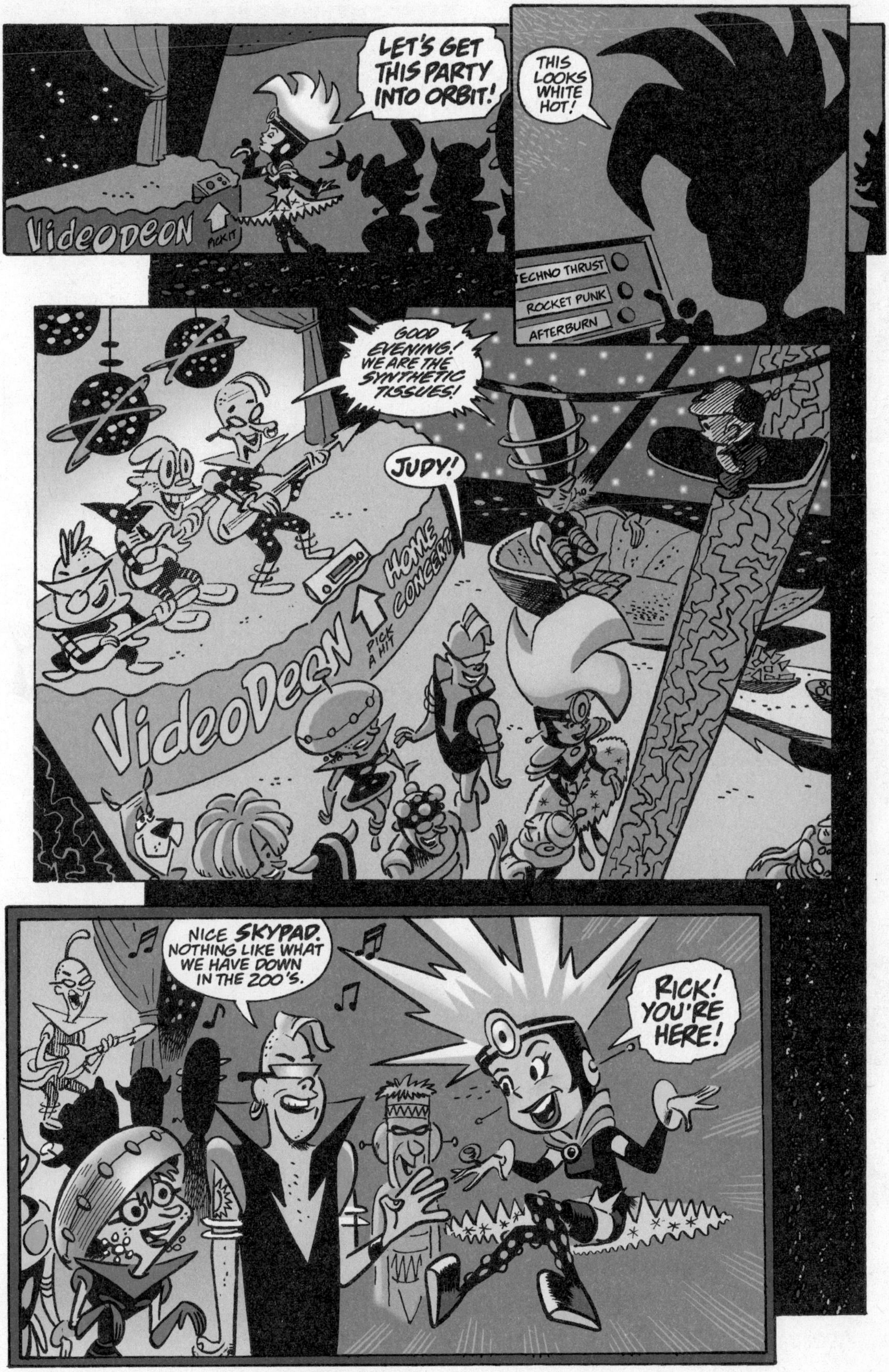
LET'S GET THIS PARTY INTO ORBIT!
VIDEODEON
PICK IT
THIS LOOKS WHITE HOT!
TECHNO THRUST
ROCKET PUNK
AFTERBURN
GOOD EVENING! WE ARE THE SYNTHETIC TISSUES!
JUDY!
VIDEODEON
PICK A HIT
HOME CONCERT
NICE SKYPAD. NOTHING LIKE WHAT WE HAVE DOWN IN THE ZOO'S.
RICK! YOU'RE HERE!

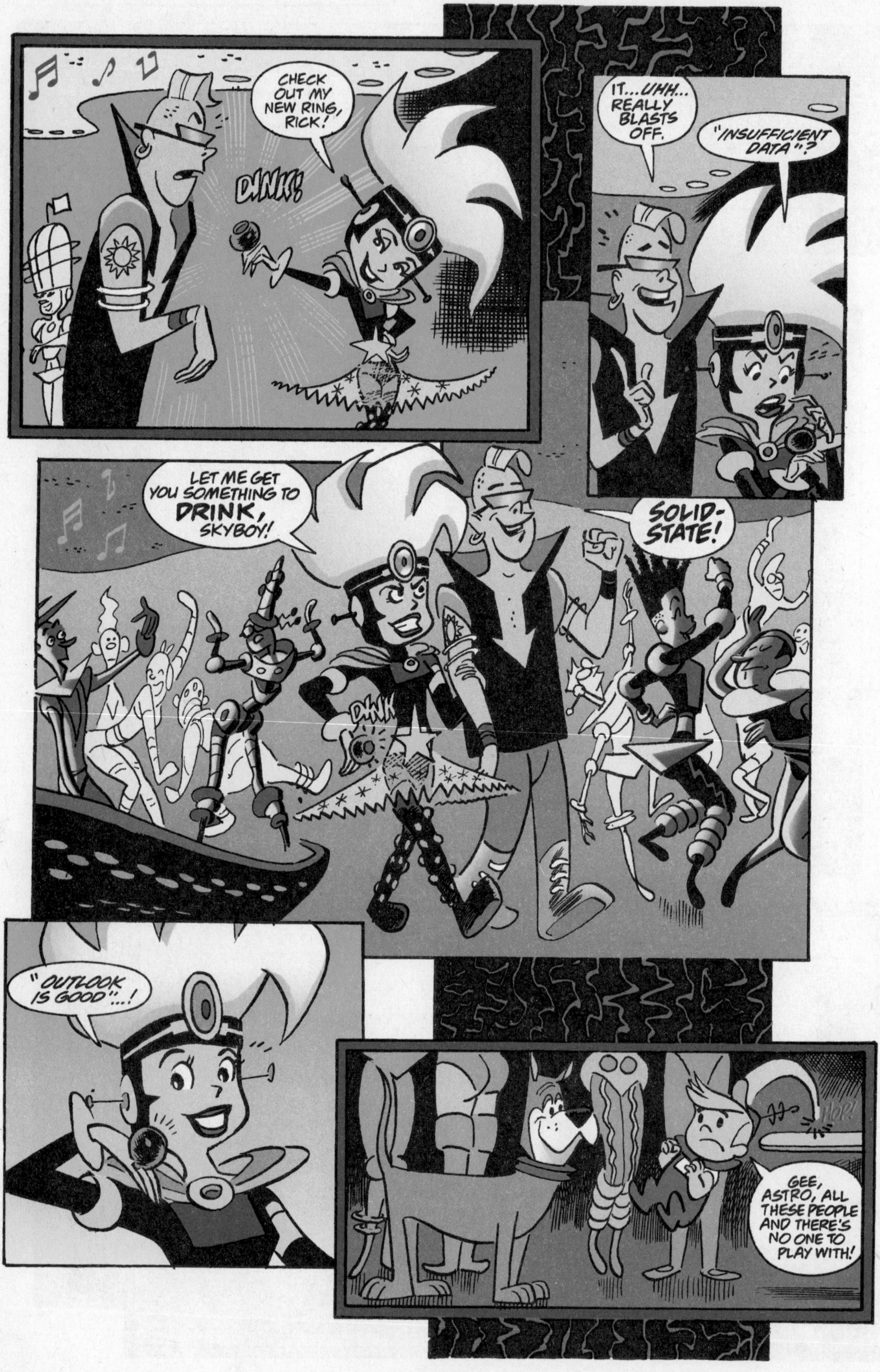
CHECK OUT MY NEW RING, RICK!
DINK!
IT... UHH... REALLY BLASTS OFF.
"INSUFFICIENT DATA"?
LET ME GET YOU SOMETHING TO DRINK, SKYBOY!
SOLID-STATE!
DINK
"OUTLOOK IS GOOD"...!
GEE, ASTRO, ALL THESE PEOPLE AND THERE'S NO ONE TO PLAY WITH!

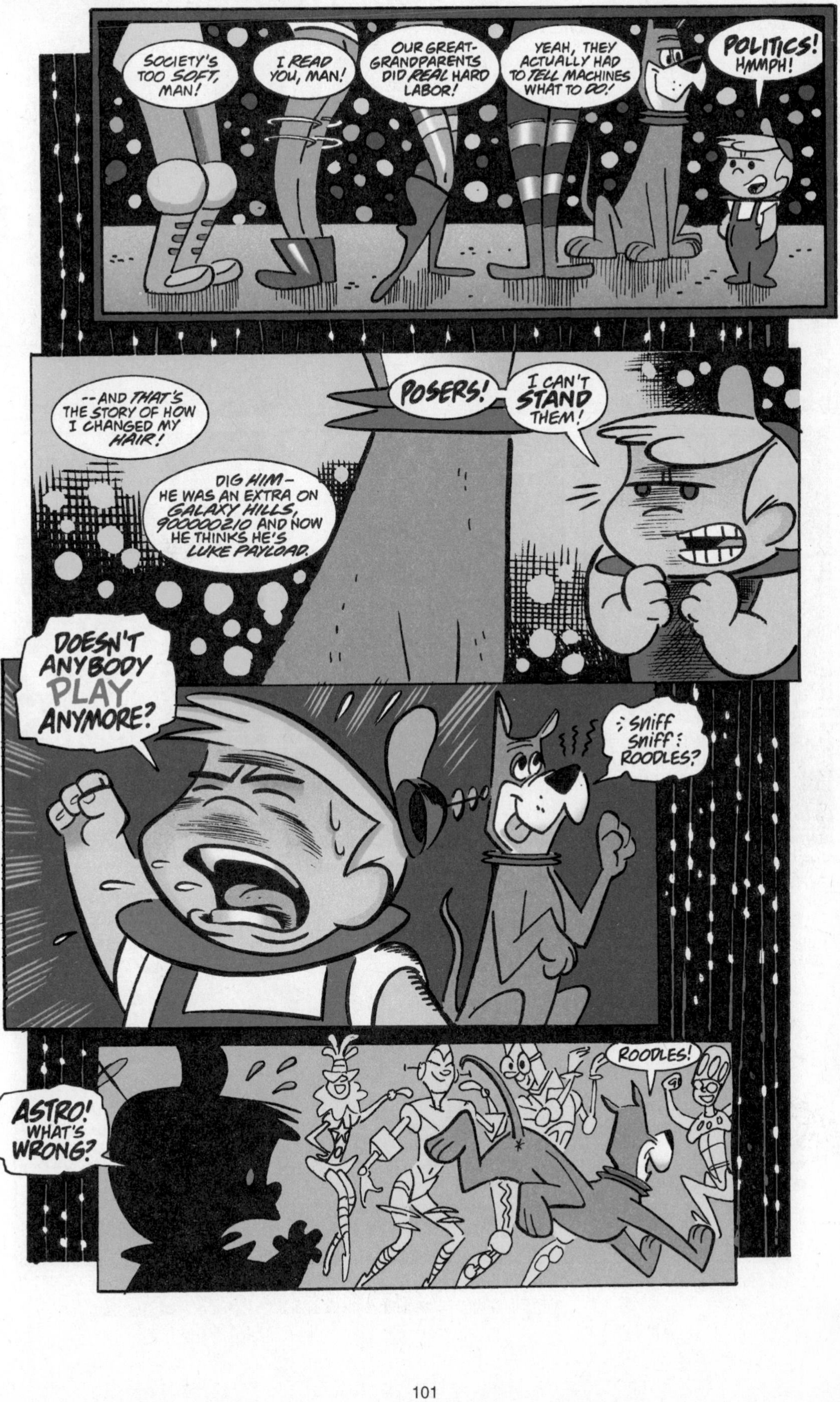
SOCIETY'S TOO SOFT, MAN!
I READ YOU, MAN!
OUR GREAT-GRANDPARENTS DID REAL HARD LABOR!
YEAH, THEY ACTUALLY HAD TO TELL MACHINES WHAT TO DO!
POLITICS! HMMPH!
--AND THAT'S THE STORY OF HOW I CHANGED MY HAIR!
DIG HIM--HE WAS AN EXTRA ON GALAXY HILLS, 900000210 AND NOW HE THINKS HE'S LUKE PAYLOAD.
POSERS!
I CAN'T STAND THEM!
DOESN'T ANYBODY PLAY ANYMORE?
: Sniff Sniff : ROODLES?
ASTRO! WHAT'S WRONG?
ROODLES!

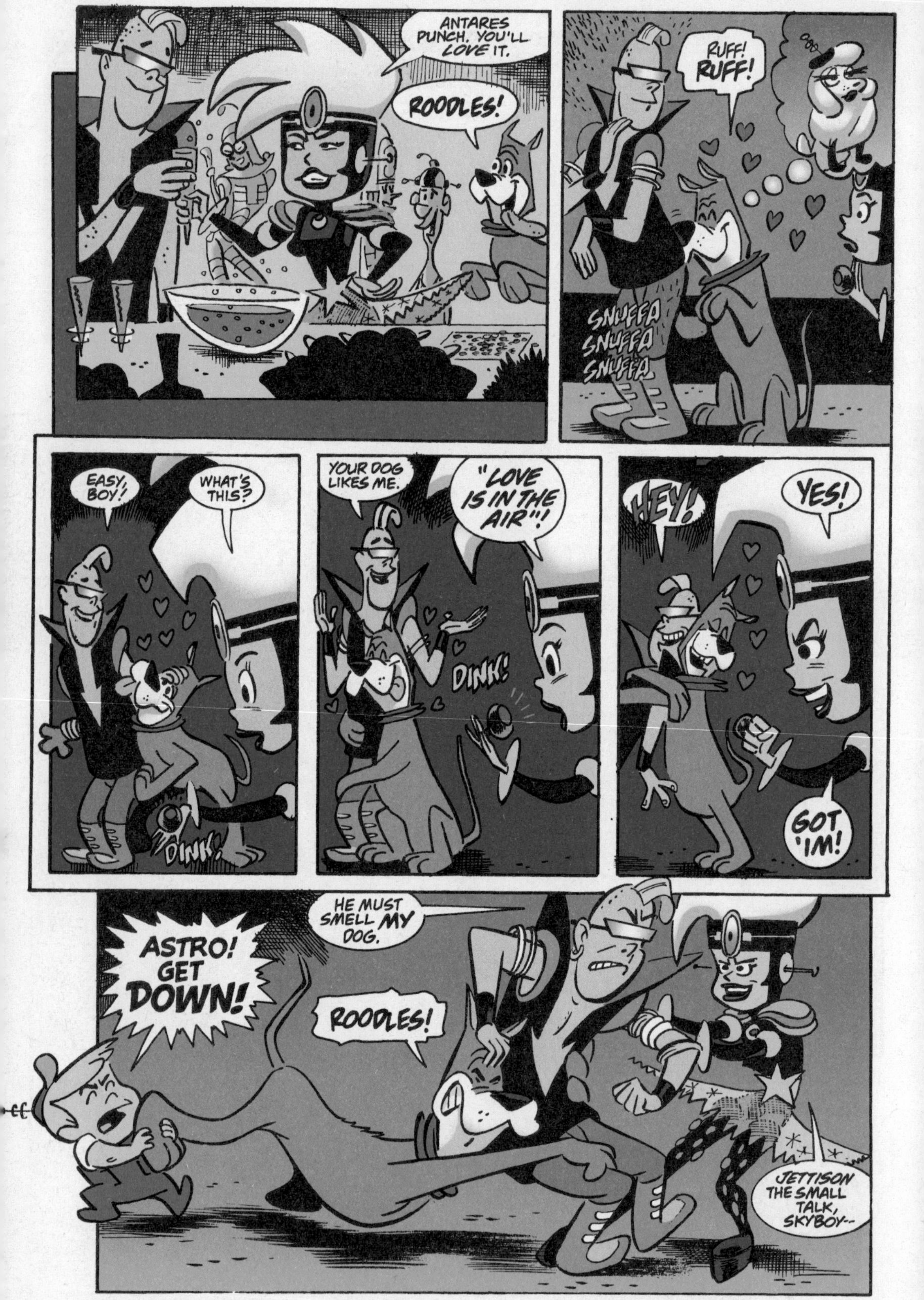

ANTARES PUNCH. YOU'LL LOVE IT.
ROODLES!
RUFF! RUFF!
SNUFFA SNUFFA SNUFFA
EASY, BOY!
WHAT'S THIS?
DINK!
YOUR DOG LIKES ME.
"LOVE IS IN THE AIR"!
DINK!
HEY!
YES!
GOT 'IM!
HE MUST SMELL MY DOG.
ASTRO! GET DOWN!
ROODLES!
JETTISON THE SMALL TALK, SKYBOY--

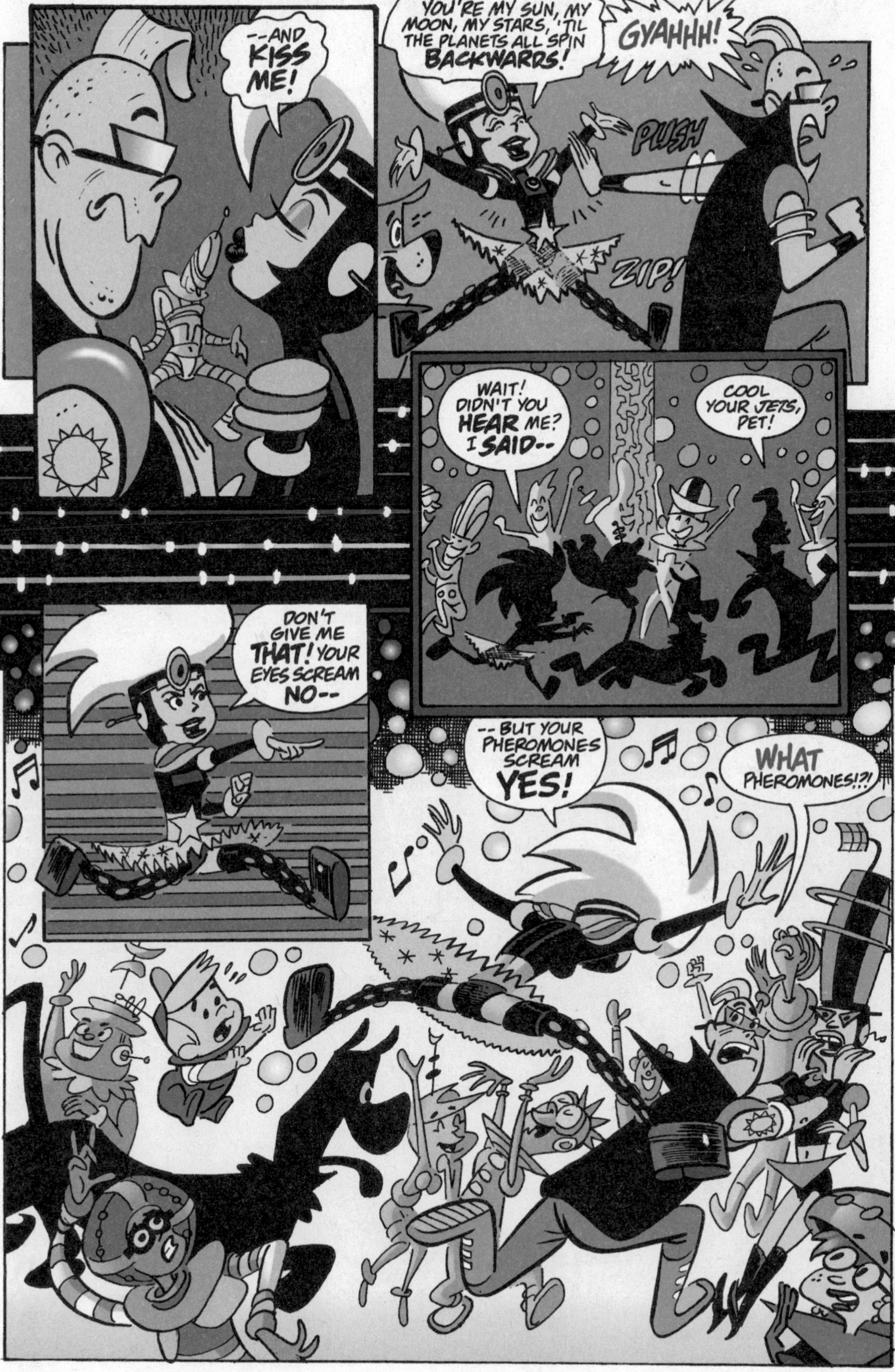
--AND KISS ME!
YOU'RE MY SUN, MY MOON, MY STARS, 'TIL THE PLANETS ALL SPIN BACKWARDS!
GYAHHH!
PUSH
ZIP!
WAIT! DIDN'T YOU HEAR ME? I SAID--
COOL YOUR JETS, PET!
DON'T GIVE ME THAT! YOUR EYES SCREAM NO--
--BUT YOUR PHEROMONES SCREAM YES!
WHAT PHEROMONES!?!

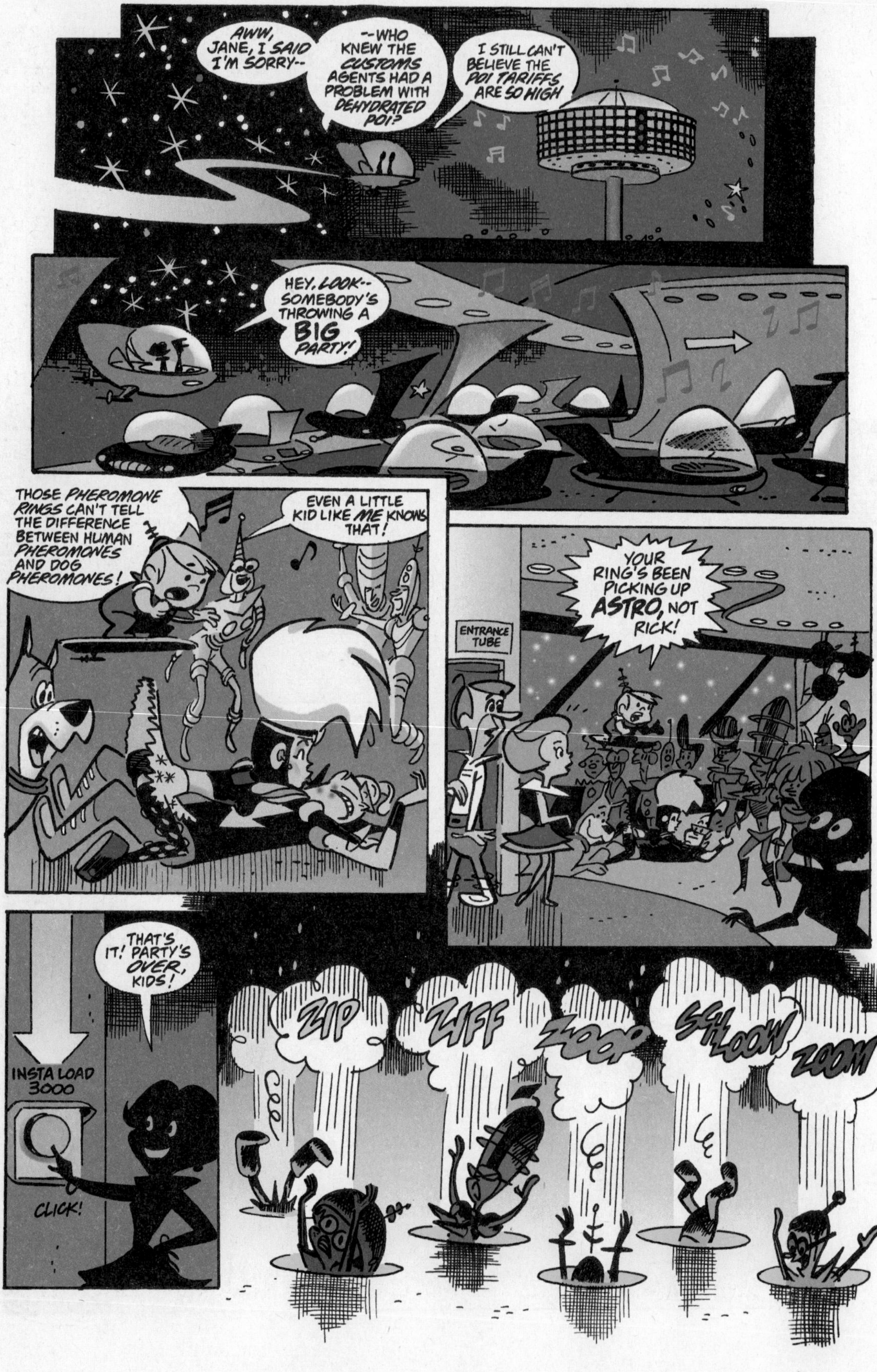
AWW, JANE, I SAID I'M SORRY--
--WHO KNEW THE CUSTOMS AGENTS HAD A PROBLEM WITH DEHYDRATED POI?
I STILL CAN'T BELIEVE THE POI TARIFFS ARE SO HIGH
HEY, LOOK-- SOMEBODY'S THROWING A BIG PARTY!
THOSE PHEROMONE RINGS CAN'T TELL THE DIFFERENCE BETWEEN HUMAN PHEROMONES AND DOG PHEROMONES!
EVEN A LITTLE KID LIKE ME KNOWS THAT!
ENTRANCE TUBE
YOUR RING'S BEEN PICKING UP ASTRO, NOT RICK!
THAT'S IT! PARTY'S OVER, KIDS!
INSTA LOAD 3000
CLICK!
ZIP
ZIFF
ZOOP
SCHLOOOM
ZOOM

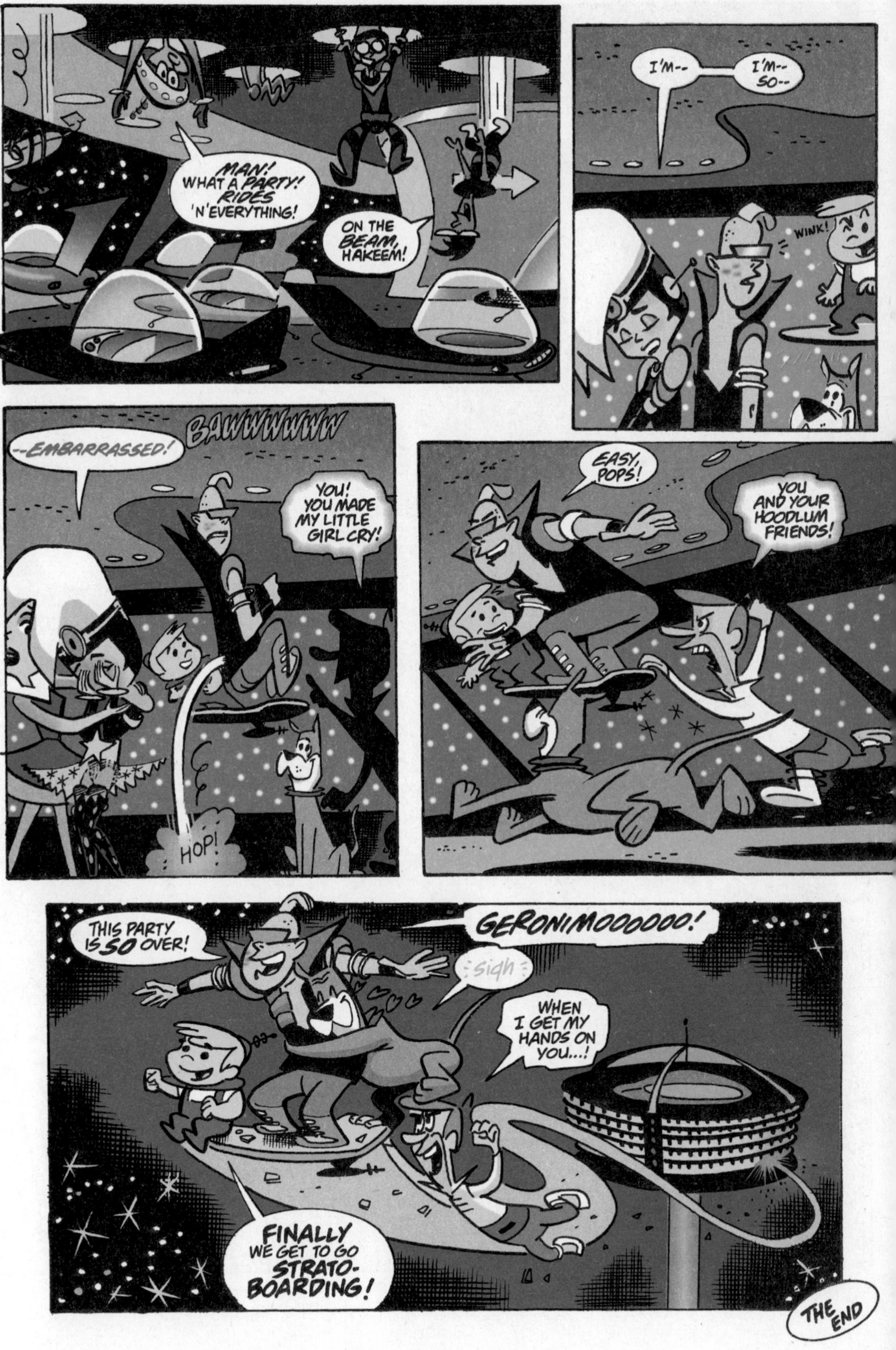

MAN! WHAT A PARTY! RIDES 'N' EVERYTHING!
ON THE BEAM, HAKEEM!
I'M--
I'M-- SO--
WINK!
--EMBARRASSED!
BAWWWWWW
YOU! YOU MADE MY LITTLE GIRL CRY!
HOP!
EASY, POPS!
YOU AND YOUR HOODLUM FRIENDS!
THIS PARTY IS SO OVER!
GERONIMOOOOOO!
sigh
WHEN I GET MY HANDS ON YOU...!
FINALLY WE GET TO GO STRATO-BOARDING!
THE END

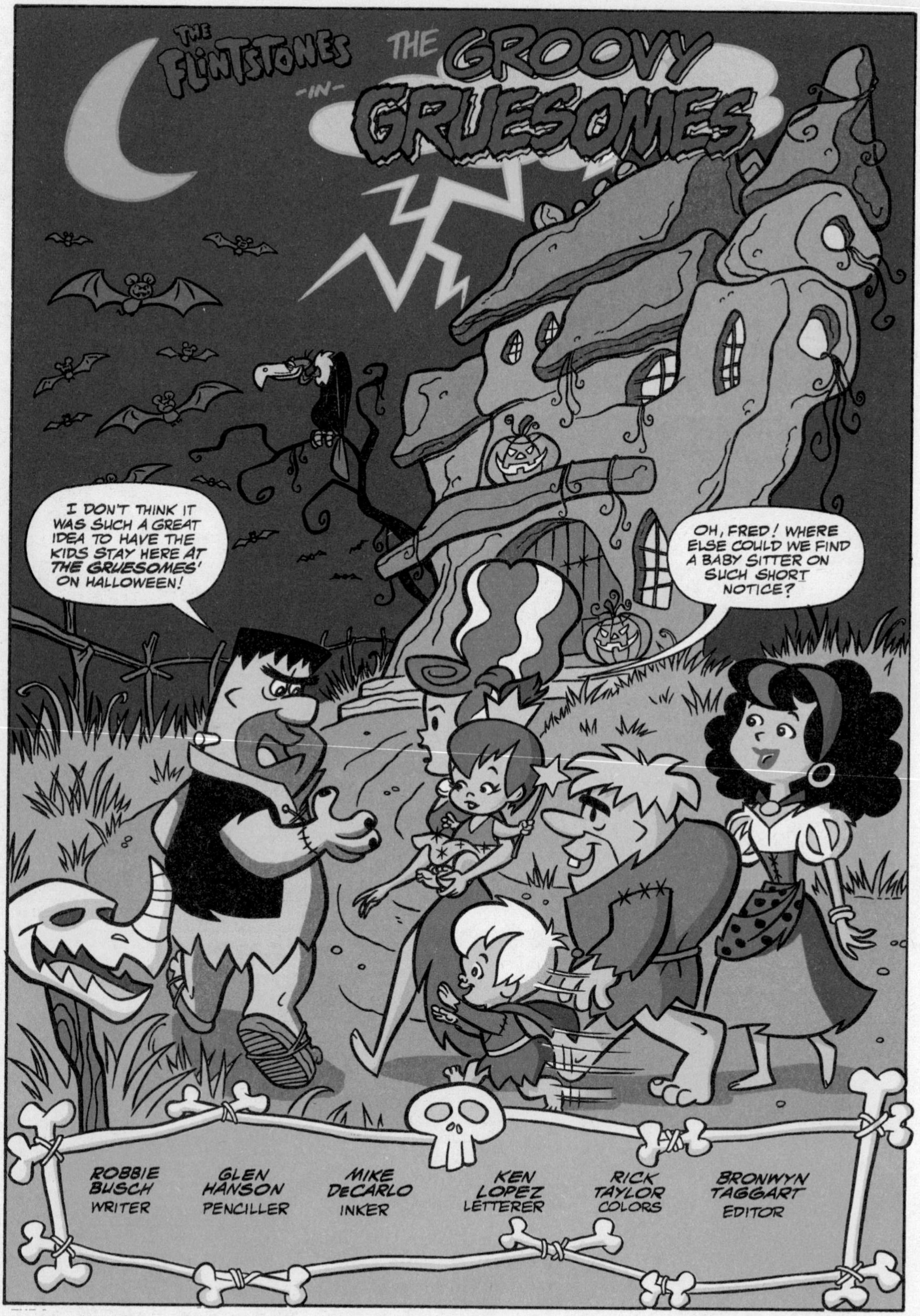
THE FLINTSTONES -IN- THE GROOVY GRUESOMES
I DON'T THINK IT WAS SUCH A GREAT IDEA TO HAVE THE KIDS STAY HERE AT THE GRUESOMES' ON HALLOWEEN!
OH, FRED! WHERE ELSE COULD WE FIND A BABY SITTER ON SUCH SHORT NOTICE?
ROBBIE BUSCH WRITER
GLEN HANSON PENCILLER
MIKE DeCARLO INKER
KEN LOPEZ LETTERER
RICK TAYLOR COLORS
BRONWYN TAGGART EDITOR

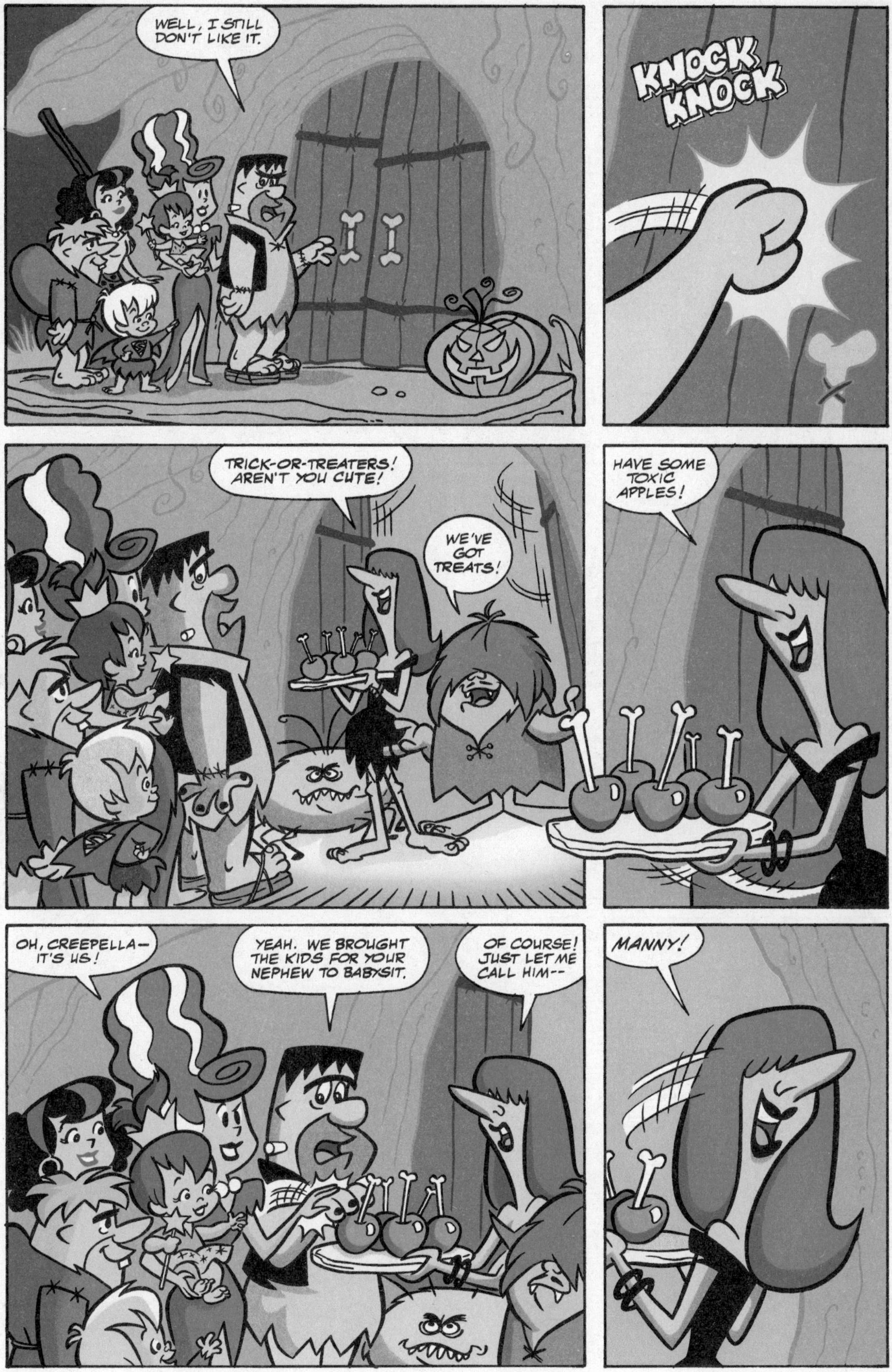
WELL, I STILL DON'T LIKE IT.
KNOCK KNOCK
TRICK-OR-TREATERS! AREN'T YOU CUTE!
WE'VE GOT TREATS!
HAVE SOME TOXIC APPLES!
OH, CREEPELLA— IT'S US!
YEAH. WE BROUGHT THE KIDS FOR YOUR NEPHEW TO BABYSIT.
OF COURSE! JUST LET ME CALL HIM--
MANNY!

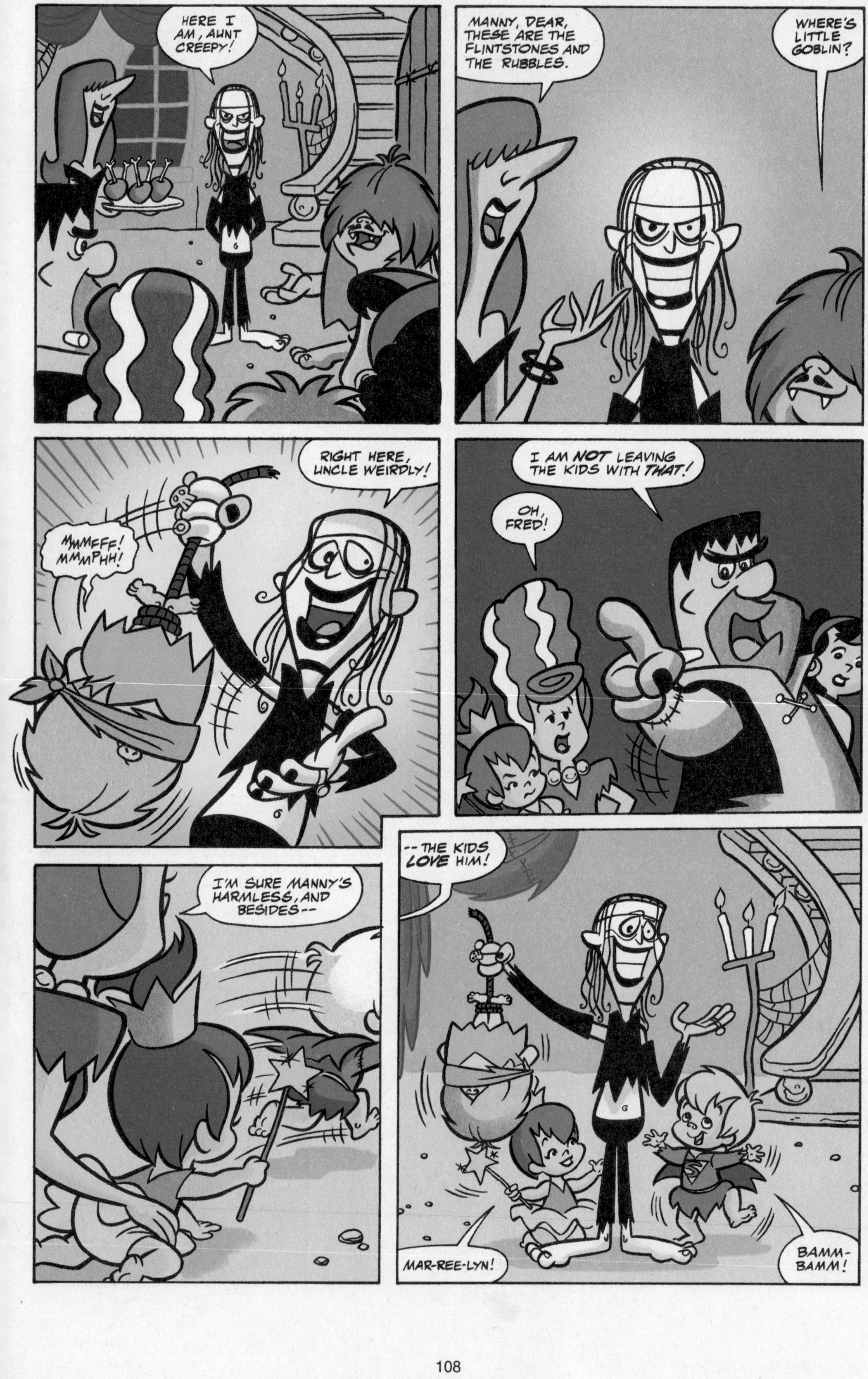
HERE I AM, AUNT CREEPY!
MANNY, DEAR, THESE ARE THE FLINTSTONES AND THE RUBBLES.
WHERE'S LITTLE GOBLIN?
RIGHT HERE, UNCLE WEIRDLY!
MMMFFF! MMMPHH!
I AM NOT LEAVING THE KIDS WITH THAT!
OH, FRED!
I'M SURE MANNY'S HARMLESS, AND BESIDES--
--THE KIDS LOVE HIM!
MAR-REE-LYN!
BAMM-BAMM!

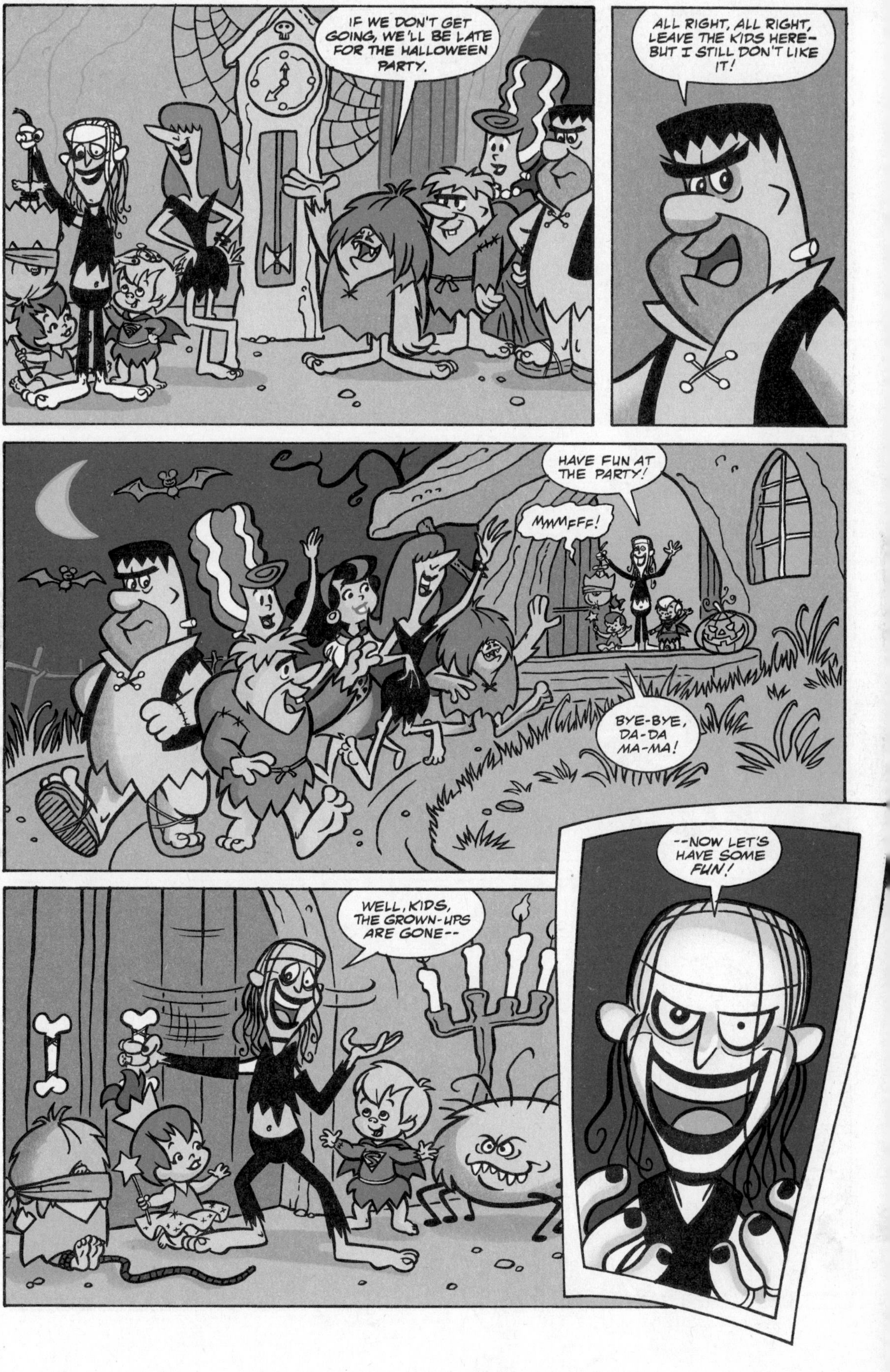
IF WE DON'T GET GOING, WE'LL BE LATE FOR THE HALLOWEEN PARTY.
ALL RIGHT, ALL RIGHT, LEAVE THE KIDS HERE-- BUT I STILL DON'T LIKE IT!
HAVE FUN AT THE PARTY!
MMMFFF!
BYE-BYE, DA-DA MA-MA!
WELL, KIDS, THE GROWN-UPS ARE GONE--
--NOW LET'S HAVE SOME FUN!

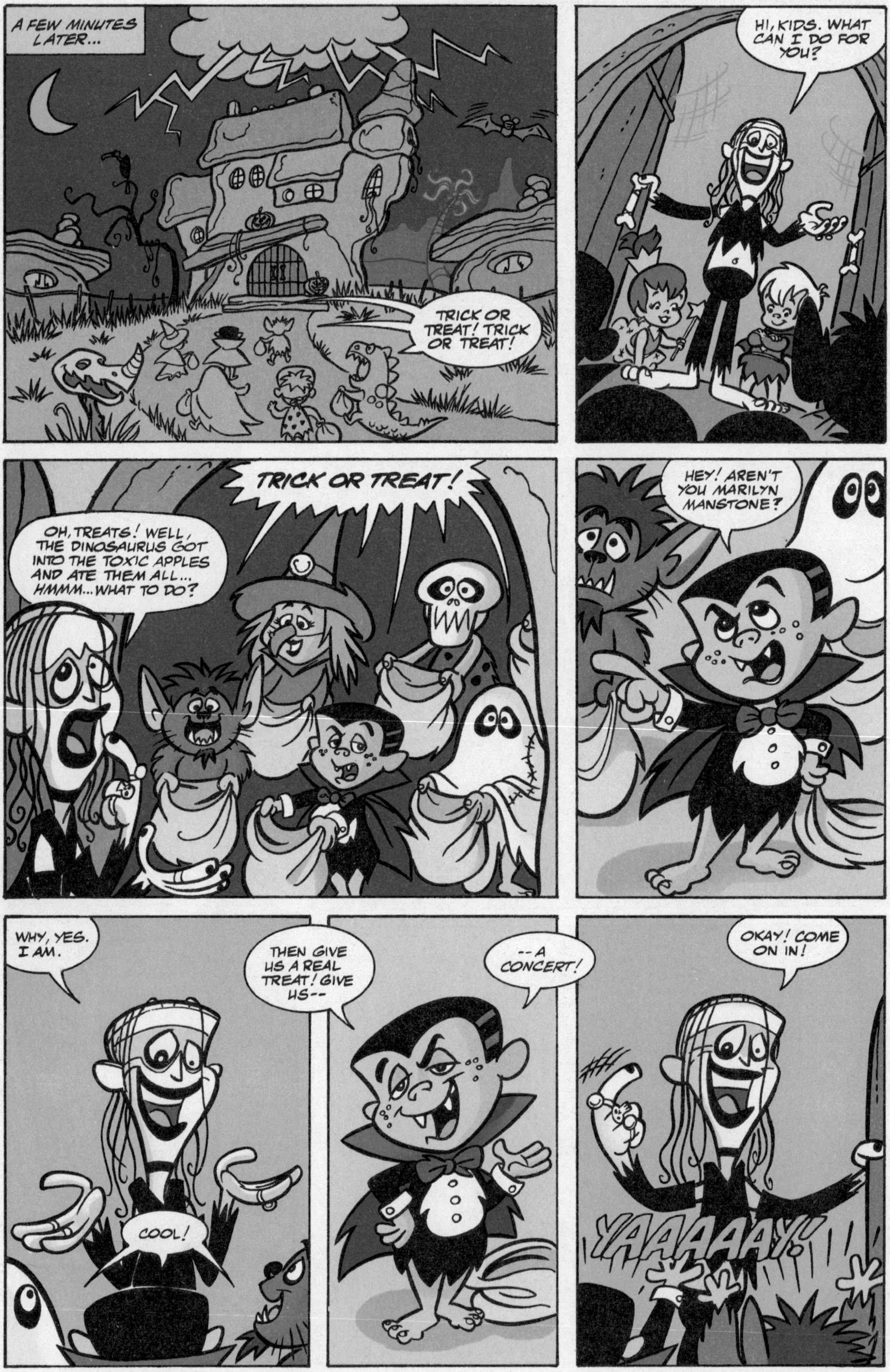
A FEW MINUTES LATER...
TRICK OR TREAT! TRICK OR TREAT!
HI, KIDS. WHAT CAN I DO FOR YOU?
TRICK OR TREAT!
OH, TREATS! WELL, THE DINOSAURUS GOT INTO THE TOXIC APPLES AND ATE THEM ALL... HMMM... WHAT TO DO?
HEY! AREN'T YOU MARILYN MANSTONE?
WHY, YES. I AM.
COOL!
THEN GIVE US A REAL TREAT! GIVE US--
--A CONCERT!
OKAY! COME ON IN!
YAAAAAY!

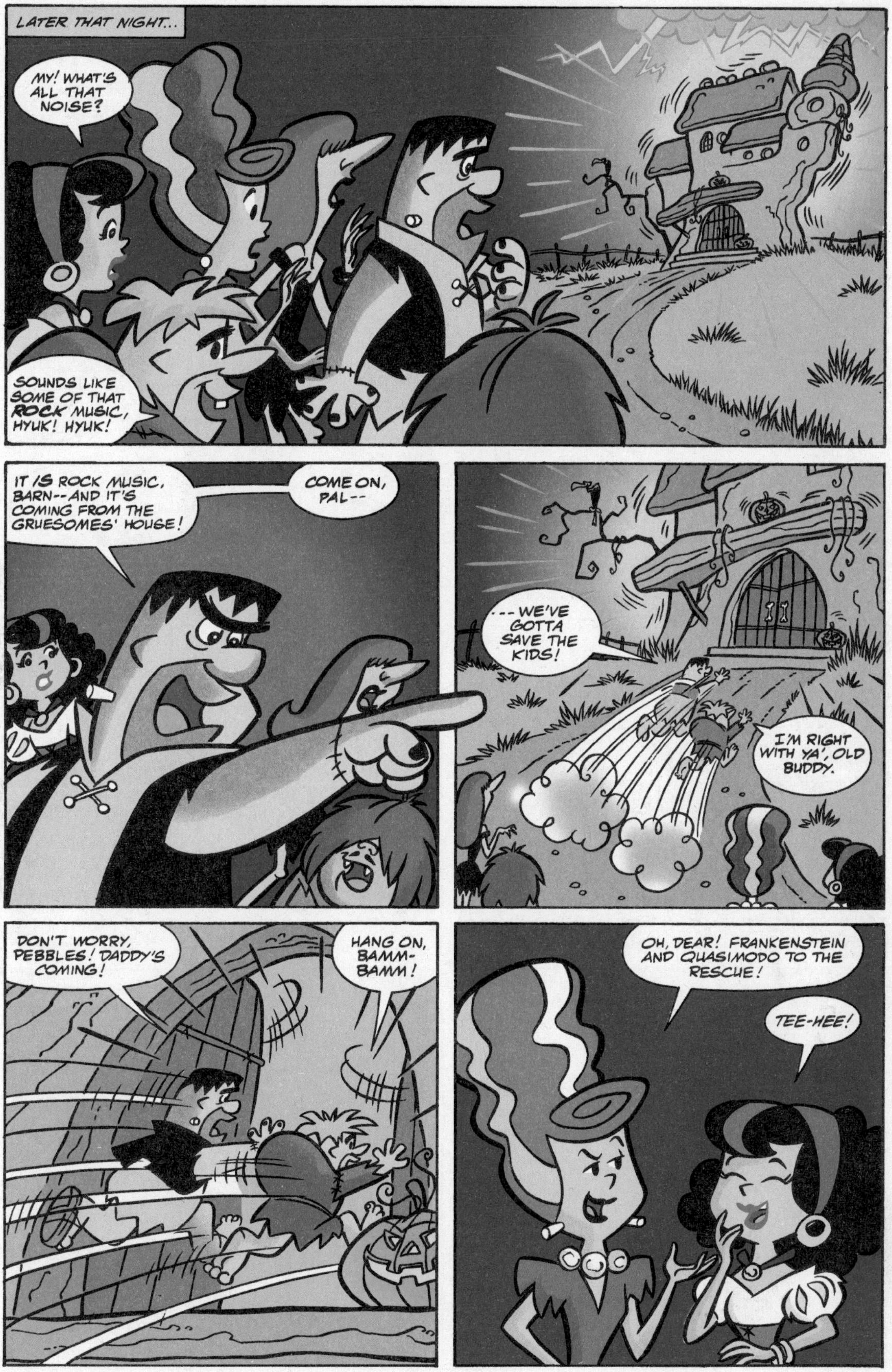
LATER THAT NIGHT...
MY! WHAT'S ALL THAT NOISE?
SOUNDS LIKE SOME OF THAT ROCK MUSIC, HYUK! HYUK!
IT IS ROCK MUSIC, BARN-- AND IT'S COMING FROM THE GRUESOMES' HOUSE!
COME ON, PAL--
---WE'VE GOTTA SAVE THE KIDS!
I'M RIGHT WITH YA', OLD BUDDY.
DON'T WORRY, PEBBLES! DADDY'S COMING!
HANG ON, BAMM-BAMM!
OH, DEAR! FRANKENSTEIN AND QUASIMODO TO THE RESCUE!
TEE-HEE!

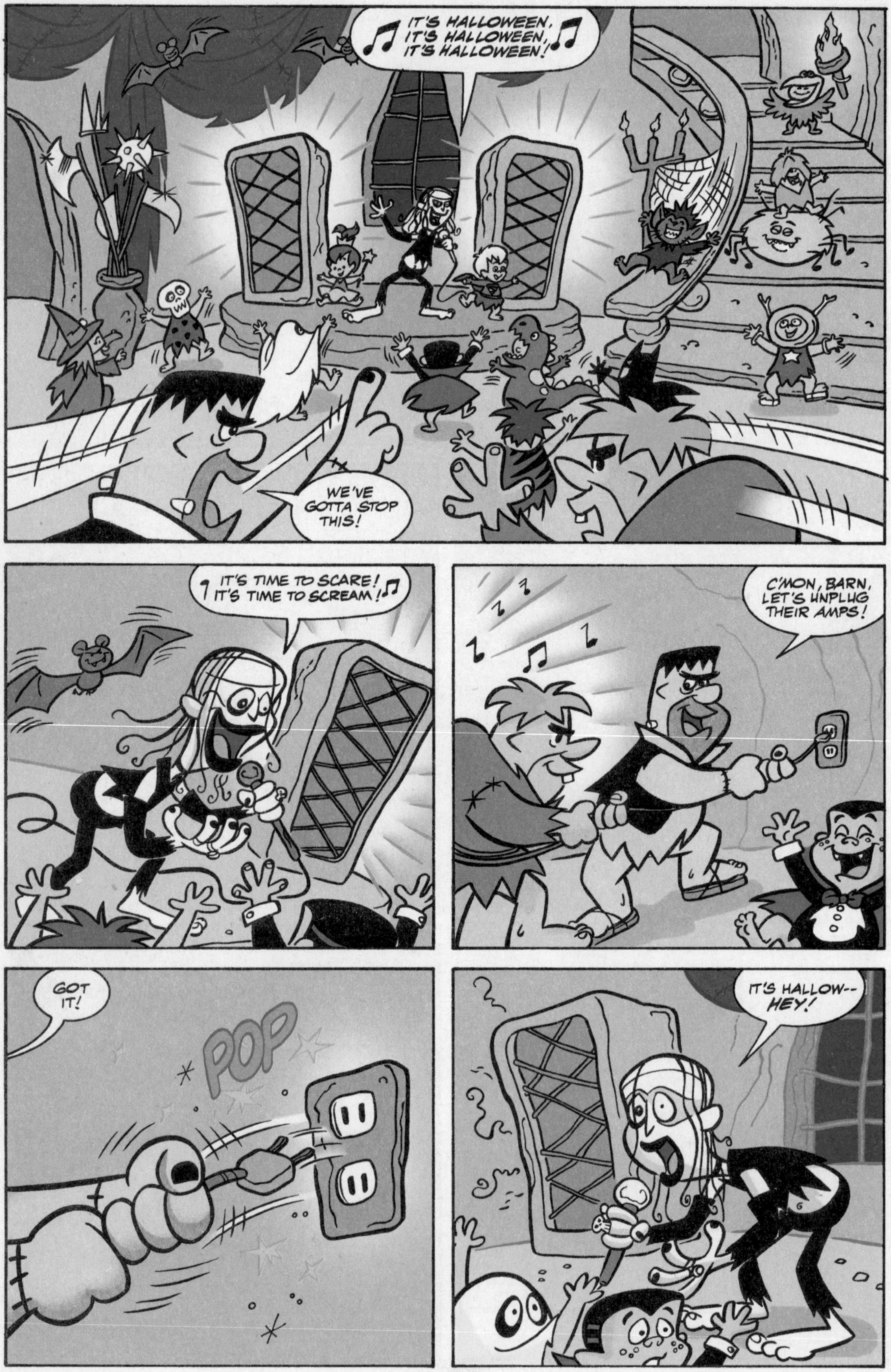

♫ IT'S HALLOWEEN, IT'S HALLOWEEN, IT'S HALLOWEEN! ♫
WE'VE GOTTA STOP THIS!
IT'S TIME TO SCARE! IT'S TIME TO SCREAM! ♫
C'MON, BARN, LET'S UNPLUG THEIR AMPS!
GOT IT!
POP
IT'S HALLOW-- HEY!

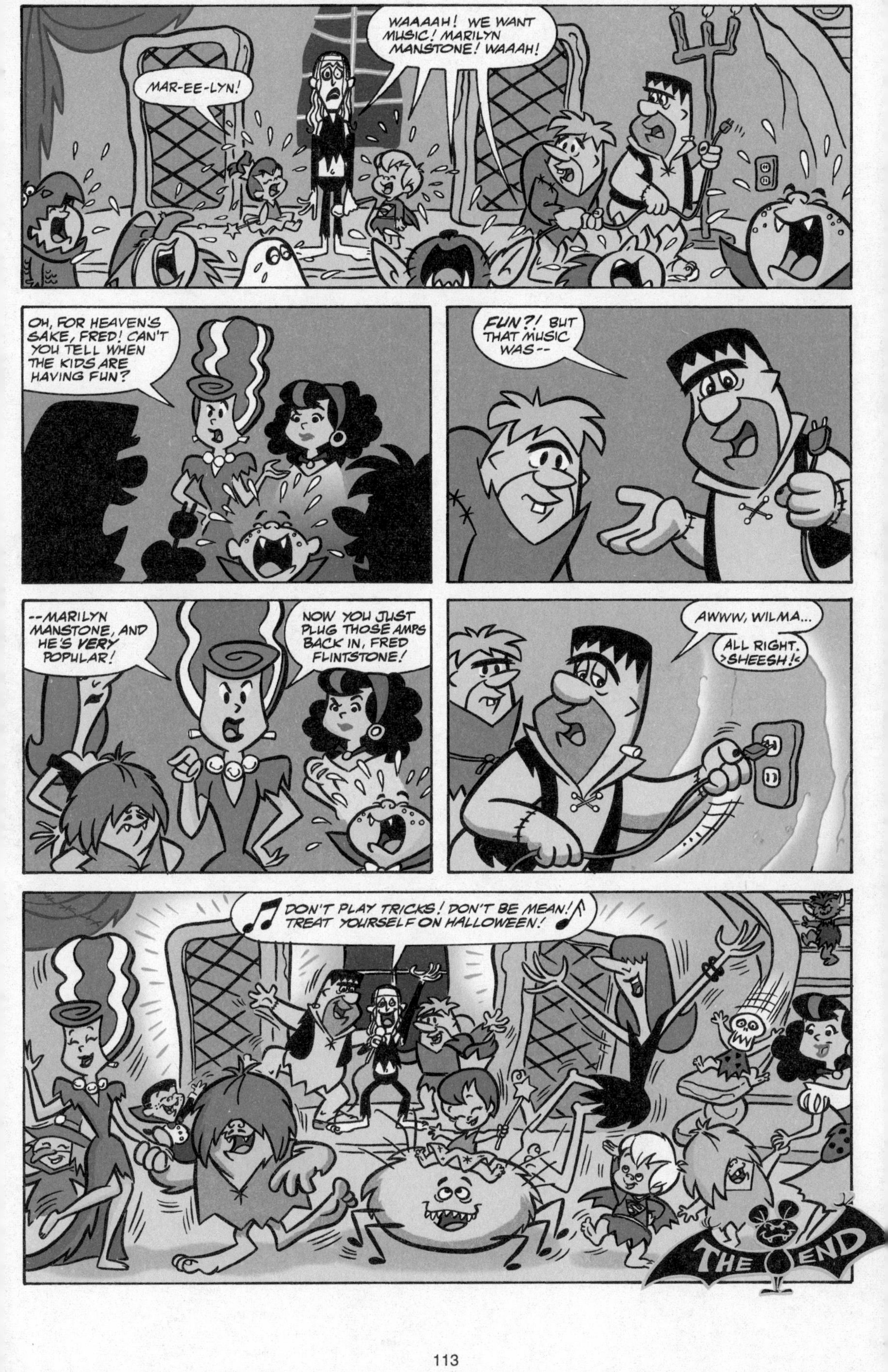
MAR-EE-LYN!
WAAAAH! WE WANT MUSIC! MARILYN MANSTONE! WAAAH!
OH, FOR HEAVEN'S SAKE, FRED! CAN'T YOU TELL WHEN THE KIDS ARE HAVING FUN?
FUN?! BUT THAT MUSIC WAS--
--MARILYN MANSTONE, AND HE'S VERY POPULAR!
NOW YOU JUST PLUG THOSE AMPS BACK IN, FRED FLINTSTONE!
AWWW, WILMA...
ALL RIGHT. >SHEESH!<
DON'T PLAY TRICKS! DON'T BE MEAN! TREAT YOURSELF ON HALLOWEEN!
THE END

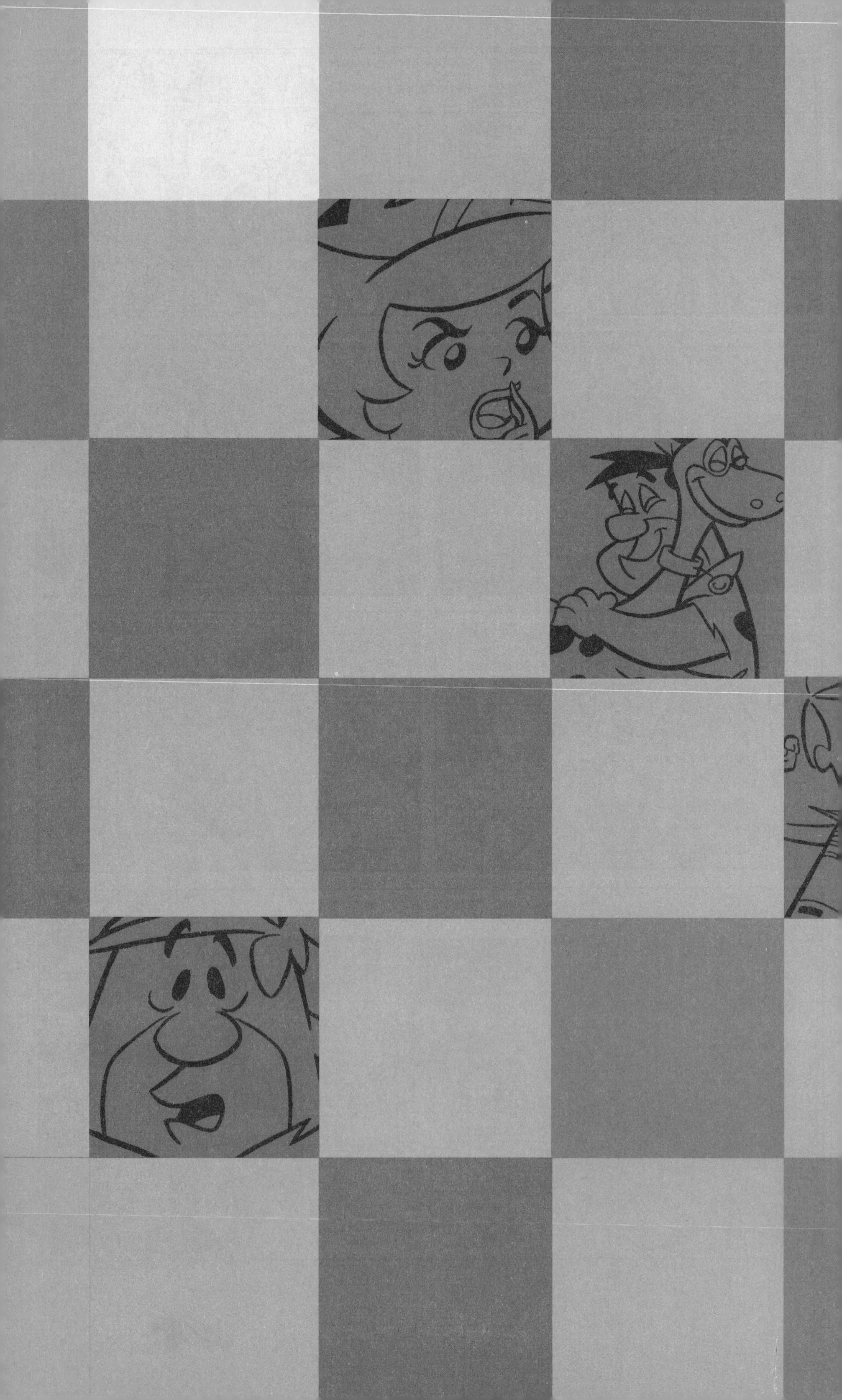

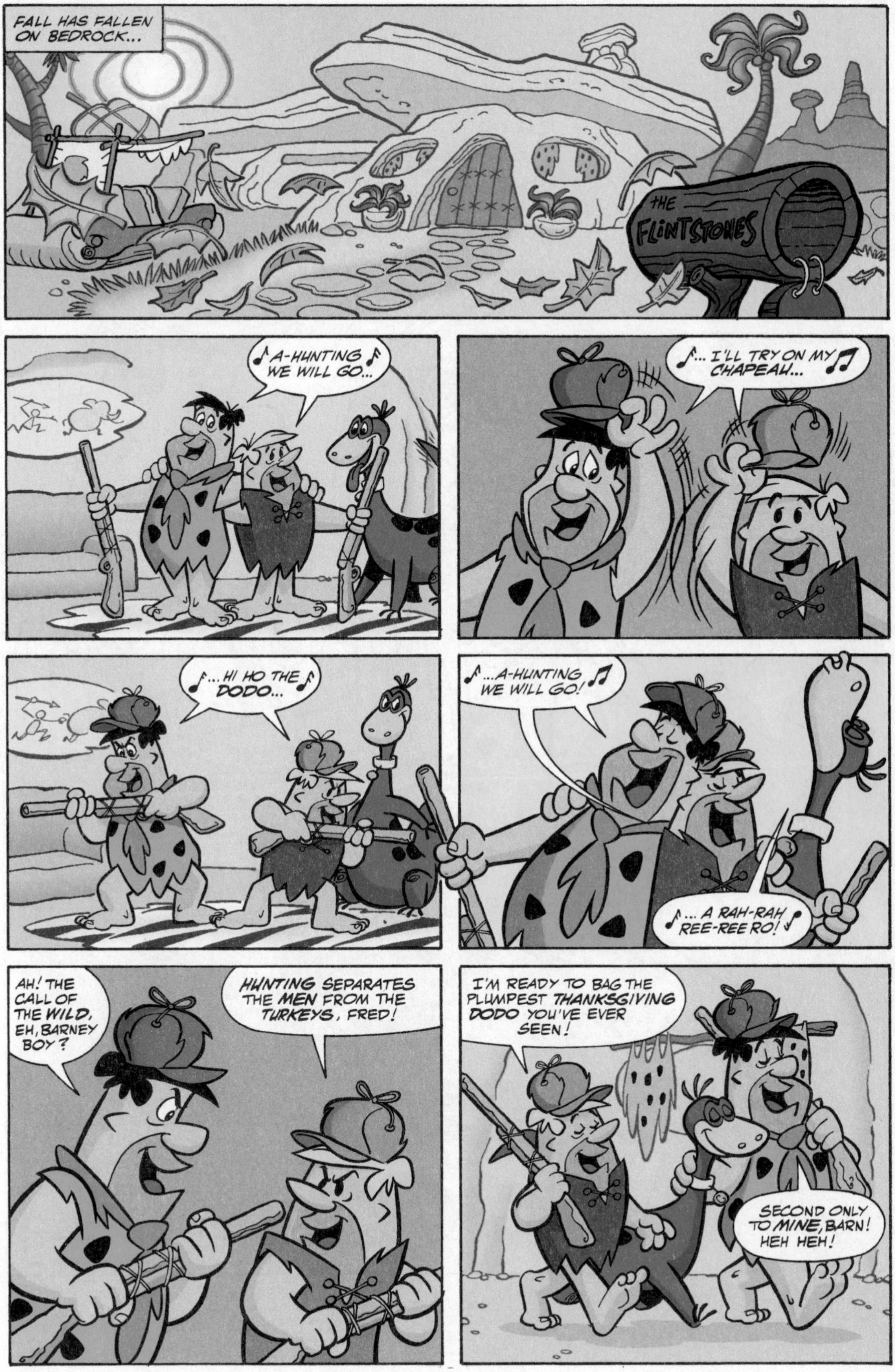
FALL HAS FALLEN ON BEDROCK...
THE FLINTSTONES
A-HUNTING WE WILL GO...
... I'LL TRY ON MY CHAPEAU...
...HI HO THE DODO...
...A-HUNTING WE WILL GO!
... A RAH-RAH REE-REE RO!
AH! THE CALL OF THE WILD, EH, BARNEY BOY?
HUNTING SEPARATES THE MEN FROM THE TURKEYS, FRED!
I'M READY TO BAG THE PLUMPEST THANKSGIVING DODO YOU'VE EVER SEEN!
SECOND ONLY TO MINE, BARN! HEH HEH!

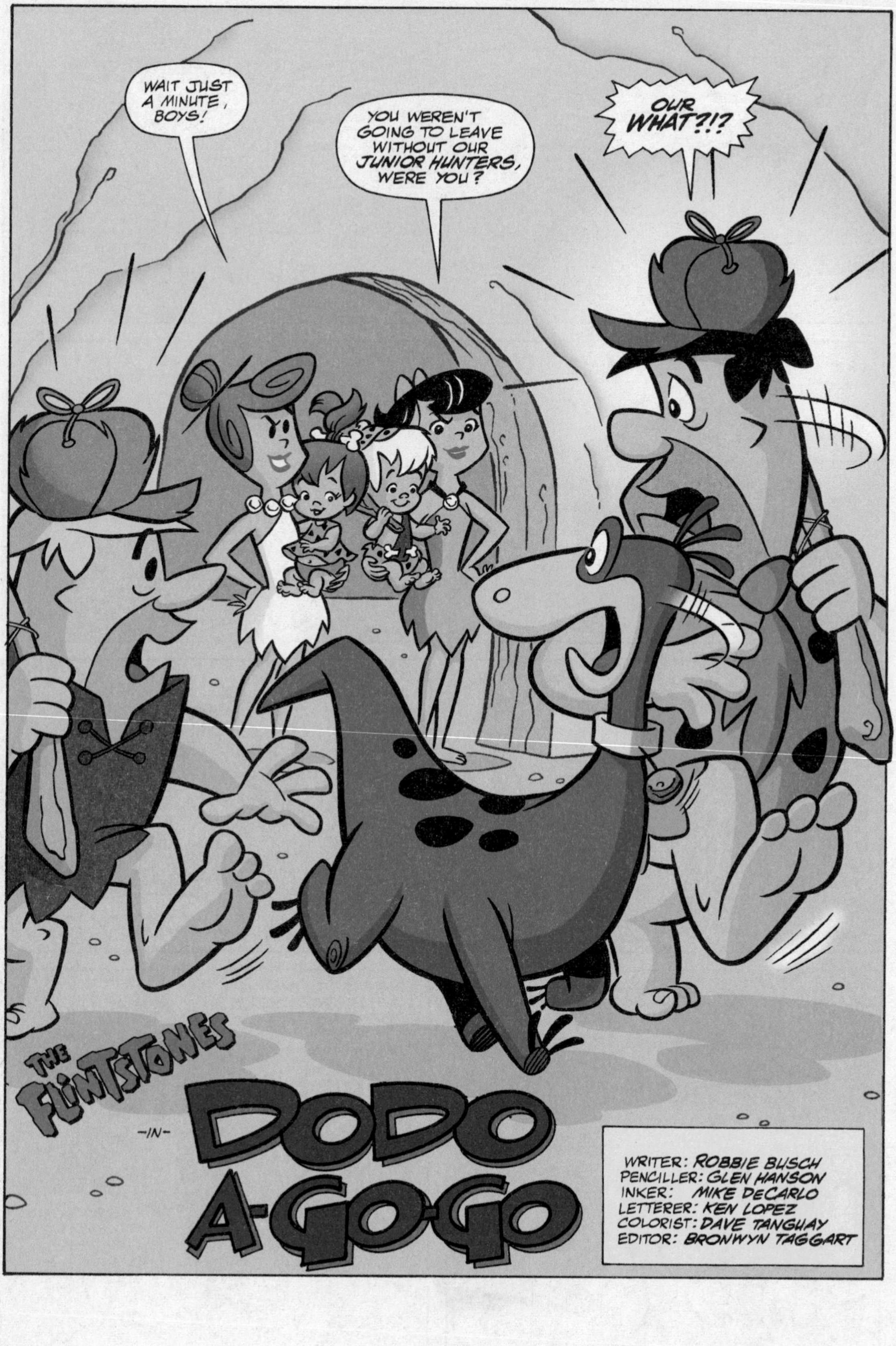
WAIT JUST A MINUTE, BOYS!
YOU WEREN'T GOING TO LEAVE WITHOUT OUR JUNIOR HUNTERS, WERE YOU?
OUR WHAT?!?
THE FLINTSTONES
-IN-
DODO A-GO-GO
WRITER: ROBBIE BUSCH
PENCILLER: GLEN HANSON
INKER: MIKE DeCARLO
LETTERER: KEN LOPEZ
COLORIST: DAVE TANGUAY
EDITOR: BRONWYN TAGGART

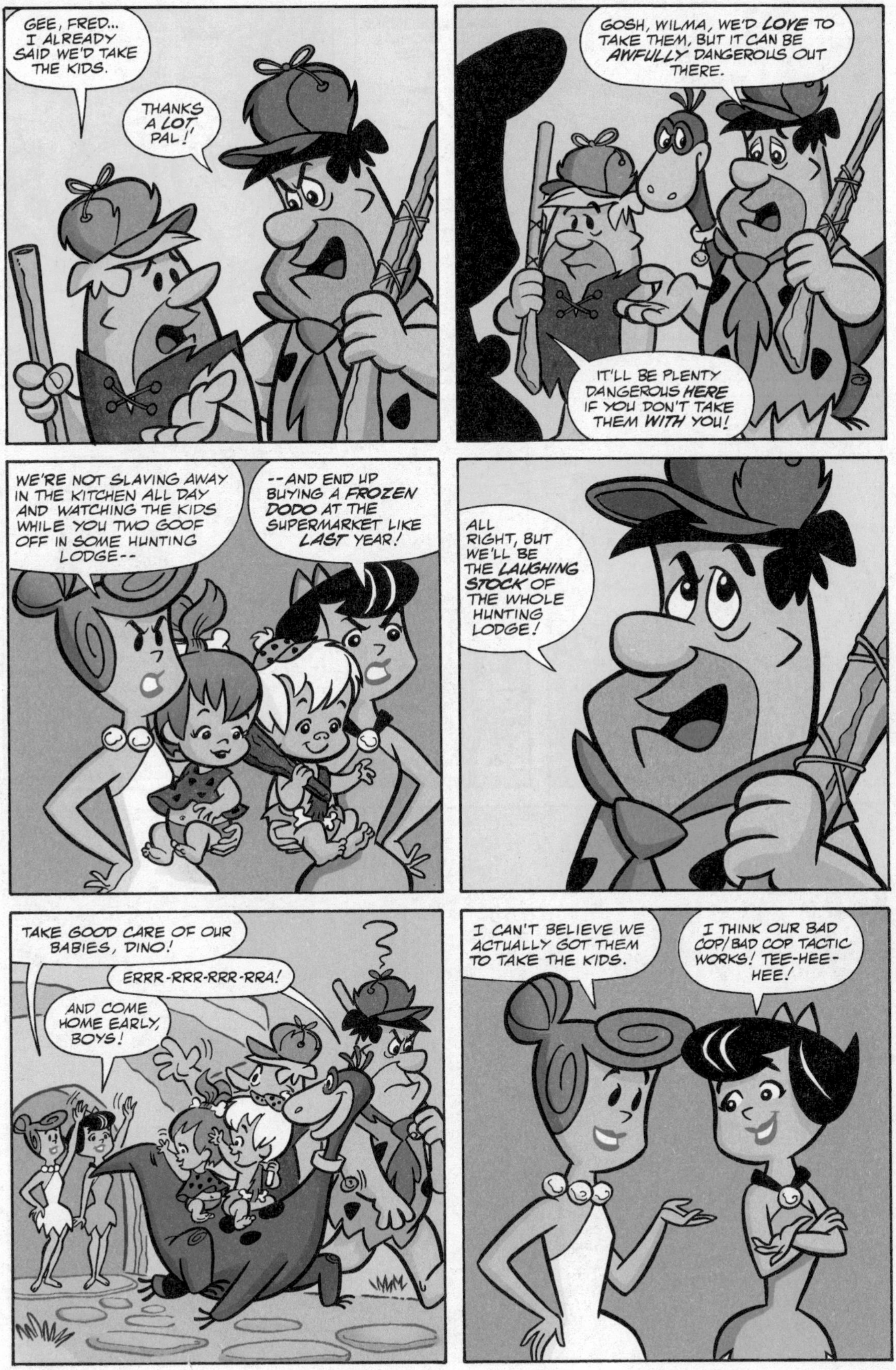
GEE, FRED... I ALREADY SAID WE'D TAKE THE KIDS.
THANKS A LOT, PAL!
GOSH, WILMA, WE'D LOVE TO TAKE THEM, BUT IT CAN BE AWFULLY DANGEROUS OUT THERE.
IT'LL BE PLENTY DANGEROUS HERE IF YOU DON'T TAKE THEM WITH YOU!
WE'RE NOT SLAVING AWAY IN THE KITCHEN ALL DAY AND WATCHING THE KIDS WHILE YOU TWO GOOF OFF IN SOME HUNTING LODGE--
--AND END UP BUYING A FROZEN DODO AT THE SUPERMARKET LIKE LAST YEAR!
ALL RIGHT, BUT WE'LL BE THE LAUGHING STOCK OF THE WHOLE HUNTING LODGE!
TAKE GOOD CARE OF OUR BABIES, DINO!
ERRR-RRR-RRR-RRA!
AND COME HOME EARLY, BOYS!
I CAN'T BELIEVE WE ACTUALLY GOT THEM TO TAKE THE KIDS.
I THINK OUR BAD COP/BAD COP TACTIC WORKS! TEE-HEE-HEE!

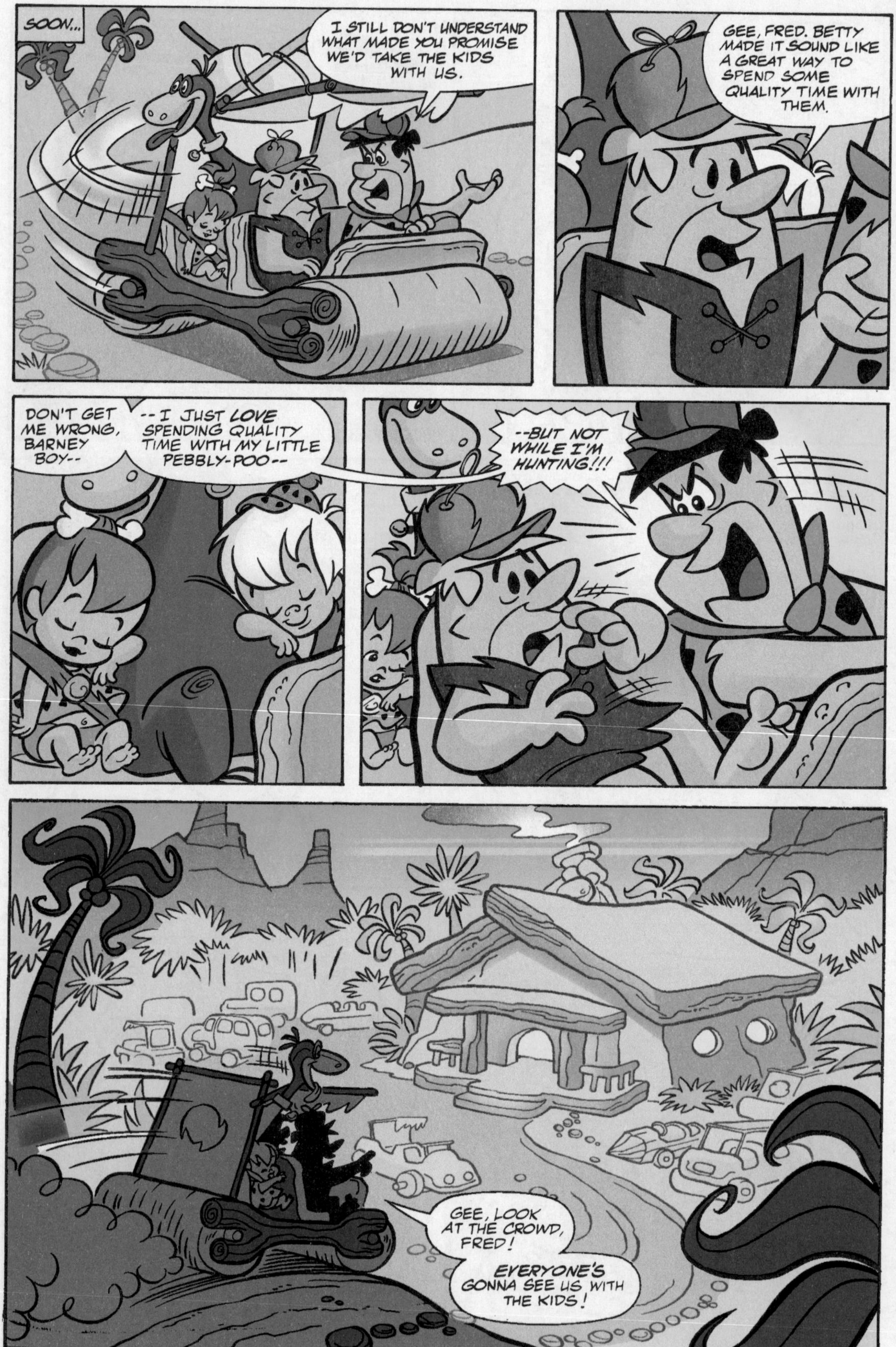
SOON...
I STILL DON'T UNDERSTAND WHAT MADE YOU PROMISE WE'D TAKE THE KIDS WITH US.
GEE, FRED. BETTY MADE IT SOUND LIKE A GREAT WAY TO SPEND SOME QUALITY TIME WITH THEM.
DON'T GET ME WRONG, BARNEY BOY--
--I JUST LOVE SPENDING QUALITY TIME WITH MY LITTLE PEBBLY-POO--
--BUT NOT WHILE I'M HUNTING!!!
GEE, LOOK AT THE CROWD, FRED!
EVERYONE'S GONNA SEE US WITH THE KIDS!

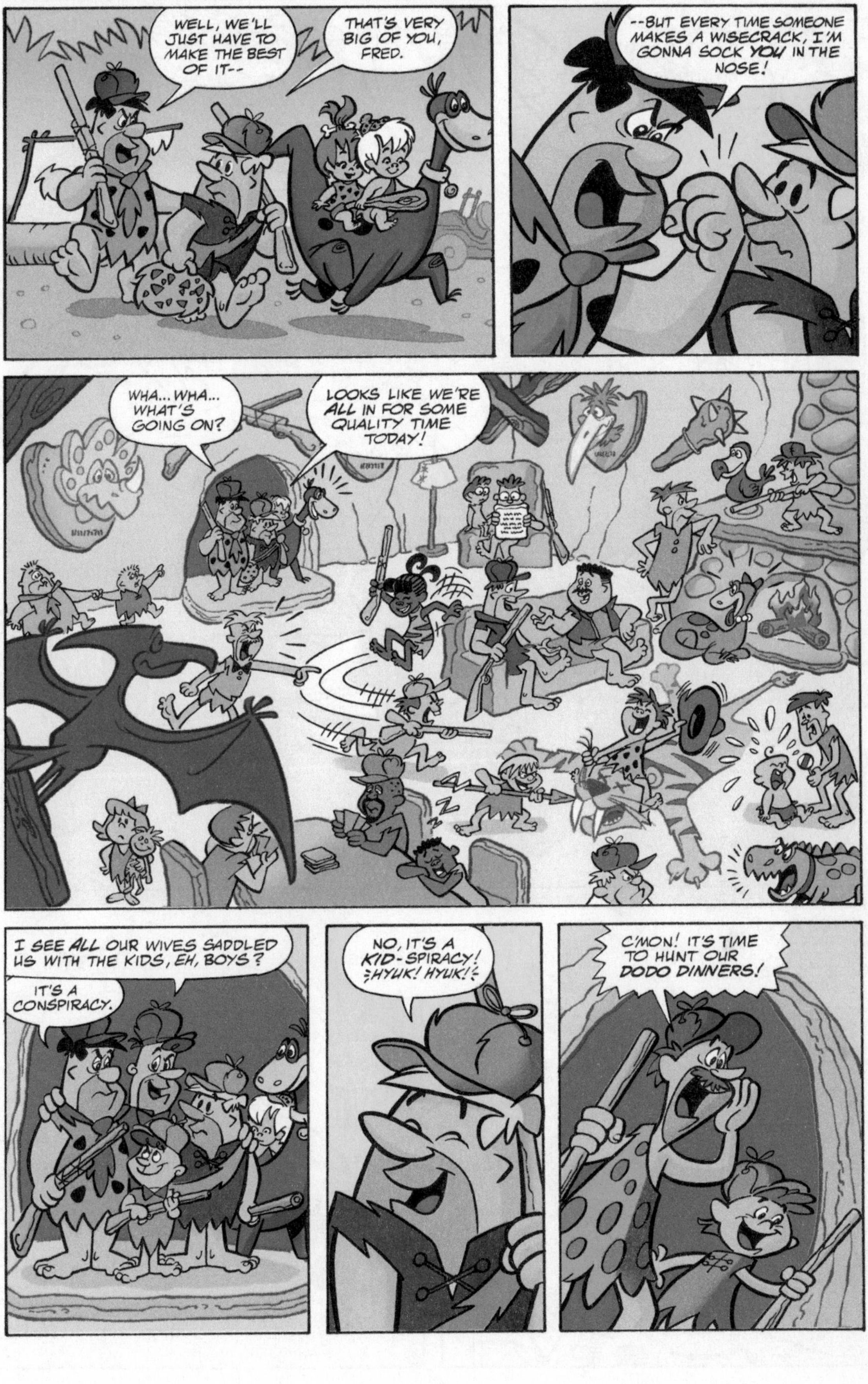

WELL, WE'LL JUST HAVE TO MAKE THE BEST OF IT--
THAT'S VERY BIG OF YOU, FRED.
--BUT EVERY TIME SOMEONE MAKES A WISECRACK, I'M GONNA SOCK YOU IN THE NOSE!
WHA... WHA... WHAT'S GOING ON?
LOOKS LIKE WE'RE ALL IN FOR SOME QUALITY TIME TODAY!
I SEE ALL OUR WIVES SADDLED US WITH THE KIDS, EH, BOYS?
IT'S A CONSPIRACY.
NO, IT'S A KID-SPIRACY! HYUK! HYUK!
C'MON! IT'S TIME TO HUNT OUR DODO DINNERS!

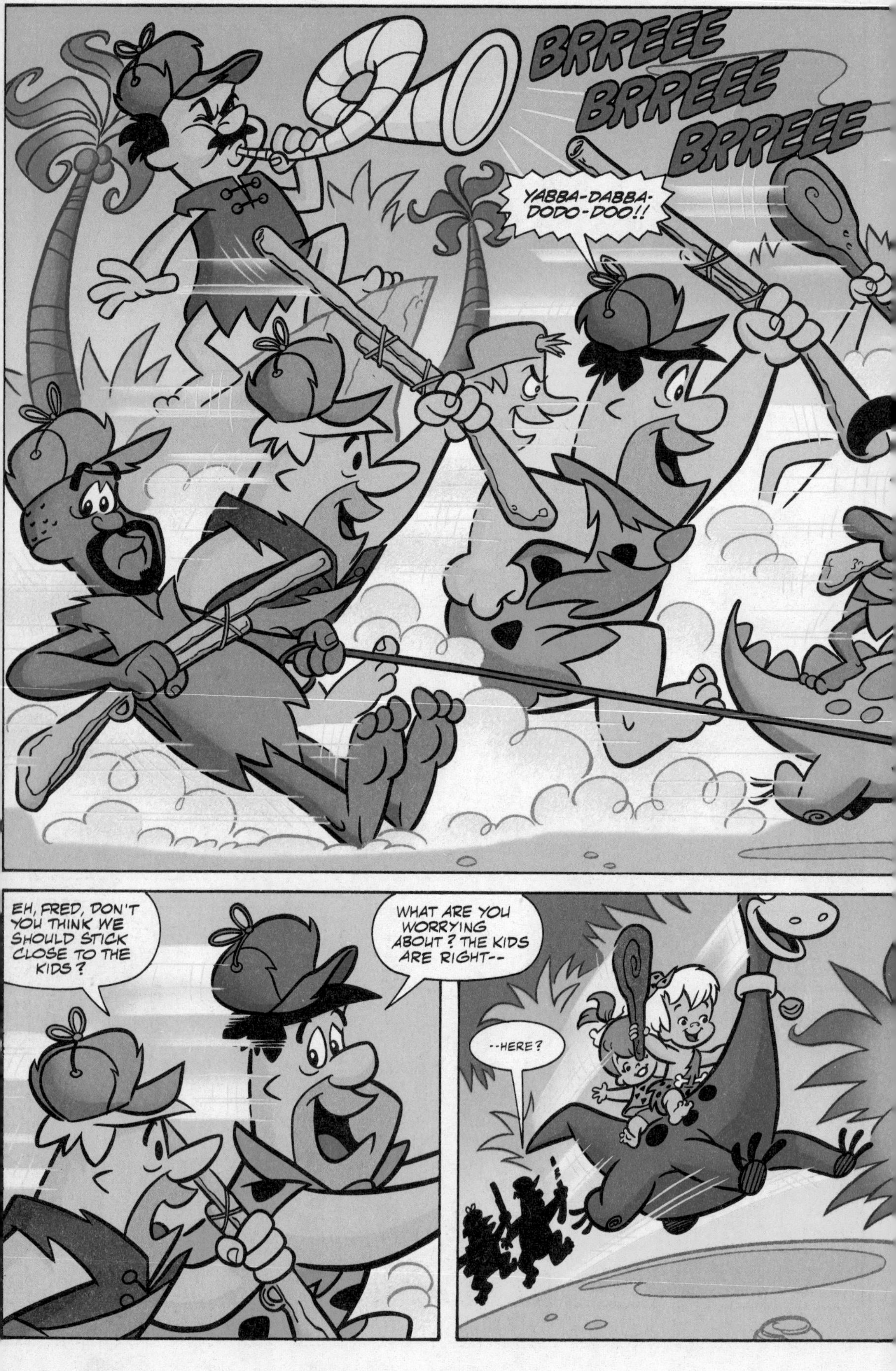
BRREEE
BRREEE
BRREEE
YABBA-DABBA-DODO-DOO!!
EH, FRED, DON'T YOU THINK WE SHOULD STICK CLOSE TO THE KIDS?
WHAT ARE YOU WORRYING ABOUT? THE KIDS ARE RIGHT--
--HERE?

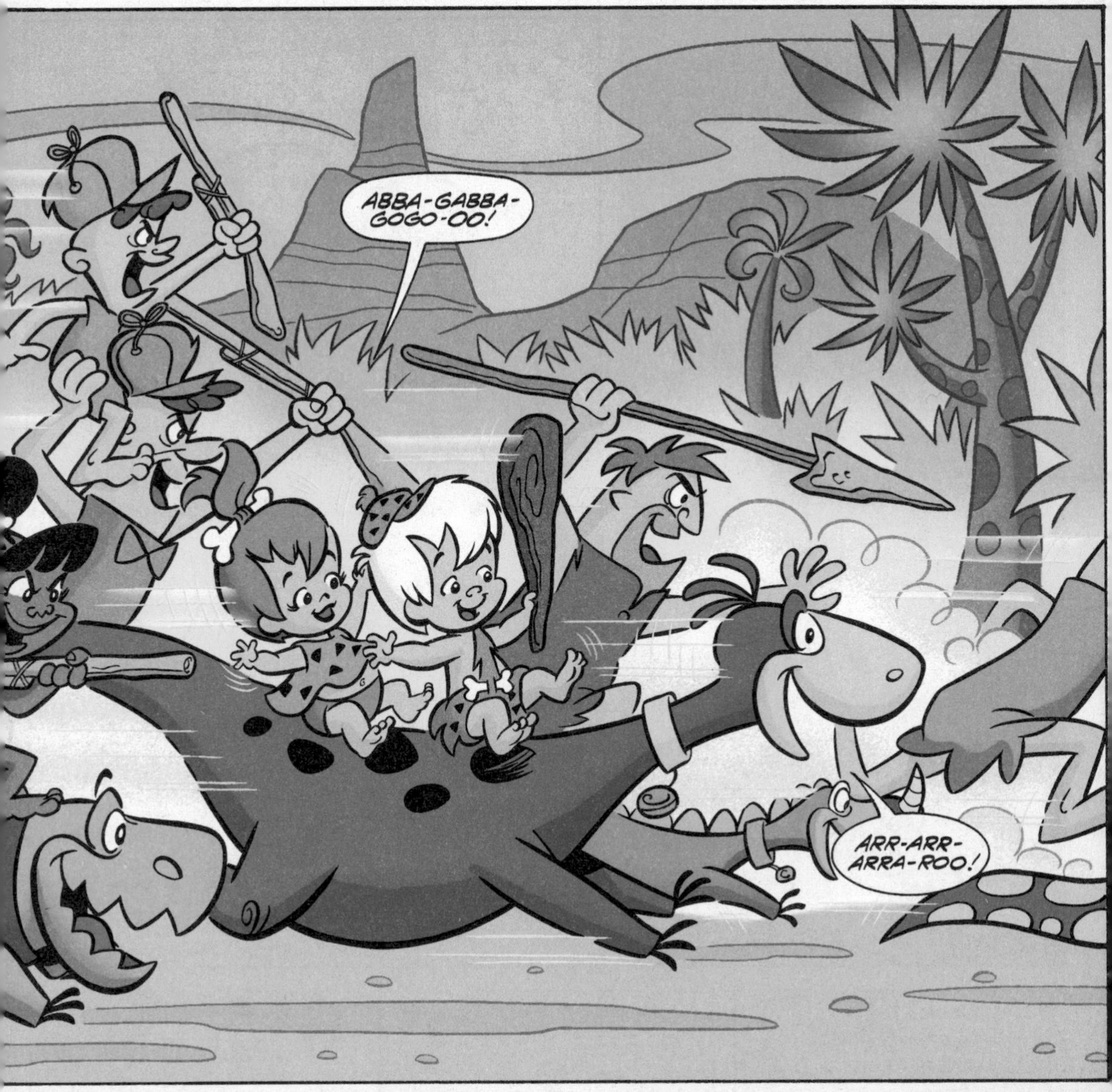
ABBA-GABBA-GOGO-OO!
ARR-ARR-ARRA-ROO!

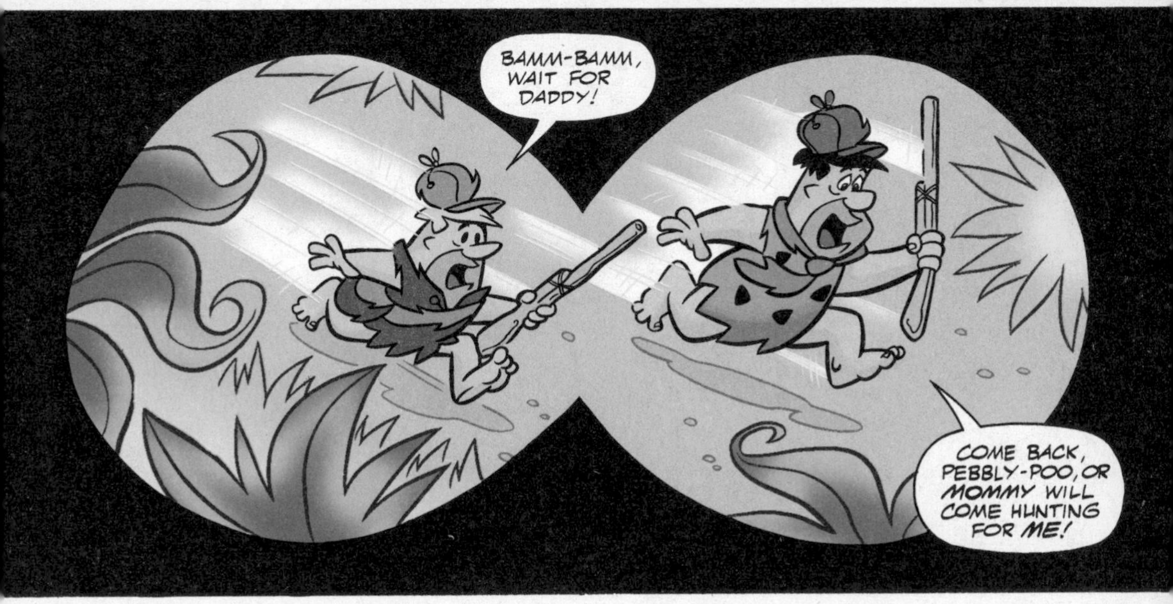
BAMM-BAMM, WAIT FOR DADDY!
COME BACK, PEBBLY-POO, OR MOMMY WILL COME HUNTING FOR ME!

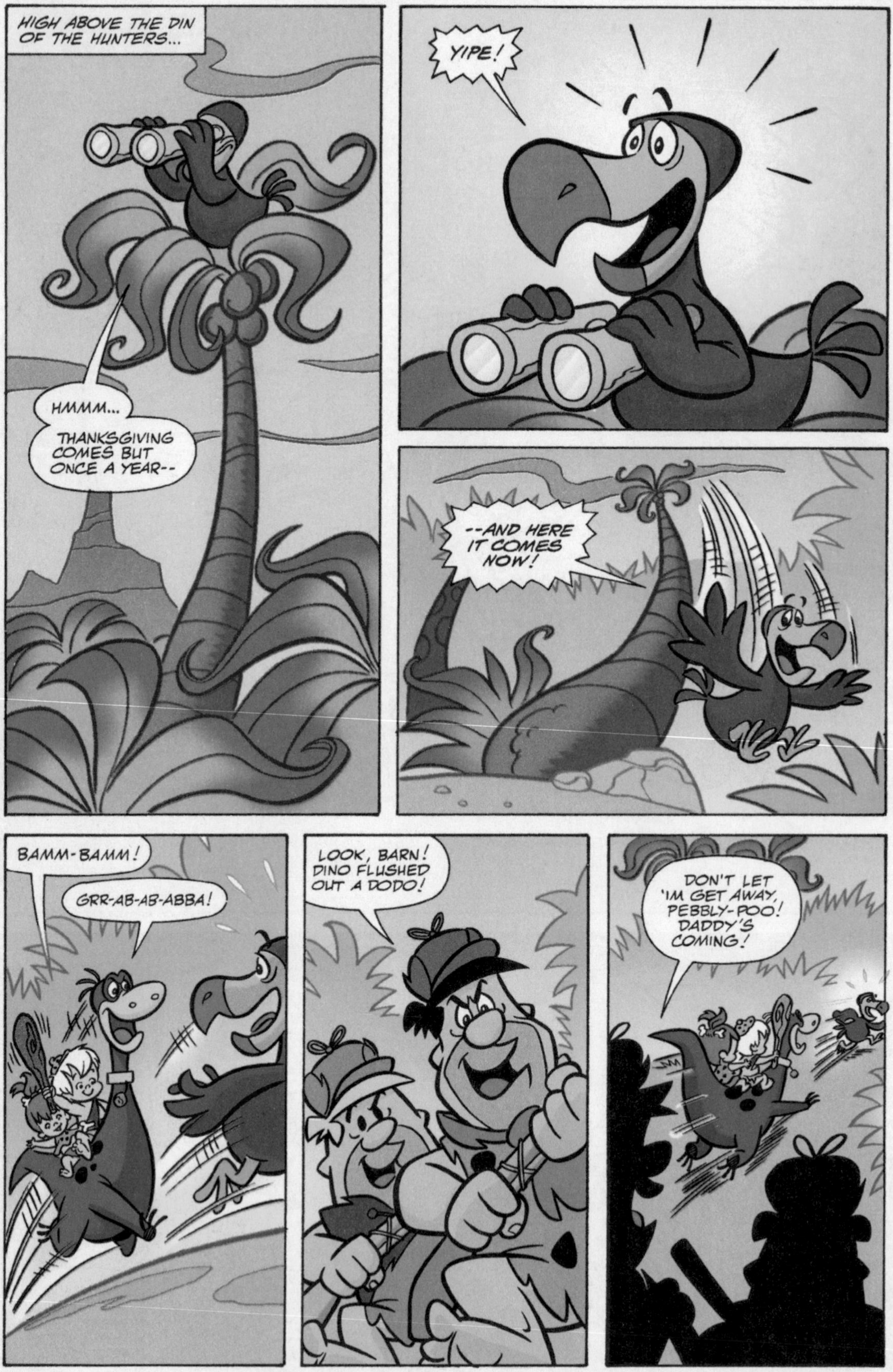
HIGH ABOVE THE DIN OF THE HUNTERS...
HMMM...
THANKSGIVING COMES BUT ONCE A YEAR--
YIPE!
--AND HERE IT COMES NOW!
BAMM-BAMM!
GRR-AB-AB-ABBA!
LOOK, BARN! DINO FLUSHED OUT A DODO!
DON'T LET 'IM GET AWAY, PEBBLY-POO! DADDY'S COMING!

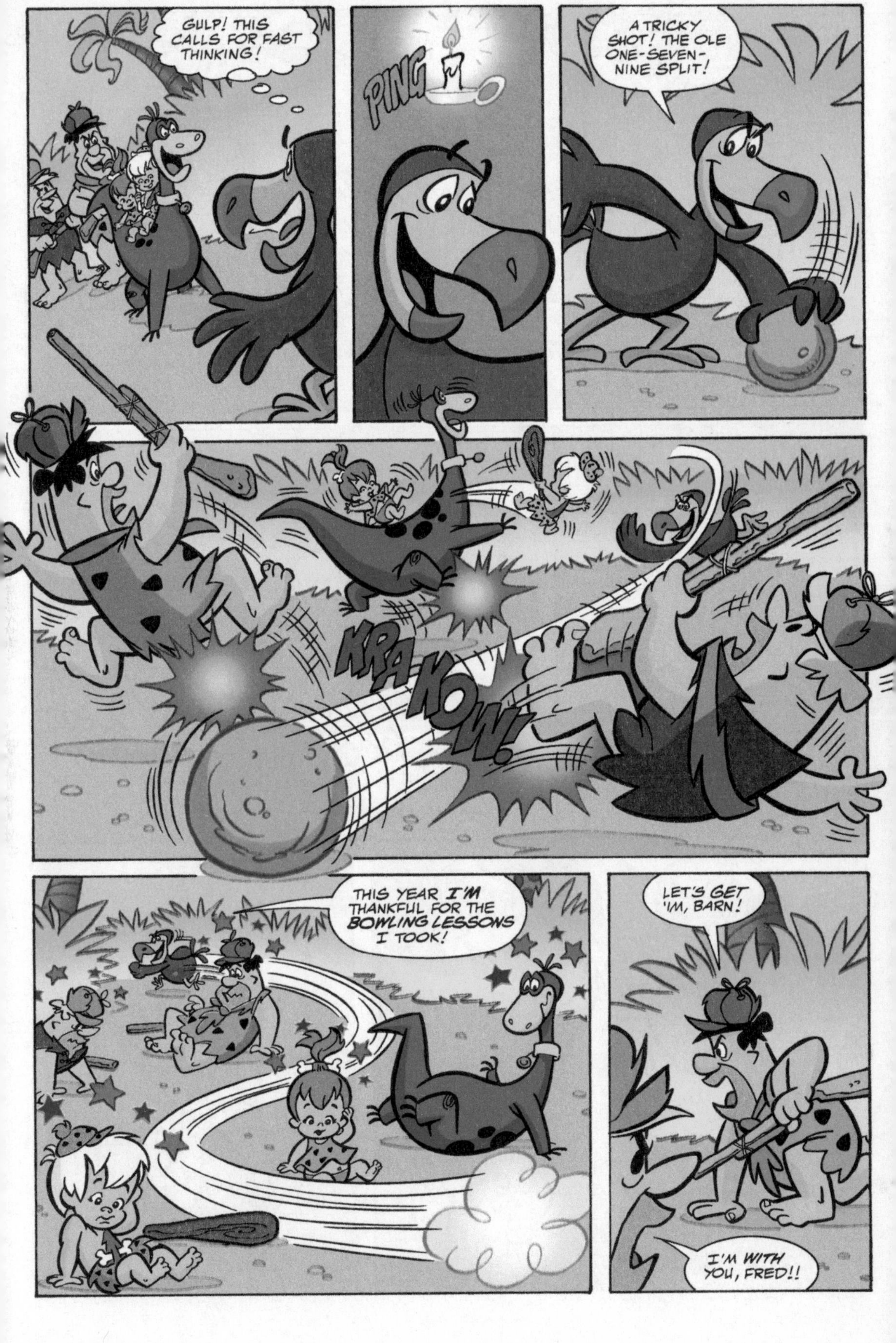
GULP! THIS CALLS FOR FAST THINKING!
PING
A TRICKY SHOT! THE OLE ONE-SEVEN-NINE SPLIT!
KRA KOW!
THIS YEAR I'M THANKFUL FOR THE BOWLING LESSONS I TOOK!
LET'S GET 'IM, BARN!
I'M WITH YOU, FRED!!

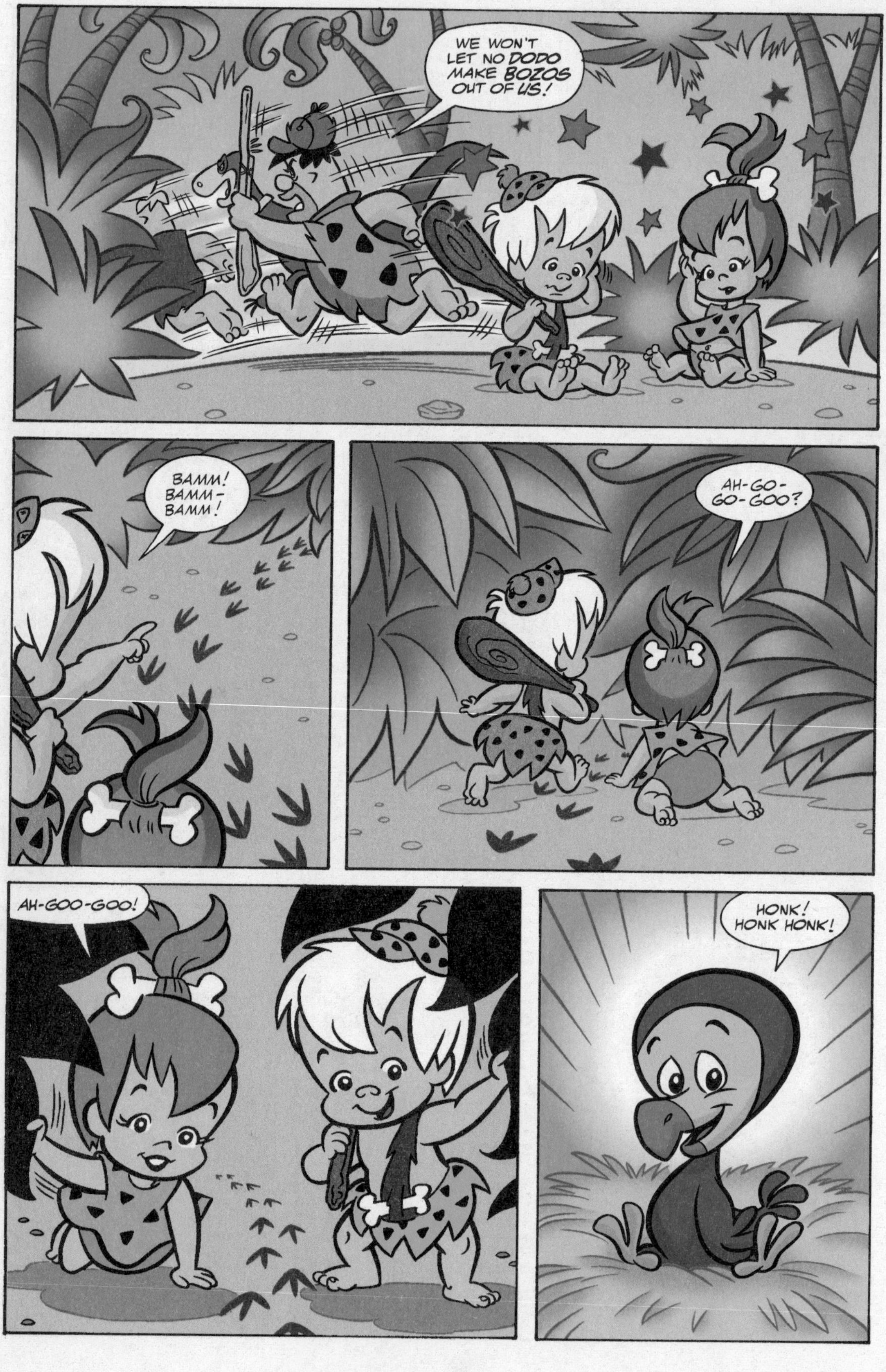
WE WON'T LET NO DODO MAKE BOZOS OUT OF US!
BAMM! BAMM-BAMM!
AH-GO-GO-GOO?
AH-GOO-GOO!
HONK! HONK HONK!

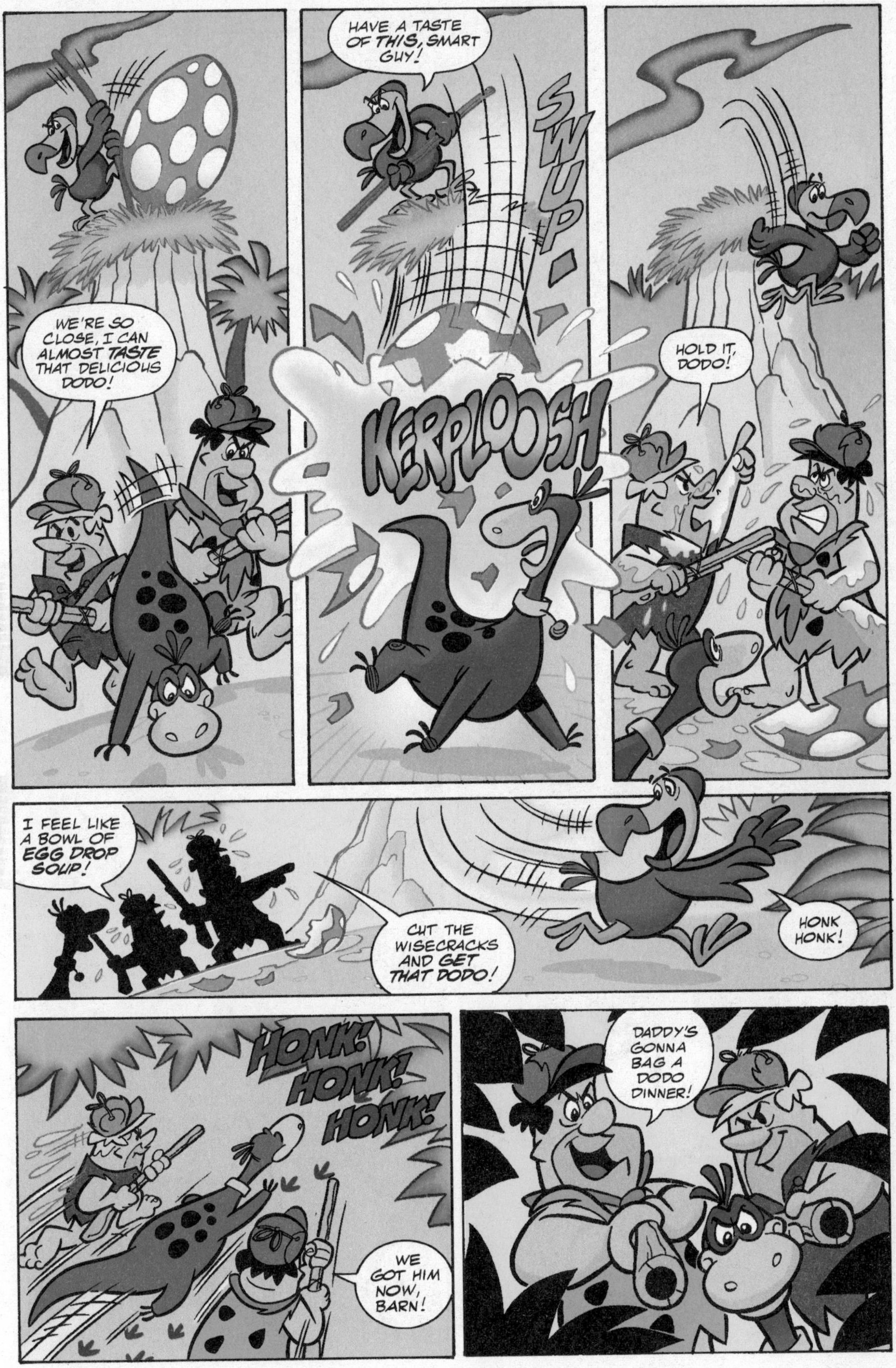
WE'RE SO CLOSE, I CAN ALMOST TASTE THAT DELICIOUS DODO!
HAVE A TASTE OF THIS, SMART GUY!
SWUP-
KERPLOOSH
HOLD IT, DODO!
I FEEL LIKE A BOWL OF EGG DROP SOUP!
CUT THE WISECRACKS AND GET THAT DODO!
HONK HONK!
HONK! HONK! HONK!
WE GOT HIM NOW, BARN!
DADDY'S GONNA BAG A DODO DINNER!

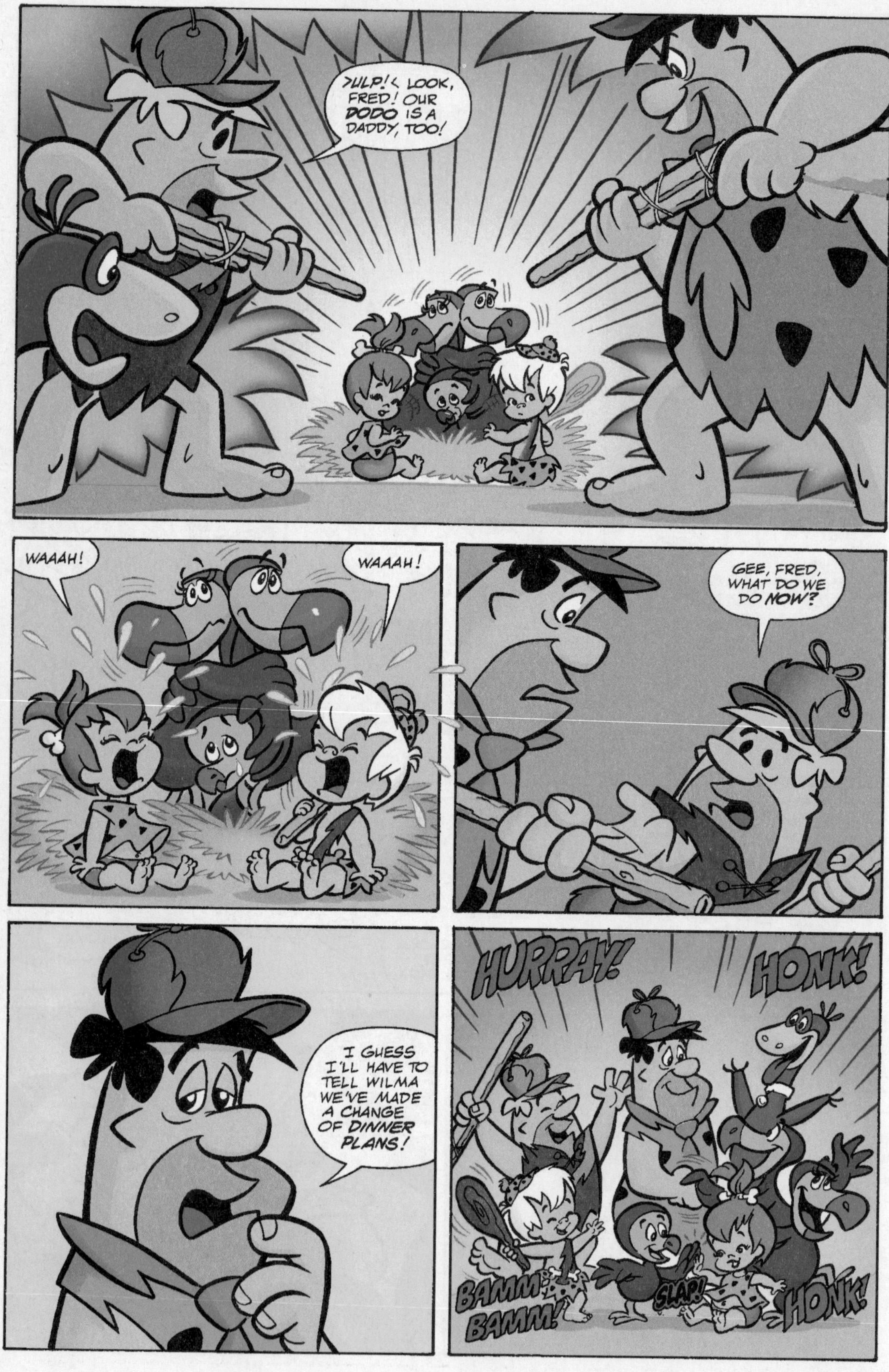

>ULP!< LOOK, FRED! OUR DODO IS A DADDY, TOO!
WAAAH!
WAAAH!
GEE, FRED, WHAT DO WE DO NOW?
I GUESS I'LL HAVE TO TELL WILMA WE'VE MADE A CHANGE OF DINNER PLANS!
HURRAY!
HONK!
BAMM! BAMM!
SLAP!
HONK!

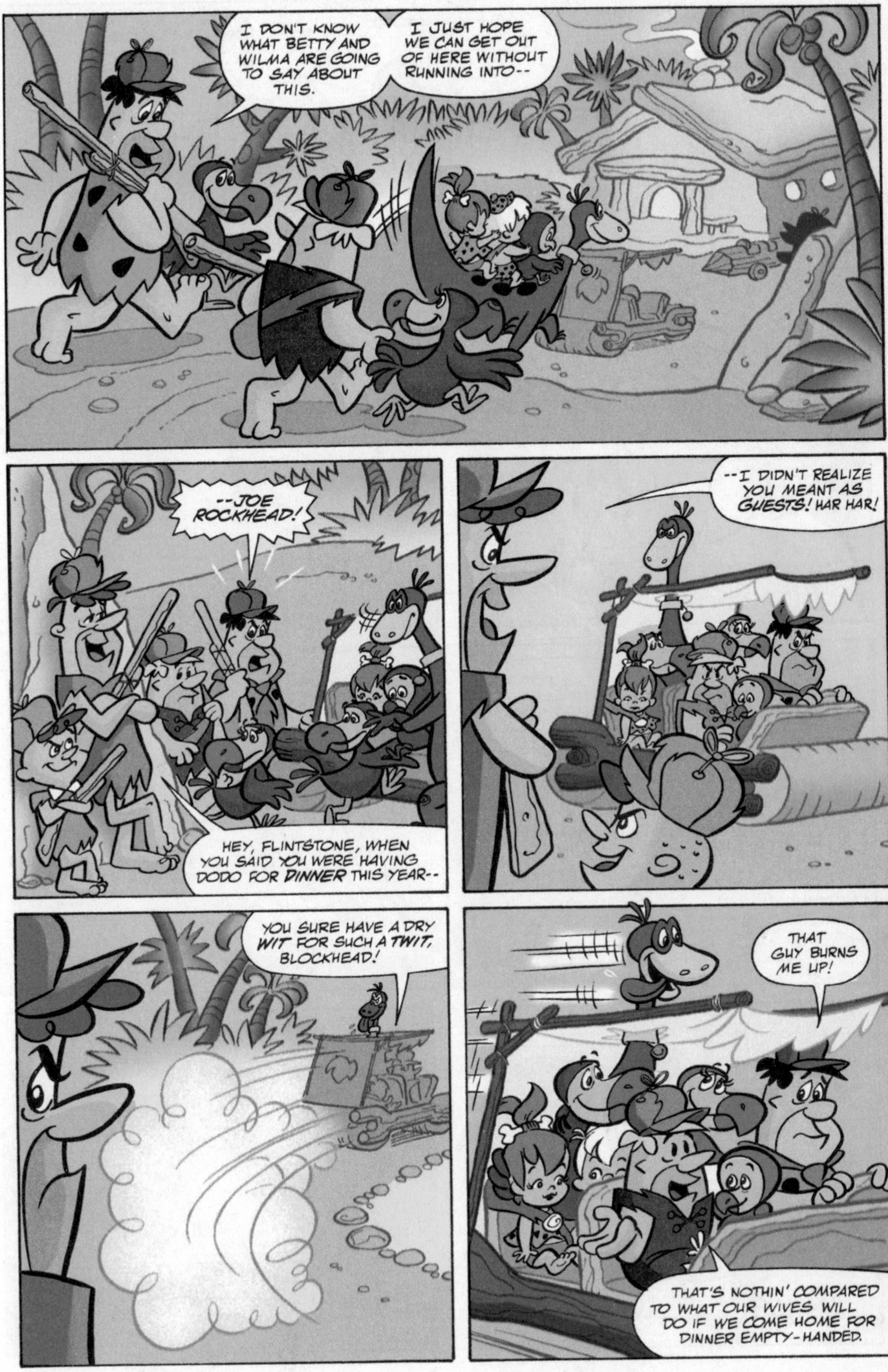

I DON'T KNOW WHAT BETTY AND WILMA ARE GOING TO SAY ABOUT THIS.
I JUST HOPE WE CAN GET OUT OF HERE WITHOUT RUNNING INTO--
--JOE ROCKHEAD!
HEY, FLINTSTONE, WHEN YOU SAID YOU WERE HAVING DODO FOR DINNER THIS YEAR--
--I DIDN'T REALIZE YOU MEANT AS GUESTS! HAR HAR!
YOU SURE HAVE A DRY WIT FOR SUCH A TWIT, BLOCKHEAD!
THAT GUY BURNS ME UP!
THAT'S NOTHIN' COMPARED TO WHAT OUR WIVES WILL DO IF WE COME HOME FOR DINNER EMPTY-HANDED.

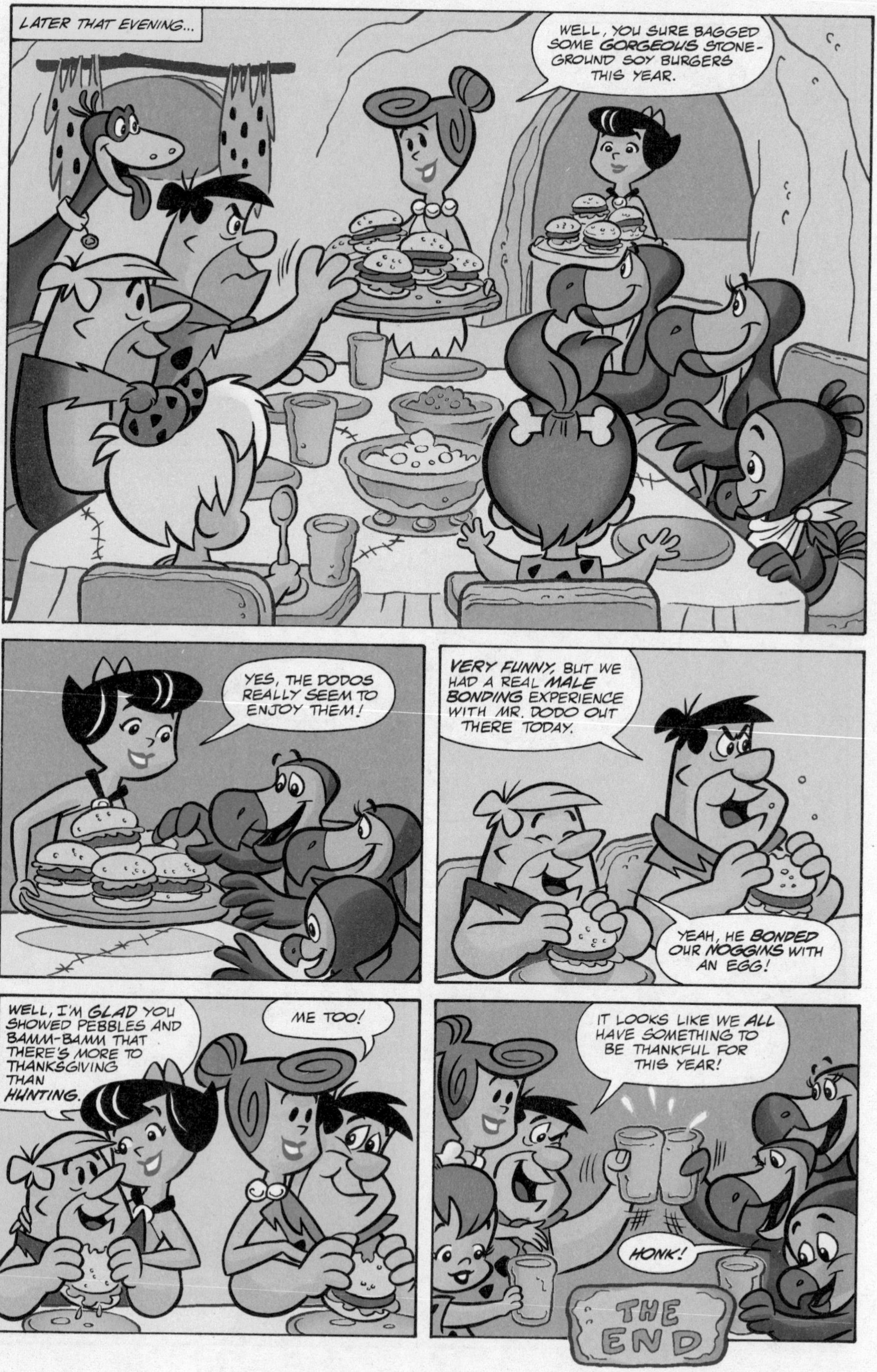
LATER THAT EVENING...
WELL, YOU SURE BAGGED SOME GORGEOUS STONE-GROUND SOY BURGERS THIS YEAR.
YES, THE DODOS REALLY SEEM TO ENJOY THEM!
VERY FUNNY, BUT WE HAD A REAL MALE BONDING EXPERIENCE WITH MR. DODO OUT THERE TODAY.
YEAH, HE BONDED OUR NOGGINS WITH AN EGG!
WELL, I'M GLAD YOU SHOWED PEBBLES AND BAMM-BAMM THAT THERE'S MORE TO THANKSGIVING THAN HUNTING.
ME TOO!
IT LOOKS LIKE WE ALL HAVE SOMETHING TO BE THANKFUL FOR THIS YEAR!
HONK!
THE END

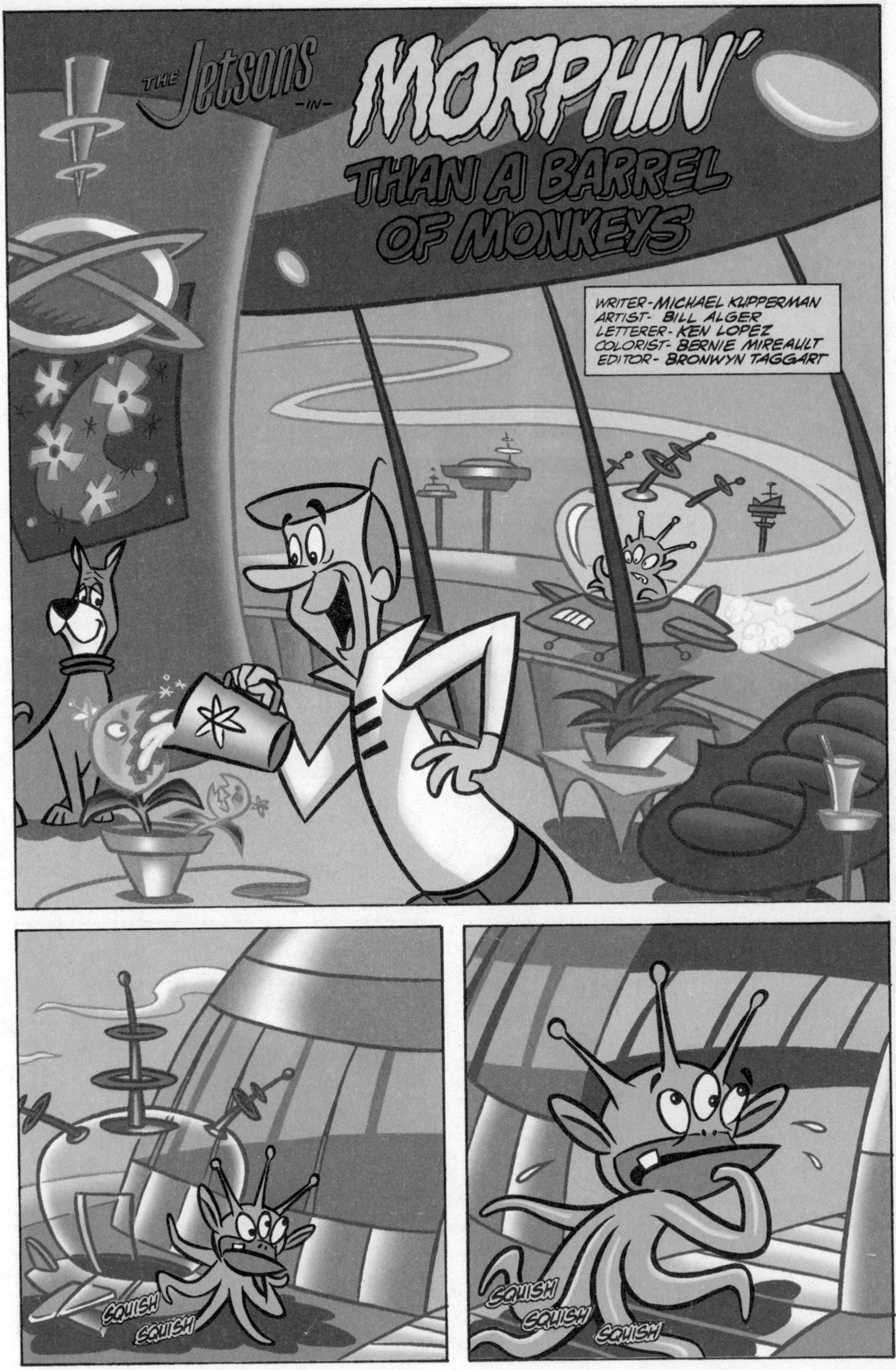
THE Jetsons -IN-
MORPHIN'
THAN A BARREL OF MONKEYS
WRITER- MICHAEL KUPPERMAN
ARTIST- BILL ALGER
LETTERER- KEN LOPEZ
COLORIST- BERNIE MIREAULT
EDITOR- BRONWYN TAGGART
SQUISH
SQUISH
SQUISH
SQUISH
SQUISH

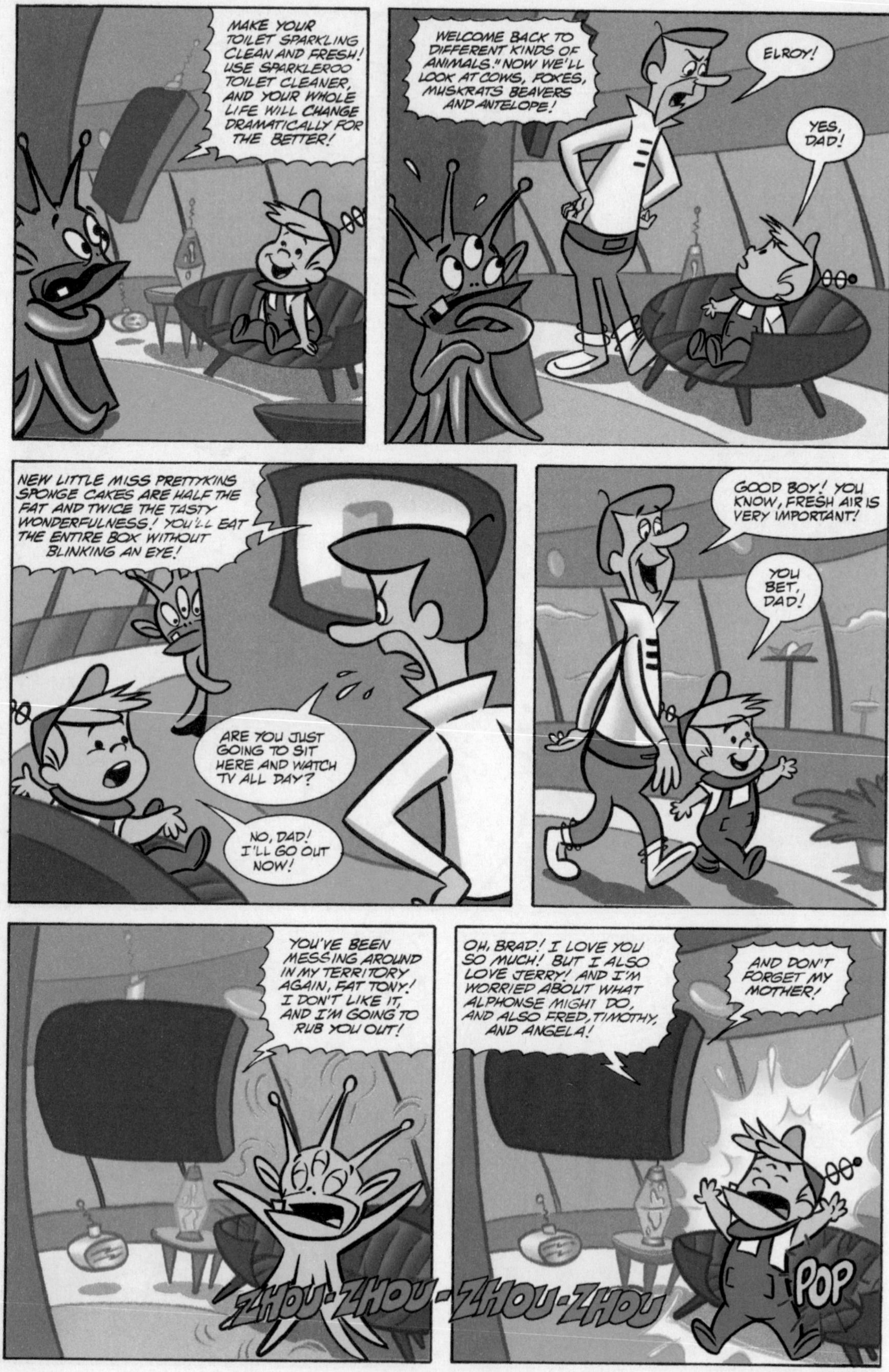
MAKE YOUR TOILET SPARKLING CLEAN AND FRESH! USE SPARKLEROO TOILET CLEANER, AND YOUR WHOLE LIFE WILL CHANGE DRAMATICALLY FOR THE BETTER!
WELCOME BACK TO "DIFFERENT KINDS OF ANIMALS." NOW WE'LL LOOK AT COWS, FOXES, MUSKRATS BEAVERS AND ANTELOPE!
ELROY!
YES, DAD!
NEW LITTLE MISS PRETTYKINS SPONGE CAKES ARE HALF THE FAT AND TWICE THE TASTY WONDERFULNESS! YOU'LL EAT THE ENTIRE BOX WITHOUT BLINKING AN EYE!
ARE YOU JUST GOING TO SIT HERE AND WATCH TV ALL DAY?
NO, DAD! I'LL GO OUT NOW!
GOOD BOY! YOU KNOW, FRESH AIR IS VERY IMPORTANT!
YOU BET, DAD!
YOU'VE BEEN MESSING AROUND IN MY TERRITORY AGAIN, FAT TONY! I DON'T LIKE IT, AND I'M GOING TO RUB YOU OUT!
OH, BRAD! I LOVE YOU SO MUCH! BUT I ALSO LOVE JERRY! AND I'M WORRIED ABOUT WHAT ALPHONSE MIGHT DO, AND ALSO FRED, TIMOTHY, AND ANGELA!
AND DON'T FORGET MY MOTHER!
ZHOU-ZHOU-ZHOU-ZHOU
POP

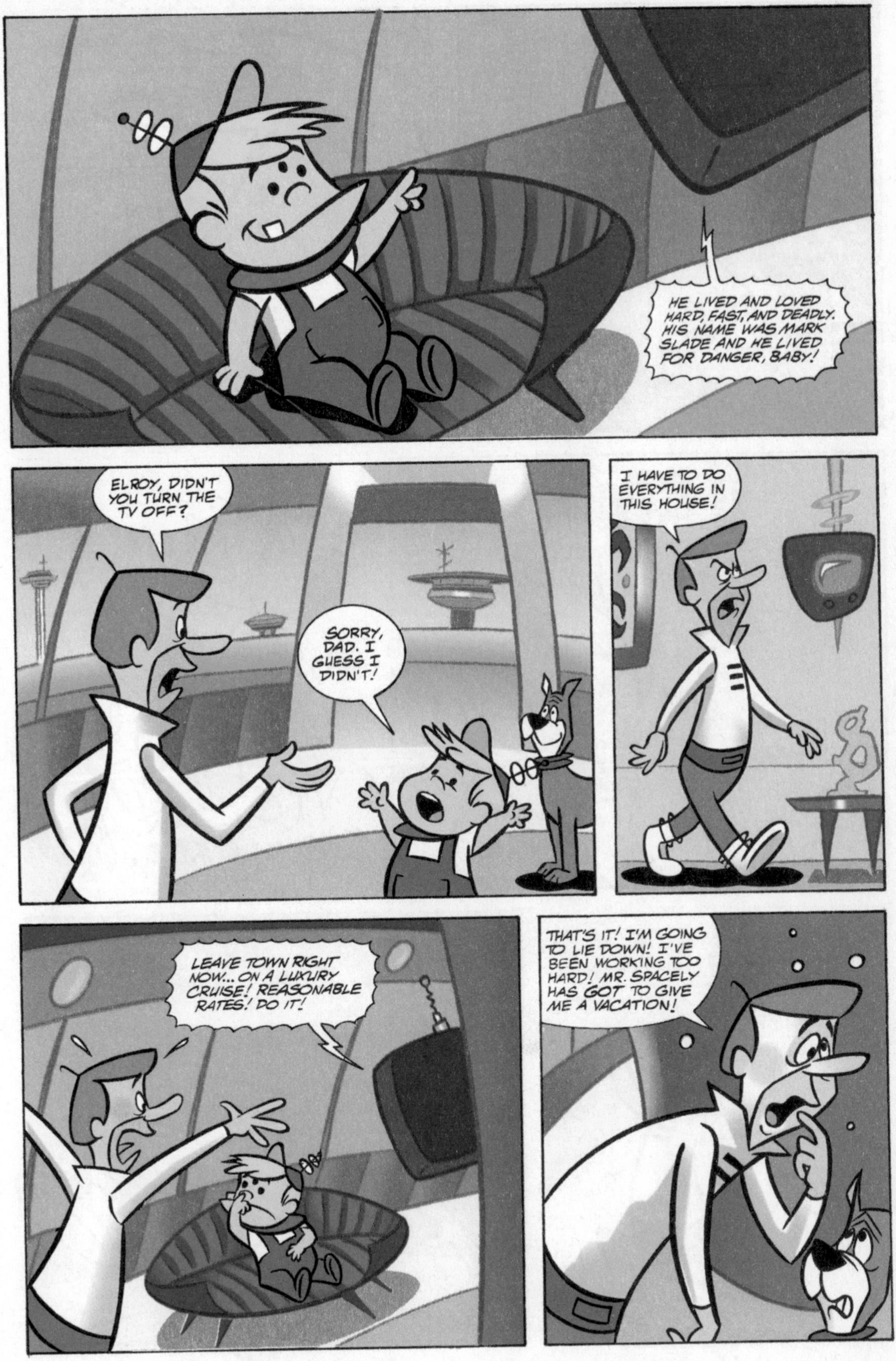
HE LIVED AND LOVED HARD, FAST, AND DEADLY. HIS NAME WAS MARK SLADE AND HE LIVED FOR DANGER, BABY!
ELROY, DIDN'T YOU TURN THE TV OFF?
SORRY, DAD. I GUESS I DIDN'T!
I HAVE TO DO EVERYTHING IN THIS HOUSE!
LEAVE TOWN RIGHT NOW... ON A LUXURY CRUISE! REASONABLE RATES! DO IT!
THAT'S IT! I'M GOING TO LIE DOWN! I'VE BEEN WORKING TOO HARD! MR. SPACELY HAS GOT TO GIVE ME A VACATION!

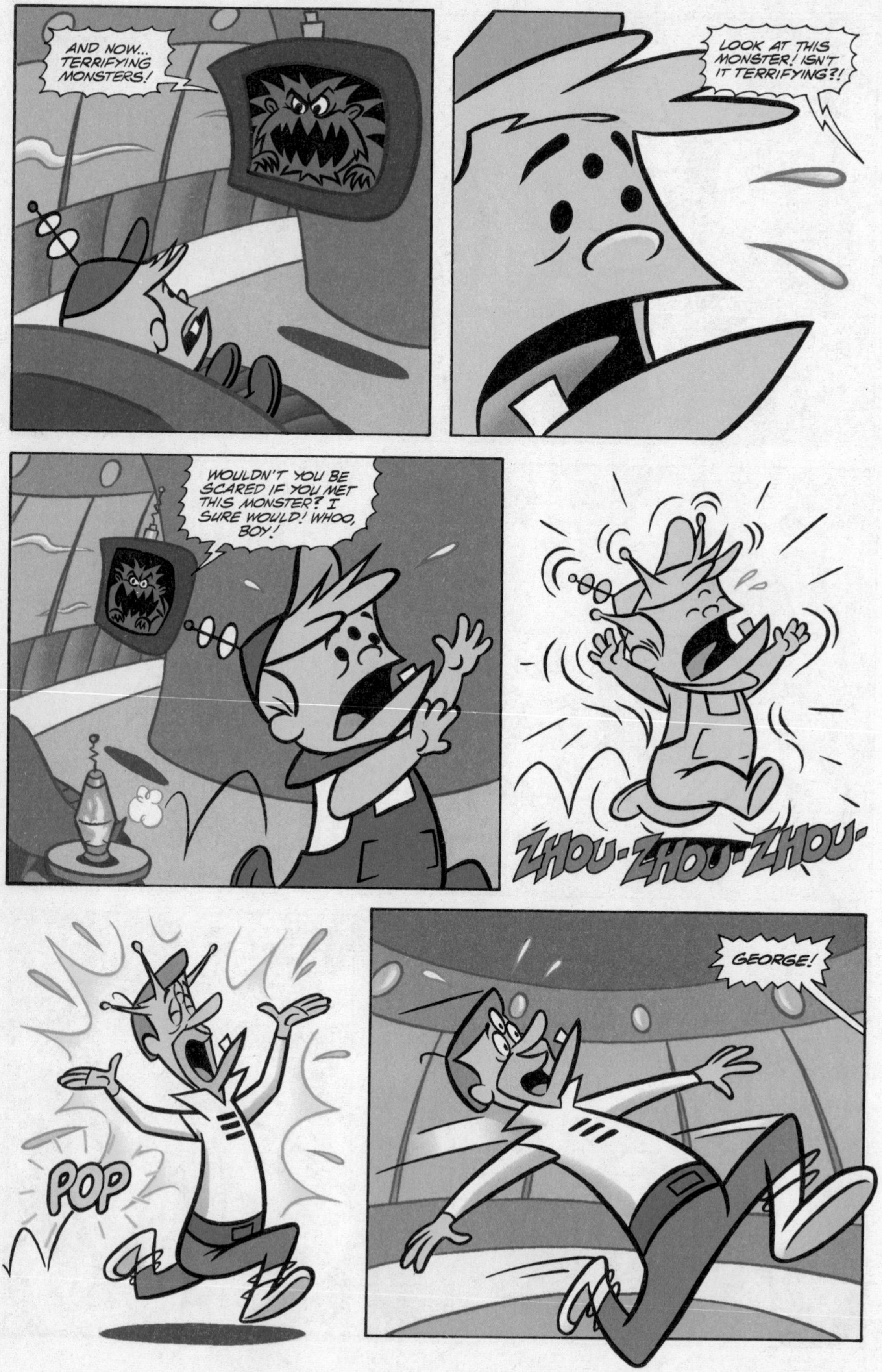
AND NOW... TERRIFYING MONSTERS!
LOOK AT THIS MONSTER! ISN'T IT TERRIFYING?!
WOULDN'T YOU BE SCARED IF YOU MET THIS MONSTER? I SURE WOULD! WHOO, BOY!
ZHOU-ZHOU-ZHOU-
POP
GEORGE!

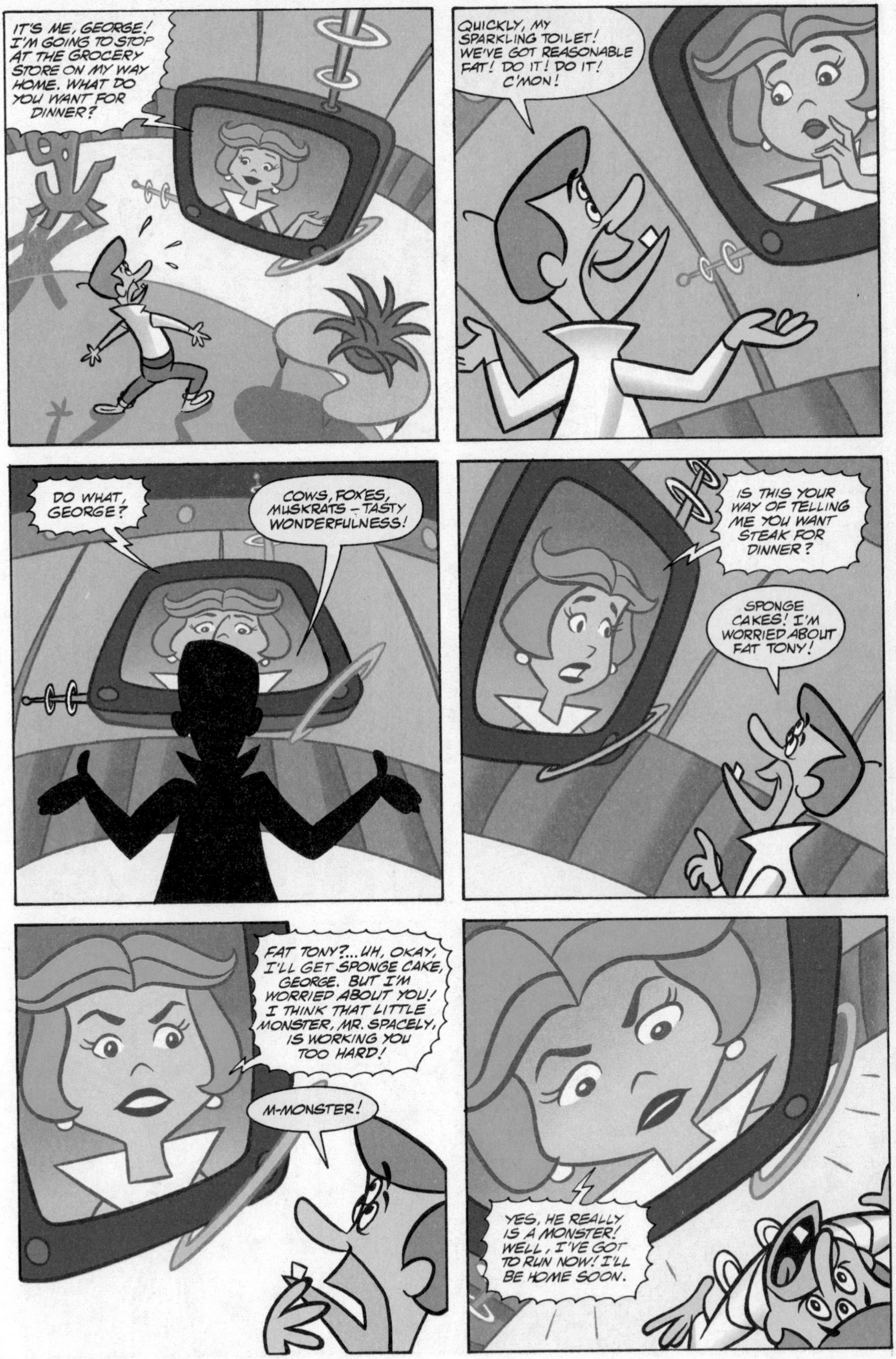
IT'S ME, GEORGE! I'M GOING TO STOP AT THE GROCERY STORE ON MY WAY HOME. WHAT DO YOU WANT FOR DINNER?
QUICKLY, MY SPARKLING TOILET! WE'VE GOT REASONABLE FAT! DO IT! DO IT! C'MON!
DO WHAT, GEORGE?
COWS, FOXES, MUSKRATS -- TASTY WONDERFULNESS!
IS THIS YOUR WAY OF TELLING ME YOU WANT STEAK FOR DINNER?
SPONGE CAKES! I'M WORRIED ABOUT FAT TONY!
FAT TONY?...UH, OKAY, I'LL GET SPONGE CAKE, GEORGE. BUT I'M WORRIED ABOUT YOU! I THINK THAT LITTLE MONSTER, MR. SPACELY, IS WORKING YOU TOO HARD!
M-MONSTER!
YES, HE REALLY IS A MONSTER! WELL, I'VE GOT TO RUN NOW! I'LL BE HOME SOON.

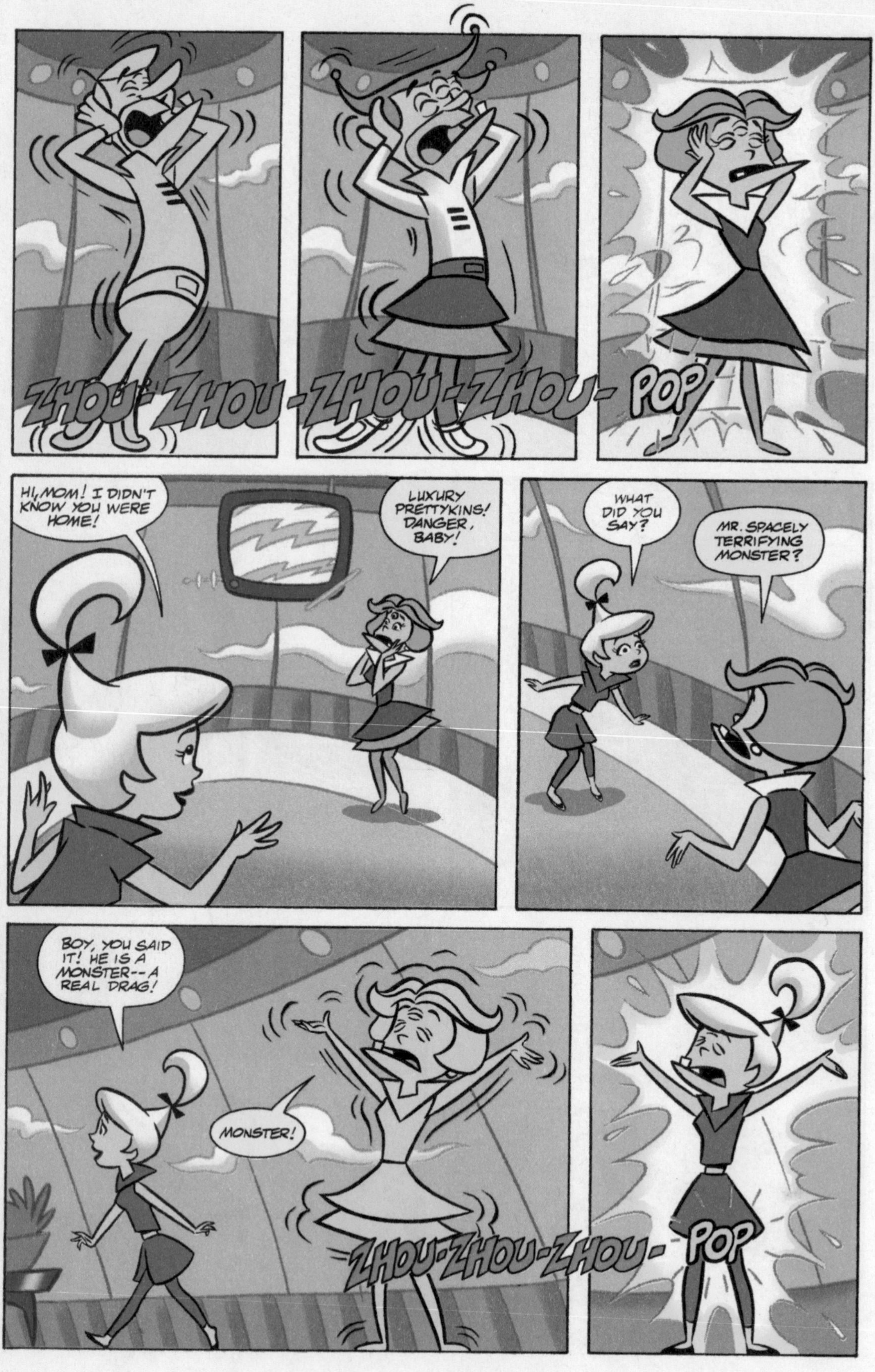

ZHOU-ZHOU-ZHOU-ZHOU-POP
HI, MOM! I DIDN'T KNOW YOU WERE HOME!
LUXURY PRETTYKINS! DANGER, BABY!
WHAT DID YOU SAY?
MR. SPACELY TERRIFYING MONSTER?
BOY, YOU SAID IT! HE IS A MONSTER--A REAL DRAG!
MONSTER!
ZHOU-ZHOU-ZHOU-POP

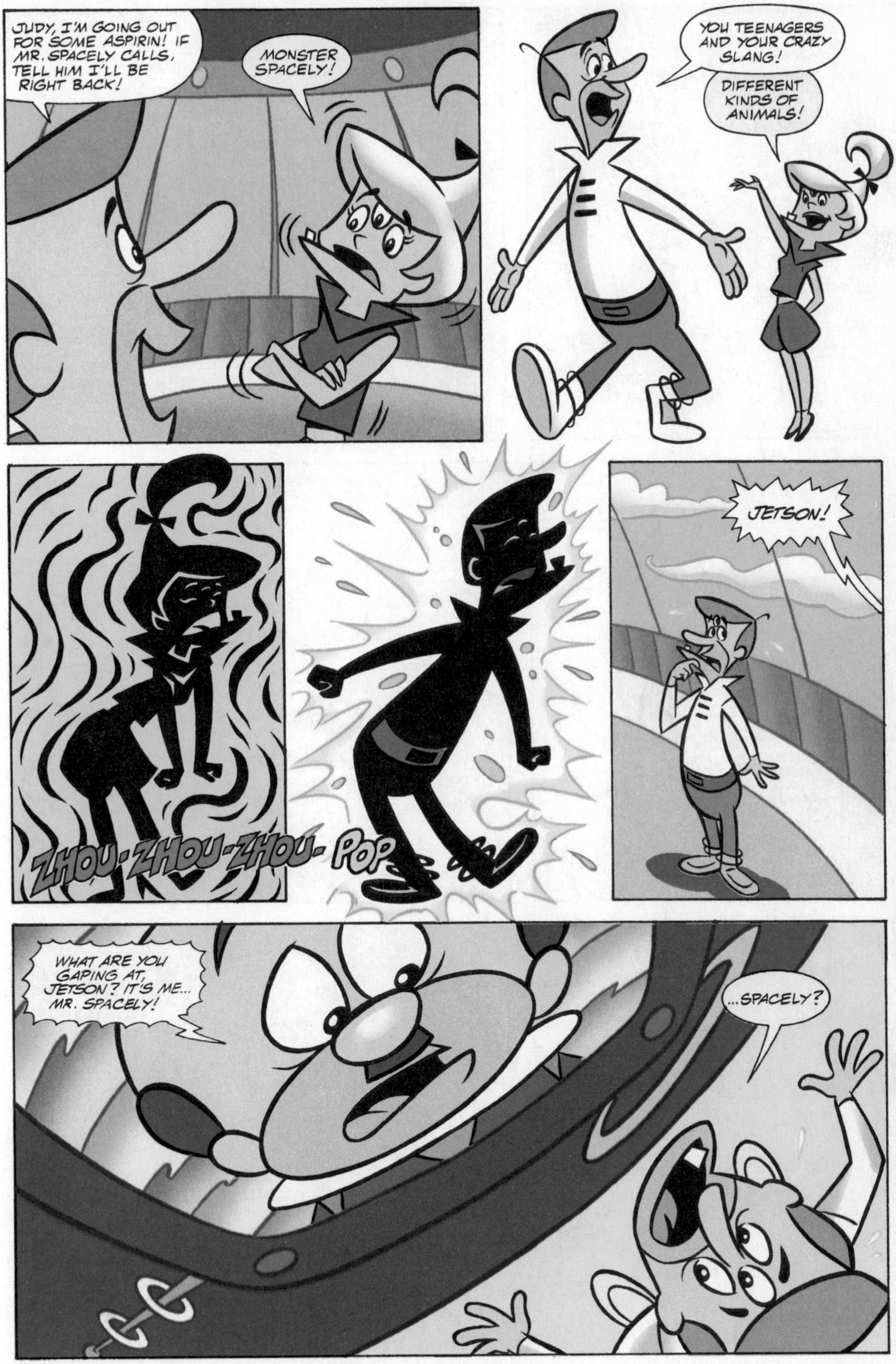
JUDY, I'M GOING OUT FOR SOME ASPIRIN! IF MR. SPACELY CALLS, TELL HIM I'LL BE RIGHT BACK!
MONSTER SPACELY!
YOU TEENAGERS AND YOUR CRAZY SLANG!
DIFFERENT KINDS OF ANIMALS!
ZHOU-ZHOU-ZHOU-POP
JETSON!
WHAT ARE YOU GAPING AT, JETSON? IT'S ME... MR. SPACELY!
...SPACELY?

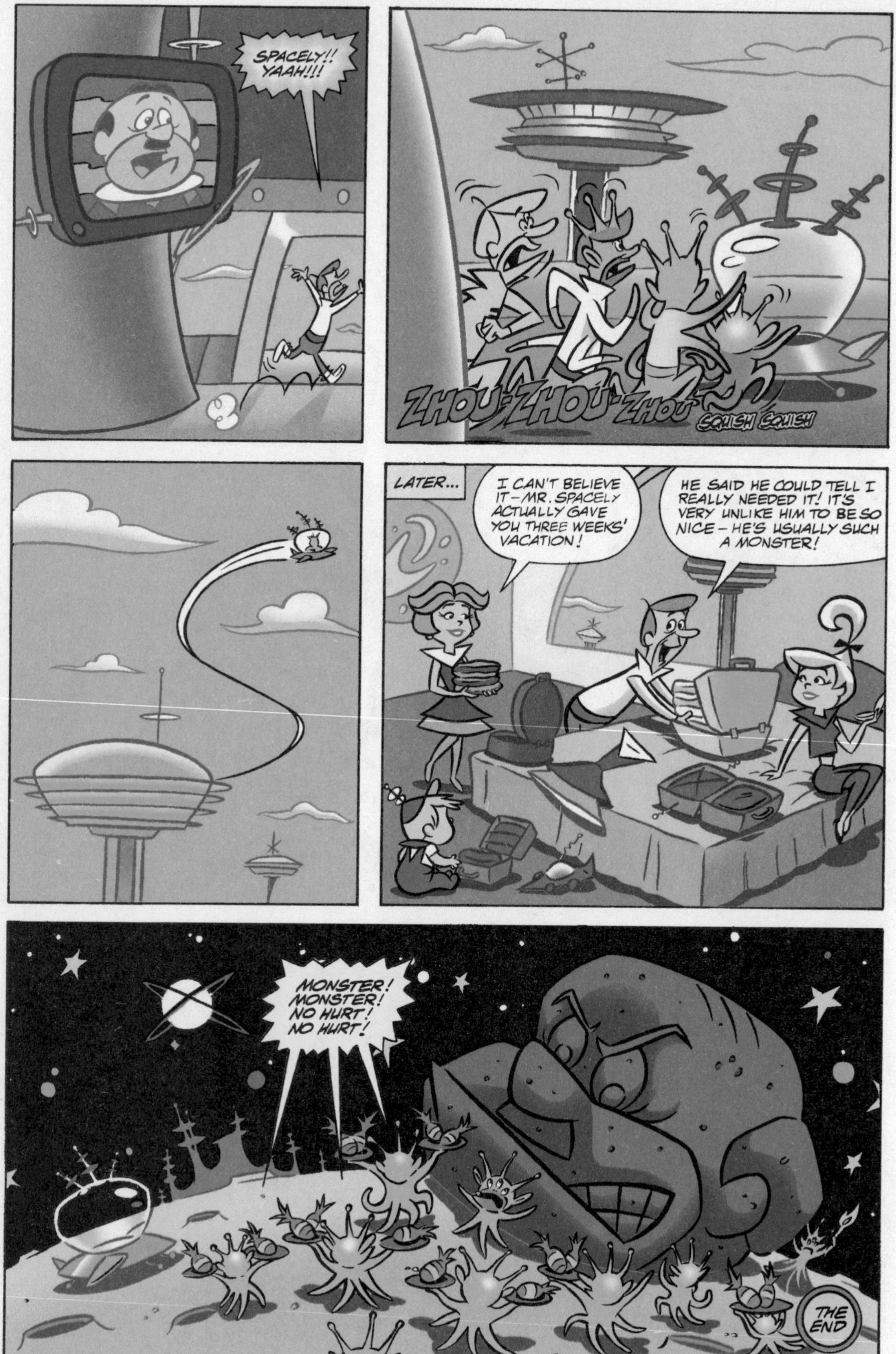
SPACELY!!
YAAH!!!
ZHOU-ZHOU-ZHOU
SQUISH SQUISH
LATER...
I CAN'T BELIEVE IT—MR. SPACELY ACTUALLY GAVE YOU THREE WEEKS' VACATION!
HE SAID HE COULD TELL I REALLY NEEDED IT! IT'S VERY UNLIKE HIM TO BE SO NICE—HE'S USUALLY SUCH A MONSTER!
MONSTER! MONSTER! NO HURT! NO HURT!
THE END

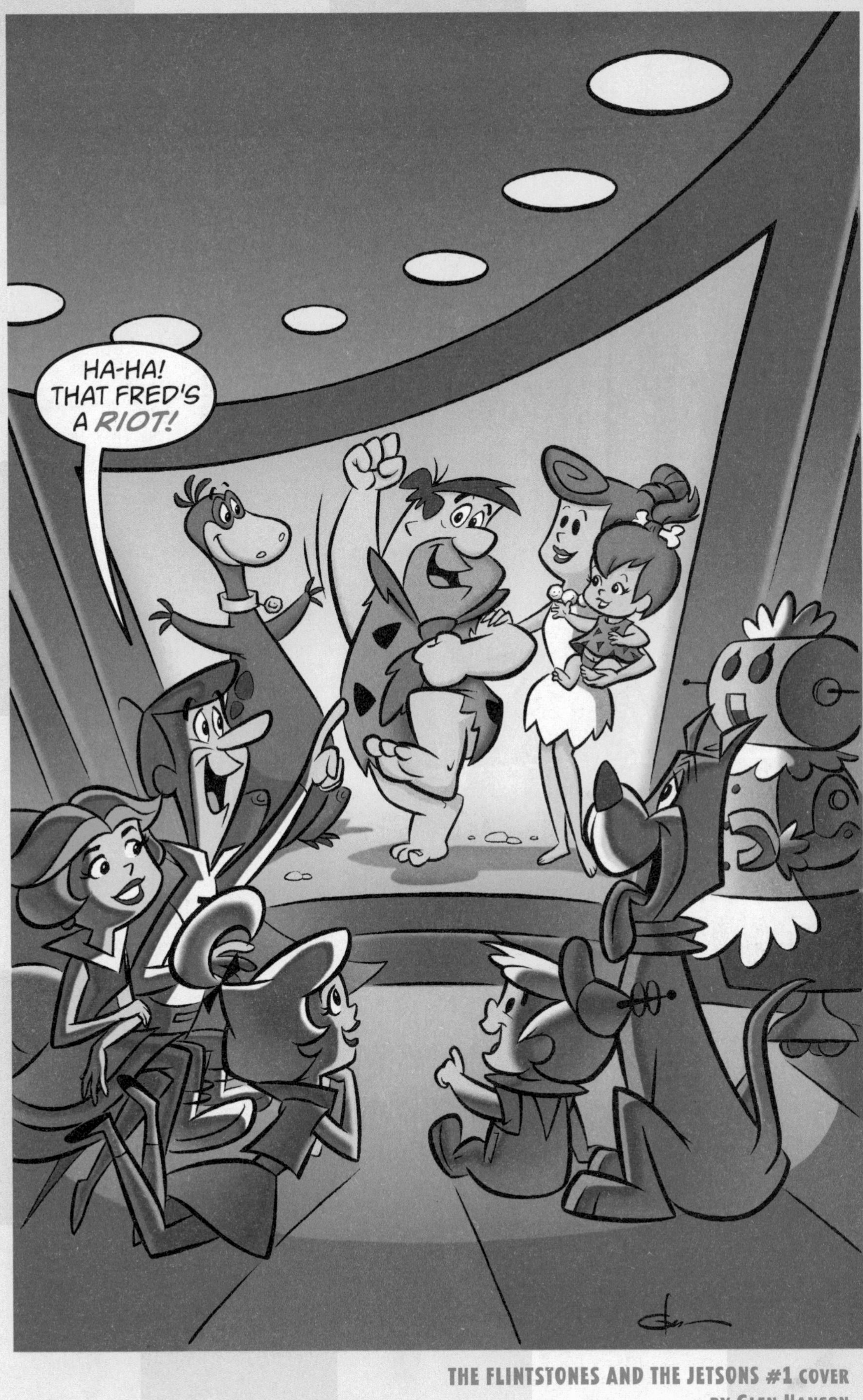
HA-HA! THAT FRED'S A RIOT!

THE FLINTSTONES AND THE JETSONS #1 COVER
BY GLEN HANSON

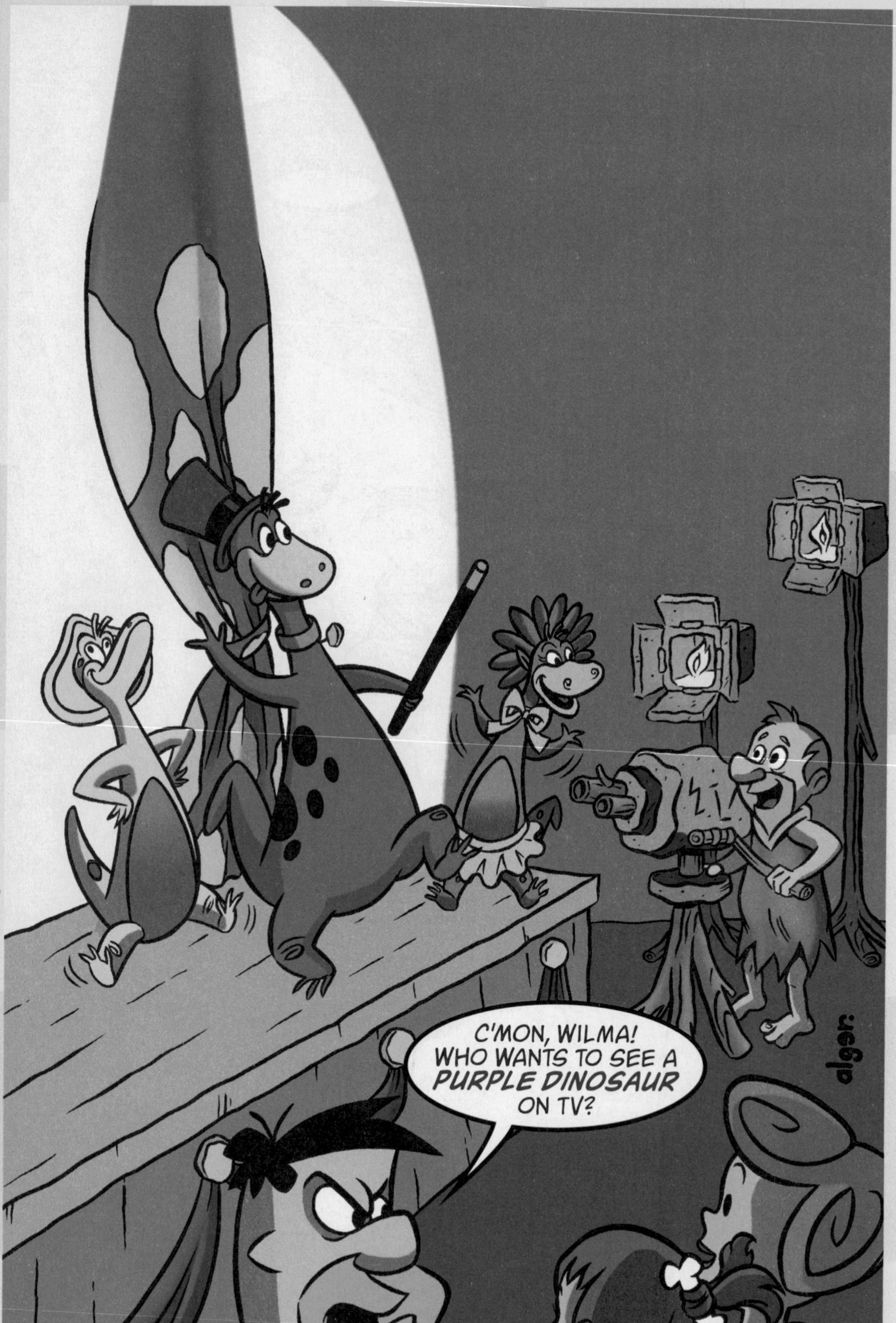
C'MON, WILMA! WHO WANTS TO SEE A PURPLE DINOSAUR ON TV?
alger

THE FLINTSTONES AND THE JETSONS #2 COVER
BY BILL ALGER AND RICK TAYLOR

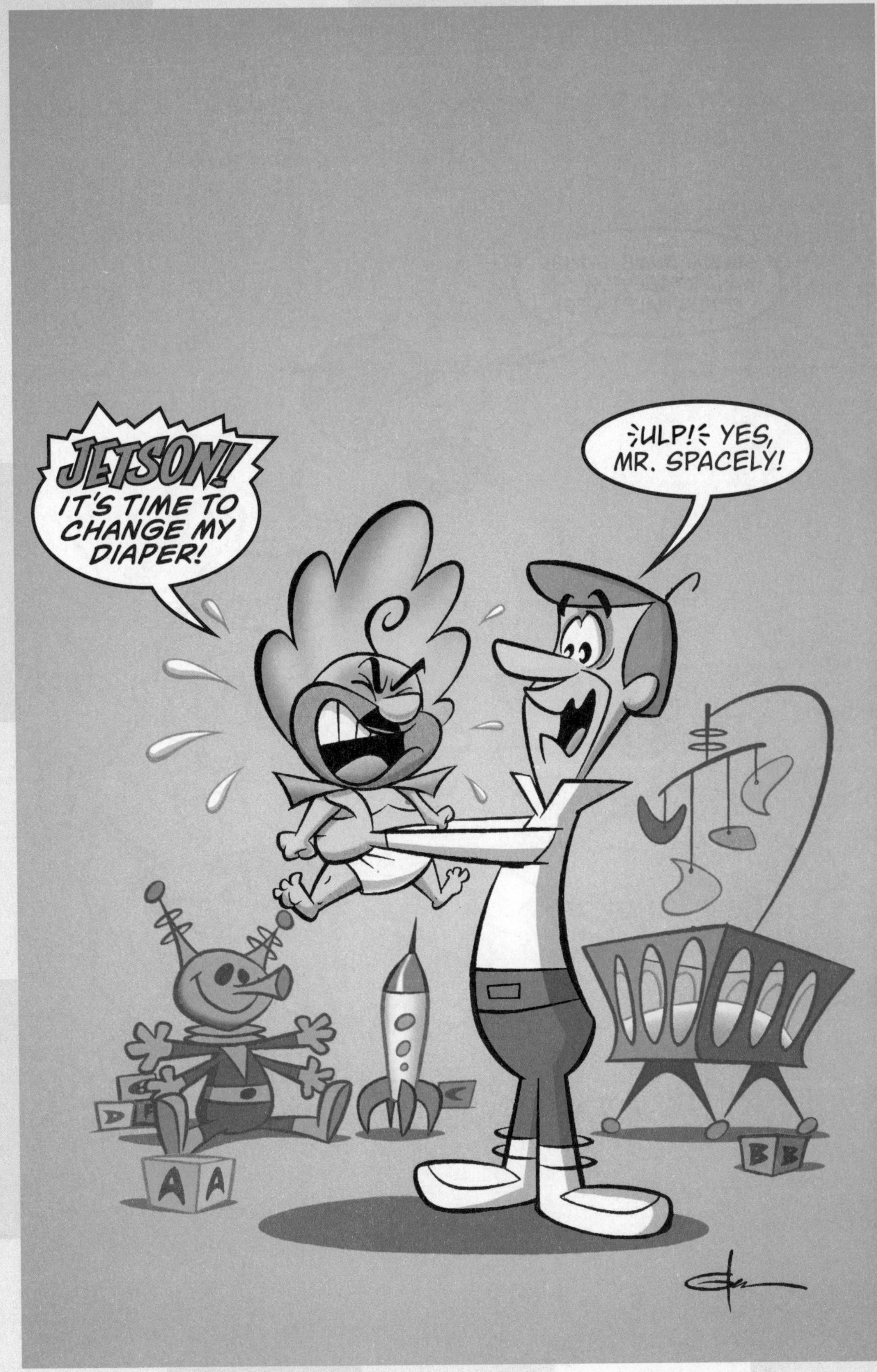

JETSON! IT'S TIME TO CHANGE MY DIAPER!
ULP! YES, MR. SPACELY!

THE FLINTSTONES AND THE JETSONS #3 COVER
BY GLEN HANSON

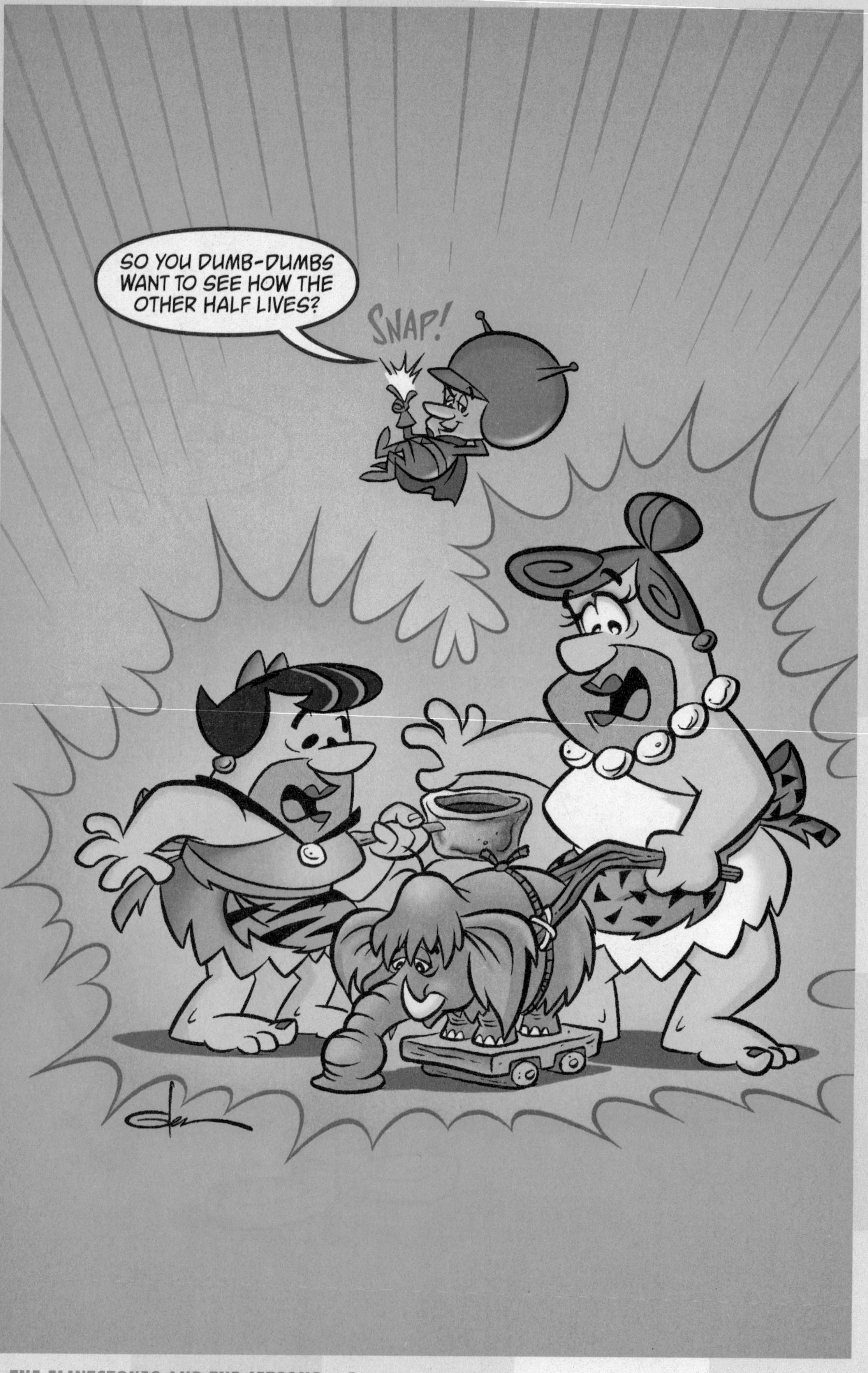
SO YOU DUMB-DUMBS WANT TO SEE HOW THE OTHER HALF LIVES?
SNAP!

THE FLINTSTONES AND THE JETSONS #4 COVER
BY GLEN HANSON

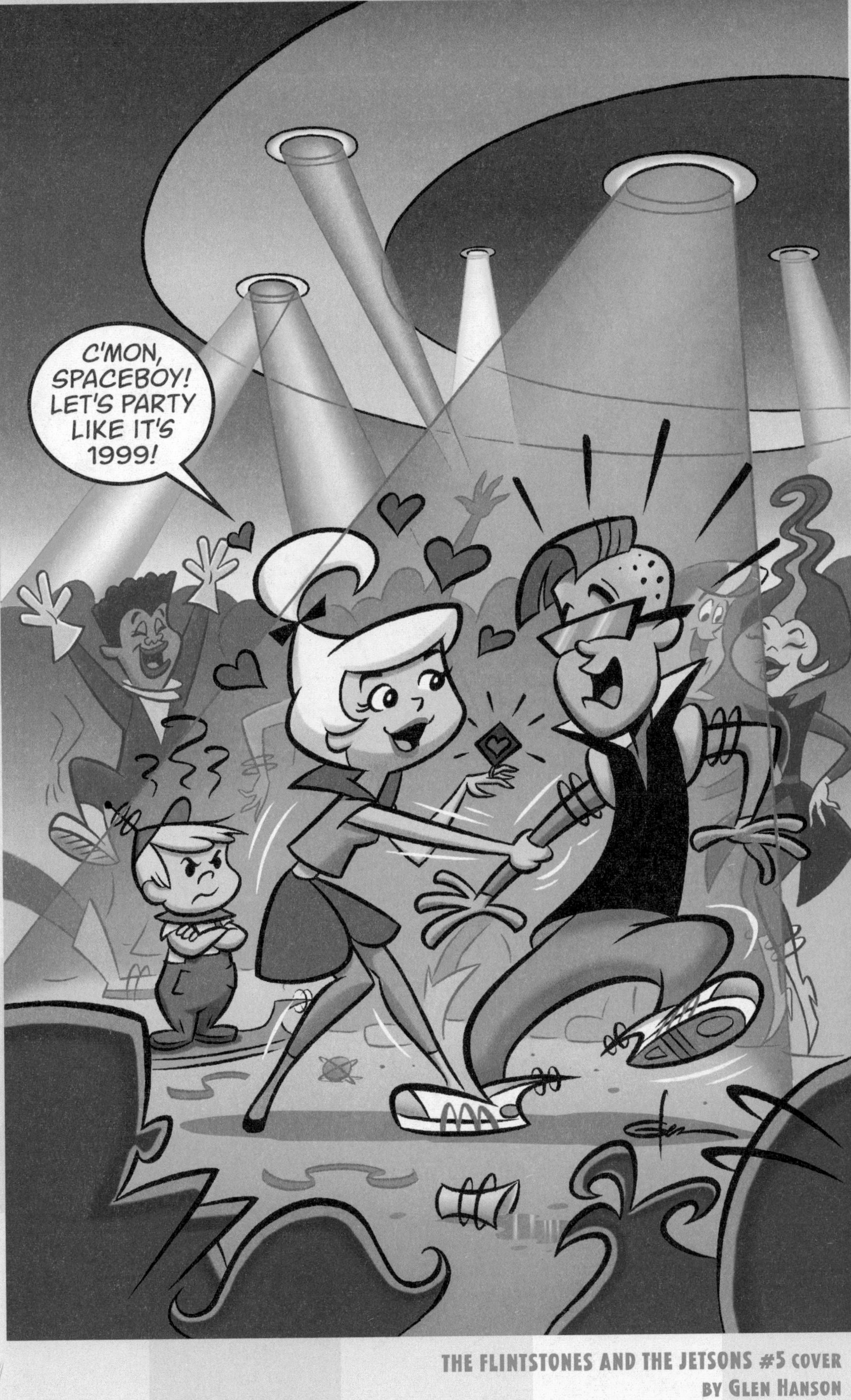
C'MON, SPACEBOY! LET'S PARTY LIKE IT'S 1999!

THE FLINTSTONES AND THE JETSONS #5 COVER
BY GLEN HANSON

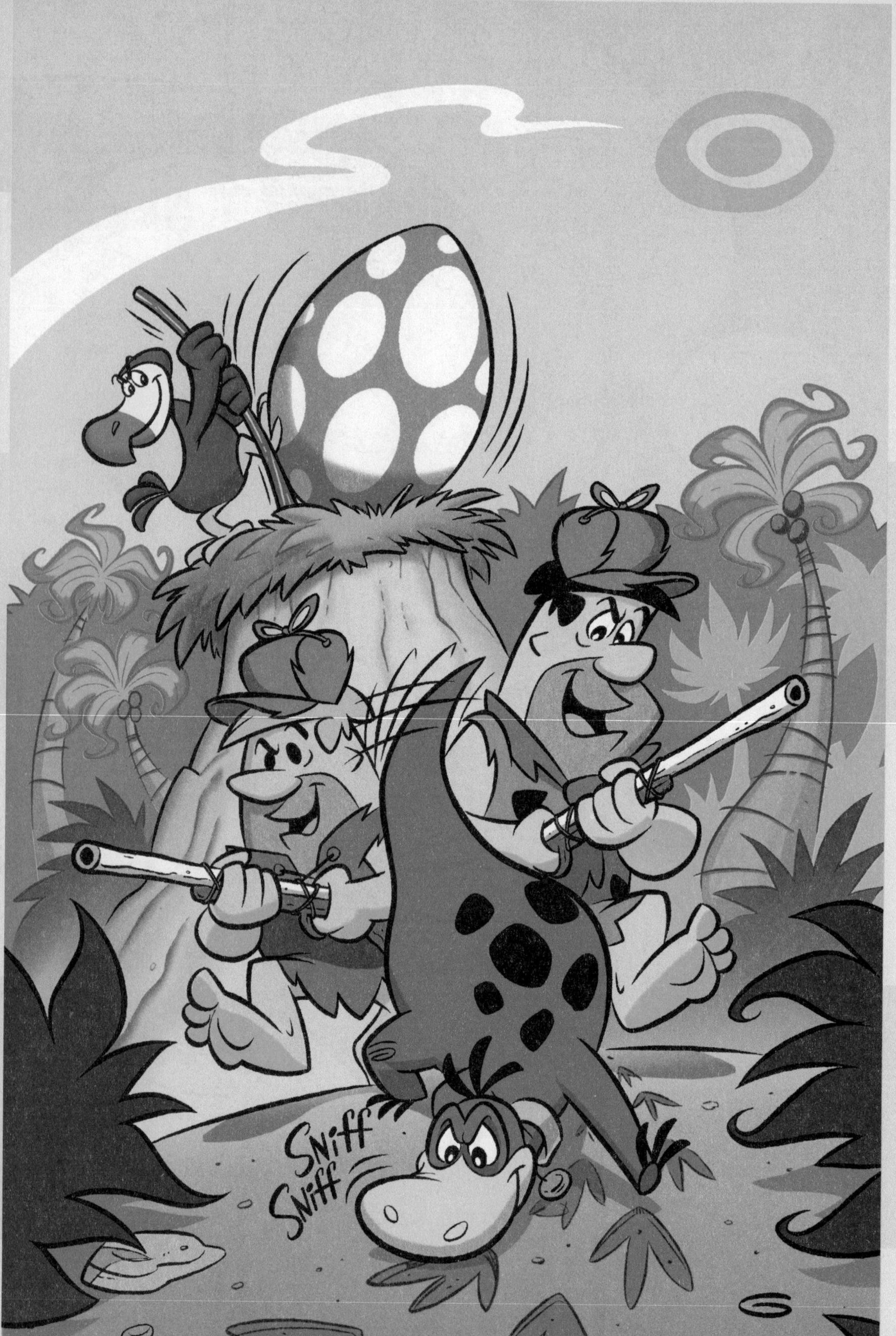
SNIFF
SNIFF

THE FLINTSTONES AND THE JETSONS #6 COVER
BY GLEN HANSON

FRED AND BARNEY PAPER DOLLS

GET OUT YOUR SAFETY SCISSORS AND PASTE--IT'S TIME FOR PAPER DOLLS! HERE'S HOW: (1) CAREFULLY CUT OR TEAR OUT THIS PAGE FROM THE COMIC. (DO IT!) (2) PASTE THE PAGE TO A PIECE OF LIGHTWEIGHT CARDBOARD. (ONE SIDE OF AN EMPTY CEREAL BOX IS FINE.) (3) CUT OUT BARNEY AND FRED AND THEIR TWO STANDS. (4) CUT THE LITTLE SLOTS MARKED 'A' ON THE DOLLS AND STANDS, AND SLIDE THE PIECES TOGETHER AS SHOWN. (5) CUT OUT THE LITTLE OUTFITS--LEAVE THE TABS ON!--AND DRESS UP FRED AND BARNEY IN THEIR BRAND-NEW CLOTHES BY FOLDING THE TABS OVER THE DOLLS. YAY! AND **DON'T EAT PASTE**. NOBODY LIKES A PASTE-EATER.

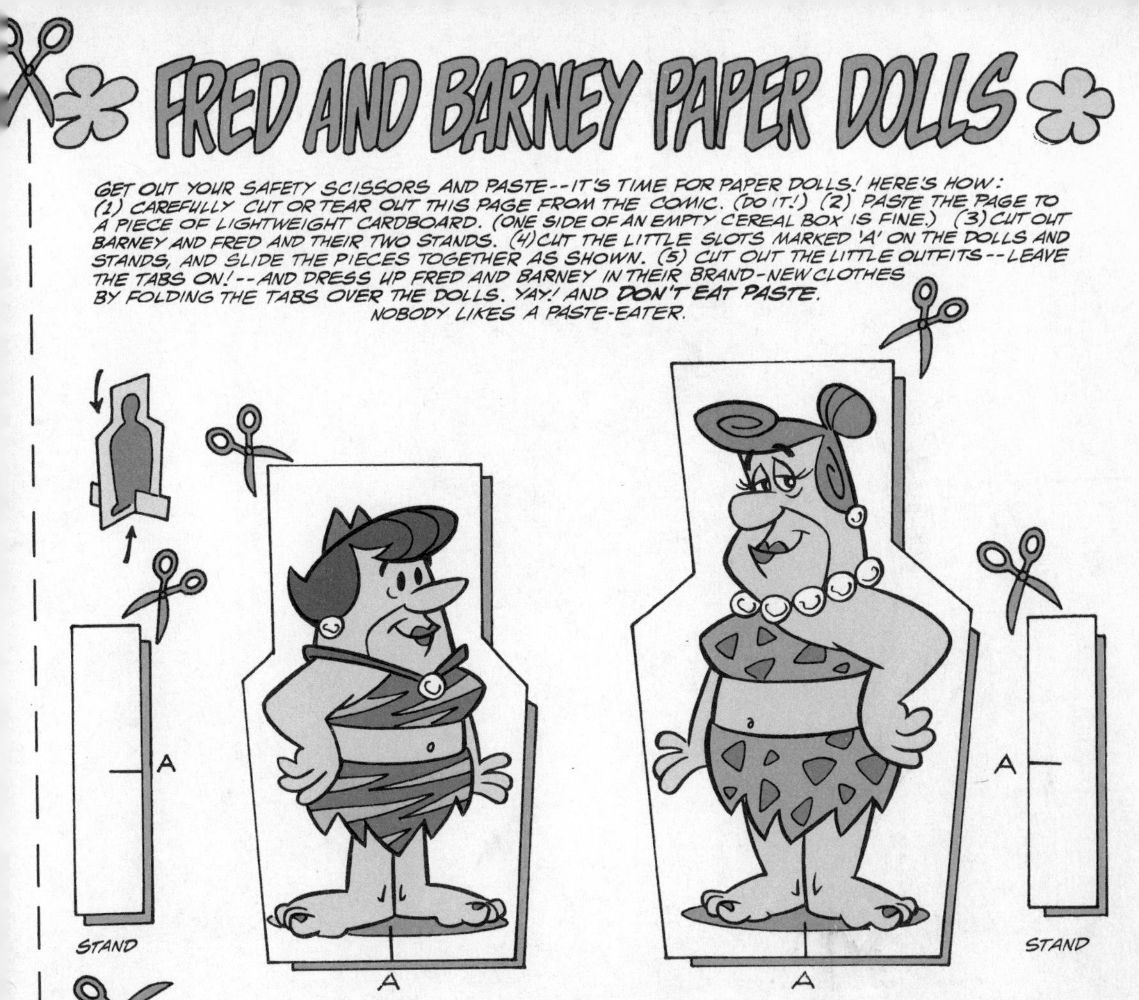
A
STAND
A
A
A
STAND

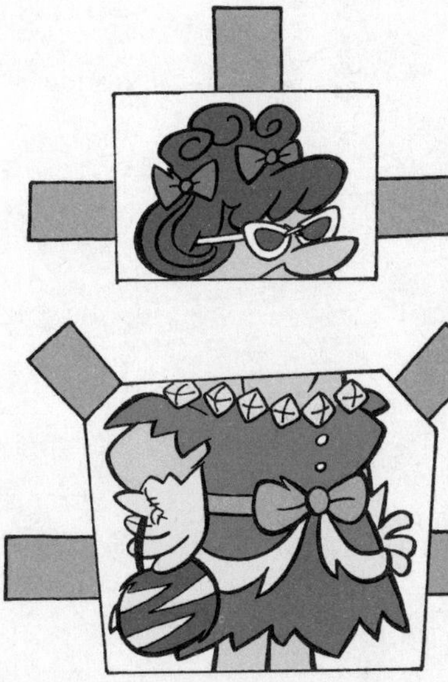

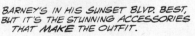

BARNEY'S IN HIS SUNSET BLVD. BEST, BUT IT'S THE STUNNING ACCESSORIES THAT *MAKE* THE OUTFIT.

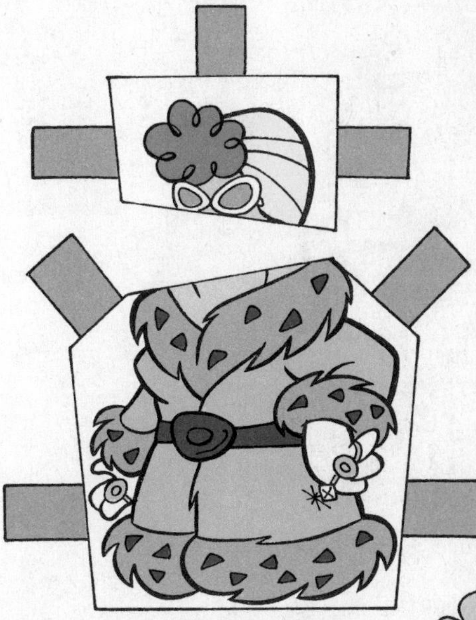

FRED IS READY FOR HIS CLOSE-UP IN A SUPER-CHIC TURBAN AND SABRE-TOOTH FUR COAT.

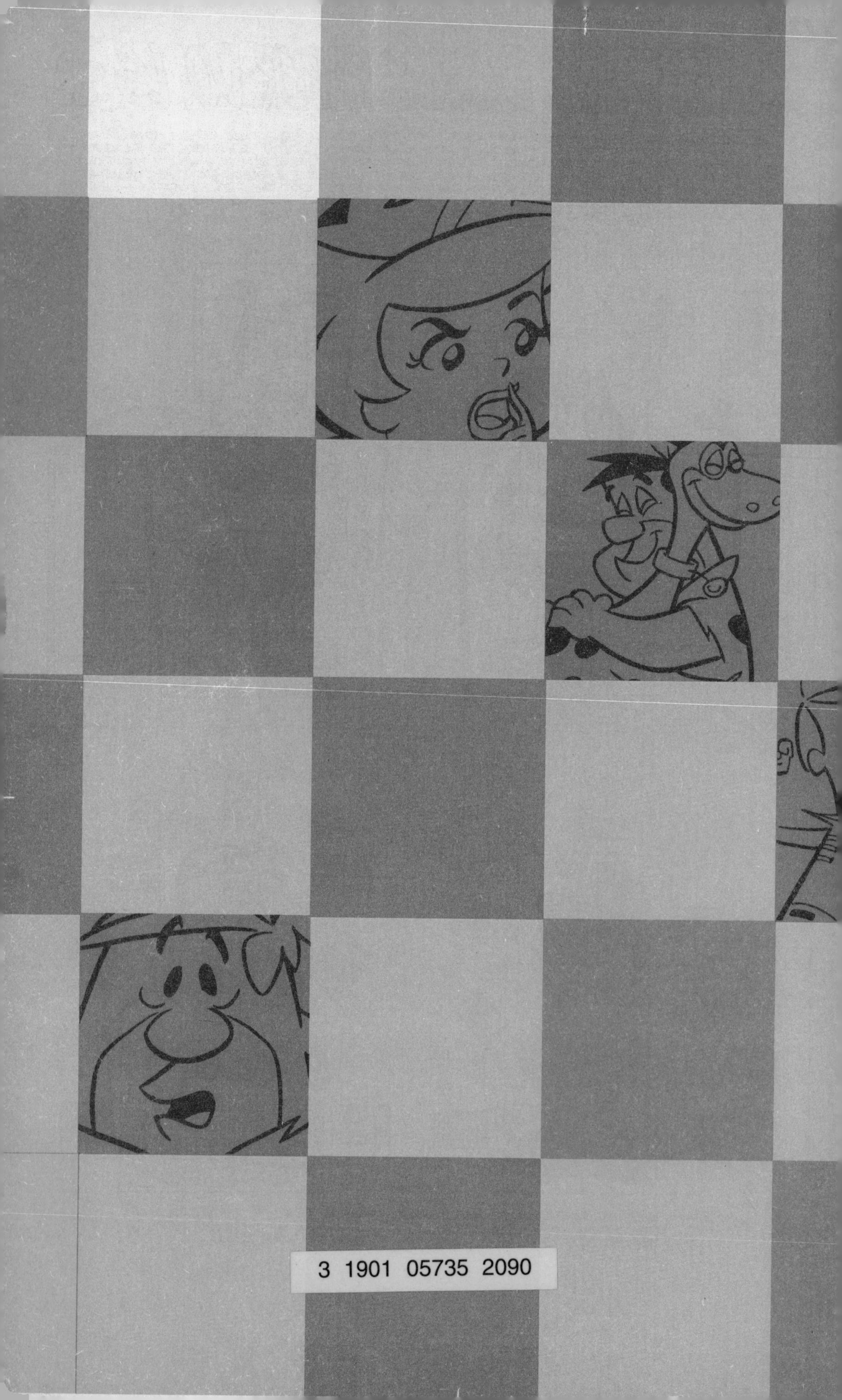